NOLO *Your Legal Companion*

"In Nolo you can trust." —**THE NEW YORK TIMES**

OUR MISSION
Make the law as simple as possible, saving you time, money and headaches.

Whether you have a simple question or a complex problem, turn to us at:

NOLO.COM

Your all-in-one legal resource

Need quick information about wills, patents, adoptions, starting a business—or anything else that's affected by the law? **Nolo.com** features free articles in our Nolopedia, legal updates, resources and all of our books, software, forrms and online applications.

NOLO NOW

Make your legal documents online

Creating a legal document has never been easier or more cost-effective! Create an online will or living trust, form an LLC, or file a Provisional Patent Application! **http://nolonow.nolo.com**.

NOLO'S LAWYER DIRECTORY

Meet your new attorney

If you want advice from a qualified attorney, turn to Nolo's Lawyer Directory—the only directory that lets you see hundreds of in-depth attorney profiles so you can pick the one that's right for you. Find it at **http://lawyers.nolo.com**.

ALWAYS UP TO DATE

Sign up for **NOLO'S LEGAL UPDATER**

Old law is bad law. We'll email you when we publish an updated edition of this book—sign up for this free service at **nolo.com/ legalupdater**.

Find the latest updates at **NOLO.COM**

Recognizing that the law can change even before you use this book, we post legal updates during the life of this edition at **nolo.com/updates**.

Is this edition the newest? **ASK US!**

To make sure that this is the most recent edition available, just give us a call at **800-728-3555**.

(Please note that we cannot offer legal advice.)

Please note

We believe accurate, plain-English legal information should help
you solve many of your own legal problems. But this text is not a
substitute for personalized advice from a knowledgeable lawyer. If
you want the help of a trained professional—and we'll always point
out situations in which we think that's a good idea—consult an
attorney licensed to practice in your state.

9th edition

Make Your Own Living Trust

by Attorney Denis Clifford

Ninth Edition	FEBRUARY 2009
Editor	BETSY SIMMONS
Cover Design	SUSAN PUTNEY
Production	MARGARET LIVINGSTON
CD-ROM Preparation	ELLEN BITTER
Proofreading	ELAINE MERRILL
Index	BAYSIDE INDEXING SERVICE
Printing	CONSOLIDATED PRINTERS, INC.

Clifford, Denis.
  Make your own living trust / by Denis Clifford. -- 9th ed.
      p. cm.
  ISBN-13: 978-1-4133-0933-1 (pbk.)
  ISBN-10: 1-4133-0933-X (pbk.)
  1. Living Trusts--United States--Popular works. I. Title.
  KF734.C58 2009
  346.7305'2--dc22

                              2008037028

Copyright © 1993, 1996, 1998, 2000, 2004, 2005, 2007, and 2009 by Denis Clifford.
ALL RIGHTS RESERVED. PRINTED IN THE U.S.A.

No part of this publication may be reproduced, stored in a retrieval system, or transmitted in any form or by any means, electronic, mechanical, photocopying, recording, or otherwise without the prior written permission of the publisher and the author. Reproduction prohibitions do not apply to the forms contained in this product when reproduced for personal use.

Quantity sales: For information on bulk purchases or corporate premium sales, please contact the Special Sales Department. For academic sales or textbook adoptions, ask for Academic Sales. 800-955-4775, Nolo, 950 Parker Street, Berkeley, CA 94710.

Dedication

Once again, to Naomi.

Acknowledgments

My thanks to all those friends who helped me with this book, both putting it together and over the years:

First, to friends at Nolo, without whose aid this book would never have remained in print: Betsy Simmons, my editor extraordinaire, and a pleasure to work with; my former editors, Mary Randolph and Shae Irving; Stephanie Harolde, who prepared so many drafts of the book so well and did much fine editing, too; and Ella Hirst, for her fine research.

Second, to Mark Peery, of Greenbrae, California, a superb estate planning lawyer (and great friend).

Third, to Jake Warner, for his brilliant editing and assistance on this book and for all his help through the years.

Fourth, to Toni Ihara, a spirit forever joyous—thanks again for getting me into all this.

Fifth, to all my other friends and colleagues at Nolo. In the past, I listed everyone, but now we have 100 or more employees, plus more outside writers and an employee manual. Still, Nolo retains the relaxed, friendly atmosphere that makes it such a pleasant (as well as productive) place to work.

Sixth, to Attorney Magdalen Gaynor, of White Plains and New York City, New York, an excellent estate planning lawyer who gave me information generously and cheerfully.

Seventh, to other friends who helped me with this book: Linda Moody, of Mill Valley, California, a law school friend who's become another superb estate planning lawyer; Ken Fisher, of Pleasant Hill, California; and the many, many other people who helped with this book and, over the years, with earlier materials I've written about living trusts.

And finally, my heartfelt thanks to my clients from past years, from whom I learned so much reality I could never have learned in books or school (sure never did in law school), and also to the many readers of earlier editions of this book who wrote me with suggestions, comments, corrections, and other thoughts that contributed greatly to this edition.

About the Author

Denis Clifford practices estate planning law in Berkeley, California. He is the author of several Nolo books, including *Plan Your Estate* and *Nolo's Simple Will Book*. A graduate of Columbia Law School, where he was an editor of the *Law Review,* he has practiced law in various ways, and has become convinced that people can do much of their own legal work.

Table of Contents

Appendixes

Index

Your Legal Companion for Making Your Own Living Trust

Would you like your property to avoid probate after your death? Would you like to learn what a living trust is and how it avoids probate? Have you thought about creating a living trust but been put off by the prospect of high legal fees? If you answered yes to any of these questions, you've come to the right place. With this book, you can understand living trusts and create one yourself, without a lawyer. If you make a trust using this book, after your death, your property can be transferred to your beneficiaries without probate courts or attorneys.

This book can also help more prosperous couples create a living trust that can reduce or eliminate federal estate taxes, in addition to avoiding probate. This type of trust is called an AB trust. As you read through the book, you'll learn whether or not it's wise for you to create an AB trust with the forms in this book.

Many so-called authorities on living trusts assert that it is foolish to try to make your own living trust. They maintain that you must hire a lawyer or even a team of experts—lawyer, accountant, financial planner. (This "team" will do their best to consume much of your estate with their fees.) Some even argue that doing your own living trust is like trying to do your own brain surgery. This is ridiculous. Preparing a simple living trust that will avoid probate and transfer property after death is not brain surgery or anything close to it. For most people, there's no reason to hire a lawyer to accomplish these goals.

The trust forms in this book have been carefully prepared to be both clear and legally acceptable. Anyone who asserts that trusts must be written in "legalese" (language that is peculiar to the legal profession) is flat-out wrong. A living trust functions just fine if it covers the basics, such as what property is in the trust, who gets it, and who manages the trust after you die. And although no legalese is mandated, it is prudent to have a trust form that, like the ones in this book, is sufficiently traditional so it looks familiar to institutions that may see it—such as banks, title companies, or stock brokerage companies.

> **CAUTION**
>
> **Louisiana residents cannot make a trust with this book.** This book is designed for residents of all states except Louisiana, which has a legal system based on the Napoleonic Code, different from all other states.

Although most people can make a living trust without the help of an expert, there are some situations that require professional help. This book is very clear about which situations warrant seeking the advice of a professional. And if you do decide to get an expert's help with preparing your living trust, this book will help you make the most of hiring a professional. It even offers information about how to find a good lawyer who will charge a reasonable fee.

Make Your Own Living Trust is a workbook. Its purpose is to help you understand and prepare your own living trust. While reading this book, take notes, record information about your own situation, use the worksheets to the extent you find them helpful, and decide how you want your trust to work. Then, draft your own living trust using one of the trust forms in Appendix B or on the CD-ROM. Before you actually start to prepare a living trust, read through the book once. You need to know how a living trust really works and how it fits in with your overall estate plan. You'll also need to resolve basic personal issues, such as what property to transfer to your trust and who will inherit what. You can do it yourself, but you must do it right, which means educating yourself about your options so you can make well-informed decisions.

Congratulations on starting your estate planning—it's a wonderful thing to do for your family. We at Nolo know from long experience that putting a sound estate plan into place can bring peace and satisfaction to those who take the time to do it.

Overview of Living Trusts

Living trusts are an efficient and effective way to transfer property at your death to the relatives, friends, or charities you've chosen. Essentially, a living trust performs the same function as a will, with the important difference that property left by a will must go through the probate court process. In probate, a deceased person's will is proved valid in court, the person's debts are paid, and, usually after about a year, the remaining property is finally distributed to the beneficiaries. In the vast majority of instances, these probate court proceedings waste time and money.

By contrast, property left by a living trust can go promptly and directly to your inheritors. They don't have to bother with a probate court proceeding. That means they won't have to spend any of your hard-earned money (at least, I presume it was hard-earned) to pay for court and lawyer fees.

You don't need to maintain separate tax records for your living trust. While you live, all transactions that are technically made by your living trust are simply reported on your personal income tax return. Indeed, while some paperwork is necessary to establish a probate-avoidance living trust and transfer property to it, there are no serious drawbacks or risks involved in creating or maintaining the trust.

These trusts are called "living" or sometimes "inter vivos" (Latin for "among the living") because they're created while you're alive. They're called "revocable" because you can revoke or change them at any time, for any reason, before you die.

While you live, you effectively keep ownership of all property that you've technically transferred to your living trust. You can do whatever you want to with any trust property, including selling it, spending it, or giving it away. A revocable living trust becomes operational at your death. At that point, it allows your trust property to be transferred, privately and outside of probate, to the people or organizations you have named as beneficiaries of the trust.

Living Trusts Explained

A trust can seem like a mysterious creature, dreamed up by lawyers and wrapped in legal jargon. But don't let the word "trust" scare you, even though it might initially sound impressive or even slightly ominous. True, trusts were an invention of medieval England, used by aristocrats to evade restrictions on ownership and inheritance of land. And true, complex trusts have traditionally been used by rich American families to preserve their wealth over generations. But happily, the types of living trusts this book covers are not complicated or beyond the reach of regular folks. Here are the basics.

The Concept of a Trust

A trust is an intangible legal entity ("legal fiction" might be a more accurate term). Beyond a few pieces of paper, you can't see a trust, or touch it, but it does exist. The first step in creating a working trust is to prepare and sign a document called a *Declaration of Trust*.

Once you create and sign the Declaration of Trust, the trust exists. There must, however, be a flesh-and-blood person actually in charge of this property; that person is called the *trustee*. With traditional trusts, the trustee manages the property on behalf of someone else, called the *beneficiary*. However, with a living trust, until you die you are the trustee of the trust you create and also, in effect, the beneficiary. Only after your death do the trust beneficiaries you've named in the Declaration of Trust have any rights to your trust property.

Creating a Living Trust

When you create a living trust document with this book, you must identify:

- Yourself, as the *grantor*—or for a couple, the grantors. The grantor is the person who creates the trust.
- The *trustee,* who manages the trust property. You are also the trustee, as long as you (or your spouse or partner, if you make a trust together) are alive.
- The *successor trustee,* who takes over after you (or you and your spouse or partner) die. This successor trustee turns the trust property over to the trust beneficiaries and performs any other task required by the trust.
- The *trust beneficiary* or *beneficiaries*, those who are entitled to receive the trust property at your death.
- The *property* that is subject to the trust.

A Declaration of Trust also includes other basic terms, such as the authority of the grantor to amend or revoke the document at any time, and the authority of the trustee.

How a Living Trust Works

The key to establishing a living trust to avoid probate is that the grantor—remember, that's you, the person who sets up the trust—isn't locked into anything. You can revise, amend, or revoke the trust for any (or no) reason, any time before your death, as long as you're legally competent. And because you appoint yourself as the initial trustee, you can control and use the property as you see fit while you live.

What Is Competence?

"Competent" means having the mental capacity to make and understand decisions regarding your property. A person can become legally "incompetent" if declared so in a court proceeding, such as a custodianship or guardianship proceeding. If a person tries to make or revoke or amend a living trust and someone challenges his or her mental capacity, or competence, to do so, the matter can end up in a nasty court battle. Fortunately, such court disputes are quite rare.

A Mini-Glossary of Living Trust Terms

- The person who sets up the living trust (that's you, or you and your spouse or partner) is called a **grantor, trustor,** or **settlor.** These terms mean the same thing and are used interchangeably.
- All the property you own at death, whether in your living trust or owned in some other form, is your **estate.**
- The market value of your property at your death, less all debts and liabilities on that property, is your net or **taxable estate.** The IRS allows your successor trustee to choose market value at your death or six months later.
- The property you transfer to the trust is called, collectively, the **trust property, trust principal,** or **trust estate.** (And, of course, there's a Latin version: the trust corpus.)
- The person who has power over the trust property is called the **trustee.**
- The person the grantor names to take over as trustee after the grantor's death (or, with a trust made jointly by a couple, after the death of both spouses) is called the **successor trustee.**
- The people or organizations who get the trust property when the grantor dies are called the **beneficiaries** of the trust. (While the grantors are alive, technically they themselves are the beneficiaries of the trust.)

And now for the legal magic of the living trust device. Although a living trust is only a legal fiction during your life, it assumes a very real presence for a brief period after your death. When you die, the living trust can no longer be revoked or altered. It is now irrevocable.

With a trust for a single person, after you die, the person you named in your trust document to be successor trustee takes over. That person is in charge of transferring the trust property to the family, friends, or charities you named as your trust beneficiaries.

With a trust for a couple, the surviving spouse or partner manages the trust. A successor trustee takes over after both spouses or partners die.

There is no court or governmental supervision to ensure that your successor trustee complies with the terms of your living trust. That means that a vital element of an effective living trust is naming someone you fully trust as your successor trustee. If there is no person you trust sufficiently to name as successor trustee, a living trust probably isn't for you. You can name a bank, trust company, or other financial institution as successor trustee, but doing so has serious drawbacks.

After the trust grantor dies, some paperwork is necessary to transfer the trust property to the beneficiaries, such as preparing new ownership documents. But because no probate is necessary for property that was transferred to the living trust, the whole thing can generally be handled within a few weeks, in most cases without a lawyer. No court proceedings or papers are required to terminate the trust. Once the job of getting the property to the beneficiaries is accomplished, the trust just evaporates, by its own terms.

There are a couple of exceptions here. First, a prosperous couple may create what's called an AB living trust to avoid probate and save on overall estate taxes. When one spouse dies, that spouse's trust keeps going until the second spouse dies. A lawyer or other financial expert must be hired to divide the trust property between that owned by the deceased spouse's trust and that owned by the surviving spouse.

Another type of trust that can last for a long time is called a child's trust. The trust forms in this book allow you to create a child's trust if you wish, to leave trust property to one or more minors or young adult beneficiaries. These trusts are managed by your successor trustee and can last until the young beneficiary reaches the age you specified in your Declaration of Trust. Then the beneficiary receives the trust property, and the trust ends.

Probate and Why You Want to Avoid It

Given that you're reading this book, you probably already know that you want to avoid probate. If you still need any persuasion that avoiding probate is desirable, here's a brief look at how the process actually works.

Probate is the legal process that includes:

- filing the deceased person's will with the local probate court (called "surrogate" or "chancery" court in some places)
- taking inventory of the deceased person's property
- having that property appraised
- paying legal debts, including death taxes
- proving the will valid in court, and
- eventually distributing what's left as the will directs.

If the deceased person didn't leave a will, or a will isn't valid, the estate must still undergo probate. The process is called an "intestacy" proceeding, and the property is distributed to the closest relatives as state law dictates.

People who defend the probate system assert that probate prevents fraud in transferring a deceased person's property. In addition, they claim it protects inheritors by promptly resolving claims creditors have against a deceased person's property. In truth, however, most property is transferred within a close circle of

family and friends, and very few estates have problems with creditors' claims. In short, most people have no need of these so-called benefits, so probate usually amounts to a lot of time-wasting, expensive mumbo-jumbo of aid to no one but the lawyers involved.

The actual probate functions are essentially clerical and administrative. In the vast majority of probate cases, there's no conflict, no contesting parties—none of the normal reasons for court proceedings or lawyers' adversarial skills. Likewise, probate doesn't usually call for legal research or lawyers' drafting abilities. Instead, in the normal, uneventful probate proceeding, the family or other heirs of the deceased person provide a copy of the will and other financial information. The attorney's secretary then fills in a small mound of forms and keeps track of filing deadlines and other procedural technicalities. Some lawyers hire probate form preparation companies to do all the real work. In most instances, the existence of these freelance paralegal companies is not disclosed to clients, who assume that lawyers' offices at least do the routine paperwork they are paid so well for. In some states, the attorney makes a couple of routine court appearances; in others, normally the whole procedure is handled by mail.

Because of the complicated paperwork and waiting periods imposed by law, a typical probate takes up to a year or more, often much more. (I once worked in a law office that was profitably entering its seventh year of handling a probate estate—and a very wealthy estate it was.) During probate, the beneficiaries generally get nothing unless the judge allows the decedent's immediate family a "family allowance." In some states, this allowance is a pittance—only a few hundred dollars. In others, it can amount to thousands.

Most states now allow simplified probate for certain types of estates. While simplified probate can speed up the process, and may even result in lower attorney fees, the truth is that probate—simplified or not—is simply a waste for most people.

Probate usually requires both an "executor" (called a "personal representative" in some states) and someone familiar with probate procedures, normally a probate attorney. The executor is a person appointed in the will who is responsible for supervising the estate, which means making sure that the will is followed. If the person died without a will, the court appoints an "administrator" (whose main qualification may sometimes be that he or she is a crony of the judge) to serve the same function. The executor, who is usually the spouse, partner, child, relative, or friend of the deceased, hires a probate lawyer to do the paperwork. The executor often hires the decedent's lawyer (who may even have possession of the will), but this is not required. Then the executor does little more than sign where the lawyer directs, wondering why the whole business is taking so long. For these services, the lawyer and the executor are each entitled to a hefty fee from the probate estate. Some lawyers even persuade clients into naming them as executors, enabling the lawyers to hire themselves as probate attorneys and collect two fees—one as executor, one as probate attorney. By contrast, most relatives and friends who serve as executors do not take the fee, especially if the person who serves is a substantial inheritor.

While probate can evoke images of greedy lawyers consuming most of an estate in fees, lawyer fees rarely actually devour the entire estate. In many states, the fees are what a court approves as "reasonable." In a few states, the fees are based on a percentage of the estate subject to probate. Either way, probate attorney fees for a routine estate with a gross value of $500,000 (these days, in many urban areas, this may be little more than a modest home, some savings, and a car) can amount to $10,000, $15,000, or more. Fees based on the "gross" probate estate means that debts on property are not deducted to determine value. For example, if a house has a market value of $300,000 with a mortgage balance of $260,000 (net equity of $40,000), the gross value of the house is $300,000.

EXAMPLE:

In California, probate fees are set by statute. (Section 10800, Cal. Prob. Code.) The fee for probate of a house is based on the gross value of that house. Given the prices of California real estate, this can result in a lot of money wasted on attorney's fees. For example, a house purchased for $150,000 some years ago may now be worth $900,000. The probate fee for transferring this house will be $23,000. That fee will be charged no matter how much equity the owners have in the house.

In addition to executor's fees and probate attorney's fees, there are court costs, appraiser's fees, and other possible expenses. Moreover, if the basic fee is set by statute and there are any "extraordinary" services performed for the estate, the attorney or executor can ask the court for additional fees.

Extreme Probate Fees

Marilyn Monroe died in debt in 1962, but over the next 18 years, her estate received income, mostly from movie royalties, in excess of $1.6 million. When her estate was settled in 1980, her executor announced that debts of $372,136 had been paid, and $101,229 was left for inheritors. Well over $1 million of Monroe's estate was consumed by probate fees.

Then there's the 1997 U.S. Tax Court case upholding an attorney's probate fee of $1,600 per hour for a total of $368,100. The court declared the fee was "reasonable under New York law."

Even England—the source of our antiquated probate laws—abolished its elaborate probate system years ago. It survives in this country because it is so lucrative for lawyers.

Avoiding Probate

The most flexible and complete probate-avoidance method is, undoubtedly, the living trust. However, there are a number of other methods.

Informal Probate Avoidance

You may wonder why surviving relatives and friends can't just divide up your property as your will directs (or as you said you wanted, if you never got around to writing a will), and ignore the laws requiring probate. Some small estates are undoubtedly disposed of this way.

For example, say an older man lives his last few years in a nursing home. After his death, his children meet and divide the personal items their father had kept over the years. What little savings he has have long since been put into a joint account with the children anyway, so there's no need for formalities there.

For this type of informal procedure to work, the family must be able to gain possession of all of the deceased's property, agree on how to distribute it, and pay all the creditors. Gaining possession of property isn't difficult when the only property left is personal effects and household items. However, if real estate, securities, bank accounts, cars, boats, or other property bearing legal title papers are involved, informal family property distribution can't work. Title to a house, for example, can't be changed on the say-so of the next of kin. Someone with legal authority must prepare, sign, and record a deed transferring title to the house to the new owners, the inheritors.

Further, whenever outsiders are involved with a deceased's property, do-it-yourself division by inheritors is not feasible. For instance, creditors can be an obstacle; a creditor concerned about being paid can usually file a court action to compel a probate proceeding.

Another stumbling block for an informal family property disposition is disagreement among family members on how to divide the deceased's possessions. All inheritors must agree to the property distribution if probate is bypassed. Any inheritor who is unhappy with the result can, like creditors, file for a formal probate. If there's a will, the family will probably follow its provisions. If there is no will, the family may look up and agree to abide by the inheritance rules established by the law of the state where the deceased person lived. Or, in either case, the family may simply agree on their own settlement. For example, if, despite a will provision to the contrary, one sibling wants the furniture and the other wants the tools, they can simply trade.

In sum, informal probate avoidance, even for a small estate, isn't something you can count on. Realistically, you must plan ahead to avoid probate.

Other Probate-Avoidance Methods

Besides the living trust, these are the most popular probate-avoidance methods:

- joint tenancy or tenancy by the entirety
- pay-on-death financial accounts
- transfer-on-death registration for stocks and bonds
- retirement accounts
- life insurance
- state laws that exempt certain (small) amounts of property left by will from probate, and
- gifts made while you are alive.

These methods are discussed briefly in Chapter 15.

RESOURCE

More on avoiding probate. These and other probate-avoidance techniques are discussed in detail in *Plan Your Estate,* by Denis Clifford (Nolo).

While I'm a fan of living trusts, I don't believe they are always the best probate-avoidance device for all property of all people in all situations. It's up to you to determine whether a living trust is the best way for you to avoid probate for all your property, or whether you want to use other methods.

Reducing Estate Taxes

A basic probate-avoidance living trust, either for a single person or a couple, does not, by itself, reduce federal estate or state inheritance taxes. The taxing authorities don't care whether or not your property goes through probate; all they care about is how much you owned at your death. Property you leave in a revocable living trust is definitely considered part of your estate for federal estate tax purposes.

Under federal law, the personal estate tax exemption allows a set dollar amount of property to pass tax-free, no matter who it is left to. This amount varies, depending on the year of death, as shown below.

The Personal Estate Tax Exemption	
Year of Death	Estate Tax Exemption
2009	$3.5 million
2010	Estate tax repealed
2011	$1 million unless Congress extends repeal

As you can tell from this chart, the amount of the federal estate tax exemption fluctuates significantly between 2009 and 2011. It does not seem sensible to have no estate tax whatsoever in 2010, and then tax all estates worth over $1 million in the next year. The consensus of estate planners is that Congress will have to revise the exemption rules, and will probably do so relatively soon after the 2008 election—but not soon enough for this ninth edition of this book. A plausible guess is that the exemption will be settled at $3 million or $4 million.

Definition: Federal Estate Tax Threshold

Because the amount of the personal exemption depends on the year of death, no one dollar figure can define the amount of an estate that can be transferred tax-free under this exemption. Rather than repeat this table each time I refer to the personal exemption, I use the term "estate tax threshold" to mean the amount of the personal exemption in any and all years. .

In addition to the personal exemption, all property left to a spouse (if that spouse is a U.S. citizen) or to a tax-exempt charity is exempt from estate tax.

Some specialized kinds of living trusts can save on estate taxes. This book contains two such tax-saving trusts: two types of an AB trust.

If you are a member of a couple with combined property worth over the estate tax threshold, you could save your inheritors substantial estate taxes by using one of Nolo's AB trusts. Basically, an AB trust allows each member of a couple to use a separate personal estate tax exemption (that is, use two exemptions in total) while leaving one spouse's property for the use of the surviving spouse. AB trusts are explained in depth in Chapters 4 and 5.

SEE AN EXPERT

When to get expert help. If the combined value of your and your spouse's estates exceeds the estate tax threshold, you would benefit from estate tax planning help that's beyond the scope of this book, although an AB trust will likely be a key component of your final plan. See Chapter 17 for information about finding and hiring a lawyer.

Other Advantages of a Living Trust

As you know, the main reason for setting up a revocable living trust is to save your family time and money by avoiding probate and perhaps estate taxes as well. But there are also other advantages. Here is a brief rundown of the other major benefits of a living trust.

Out-of-State Real Estate Doesn't Have to Be Probated in That State

The only thing worse than regular probate is out-of-state probate. Usually, an estate is probated in the probate court of the county where the decedent was living before he or she died. But if the decedent owned real estate in more than one state, it's usually necessary to have a whole separate probate proceeding in each one. That means the surviving relatives must find and hire a lawyer in each state, and pay for multiple probate proceedings.

With a living trust, out-of-state property can normally be transferred to the beneficiaries without probate in that state.

You Can Avoid the Need for a Conservatorship

A living trust can be useful if the person who created it (the grantor) becomes incapable, because of physical or mental illness, of taking care of his or her financial affairs. The person named in the living trust document to take over as trustee at the grantor's death (the successor trustee) can also take over management of the trust if the grantor becomes incapacitated. (See Chapter 7.) When a couple sets up a trust, if one person becomes incapacitated, the other takes sole responsibility. If both members of the couple are incapacitated, their successor trustee takes over. The person who takes over has authority to manage all property in the trust, and to use it for the grantor or grantors' benefit.

EXAMPLE:

Wei creates a revocable living trust, appointing herself as trustee. The trust document states that if she becomes incapacitated, her daughter Li-Shan will replace her as trustee and manage the trust property for Wei's benefit.

If there is no living trust and no other arrangements have been made for someone to take over property management if you become incapacitated, someone must get legal authority, from a court, to take over. Typically, the spouse, partner, or adult child of the person seeks this authority and is called a conservator or guardian. Conservatorship proceedings are intrusive and often expensive, and they get a court involved in your personal finances on a continuing basis.

Durable Power of Attorney

You should also give your successor trustee (or spouse) the authority to manage property that has not been transferred to the trust if you become incapacitated. The best way to do that is to prepare and sign a document called a "Durable Power of Attorney for Finances." (See Chapter 15.)

Your successor trustee has no power to make health care decisions for you if you become incapacitated. If your preference is to die a natural death without the unauthorized use of life support systems, you'll want to prepare and sign health care directives. (This is discussed in Chapter 15.)

Your Estate Plan Remains Confidential

When your will is filed with the probate court after you die, it becomes a matter of public record. A living trust, on the other hand, is a private document. Because the living trust document is never filed with a court or other government entity, what you leave, and to whom, generally remains private. There are just a couple of exceptions. First, records of real estate transfers are always public, so if your successor trustee transfers real estate to a beneficiary after your death, there will be a public record of it. Second, some states require the successor trustee to disclose information about your living trust to trust beneficiaries. These requirements are explained in Chapter 14.

A handful of states require that you register your living trust with the local court, but there are no legal consequences or penalties if you don't. (Registration is explained in Chapter 12.) Also, registration of a living trust normally requires that you just file a paper stating the existence of the trust and the main players—you don't file the document itself, so the terms aren't part of the public record.

In most cases, the only way the terms of a living trust might become public is if—and this is very unlikely—after your death someone files a lawsuit to challenge the trust or collect a court judgment you owe them.

You Can Change Your Mind at Any Time

You have complete control over your revocable living trust and all the property you transfer to it. You can:

- sell, mortgage, or give away property in the trust
- put ownership of trust property back in your own name
- add property to the trust
- change the beneficiaries
- name a different successor trustee (the person who distributes trust property after your death), or
- revoke the trust completely.

If you and your spouse or partner create the trust together, both of you must consent to changes, although either of you can revoke the trust entirely. (See Chapter 13.)

No Trust Record Keeping Is Required While You Are Alive

Even after you create a valid trust that will avoid probate after your death, you do not have to maintain separate trust records. This means you do not have to keep a separate trust bank account, maintain trust financial records, or spend any time on trust paperwork.

As long as you remain the trustee of your trust, the IRS does not require that a separate trust income tax return be filed. (IRS Reg. § 1.671-4.) You do not have to obtain a trust taxpayer ID number. You report all trust transactions on your regular income tax returns. In sum, for tax purposes, living trusts don't exist while you live.

You Can Name Someone to Manage Trust Property for Young Beneficiaries

If there's a possibility that any of your beneficiaries will inherit trust property while still young (not yet 35), you may want to arrange to have someone manage that property for them until they're older. If they might inherit before they're legally adults (age 18), you should definitely arrange for management. Minors are not allowed to legally control significant amounts of property, and if you haven't provided someone to do it, a court will have to appoint a property guardian.

When you create a living trust with this book, you can arrange for someone to manage property for a young beneficiary. In most states, you have two options:

- Have your successor trustee (or your spouse, if you created a shared living trust) manage the property in a child's trust until the child reaches an age you designate.
- In all but two states (South Carolina and Vermont), you can appoint an adult as a "custodian" to manage the property until the child reaches an age specified by your state's Uniform Transfers to Minors Act (18 in a few states, 21 in most, but up to 25 in a few).

Both methods are explained in Chapter 9.

No Lawyer Is Necessary to Distribute Your Property

With a living trust, the person you named as your successor trustee has total control over how the property is transferred to the beneficiaries you named in the trust document. With a will, the executor is technically in charge of the property that passes under the terms of the will, but the probate lawyer usually runs the show. This can include the personal show as well as the silly court show. I've heard of a lawyer calling a family in for a reading of the deceased's will immediately after the funeral service, which some family members found highly insensitive. There's much less chance of this type of crassness if only close personal relations are involved in the transfer of the property.

Possible Drawbacks of a Living Trust

A basic living trust can have some drawbacks. They aren't significant to most people, but you should be aware of them before you create a living trust. Aside from the problems discussed below, an AB living trust, which is designed to save on estate taxes as well as avoid probate, has a whole set of its own potential drawbacks, which are covered in Chapter 4.

Initial Paperwork

Setting up a living trust requires some paperwork. The first step is to create a trust document, which you must sign in front of a notary public. So far, this is the same amount of work as is required to write a will.

There is, however, one more essential step to make your living trust effective. *You must make sure that ownership of all the property you listed in the trust document is legally transferred to the living trust.* (Chapter 11 explains this process in detail.) Transferring property into your trust is simply a matter of doing the paperwork correctly. What you have to do depends on the kind of property you're putting in the trust.

- If an item of property doesn't have a title (ownership) document, then in most states, listing it in the trust document is enough to transfer it. So, for example, no additional paperwork is legally required for most books, furniture, electronics, jewelry, appliances, musical instruments, paintings, and many other kinds of property.
- If an item has a title document—real estate, stocks, mutual funds, bonds, money market accounts, or vehicles, for example—you must change the title document to show that the property is owned by the trustee of the trust. For example, if you want to put your house into your living trust, you must prepare and sign a new deed, transferring ownership from you to your living trust.

After the trust is created, you must keep written records sufficient to identify what's in and out of the trust whenever you transfer property to or from the trust. This isn't burdensome unless you're frequently transferring property in and out, which is rare.

EXAMPLE:

Misha and David Feldman put their house in a living trust to avoid probate, but later decide to sell it. In the real estate contract and deed transferring ownership to the new owners, Misha and David sign their names "as trustees of the Misha and David Feldman Revocable Living Trust, dated March 18, 20xx."

Transfer Taxes

In virtually all states, including California, New York, Florida, and Texas, transfers of real estate to revocable living trusts are exempt from transfer taxes usually imposed on real estate transfers. Washington, DC, used to tax transfers of real estate to living trusts, but repealed those laws.

If you're the cautious type, you can check with your county tax assessor to learn if there will be any transfer tax imposed on transfer of your real estate to your trust. Your county land records office (county recorder's office or registry of deeds) may also be able to provide this information. As I've said, you're very likely to learn that no tax is imposed. If there is a tax but it is minor, it may impose no serious burden on creating your trust. If the tax is substantial, you may decide it's too costly to place your real estate in a trust.

Difficulty Refinancing Trust Real Estate

Because legal title to trust real estate is held in the name of the trustee of the living trust—not your name—some banks, and especially title companies, may balk if you want to refinance it. They should be sufficiently reassured if you show them a copy of your trust document, which specifically gives you, as trustee, the power to borrow against trust property.

In the unlikely event you can't convince an uncooperative lender to deal with you in your capacity as trustee, you'll have to find another lender (which shouldn't be hard) or simply transfer the property out of the trust and back into your name. Later, after you refinance, you can transfer it back into the living trust. It's a silly process, but one that does work.

No Cutoff of Creditors' Claims

Most people don't have to worry that after their death creditors will try to collect large debts from property in their estate. In most situations, there are no massive debts. Those that exist, such as outstanding bills, taxes, and last illness and funeral expenses, can be readily paid from the deceased's property. But if you are concerned about the possibility of large claims, you may want to let your property go through probate instead of a living trust.

If your property goes through probate, creditors have only a set amount of time to file claims against your estate. A creditor who was properly notified of the probate court proceeding cannot file a claim after the period—about six months, in most states—expires.

EXAMPLE:

Elaine is a real estate investor with a good-sized portfolio of property. She has many creditors and is involved in a couple of lawsuits. It's sensible for her to have her estate transferred by a probate court procedure, which allows creditors to present claims, resolves conflicts, and cuts off the claims of creditors who are notified of the probate proceeding but don't present timely claims.

On the other hand, when property isn't probated, creditors still have the right to be paid (if the debt is valid) from that property. In most states, there is no formal claim procedure. (California has enacted a statutory scheme for creditors to get at property transferred by living trust.) The creditor may not know who inherited the deceased debtor's property, and once the property is found, the creditor may have to file a lawsuit, which may not be worth the time and expense.

If you want to take advantage of probate's creditor cutoff, you must let all your property pass through probate. If you don't, there's a good chance the creditor could still sue (even after the probate claim cutoff) and try to collect from the property that didn't go through probate and passed instead through your living trust.

Human Realities and Living Trusts

Before plunging deeper into the mechanics of creating your own living trust, I want to switch gears and acknowledge the underlying realities we're talking about here: death, and the transfer of your property after death. Although property concerns can be minor indeed in the face of the overwhelming force and mystery of death, these deep imponderables are beyond the scope of this book and are appropriately left to poets, philosophers, clergy, and—ultimately—to you.

Planning for the transfer of property on your death can raise deep emotional concerns, problems, or potential conflicts. No matter how well you deal with the legal technicalities of making your living trust, it won't achieve what you want unless you take human concerns into account.

For many people—probably most—no serious personal problems arise when preparing a living trust. They know to whom they want to give their property. They have no difficulty deciding whom to name as successor trustee. They do not foresee conflict among their beneficiaries or threat of a lawsuit by someone angry at not being named a beneficiary. These people can, happily, focus on the satisfactions they expect their gifts to bring.

However, not everyone's situation is so clear and straightforward. Some people must deal with more difficult human dynamics, such as possible family conflicts, dividing property unequally between children, providing care for minor children, or handling complexities arising from second or subsequent marriages.

Before beginning the work of preparing your living trust, it's vital that you assess your personal circumstances and resolve any potential human problems regarding distribution of your property. If you're sure you don't face any such problems, wonderful. If, however, you think you might face complications—or if you're not sure what kinds of problems can come up—try to identify and resolve those problems now, or as you go along. After all, you surely don't want the distribution of your property to result in bitterness, family feuds, or fights between former friends.

A self-evident truth about a living trust is that it transfers property—money or things that can be converted into money. Money, as most of us have learned, is strange stuff indeed. It has power to do good in a number of material ways, and can alleviate anxiety and provide security. Unfortunately, however, human flaws and fears can be unleashed when substantial sums of money are involved; meanness, greed, and dishonesty have certainly been known to surface. Naturally, in making your gifts, you don't want to unnecessarily stir up negative feelings or emotions.

Sadly, bitterness, strife, and lawsuits are far from unheard of upon distribution of property after one's death. This chapter discusses a number of personal concerns, based on examples drawn from my living trust legal practice.

Leaving Unequal Amounts of Property to Children

Most parents feel it's very important to treat their children equally regarding the distribution of property, to avoid giving the impression that they value one child more than another. However, in some situations, parents sensibly conclude that the abstract goal of equal division of property isn't the fairest or wisest solution for their children. The most important issue here, I suggest, is to explain your reasoning to your children.

EXAMPLE:

A single mother with three grown children feels that one, a struggling pianist, needs far more financial support than her other two, who have more conventional and well-paying jobs. She wants to give the pianist the bulk of her money, but worries this might cause problems among her children. So she writes a letter explaining that she loves all three children equally and that her decision to give the pianist more is a reflection of need, not preference. She attaches the letter to her living trust. She also leaves most family heirlooms, which are emotionally but not monetarily valuable, to the other two children to emphasize how much she cares for them.

EXAMPLE:

An elderly couple owns a much-loved summer home in the Poconos. Only one of their four children, Skip, cares about the home as much as they do, and they plan to give it to him. But they question whether they should reduce his portion of the rest of their estate by the value of the home, or divide the rest of their estate equally among their four children, and on top of this, give the summer home to Skip.

As the family is a close one, they discuss the problem with the kids. One of them doesn't think their last alternative is fair. Skip doesn't think so either. The parents decide to give Skip less than one-fourth of the rest of their estate, but not to reduce his share by the full value of the summer home. They explain their decision to the others on the basis that Skip helped maintain the summer home for many years, and that his work should be recognized. It is, and the plan is accepted in good grace by all.

Second or Subsequent Marriages

People who marry more than once may face problems reconciling their desires for their present spouse (and family) with their wishes for children from prior marriages. Individual situations vary greatly here, and you must work carefully through your needs and desires. How much of one spouse's property might a surviving spouse need? How much property does each spouse want to leave to his or her own children? Sometimes, spouses can readily resolve such concerns and use a Nolo living trust to leave their property.

EXAMPLE:

Ben and Estelle met in the 1970s, as teachers in an alternative school. They fell in love, ran away to Oregon to live in a commune, and had two daughters. What a long, strange trip it was; they wound up, to their considerable surprise, owning a prosperous business in San Francisco. Now that it is time to draw up their living trust, Ben and Estelle are in complete accord about how to distribute their property, with one exception—Ben's daughter, Susan (now age 47), from his first marriage. Ben wants to leave her a substantial part of his estate; he suggests 20%. Estelle thinks that is outrageous, since his daughter has treated him terribly for decades, and is a wastrel with money besides. Estelle says it's too late to try to buy her love. Ben insists he feels a duty to his child no matter how she treats him.

Fortunately, both Ben and Estelle recognize signs of trouble and understand they're talking about a lot more than property here. What, if anything, does Ben owe his child? Will his ex-wife get involved if his daughter inherits money? If so, so what? Ben and Estelle discuss these problems themselves and with a therapist they see from time to time.

Eventually, they reach a compromise. Ben will leave some property to Susan, but not a percentage of his total estate. He and Estelle agree on a figure of $40,000.

You may, however, want more control than a Nolo living trust offers. Many couples with substantial assets create a trust leaving property to the surviving spouse for his or her life, with specific, limiting controls over how that property can be spent for that spouse. Then, when that spouse dies, the trust property goes to children from the other spouse's prior marriage(s). These types of "life estate" trusts are briefly discussed in Chapter 15. (They are discussed in more depth in Nolo's *Plan Your Estate,* by Denis Clifford.) You need a lawyer to draft this kind of trust.

Couples in subsequent marriages have additional estate-planning concerns. First, spouses need to make legal provisions for what is to be done medically if one spouse becomes incapacitated—that is, if he or she can no longer make decisions for himself or herself. Family members have been known to disagree about appropriate medical care needed. Fortunately, there are standard legal documents you can prepare to make your wishes for medical care clear and mandatory. (See "Planning for Incapacity" in Chapter 15.)

Another concern can be characterization of assets: What's hers, what's his, and what's theirs? You'll want to be sure that property is properly classified, so there can be no confusion about who owns what. (See Chapter 6.)

EXAMPLE:

Ellen and Alex, a married couple, each have children from prior marriages. Both spouses want to eventually leave their property to their own children, but both also want to protect the interest of the survivor. They own a house in equal shares. If the first spouse to die leaves half directly to his or her children, they may want to sell it or use it before the other spouse dies. At best, the surviving spouse will be insecure and, at worst, may be thrown out of the house. Neither spouse wants to risk that.

They decide to each leave the other what's called a "life estate" in their one-half of the house, specifying that the surviving spouse cannot sell the house. For instance, if Alex dies first, Ellen can live in the house during her lifetime, but when she dies, Alex's share automatically goes to his children. Because Ellen's share will go to her kids, the house will probably be sold, and the proceeds divided, when she dies.

Single People

A living trust can be every bit as desirable for a single person as for a couple. Any person, single or not, who wants to avoid probate, can successfully use a living trust.

EXAMPLE:

Alina, in her 50s, is a single mother with two teen-age children. Alina's major asset is her house, which is mostly paid for. Alina wants to leave all her property equally to her children. She sensibly does not want probate fees paid on the transfer of her house after she dies. So she sets up a living trust and transfers ownership of her house to it. In the trust, she also creates a child's trust for each of her two children. If either child is under 35 when Alina dies, that child's trust property will be held in a child's trust until that child reaches age 35. Alina names her sister Natasha to serve as trustee of any child's trust that becomes operational.

Disinheriting a Child

Sometimes people are troubled by deciding how much, if any, property to leave to a child. Legally, you can completely disinherit a child if you want to. (However, those who are accidently disinherited by their parents can claim part of their parents' estate.) But deciding to disinherit a child is often not emotionally easy to do. Many people decide that something less harsh than disinheritance is desirable. Rather than completely cutting off a child by direct words, they decide that it's wiser to leave some small, lesser amount to this out-of-favor child.

EXAMPLE:

Toshiro and Miya have three daughters and a substantial estate. They are very close to two of the daughters, but are bitterly on the outs with the third, Kimiko. Toshiro and Miya had originally intended to leave most of their property to the surviving spouse, and some to the two daughters they're close to. Then, when the surviving spouse dies, the remaining property is to be divided between these two daughters.

But they have second thoughts. Do they really want to cut Kimiko out entirely? If they do, aren't they creating an incentive for her to sue and try to invalidate their estate plan? They decide that good hearts and prudence both dictate the same decision. Each will leave Kimiko $25,000 in their living trust and include a "no-contest" clause in both their wills and trusts. This clause states that if any beneficiary challenges a will or trust, she gets nothing if her challenge is unsuccessful. The parents expect Kimiko to take the certain $50,000 rather than risk an expensive lawsuit she's very likely to lose. Also, Toshiro and Miya are relieved that they haven't had to formally disinherit one of their own children.

If you decide to disinherit a child, you must make that explicitly clear in your will.

Unmarried Couples

Unlike married couples, unmarried couples in most states have no automatic legal right to inherit any of each other's property.

A major concern of most unmarried couples is to ensure that each will inherit property from the other. Happily, people have the right to leave their property by living trust to whomever they want.

EXAMPLE:

Ernesto and Teresa have lived together for several years. Aside from a few small gifts to friends or family, each wants to leave all their property to the other after death. They're concerned with efficiency and economy, but above all they want to be sure that their estate plan can't be successfully attacked by several close relatives who have long been hostile to their lifestyle. Each then prepares a living trust, leaving their property as they desire. They videotape their signing and the notarization of this document to provide additional proof they were both mentally competent and not under duress.

If either member of an unmarried couple has children, they'll want to do specific planning for each child.

EXAMPLE:

John and Byron have been together for 15 years. Six years ago, John adopted a son, Max. John and Byron both serve as parents for Max. John and Byron each prepare a living trust, leaving property to Max in a child's trust and naming the other partner as successor trustee of that trust.

In his will, John specifies that if Max is a minor when he dies, he desires that Byron be appointed Max's guardian. John consults an attorney to discuss how he can prepare the most persuasive case for Byron, so that, if the need arises, a judge (who gets the final, official say) will be mostly likely to appoint Byron as guardian.

Same-Sex Couples

Now that a number of states offer same-sex couples the option of marriage or marriage-like relationships, surviving members of these couples may have inheritance rights similar to those of spouses.

Connecticut and Massachusetts are the only states that allow gay and lesbian couples to marry. When one member of any married couple dies, the surviving spouse has certain inheritance rights. (See Chapter 6.)

Lesbian and gay couples can register as domestic partners in the states listed below. The terminology in each state is different—for example, in Vermont and Connecticut, couples go through a "civil union"—and the particulars differ, but the couples get a status that is close or identical to that of married couples. Below is a summary of the inheritance rights offered by each state.

If you registered your same-sex partnership in one of these states (and if you still live in that state), you may have these rights. Specifically, if you die intestate (without a living trust or will) your estate will pass to your partner rather than to another member of your family.

A strong note of caution, however. While some folks work to expand protections for same-sex couples, others work just as hard to thwart them. Laws here today, could be repealed tomorrow. Additionally, you cannot rely on other states to enforce the rights your state gives to same-sex couples.

You should not rely on your state's law to transfer your property on your death. Make your own decisions defining who gets what. Then prepare the appropriate documents to ensure that your desires are carried out. It's never wise to allow the state to do your financial planning, and particularly not for a matter as important as who inherits your property.

State	Type	Inheritance Rights for Surviving Partner
California	Domestic Partnerships	No (community property instead)
Connecticut	Civil Unions and Marriage	Yes
Hawaii	Reciprocal Beneficiaries	Yes
Maine	Domestic Partnerships	Yes
Massachusetts	Marriage	Yes (spousal rights)
New Hampshire	Civil Unions	Yes
New Jersey	Civil Unions	Yes
Oregon	Domestic Partnerships	Yes
Vermont	Civil Unions	Yes
Washington	Domestic Partnerships	Yes

Communicating Your Decisions to Family and Friends

Most of the examples in this chapter demonstrate my belief that talking can help resolve many potential difficulties with family and friends. But talking is not a panacea. Certainly, there are times when someone doesn't want to listen or talk, or times when communication reveals only a deep and unbridgeable gulf. Still, most of the people I've worked with have been aided by talking openly about what they want to accomplish with their living trusts. If you have a personal problem or two, something to work out on an emotional level, it can require a good deal of thought, understanding, and consideration. For these problems, two or more heads do seem better than one. ●

Common Questions About Living Trusts

Complexities and doubts sometimes arise between considering a living trust and deciding to prepare one, so before you move into the heart of this book, read through this chapter. It answers a number of questions about living trusts I've been asked over the years, both by clients and by readers of my estate planning books.

Does Everyone Need a Living Trust?

For those who want to plan now to avoid probate, living trusts are usually the best probate-avoidance device. Indeed, most people who plan their estates ultimately choose a living trust to transfer their property, at least their big-ticket assets—house, stocks and bonds, and other valuable items.

Given the advantages of avoiding probate, shouldn't every prudent person use a living trust for all of his or her property? A number of lawyers make that claim in advertisements and seminars, but it's too extreme. First, some people don't really need to plan now to avoid probate. Second, other probate-avoidance methods may fit an individual's needs better, at least for certain types of property.

Generally, you may not need a living trust, at least not right now, if:

- **You are young and healthy.** Your primary goals probably are to be sure your property will be distributed as you want, and to provide financial resources and arrange for someone to care for your minor children, if you have any. A will (perhaps coupled with life insurance) often achieves these goals more easily than a living trust.

  Here's why: A will is simpler to prepare than a living trust. While using a will usually means property goes through probate, probate occurs only after death. As long as you are alive, the fact that probate will be avoided is of no benefit. Because very few healthy younger people die without any warning (and because they often don't yet own enough property that would make probate fees amount to much), it can make good sense to use a will for a number of years. Later in life, when the prospect of death is more imminent and you have accumulated more property, you can create a living trust to avoid probate.

Different Views on Living Trusts for Young People

Some attorneys maintain that living trusts are desirable for younger people because they provide protection if you can longer manage your estate. If you become incapacitated without having named a person to make decisions for you, a court will have to hold a conservatorship proceeding to appoint a guardian. A living trust could protect against this possibility.

This view may (or may not) make sense for your situation. The risk of a young person suddenly becoming incapacitated is low. Further, most young people don't own substantial assets or an estate that needs to be "managed." For these reasons, many young people conclude that they have enough to deal with already, and choose not to create a living trust in their youth. On the other hand, some very cautious young people may decide to plan for incapacity by making a living trust.

- **You can more sensibly transfer your assets, or at least some of them, by other probate-avoidance devices.** Other easy ways to avoid probate include joint tenancy, pay-on-death bank accounts, transfer-on-death securities accounts, life insurance, and gifts. In addition, the laws in some states allow certain amounts or types of property (and occasionally all property left to certain classes of beneficiaries, such as a surviving spouse) to be transferred without probate even if a will is used. None of these devices has the breadth of a living trust, which can be used to transfer virtually all types of assets. However, each can be easier to use, and equally efficient, in particular circumstances. It's best to understand all probate-avoidance methods and then to decide which ones will work best for you. (See Chapter 15.)

- **You have complex debt problems.** If you have a serious debt problem, such as a business that has many creditors, probate provides an absolute cutoff time for notified creditors to file claims. If they don't do so in the time permitted (a few months, in most states), your inheritors can take your property free of concern that these creditors will surface later and claim a share. A living trust normally doesn't create any such cutoff period, which means your property could be subject to creditors' claims for a much longer time.

- **Your primary goal is to name a personal guardian to care for your minor children.** A living trust shouldn't be used for this purpose. You do this in your will.

Naming a Guardian for Minor Children in a Living Trust

A few states' laws, such as California's, can be read to allow the appointment of your minor children's personal or property guardian in your living trust. However, this is most definitely not common practice. A judge must confirm the appointment of any acting personal or property guardian. It's unwise to present judges with novel legal documents when important matters are at stake.

A will can always be used to name a personal guardian for your minor children. (See Chapter 16.) If you have a great deal of valuable property, you will probably create a living trust (or other probate-avoidance device) to transfer it, and name a personal guardian for your minor children in a "backup" will.

- **Your state has streamlined probate procedures.** Wisconsin lets married couples avoid probate altogether for their marital property by using a written agreement. For Wisconsin couples who don't want a tax-saving AB trust, this procedure could work fine. By contrast, in most other states with simplified probate, you still have to pay a lawyer. For example, in Texas, probate is usually not very complicated, but property still must go through court, and a lawyer will take fees. The process will probably be more costly than using one of Nolo's do-it-yourself living trusts.
- **You are separated but not yet divorced.** To protect the rights of divorcing spouses, your state may have very specific rules about what you can and cannot do with property after separation but before your divorce is final. See a lawyer before trying to create a living trust or transferring property in or out of one.

- **You own little property.** If you don't have a lot of assets, there isn't much point in bothering with a living trust and probate avoidance, because probate won't cost that much. Often parents in this situation provide money for their young children, in case of a parent's death, by purchasing life insurance. (Insurance proceeds do not go through probate.) However, insurance proceeds (above a minimal amount) cannot be turned over to children under 18. So you may need to leave the proceeds under your state's Uniform Transfers to Minors Act (available in all states except South Carolina and Vermont). Using this act, you name an adult custodian to manage the money for the benefit of the child until the child becomes an adult. (See Chapter 9.)

How large should your estate be before you need to concern yourself with avoiding probate? There's no mathematical rule here. Even a relatively small estate—say $50,000—might cost $1,000 or more to transfer by probate. If you have a small estate, you may want to check out the dollar amount of property your state allows to be transferred by a will without formal probate. This varies widely from state to state. California, one of the more generous states, allows you to transfer up to $100,000 by will free of probate. Most states allow much less. You can find a state-by-state list of each state's rules in *Plan Your Estate*, by Denis Clifford (Nolo). Basically, if you own any significant amount of property, it's desirable to avoid probate.

If I Prepare a Living Trust, Do I Need a Will?

Yes. Even if you arrange to transfer almost all your property by a living trust, you should always prepare a backup will. A backup will can serve several purposes. Use your backup will to:

- name beneficiaries for property that is generally not desirable to transfer to a living trust, such as your personal checking account or car
- name beneficiaries for any property that you haven't transferred to your trust or that you may not yet officially own (for example, lottery winnings, a lawsuit settlement, or an inheritance)

- name a personal guardian who will look after your young, and
- name a property manager who will look after your children's property.

Backup wills are covered in Chapter 16. Tear-out will forms are included in Appendix B and on the CD-ROM.

How Can I Leave Trust Property to Children and Young Adults?

Chapter 9 covers how you can use your living trust to leave property to minor children or young adults. Here I cover some basic, preliminary questions.

Providing for Minor Children

You can leave property to minor children (those under 18) in your living trust and name an adult to manage that trust property.

If any of your living trust property is left to a beneficiary who's a minor when you die, an adult must manage that property for the minor.

What Your Living Trust Can't Do for Children

Do not use a living trust to name a personal guardian to care for your minor children if you die. Similarly, do not use a living trust to name a general property guardian to manage all property owned by your minor children. You must use your will for those purposes.

Various legal devices can be used to leave property to minors:

- **Small gifts for children's benefit.** If your estate is relatively modest and there is a trusted person to care for the child (usually the other parent), it's often easiest simply to leave property directly to the adult who will care for the child.
- **Larger gifts.** If the gift is larger—as a rough rule, say between $50,000 and $100,000—it can be desirable to leave the property by using the Uniform Transfers to Minors Act (UTMA) in your living trust. You name an adult custodian to manage the property you leave to the child.

The trust forms in this book have specific provisions allowing you to use the UTMA if your state has it. All states but South Carolina and Vermont have it.

- **Very large gifts.** The best way to leave even larger gifts—over $100,000—to minor children is generally by using a child's trust as part of your living trust. A child's trust allows you to designate the age at which the child will receive the property. Your successor trustee manages the trust property for the child's benefit until the child receives it outright.

The forms in this book allow you to create a child's trust as a part of your living trust. If you die before a minor beneficiary has reached the age you've chosen, that child's trust property is held in a child's trust. If you don't specify an age, the trust provides that the property remains in the child's trust until that child becomes age 35. This trust is irrevocable after your death. If the child has already reached that age when you die, she receives her property outright, and no child's trust is needed.

EXAMPLE:

One of the beneficiaries of Edward's living trust is Abigail, age 17. Edward establishes a child's trust for her, as part of his living trust. His trust states that she will receive her trust property when she becomes 35. Edward dies when Abigail is 26. Her property is maintained in the trust until she becomes 35.

While a child's trust is operational, the trustee (the successor trustee of your living trust) has broad powers to spend any of that trust's income or principal for the child's health, support, maintenance, or education. When the child reaches the age you specified for her to receive her property outright (or age 35, if you didn't specify an age), the successor trustee turns the trust property over to her.

Young Adult Beneficiaries Who Can't Handle Money Responsibly Now

A child's trust does not have to be used solely for minors. You can leave a gift in a child's trust for any beneficiary who is under 35 when you create your trust.

EXAMPLE:

Julio's son Enrique is 22. Julio wants to leave Enrique valuable property, worth over $250,000. Julio worries (sadly, with good reason) that Enrique isn't mature enough to handle this money responsibly if he inherits it soon. So Julio creates a child's trust for this gift to Enrique, and provides that Enrique will receive the gift outright at age 35.

Will My Living Trust Reduce Estate Taxes?

When some people hear the word "trust," they feel it must mean "tax savings." Not necessarily. Indeed, most living trusts are designed solely to avoid probate. A basic trust for a single person (Form 1 in this book), or a basic shared living trust for a couple (Form 2), will not reduce federal estate taxes.

By contrast, an AB living trust (Forms 3 and 4) can achieve substantial federal estate tax savings for a couple with a combined estate that may be liable for estate taxes.

Before you worry about estate taxes, check out whether your estate will be liable for them. Very few are. Read more about trusts and estate taxes in Chapters 4, 5, and 15.

Will I Have to Pay Gift Taxes?

Some people worry that by creating a living trust, they'll become enmeshed in gift taxes. Not to worry.

No gift tax is assessed when you transfer property to your living trust. To make a taxable gift, you must relinquish all control over the property. Since you keep complete control over property in your living trust (and you can revoke the trust at any time before you die), you don't make a gift simply by transferring property to the trust. (See Chapter 15 for a discussion of gifts and gift taxes.)

Will a Living Trust Shield My Property From Creditors?

Some people think that a living trust can protect their assets from creditors. No such luck.

While You're Alive

Property in a revocable living trust is not immune from attack by your creditors while you're alive. Some "authorities" have inaccurately stated that property in a revocable living trust can't be grabbed by the grantor's creditors, because for collection purposes a revocable living trust is legally distinct from its creator. I know of no law or court ruling that supports this position. It's most unlikely that any judge would accept it, because during your life you have complete and exclusive power over the trust property.

On the other hand, if property is put in an *irrevocable trust*—and you no longer have any control over it—it's a different legal matter. Property transferred to a bona fide irrevocable trust is immune from your creditors. The key words here are "bona fide." If an irrevocable trust is set up to defraud creditors, it's not bona fide. This book does not include irrevocable trusts.

 SEE AN EXPERT

Keeping creditors away from your property. If you're concerned about protecting your assets from creditors, see a lawyer.

After Your Death

A living trust won't shield your assets from your creditors after your death either, even after the property has been turned over to your beneficiaries.

One advantage claimed for probate is that it ensures that one's debts and taxes are paid before property is distributed to inheritors. If duly notified creditors don't make their claims within an allotted time, they're simply cut off. Does that mean you should worry about how your debts, including estate taxes, get paid if there's no probate and no probate court supervision? In most cases—no.

Many people leave no significant debts, and even if they do, they normally leave sufficient assets to pay them. The most common kinds of large debts—mortgages on real estate or loans on cars—don't have to be paid off when the owner dies. Normally, these kinds of debts are transferred with the asset to an inheritor, who then becomes liable for the mortgage or loan. In other words, mortgages or car loans pass with the property and don't need to be paid off separately.

Your successor trustee (who should also be named as executor of your will) has the legal responsibility of paying your debts. If no probate occurs to cut off creditors' claims, all your property, including all property that was in the living trust, remains liable for your debts. This is true even after the property is transferred to inheritors. If only one person inherits from you, that person will wind up paying your debts and any estate taxes from the inherited property.

If there are several inheritors, who will pay your last debts and taxes might cause more confusion. You can eliminate this problem by designating a specific trust asset—often a bank account or stock market account—to be used to pay your debts. If you don't have a suitable asset available to do this, consider purchasing insurance to provide quick cash to pay debts. (Providing in your trust for payment of your debts is covered in Chapter 10.)

Do I Need a "Catastrophic Illness Clause" in My Trust?

The term "catastrophic illness clause" commonly refers to a clause that, hopefully, prevents assets from being used for the costs of a major illness that strikes you or your spouse when you want government aid to help pay the bills. Many people are concerned with becoming eligible for federal benefits without having to use up all (or even any) of their assets. They don't want their assets counted when eligibility for government aid is determined. Married couples want to protect at least the assets owned by the healthier spouse.

A catastrophic illness clause certainly sounds like a good idea. But unfortunately, no simple clause can protect your assets. Bluntly put, the law doesn't easily allow people to retain their assets and still become eligible for federal aid. There are various, more complex ways of protecting some of your assets if you're faced with huge medical bills, including making gifts, paying children for services, or using certain complex types of trusts.

RESOURCE

More information on protecting assets. Methods of hanging onto your assets are discussed in *Long-Term Care: How to Plan & Pay for It,* by Joseph Matthews (Nolo).

SEE AN EXPERT

Individualized advice on protecting assets. If you want to take concrete actions to protect your assets from possible medical costs, see a lawyer knowledgeable in this distinct legal area. To help you, a lawyer must be up to date on relevant federal and state statutes and regulations, which can change fast.

How Does Where I Live Affect My Living Trust?

Living trusts are valid under the laws of every state. Still, a number of questions can arise about living trusts and where you live.

Determining Your Legal Residence

In your trust document, you'll name the state where you live; that state's laws govern the document. If you live in one state but work in another, it's the state where you live whose laws apply. You must also sign appropriate documents to transfer property to your trust in that state. (See Chapter 11.)

For most people, the state they reside in (in legalese, their "domicile") is self-evident. But for others, it can be more complex.

If during the course of a year you live in more than one state, your residence is the state with which you have the most significant contacts—where you vote, register vehicles, own valuable property, have bank accounts, or run a business.

If you might be justified in claiming more than one state as your legal residence, you may want to arrange your affairs so that your legal residence is in the state with the most advantageous state inheritance tax laws. Some states (such as New Jersey and Iowa) impose inheritance taxes; others (California and Florida, for example) essentially have no inheritance tax. (See Chapter 15.)

EXAMPLE:

Carlo and Sophia, a couple in their 60s, spend about half the year in Florida and the other half in Pennsylvania, which has an inheritance tax. They have bank accounts and real estate in both states. To take advantage of Florida's lack of a state estate tax, they register their car in Florida, vote there, and move their bank accounts there. This leaves them owning nothing in Pennsylvania but a condominium near where their son lives. They decide to sell him the condo and lease it back six months of every year, severing their last important property ownership contact with Pennsylvania.

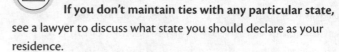

SEE AN EXPERT

Advice about your domicile. If you have significant contacts with more than one state, and a substantial estate, it may be worthwhile to have a lawyer with tax and estate planning experience advise you.

If You Live Outside the Country

If you are currently living outside the United States but are a permanent resident of the United States, you can prepare a valid living trust for property physically located within this country—usually real estate.

A problem here can be getting your living trust properly acknowledged (notarized or an equivalent). You need an acknowledgment that is legal in the state where the property is. That state's law may allow acknowledgment by officials outside the country. (California, for example, permits certain diplomatic personnel and foreign judges and notaries to acknowledge signatures.) However, it's risky to rely on a foreign acknowledgment, because title companies or other financial institutions that will be involved with the transfer of trust property after you die may not accept it. A title company may balk at accepting a trust (or deed) that has an unfamiliar kind of acknowledgment, even if it's legal under state law. (And, as an astute lawyer friend put it, "In real estate, the law is whatever a title company says it is.")

This leaves you three options:

- Have your trust notarized in the state where the property is located.
- Check to see whether that state allows foreign acknowledgments. If it does, contact a title company, and any other institution that will be involved in the transfer of in-state property, to see if it will accept a living trust (and real estate deed) with a foreign acknowledgment.
- Leave the property by will, not a living trust.

SEE AN EXPERT

If you don't maintain ties with any particular state, see a lawyer to discuss what state you should declare as your residence.

If you are in the Armed Forces and living out of the country temporarily, your legal residence is the state you declared as your Home of Record—the state you lived in before going overseas, or where your spouse or parents live.

If you acquire property, such as real estate, in a foreign country, you must check out that country's laws regarding transfer of real estate on death.

If You Move to Another State or Country

Revocable living trusts are valid and used in every state, and your trust remains valid if you move to a different state. However, if you're married and you move from a community property state to a common law state, or vice versa, you may want to check the marital property ownership laws of your new state. (See "Marital Property Laws" in Chapter 6.) Also, if you moved from a state that allows gifts to be made under the Uniform Transfers to Minors Act to a state that has not adopted the Act, and you made a gift using that Act, you'll have to amend this portion of your trust.

If you move to another country after creating a living trust, the trust remains valid. Under the 1961 Hague Convention (effective for U.S. citizens since 1981), a document notarized as a valid document in one country is recognized as valid by other countries that agreed to the treaty.

Out-of-State Beneficiaries or Successor Trustee

Your trust beneficiaries and your successor trustee can live in any state or any country.

Registration

Some states require "registration" of living trusts. These requirements are neither a serious burden nor reason not to use a trust. (See "Registering the Trust" in Chapter 12.)

Can I Place Real Estate in a Living Trust?

Generally, it's easy—and quite common—to place valuable real estate (usually your home, whether house or condominium) in a living trust. You simply prepare and record a deed, transferring the real estate from you, personally, to you as trustee of your trust. (See "Real Estate" in Chapter 11.)

Property Tax Reassessment

In some states, certain real estate transfers, such as sales to new owners who aren't family members, result in property being immediately reappraised for property tax purposes. By contrast, if the property is not transferred to new owners, it usually won't be reappraised for a set period of years, or is reappraised at a reduced rate.

In states that reappraise property when it's transferred to a new owner, placing title to property in a living trust very rarely, if ever, triggers a property tax reappraisal. For instance, California law (Cal. Rev. & Tax. Code § 62) expressly prohibits reappraisals for transfers to a living trust where the grantor is a trustee. To be absolutely sure that this is true in your state if you're transferring real estate into a living trust, you can check with your local property tax collector to learn exactly what reappraisal rules apply.

Transfer Taxes

Very rarely, if ever, are transfer taxes imposed when you transfer your real estate to your living trust. But to be absolutely safe here, check this out with your county assessor or recorder's office.

Deducting Mortgage Interest

For income tax purposes, the trust doesn't exist. You retain the right to deduct all mortgage interest from your income taxes, even though your home is technically owned by the trustee of your trust.

Insurance Policies

Insurance policies on your home—fire, liability, theft, and other particular policies—do not have to be reregistered in the trust's name. Like the IRS, insurance companies are concerned with the real ownership, not legal technicalities to avoid probate or reduce estate taxes. So there's no reason at all to contact your insurance company when you transfer your home or other real estate to your living trust.

Tax Breaks for Sellers

You have the right to sell your principal home once every two years and exclude $250,000 of profit from income taxation. A couple can exclude all profits up to $500,000. During your life, you retain that right even if you have transferred that home to a living trust (I.R.C. § 121).

Homestead Rights

Generally, transferring your home to a living trust does not affect the protection offered by state homestead laws. These laws typically protect a homeowner's equity interest in a home, up to a designated amount, from creditors. The living trust forms in this book each contain a specific statement that the grantor(s) intend to remain eligible for the state homestead exemption they would be entitled to if they still owned the real estate outside the trust.

Homestead Defined

A homestead is a legal device, available under the laws of most states, to protect a limited amount of equity in your home from creditors. In some states that allow homesteads, you record a Declaration of Homestead with the county land records office; in others, the protection is automatic. In either case, if you qualify for a homestead, your home is protected against forced sale by creditors (other than mortgage holders) if your equity is below the dollar limit set out in the statute.

However, if you're in debt and concerned that a creditor may try to force a sale of your house, check your state's homestead rules carefully. If you are not seriously in debt, there is no need to worry about this one.

Selling or Refinancing Your House

If you try to sell or refinance a house that is in a living trust, you might encounter some paperwork hassles, but nothing more serious. Some banks balk at refinancing a home that technically is owned by the trustee of a living trust, even if you show them the original trust document. Similarly, some title companies are reluctant to insure sales of a home by a trustee while the grantor is alive. By contrast, once an owner dies and a house is transferred to the beneficiaries, title companies routinely approve the sale of that real estate, even though it is transferred by a successor trustee.

If you encounter a problem trying to sell or refinance a house owned by your trust, you have two options:

- Seek a bank or title company that is reasonable and will allow the transaction in the trustee's name, which is fully legal.
- Transfer the property out of the trustee's name back into your individual name. Then go ahead with the sale or refinancing. Once the refinancing is completed, you can prepare yet another deed, again transferring the property back to the trustee. Convoluted, yes, but not really onerous.

Due-on-Sale Clauses

Federal law expressly prohibits enforcing a "due-on-sale" clause in a mortgage because of a transfer of one's home ("principal residence") to one's own revocable living trust. (The Garn-St. Germain Depository Institutions Act, 12 U.S.C. §§ 1464, 1701.)

Citations to Federal Statutes

Federal laws are codified in the United States Code, cited as U.S.C. A citation to a law lists the appropriate volume and sections of the U.S.C. For example, in the citation above, you can find the Garn-St. Germain Depository Institutions Act in Volume 12 of the United States Code, Sections 1464 and 1701.

The Internal Revenue Code is contained in Volume 26 of the U.S.C. This volume is often cited simply as I.R.C.

No statute expressly prohibits a bank from enforcing a due-on-sale clause when other real estate is transferred to a trust. However, I've never heard of it happening, probably because banks know it wouldn't make sense. After all, the transfer is flatly not a sale. No money changes hands. The IRS doesn't consider the transaction a sale. If a bank did try to claim that a due-on-sale clause was activated by a transfer of, say, investment or commercial real estate to a trust, you could always rescind the transaction and transfer the property back to your individual name.

Some cautious lawyers do obtain a bank's (mortgage holder's) prior consent to transfers of commercial real estate to a living trust. Sometimes banks charge a fee of $100 or $200 for consenting to the transfer.

Transferring Part Interests in Real Estate

Any portion of real estate you own, such as a time-share or percentage of ownership, can be transferred to a living trust. (See "Real Estate" in Chapter 11.)

Owning Real Estate in More Than One State

You must record a transfer deed in the land records office of the county where the real estate is located. So if you own one piece of real estate in Arizona, one in New York, and another in Vermont, you must record transfer deeds in all three states.

Rental (Income) Property

Under federal tax law, net profits received from rental property are "passive income." Losses in passive income cannot be used to offset profits or gains from "active income." However, there is a limited $25,000 exception to this rule for owners who "actively participate" in operation of the rental property. This $25,000 exception remains applicable if the rental property is placed in a living trust. (I.R.C. § 469.)

Contaminated Property

Under federal law, "responsible parties" are liable for the costs of cleaning up contaminated land. Responsible parties include past and current owners of the real estate—whether or not the present owners contributed to the contamination. Contamination includes pollution from various toxic or dangerous substances, such as petroleum products, dry cleaning solvents, and many other chemicals.

SEE AN EXPERT

If you own land that may be contaminated. If you own real estate that you know, or suspect, is contaminated, do not simply leave that property under your living trust, or by other means. You may be leaving someone a massive, very costly problem. See a lawyer experienced with problems of contaminated property.

Can I Sell or Give Away Trust Property While I'm Alive?

You can readily sell, transfer, or give away property in your trust.

Making Gifts

While you are alive, you can give away property held in your living trust. There are no restrictions on your power to make gifts from your trust. However, federal gift tax rules apply to gifts you make from trust property, as well as to gifts you make from your own nontrust property. (See "Federal Gift and Estate Taxes" in Chapter 15.)

Selling Trust Property

You can readily sell any property in your trust. There are two ways to go about it:

- Sell the property directly from the trust, acting in your capacities as grantor and trustee to sign the title document, bill of sale, sales contract, or other document. The trust documents in this book specifically state that the trustee has the power to sell trust property, including stocks or bonds.
- In your capacity as trustee of the living trust, first transfer title of the particular item of trust property back to yourself as an individual, and then sell the property in your own name.

The only reason for using the second option, which requires more paperwork, is if some institution involved in the sale insists you sell it in your own

name. This rarely happens. For instance, stock brokerage companies are familiar with sales by a trustee from a living trust. At most, you might have to point out to some overcautious bureaucrat that the specific trustee powers clause of your trust document specifically gives you authority to make the sale.

> **Amending Your Trust After Sale or Gift of Trust Property**
>
> You should amend your revocable living trust if you sell or give away property that the trust leaves to a particular trust beneficiary. Obviously, the trust document cannot give away what the trust no longer owns. (Amending living trusts is discussed in Chapter 13.)

Is a Bank Account Held in Trust Insured by the FDIC?

Yes. If the bank is covered by the FDIC, any bank account in the trust's or trustee's name is insured up to the $100,000 maximum per institution.

Banks also offer "pay-on-death" accounts, which function as de facto living trusts for the funds in the accounts, and which also are protected by the FDIC.

Will Property in My Living Trust Get a "Stepped-Up" Tax Basis When I Die?

Yes. Property left through any type of revocable living trust does get a stepped-up tax basis. This is an important concern for many people, who understand that, for inheritors of their property, a stepped-up basis is highly desirable for income tax reasons. Here's how it works.

To understand the concept of stepped-up basis, you must first understand what "basis" means. Put simply, the basis of property is the figure used to determine taxable profit when the property is sold. Usually, the basis of real estate is its purchase price, plus the cost of any capital improvements, less any depreciation. Once you know the basis, you subtract that figure from what you sell the property for. The result is your taxable profit.

EXAMPLE:

Phyllis bought a home for $140,000. She puts $25,000 into capital improvements (new roof and foundation). So her basis in the property is $165,000. If she sells the property for $375,000, her profit is $210,000.

Under federal law, the basis of inherited property is increased, or "stepped up," to its market value as of the date the deceased owner died. (This is only fair, as the same property is valued, for estate tax purposes, at its market value as of the date the owner died.) At your death, the inheritors' basis of living trust property becomes the market value of that property at your death, not your original acquisition cost. Of course, if the property has declined in value since you bought it, the change in basis is a negative. However, given the long-term inflationary economy, property owned for a while usually increases in value. Thus, for most estates, the basis is stepped up.

EXAMPLE:

Continuing the example above, Phyllis dies and, through her living trust, leaves the house (with a market value of $375,000) to her niece, Nancy. Nancy's basis in the house is $375,000. If she promptly sells it for that amount, she has no taxable profit.

In community property states (see the list in Chapter 8), both halves of property owned jointly by both spouses receive a stepped-up basis when one spouse dies. This includes both spouses' property held in an AB trust. In all other states (called "common law" states), the property of a married person who dies receives a stepped-up basis. However, property already owned by the surviving spouse does not get a stepped-up basis; it retains the basis it had. Thus, with an AB trust in a common law state, when one spouse dies, that spouse's trust property receives a stepped-up basis. However, the trust property of the surviving spouse does not.

EXAMPLE:

Alexander and Harriet, residents of New York, share ownership of a house with a basis of $200,000. When Alexander dies, the house is worth $800,000. The basis of Alexander's share is stepped up to its value at the time of death, or $400,000. However, Harriet's share retains its original basis, which is one-half of $200,000, or $100,000.

If Alexander and Harriet lived in Texas, a community property state, and had the same property situation, each spouse's share of the house would receive a stepped-up basis to $400,000 when Alexander died.

> **CAUTION**
>
> **Stepped-up basis rules repealed for 2010.** Under the estate tax law on the books when this edition was printed, in 2010 inheritors will receive a stepped-up basis only for inherited property worth a total of $1.3 million when the deceased person dies (plus an additional $3 million for a surviving spouse). During 2010, all property above this $1.3 million limit received by inheritors will carry the same basis as it had before the deceased person died. As of now, in 2011 the estate tax will return. Whether the stepped-up basis rules will also return is not certain. Indeed, the entire estate tax "repeal" is so confusing that it seems likely that Congress will have to reexamine that question sometime before 2010.

Who Must Know About My Living Trust?

Normally, the only person who must know about your living trust before you die is your successor trustee. And even he or she need know only where the trust document is, not what's in it. However, most people do show the trust document to their successor trustee. After all, you should fully trust this person. And it should make the job easier to know in advance what property the trust owns, and who gets it after your death.

Whether or not to tell your beneficiaries what's in your trust and who gets what is entirely your personal decision. Personally, I believe it's wisest to inform at least your major beneficiaries of your trust gifts, unless you have a compelling reason not to do so.

What About Free Living Trust Seminars?

Advertisements for free living trust seminars or talks are common these days. Be cautious about these. Some are given by reputable attorneys or other financial professionals who are seeking new clients and offer legitimate information. Others are given by scam artists, high-pressure salespeople who pressure you to buy an expensive trust (and perhaps life insurance or an annuity as well). Do not agree to buy anything on the spot. You should never have to rush to prepare a living trust. Take time to be sure you are getting something you need and want.

Could Someone Challenge My Living Trust?

A trust can be challenged in court. In our judicial system, any legal document, including a living trust, can be challenged this way. But theory doesn't matter here, reality does. The important questions to ask are:

- Is there any likelihood someone will challenge my living trust?
- If there is, what can I do to protect myself?

Legal challenges to a living trust are quite rare. You don't need to concern yourself unless you think a close relative might have an axe to grind after your death.

Some people ask about including a "no-contest" clause as a protection against a lawsuit attacking their trust. A no-contest clause doesn't prevent anyone from contesting the validity of your trust. It simply says that if a beneficiary contests your living trust and loses, he or she gets nothing. Thus, a no-contest clause will not discourage a nonbeneficiary from suing. Nor will a no-contest clause necessarily deter a disgruntled beneficiary who wants more, and is willing to risk losing what you've given him or her by suing.

SEE AN EXPERT

Adding a no-contest clause. If you think you need a no-contest clause, it's an indication you have a potentially serious problem—someone who might challenge your trust. See a lawyer.

Following are the kinds of legal challenges that can theoretically be made against a living trust.

Challenges to the Validity of the Trust

Someone who wanted to challenge the validity of your living trust would have to bring a lawsuit and prove that:

- when you made the trust, you were mentally incompetent or unduly influenced by someone, or
- the trust document itself is flawed—for example, because the signature was forged.

Proving any of this is not easy. It's generally considered more difficult to successfully challenge a living trust than a will. That's because your continuing involvement with a living trust after its creation (transferring property in and out of the trust, or making amendments) is evidence that you were competent to manage your affairs.

Lawsuits by Spouses

Most married people leave much, if not all, of their property to their spouses. But if you don't leave your spouse at least half of your property, your spouse may have the right to go to court and claim some of your property after your death. Such a challenge wouldn't wipe out your whole living trust, but might take some of the property you had earmarked for other beneficiaries and give it to your spouse.

The rights of spouses vary from state to state. (See "Disinheritance" in Chapter 8.)

Lawsuits by a Child

Children usually have no right to inherit anything from their parents. There are two exceptions: laws that give minor children certain rights and laws that are designed to protect children who are unintentionally overlooked in a will.

Minor Children

State law may give your minor children (those under age 18) the right to inherit the family residence. The Florida constitution, for example, prohibits the head of a family from leaving his residence in his will (except to his spouse) if he is survived by a spouse or minor child. (Fla. Const. Art. 10, § 4.)

Overlooked Children

Some state laws protect offspring who appear to have been unintentionally overlooked in a parent's will. The legal term for such an overlooked offspring is a "pretermitted heir." In most states, this term means a child born after the will was signed. Though the law is unclear, it could be argued that a child omitted from a living trust was also a pretermitted heir. Fortunately, it's easy to avoid these problems. See Chapter 8 and Chapter 16. ●

What Type of Trust Do You Need?

No law specifies the form a living trust must take. As a result, there is no such thing as a standard living trust. Indeed, there are a bewildering variety of living trust forms. Some attorney-created forms contain vast piles of verbiage, which serve little real-world purpose except to generate attorney fees.

This book offers four types of legal living trusts, as clear and understandable as I can make them:

- a probate-avoidance trust for an individual
- a probate-avoidance trust for a couple that owns property together, called a "basic shared living trust"
- a probate-avoidance and estate tax-saving AB trust for a prosperous couple, and
- an AB disclaimer trust, which can provide more flexibility concerning estate tax decisions than a standard AB trust.

Both of Nolo's AB trusts can be beneficial for couples with a net combined estate worth more than the estate tax threshold. To remind you, as of the date of the printing of this edition of this book, the estate tax threshold may be reduced to $1 million in 2011 and thereafter. So the cautious approach is to use an AB trust if your combined estates may exceed $1 million. This is discussed more in Chapter 5.

Using More Than One Living Trust

Legally, you can have more than one living trust, for different types of property. Although it isn't necessary for most people, in complex property ownership situations, using more than one trust can make sense. For example, you might set up one trust for your business and another for the rest of your property, if you want one of your business associates to act as successor trustee to handle and transfer your business property, but a spouse, friend, or close relative to distribute your other property.

If You Are Single

If you are single and making a living trust by yourself, use Nolo's living trust for one person (Form 1). If you are a single parent, you can use Form 1 to create a living trust to leave property for your minor children.

You can use this form to leave all of your property, or any part of it, including your share of co-owned property. For instance, if you own a house together with your sister, you simply transfer your share of that house into your trust. Similarly, you can transfer your share of a partnership or shares in a small corporation to your trust, assuming the partnership agreement or corporate charter and by-laws permit it.

With Nolo's individual trust, you can also:

- name your successor trustee or trustees, and
- leave property to minors or young adults— including your own children, of course—through a child's trust, or a gift under the Uniform Transfers to Minors Act. (See Chapter 9.)

EXAMPLE:

Alfonso is a single parent of two teenage daughters. His major assets are a house and a solely owned electrical supply business. He creates an individual living trust, and transfers the house and business to it. In the trust, he leaves his property equally to his two daughters. Because they are minors, he creates a child's trust for each daughter to last (if needed) until that daughter becomes 30. He names his sister Grace to be trustee of each trust. He also creates a will, and names Grace to be guardian of his children if he dies before both have become legal adults.

If you decide to make an individual trust, go to Chapter 6, which explains what property to put in your living trust.

A More Complex Trust

Some single people want to create a trust that does more than avoid probate. For example, a sibling might want to create a "life estate" trust that first avoids probate, then leaves property for the benefit of a brother for his life, and then at the brother's death leaves the property outright to other beneficiaries.

SEE AN EXPERT

Preparing a complex trust. If you are single and want to create a living trust that accomplishes goals other than avoiding probate and, if you need it, establishing a child's trust, see a lawyer. Drafting a complex trust requires careful attention to the specifics of your situation. You cannot use Nolo's individual living trust to accomplish these goals.

If You Are Part of a Couple

Couples—married or unmarried—often own property together. They can legally set up a living trust that doesn't change that shared ownership. In their trust, they can also include property that is separately owned by either spouse.

Terminology for Unmarried Couples

Because most couples who use shared living trusts are married, my discussion of these trusts is cast in terms of "spouses" and "marital property." However, the discussion applies equally to unmarried couples. It's too awkward to restate this point in each sentence or sprinkle the text with terms such as "partners" or "significant others." Please, if you are a member of an unmarried couple, make the necessary semantic substitutions for yourself.

This book provides three ways for members of a couple to create a living trust:

- Each spouse prepares an individual trust.
- Both spouses prepare one basic shared living trust.
- Both spouses prepare one AB trust or one AB disclaimer trust.

The next sections examine each option in detail.

Individual Trusts for Members of a Couple

A member of a couple can legally use a separate, individual trust for all of his or her property, or can use two living trusts: one trust for separately owned property and another trust for property shared with the other spouse. But this is rarely necessary or advisable. As you'll see below, both separately owned and shared property can be conveniently handled in one shared living trust.

Most couples prefer not to create two individual trusts because it requires dividing property they own together, which is normally the bulk of their property. Splitting ownership of co-owned assets can be a clumsy process. For example, to transfer a co-owned house into two separate trusts would require the spouses to sign and record two deeds transferring a half-interest in the house to two separate trusts. And to transfer household furnishings to separate trusts, spouses would have to allocate each item to a trust or do something as silly as each transferring a half-interest in a couch to his or her trust.

In some common law states (see the list in Chapter 6), some attorneys advise couples to go this route. The claimed advantage for this is that it's then easier, upon the death of a spouse, to tell what property each spouse owns. I think this type of caution is unnecessary, and not worth the drawbacks of dividing shared property while both members of the couple are living. With a properly drafted trust—either a basic shared living trust or an AB trust—there should be no difficulty identifying what property belonged to which spouse.

If, however, you and your spouse own most or all of your property separately, you may each want to make an individual trust. Most couples who want this fit one of these profiles:

- You live in a community property state, and you and your spouse signed an agreement stating that each spouse's property, including earnings and other income, is separate, not community property. (See Chapter 6 for a discussion of community property.)

- You don't want to give your spouse legal authority as your successor trustee over your property when you die. (See Chapter 7.)

- You are recently married, have little or no shared or community property, and want to keep future property acquisitions separate. (To accomplish this, you'll both need to sign a written statement of your intentions.)

- You each own mostly separate property acquired before your marriage (or by gift or inheritance), which you conscientiously keep from being mixed with any shared property you own. Couples who marry later in life and no longer work often fit into this category. Not only is the property they owned before the marriage separate, but Social Security benefits and certain retirement plan benefits are also separate, not shared, or community, property.

EXAMPLE:

Howard and Luisa live in Indiana, a common law state. Both have adult children from prior marriages. When they married, they moved into Howard's house. They both have their own separate bank accounts and investments, and one joint checking account that they own as joint tenants with right of survivorship.

Each makes an individual living trust. Howard, who dies first, leaves his house (and furnishings) to Luisa, but his other property to his children. The funds in the joint checking account are not included in his living trust, but pass to Luisa, also without probate, because the account was held in joint tenancy. Howard's other bank accounts go to his children, under the pay-on-death arrangement he has with the bank. (Joint tenancy, pay-on-death accounts, and other probate-avoidance methods are discussed in Chapter 15.)

If you and your spouse decide on separate living trusts, each of you will transfer your separately owned property to your individual trust. If you own some property together—a house, for example—you each transfer your portion of it to your individual trust.

SEE AN EXPERT

Preparing separate trusts. If you and your spouse decide to prepare two separate trusts and do not name each other as successor trustees, you may want to see a lawyer to be as certain as you can that there won't be any conflict between your spouse and your successor trustee.

Basic Shared Living Trusts

If you and your spouse own most or all of your property equally together and don't want to divide it up and transfer it into two separate trusts, you'll probably choose to make one living trust and transfer all of your property—both shared and separately owned—to it. While you live, each of you retains full ownership of all your separate property, as well as your share of jointly owned property.

EXAMPLE:

Lorenzo and Marsha are married and own a house together. Marsha also owns, as her own property, some valuable jewels left to her by her mother. Lorenzo owns, as his separate property, some stock his uncle gave him.

Lorenzo and Marsha create one shared living trust and transfer all of their jointly owned property to it. Marsha's jewelry is also placed in this trust, identified as her separate property. Similarly, Lorenzo's stock is placed in this trust, identified as his separate property. Neither loses any ownership rights to her or his separate property by placing it in the shared living trust.

If probate avoidance is your only goal, you can use a basic shared living trust no matter how much all of your property is worth. But if your and your spouse's combined estates exceed the estate tax threshold, you should at least consider an estate tax-saving trust, such as Nolo's standard AB trust or AB disclaimer trust, explained below.

How a Basic Shared Trust Works

With this book's basic shared marital trust, designed to avoid probate, you and your spouse will be cotrustees of your living trust. You'll both have control over your shared ownership property in the trust. In theory, this means either spouse can act alone to sell or give away shared trust property. However, because banks, title companies, and others often have their own rules requiring both spouses' signatures, as a practical matter, the consent of both to sell or transfer shared property is commonly necessary.

SEE AN EXPERT

If one spouse will not be a trustee. If for any reason—health, mistrust, whatever—you don't want your spouse to serve with you as a trustee of your basic shared trust, see a lawyer.

As I've said, each of you retains sole control over your separate property, because in the trust document it's identified and listed as property owned by only one spouse. With your separate trust property, you may:

- sell it, give it away, or leave it in the trust
- in the trust document, name a beneficiary or beneficiaries to inherit that property, or
- amend the trust document to name a new beneficiary or beneficiaries for that property. Technically, trust amendments require consent of both spouses, but this should be a mere formality where a spouse wants to amend the trust to name new beneficiaries for his or her property. If the other spouse proves recalcitrant—say the couple is getting divorced—either spouse can revoke the entire trust and prepare a new one for his or her property.

Each spouse is also free to add separately owned property to the trust later.

In the trust document, each spouse names beneficiaries for his or her share of shared ownership property, as well as all of his or her separate property. Commonly, spouses leave all, if not the bulk, of their property to each other. But leaving all or most of your property to your spouse isn't legally required. Each spouse has complete freedom in choosing beneficiaries, except that married couples are subject to legal restrictions in many states that entitle a surviving spouse to claim a certain share of a deceased spouse's estate. (See "Marital Property Laws" in Chapter 6.)

A spouse's separate property is kept separate in a shared trust by means of trust "schedules," which are lists of trust property attached to the trust document. Schedule A lists co-owned property. Property listed on Schedule B is the separate property of one spouse (traditionally, the wife), and all property listed on Schedule C is the separate property of the other spouse (traditionally, the husband).

If spouses want to leave significant amounts of property to each other, a basic shared living trust provides another big advantage over individual trusts. With a basic shared trust, property left by one spouse to the survivor automatically stays in the living trust when the first spouse dies. It becomes part of the property the surviving spouse has in what is now his or her individual living trust. No formal transfer documents are needed. If separate, individual trusts were used, property left to the surviving spouse would need to be transferred first from the deceased spouse's trust to the name of the surviving spouse and then, to avoid probate, the second spouse would have to transfer it into his or her own living trust.

Either spouse can revoke the trust at any time. If either spouse revokes the trust, the couple's property ownership situation returns to exactly what it was before the trust was formed. Shared property is returned to the ownership of both spouses, and separately owned property goes to the spouse who owned it. By contrast, amendments to the trust document require the consent of both spouses. For example, both must agree to change the successor trustee.

What Happens When One Spouse Dies

When one spouse dies, the shared living trust is split into two trusts, Trust 1 and Trust 2; this is automatic under the terms of the basic living trust document. The surviving spouse is sole trustee of both trusts. (The surviving spouse's duties are discussed in Chapter 14.)

Trust 1 contains the deceased spouse's share of trust property, except any trust property left to the surviving spouse. Trust 1 is irrevocable; that is, the surviving spouse can't change its terms, which dictate what happens to the property in it.

Trust 2, the survivor's trust, contains the surviving spouse's share of the trust property, plus any trust property left to him or her by the deceased spouse. Trust 2 remains revocable—the surviving spouse can make changes to it during his or her lifetime.

In many situations, since all property is left to the survivor, nothing need be done at this point. However, if the deceased left property in Trust 1 to others, the surviving spouse, as sole trustee of Trust 1, distributes that property to the named beneficiaries.

The trustee simply hands over the property to the beneficiaries, except for gifts left to minors or young adults in a child's trust or through the Uniform Transfers to Minors Act (UTMA). (See Chapter 9.) If the property is left in a child's trust, the surviving spouse manages that trust for the child until the child reaches the age specified by the deceased spouse in the trust document to receive the property outright. If the property is left to a custodian under the UTMA, the custodian manages the property until the child is old enough to be legally entitled to the property.

When all the property in Trust 1 has been distributed to the beneficiaries, including any property placed in a child's trust, Trust 1 ceases to exist. No formal documents need be prepared or filed to officially end the trust. Once its mission is accomplished, it simply evaporates.

Trust 2 (the survivor's trust) is basically a continuation of the original revocable living trust. As discussed, it contains any trust property the survivor inherited from the deceased spouse, as well as the surviving spouse's share of shared trust property and any separately owned trust property that belongs to the survivor. The surviving spouse is free to change or amend Trust 2 if he or she wishes to. For example, the surviving spouse might name a new successor trustee or name a new beneficiary for property that was to have gone to the deceased spouse.

EXAMPLE:

Harry and Maude, a married couple, set up a basic shared living trust to avoid probate. In their trust document, they name themselves cotrustees and appoint Maude's brother Al as successor trustee, to take over as trustee after they have both died. They transfer much of their shared ownership property—their house, money market accounts, and stocks—to the living trust. Maude also puts some of her family heirlooms, which are her separate property, in the trust.

The trust document states that Maude's brother Al is to receive the heirlooms when she dies; everything else goes to Harry. Harry leaves all his trust property to Maude. Both name their son, Edward, as alternate and residuary beneficiary. (The residuary beneficiary is the person who receives all property not left to other named beneficiaries. See Chapter 8.)

Maude dies first. The basic shared living trust splits into Trust 1, which contains Maude's heirlooms, and Trust 2, which contains everything else—Harry's half of the co-owned trust property and the trust property he inherits from Maude. Harry becomes the sole trustee of both trusts.

Following the terms of the trust document, Harry distributes Maude's heirlooms (from Trust 1) to Al, without probate. Trust 1 then ceases to exist. Harry doesn't have to do anything with the trust property Maude left him; it's already in Trust 2, his revocable living trust.

Harry later decides that Al is getting too ill and old to be a wise choice as successor trustee for Harry's trust. So Harry amends his trust, naming Edward to be his successor trustee. (See Chapter 13 for how to amend a living trust.)

With a shared trust, when the second spouse dies, the successor trustee takes over as trustee of Trust 2. This successor trustee is responsible for distributing the surviving spouse's trust property to the surviving spouse's beneficiaries, named in the trust document. If any trust property is left to a young beneficiary in a child's trust, the trustee will also manage it. Again, no formal documents are required to terminate Trust 2.

When a spouse dies, the surviving spouse may need to amend his or her living trust to name new beneficiaries or alternate beneficiaries.

EXAMPLE:

Continuing with Harry and Maude, after Maude's death, Harry names his son, Edward, as his trust's beneficiary and residuary beneficiary. Harry needs to name new alternate beneficiaries and chooses Edward's two children.

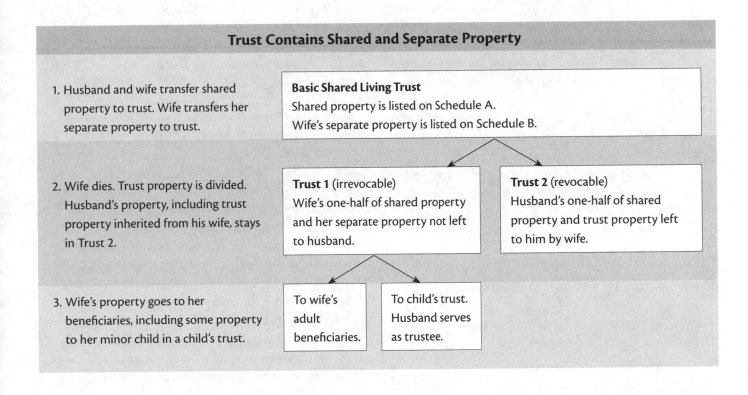

If your combined estate might be large enough to trigger estate taxes, then continue on to the next section. Otherwise, you can to skip to Chapter 6.

Tax-Saving AB Trusts

If you and your spouse have a large estate, you may well want to avoid estate taxes with an AB trust. This type of trust works by having each spouse maximize his or her use of the personal estate tax exemption.

To remind you, the personal estate exemption allows a set amount of property to pass free of federal tax. The amount depends on the year of death.

The Federal Estate Tax

You might have heard that Congress has "repealed" the estate tax. Actually, it has passed a law that's much more confusing than a simple repeal. The current federal estate tax law:

- increases the personal exemption to $3.5 million in 2009
- repeals the estate tax entirely for one, and only one, year—2010
- revives the estate tax, with an exemption of $1 million, for 2011 and thereafter, and
- greatly restricts the stepped-up basis rules for inherited property in 2010. (Stepped-up basis rules are discussed in Chapter 3.)

For both technical and political reasons, Congress could not flat-out repeal the estate tax law. The law it passed is a mess, in estate planners' opinions.

So how can anyone with substantial assets sensibly engage in estate tax planning? It would be extremely difficult to create three different plans—one if you die before 2010, another if you die in 2010, and yet another if you die in 2011. Worse, even if you could prepare a tri-part plan with the help of experts, it couldn't cover what you should do if Congress revises the estate tax law, which it is likely to do. It is the consensus of estate tax experts that Congress will need to revise the law before 2010. It's ridiculous to repeal the estate tax law in one year, and bring it back the next year with an exemption reduced to $1 million. Among the other oddities of that situation, it could make wealthy elderly people quite nervous during 2010, when their inheritors would have a huge financial interest in their dying during that year.

How Congress might revise the estate tax law is uncertain. It will depend upon political and economic realities that cannot be predicted now. For instance, Congress could decide to make the exemption $2 million or $5 million, and eliminate both further increases and the repeal.

For now, what you can sensibly do is devise a plan that provides flexibility. You may have to revise your plan when Congress revises the estate tax law.

You can find up-to-date estate tax rules by visiting Nolo's website, www.nolo.com.

Definition: Estate Tax Threshold

Because the amount of the personal exemption depends on the year of death, no set dollar figure can define the worth of an estate that can be left tax-free under the personal estate tax exemption. Rather than repeat this table each time I refer to the personal exemption, I use the term "estate tax threshold" to mean the amount of this exemption in any and all years.

Unmarried Couples

An unmarried couple can use an AB trust if it fits their needs. As with a basic shared trust, when describing an AB trust I refer to husbands, wives, and spouses, but no exclusion of unmarried couples is implied. In my experience, it's not common for an unmarried couple to want to use this type of trust, but it's certainly possible.

Suppose Anne and Frank—or Anne and Sylvia—have been an unmarried couple for a long while and have a child they both deeply love, whether both are biological parents or not. If this couple has a combined estate large enough to trigger estate taxes, they can use an AB trust and reap exactly the same benefits of probate avoidance and estate tax reduction as a married couple in a similar situation.

The Federal Personal Estate Tax Exemption

Year	Estate Tax Exemption	Highest Estate Tax Rate
2009	$3.5 million	45%
2010	Estate tax repealed	Top individual income tax rate for gift tax only
2011	$1 million unless Congress extends repeal	55% unless Congress extends repeal

Why Worry About Federal Estate Taxes?

Under U.S. tax law, a spouse can leave any amount of property, no matter how much it is worth, to the surviving spouse free of estate tax (unless that spouse is not a citizen). This is called the "marital deduction."

CAUTION

No marital deduction for unmarried couples. There is no exemption similar to the marital deduction for partners or "significant others" or whatever other name unmarried couples, whether gay or heterosexual, use for their mates. Quite simply, the estate tax laws are written to encourage and reward traditional relationships. (Don't blame or praise me; I didn't write the laws.)

Common Law Marriages

The marital deduction is available for couples in legal common law marriages. Such marriages may be created in Alabama, Colorado, District of Columbia, Georgia (only before January 1, 1997), Idaho (only before January 1, 1996), Iowa, Kansas, Montana, New Hampshire (for inheritance only), Ohio (only before October 10, 1991), Oklahoma, Pennsylvania (before January 1, 2005), Rhode Island, South Carolina, Texas, and Utah. If a couple creates a common law marriage in one of these states and then moves to another state, they are still legally married.

So what's the tax worry? After all, under the marital deduction, no tax will be assessed against any amount of property one spouse leaves another. In a nutshell, here's the problem: If a spouse leaves most, or all, of his or her property to the surviving spouse, the estate of the survivor can suddenly total more than the estate tax threshold. If this happens, estate taxes will have to be paid when the surviving spouse dies.

Estate planners call a tax due on the death of the surviving spouse the "second tax." The result of the second tax is to reduce the amount of money available to a couple's final inheritors, usually their children.

EXAMPLE:

Sven and Ingrid have a shared combined estate of $6 million. Each leaves his or her property to the surviving spouse. Eventually, when the second spouse dies, they want everything to go to their child Heidi.

Sven dies in 2007. No estate taxes are due, because his property is left to his wife.

After Sven's death, Ingrid's estate is worth $6 million. It has the same value when she dies in 2009. The personal exemption for that year is $3.5 million. So $2.5 million is subject to estate tax. This is the second tax. The tax owed is $1,125,000—money Heidi doesn't get.

It is this second tax that an AB trust is designed to eliminate. In the example above, if Sven and Ingrid had used an AB trust, when Sven died his half of the estate would have gone into trust, rather than to Ingrid. At Ingrid's death, there would have been no second tax because her estate would have been only $3 million—one-half million below the estate tax threshold for 2009.

The Purpose of an AB Trust

An AB trust is designed for couples with a combined estate over the estate tax threshold who want to leave most or all of their property to each other. Couples in this situation often have a clear goal: to keep the estate of the deceased spouse legally separate from the estate of the surviving spouse, while allowing the surviving spouse to benefit from the deceased spouse's property. An AB trust accomplishes this goal. The surviving spouse can receive all income from the deceased spouse's trust property and can even use that trust's principal for basic needs. But the deceased spouse's trust property is never legally owned by the surviving spouse.

This book presents two types of AB trusts:

- a standard AB trust, which mandates legal separation of each spouse's trust property when the first spouse dies, and
- an AB disclaimer trust, which allows the surviving spouse to decide whether to legally separate trust property a deceased spouse leaves to him or her.

The differences between these types of AB trusts are explained below and also in Chapter 5. For now, let's focus on how a standard AB trust can lower overall estate taxes.

Paying Trust Expenses

With both types of AB trust, the successor trustee (the surviving spouse) has authority to pay any expenses incurred in establishing Trust A, the deceased spouse's trust. With a probate-avoidance living trust, there shouldn't be any expenses when transferring property after a spouse dies except perhaps for minor fees for official document filings, such as to file a real estate deed.

How an AB Trust Can Solve the Second Tax Problem

With a standard AB trust, spousal estates are never combined. Rather, for tax purposes, each estate is kept separate. So each spouse's estate is subject to tax when that spouse dies. If each estate is under the estate tax threshold, no tax will be paid.

EXAMPLE:

Sam and Cynthia, an elderly couple, had an estate worth $4 million, owned equally. If each had left his or her half outright to the other, the survivor's estate would have been taxed unless the survivor were to die in 2010 because their combined estate exceeds the estate tax exemption in all years except 2010 (when the estate tax is repealed).

So instead of leaving their property outright to each other, Sam and Cynthia created a standard AB trust. Sam died in 2006 with trust property worth $2 million. The personal exemption for 2006 was $2 million, so no tax was due.

Sam's estate is never combined with Cynthia's and Cynthia still has $2 million in her estate. If Cynthia dies before 2011, no tax will be due on her estate because her estate is worth less than the estate tax threshold in 2009 ($3.5 million) and there is no estate tax in 2010. If she dies in 2011 or thereafter, her estate will be subject to tax, because it is over the current $1 million exemption. However, only $1 million will be taxable, resulting in much less

tax than it would be if the two estates had been combined. In that case, $3 million of the combined $4 million combined estate would be taxable.

An AB disclaimer trust works like a standard AB trust, with one crucial difference. With an AB disclaimer trust, when one spouse dies, the surviving spouse (acting as trustee) decides how much of the deceased spouse's property, if any, shall be placed in Trust A. Any property not placed in Trust A goes directly to the surviving spouse. If no property is placed in Trust A, that trust never becomes operational.

Given the current uncertainty about the amount of the estate tax exemption in the future, using an AB disclaimer trust is generally the best choice for a prosperous couple. Because the amount of the estate tax exemption varies so greatly over the next few years, and given the possibility that the estate tax law will be revised, it's wise to allow flexibility in determining how to allocate property between the estate of the deceased spouse and the taxable estate of the surviving spouse. (Remember, by contrast, with a standard AB trust, all of a deceased spouse's trust property must go to Trust A.)

EXAMPLE 1:

Maurice and Charlene have a combined estate of $5 million. They create an AB disclaimer trust. Maurice dies in 2009, with an estate of $2.5 million. Charlene disclaims the entire $2.5 million, so it goes to Trust A. The estate tax exemption for 2009 is $3.5 million, so no taxes are assessed on Maurice's property.

EXAMPLE 2:

The exact same situation, except Maurice dies in 2011 (and the estate tax exemption has not been changed, so it remains at $1 million). Now Charlene faces some more complicated choices. If she disclaims all of Maurice's $2.5 million, $1.5 million will be subject to estate tax. If she disclaims only $1 million, and keeps $1.5 million, no estate tax will be due on Maurice's death. However, her estate will now become worth $4 million, subject to estate tax when she dies. After consultation with her tax adviser, Charlene decides she'd rather pay no tax now, upon Maurice's death (even if the total tax burden is eventually higher). So she disclaims only $1 million to Trust A.

Another way to look at the tax benefit of an AB trust is that it allows each spouse to use the personal estate tax exemption. By contrast, if the estates are combined, only one spouse, the second to die, can use this exemption—and, as we've seen, it will be applied to a much larger estate than if the estates hadn't been combined.

With an AB trust, the surviving spouse can be given substantial rights to the deceased spouse's trust property without becoming the legal owner of it. Specifically, under IRS rules the surviving spouse can have the rights to use the trust property, to receive all income from it, and to spend trust principal for "support, health, education, or maintenance in accord with his or her accustomed manner of living." So with an AB trust, the surviving spouse is most definitely not left out in the cold from the deceased spouse's property.

A Trust by Any Other Name

The AB trust explained in this chapter goes by a variety of names in the world at large. You may hear the same type of trust called a "bypass" trust, an "exemption" trust, a "family" trust, or a "credit shelter" trust.

How an AB Trust Works

Here's a summary of how AB trusts actually work. (Nolo's two versions of AB trusts are explained briefly in the next section, and in more depth in Chapter 5.)

Together, both spouses create a shared living trust like the one described earlier in this chapter, with one crucial difference. (Sorry if I sound like a nudge, but please be sure you read carefully "Basic Shared Living Trusts," above.) What's different is that as part of their living trust, each spouse creates a separate AB trust—a trust within a trust. Actually, each AB trust contains two separate trusts, Trust A and Trust B.

With a standard AB trust, each spouse leaves all, or at least the bulk, of his or her property to Trust A, instead of outright to the survivor. As long as both spouses live, the couple's property remains in the living trust, which can be revoked or changed. When the first spouse dies, the living trust property is split into two separate trusts: Trust A, the deceased spouse's

trust, which now becomes irrevocable, and Trust B, the surviving spouse's revocable living trust.

Each spouse names the other as the "life beneficiary" of his or her Trust A. This means that the surviving spouse can use and benefit from the Trust A property for the rest of his or her life, with certain restrictions, but is not given outright ownership of it.

Each spouse also names the "final beneficiaries" of his or her AB trust. Final beneficiaries receive the Trust A property after the surviving spouse dies, and also receive the Trust B property after this spouse dies.

All trusts must have a trustee to supervise and manage trust property. With an AB trust, each spouse normally names the other as trustee. So the surviving spouse is both the life beneficiary and trustee of Trust A.

An AB disclaimer trust works the same, except that the surviving spouse has the crucial right to determine how much property, if any, goes to Trust A. Both spouses follow the above process in creating a disclaimer trust. They create a shared trust, operational while both live. Each creates a Trust A and names final beneficiaries for that trust. So a Trust A can become operational if the surviving spouse decides that's a good idea.

Only one of the couple's Trust As can become operational—that of the first spouse to die. The surviving spouse now has no use for his or her own Trust A, since there's no other living spouse. (If the surviving spouse remarries, however, a new AB trust can then be prepared.) The surviving spouse's property goes into Trust B. The reason each spouse prepares an individual AB trust (within the one overall living trust document) is that when they're setting up their estate plan, they can't know which spouse will be the first to die. So each spouse must have a Trust A, though only one will ever go into effect.

When a Trust A becomes operational, the survivor gets only a "life estate" interest in all property in Trust A. Because of this limited interest, the Trust A property is not entitled to the marital deduction. Rather, the Trust A property is subject to estate tax when the first spouse dies. If this property is worth less than the amount of the personal exemption for the year of death, no federal estate taxes are assessed. When the second spouse dies, the Trust A property is not subject to tax.

Leaving Property to Children

If you couldn't leave your spouse property without also saddling his or her estate with a large tax bill, one obvious alternative would be to leave much of your property directly to your children or other inheritors. This would make use of your personal estate tax exemption and wouldn't combine spousal estates, which causes the "second-tax" problem. But leaving property to others often conflicts with many couples' primary goal—providing the most financial security possible for the surviving spouse without tax detriment. Hence the popularity of the AB trust.

Complexities of AB Trusts

When one spouse dies, the surviving spouse has work to do. If a disclaimer trust was used, the spouse must decide whether to create an operational Trust A or not. If Trust A becomes functional, the surviving spouse must determine the value of property placed in it. With a standard AB trust, the surviving spouse must divide the trust property into Trust A and Trust B (at least on paper). This requires expert help. (See Chapter 14.) For any operational Trust A, new title documents must be prepared. Then the surviving spouse must obtain a taxpayer ID number for Trust A, maintain accurate Trust A financial records, and file an annual trust income tax return. This work is, for most people, worth it in light of the overall estate tax savings it achieves. But unless Trust A will, or seems likely to, save on taxes, there's no reason to establish it.

How an AB Disclaimer Trust Works

Technically, an AB disclaimer trust works by using the legal tool called (surprise!) a "disclaimer." A disclaimer is simply a written declaration by a beneficiary that she or he declines to accept property left to her or him. All beneficiaries have the legal right to disclaim property left to them; no one can be compelled to accept an inheritance. With a disclaimer trust, it's the surviving spouse who may disclaim trust property left to him or her by the deceased spouse.

With an AB disclaimer trust, spouses leave most or all of their trust property to the other. The trust document specifies that each spouse can disclaim any of the other's property. If the survivor does disclaim any property, it goes into Trust A. If the surviving spouse does not disclaim any of the deceased spouse's trust property, no Trust A is created. So the surviving spouse can decide whether or not to establish a Trust A based on the estate tax situation at the time of the first spouse's death—something impossible to be sure of now.

EXAMPLE:

A couple has a shared-property estate worth $6 million. The wife dies in 2009, when the exempt amount is $3.5 million. The surviving husband could disclaim all of his wife's property ($3 million), so that none of it could be combined with his taxable estate.

Now suppose that the wife dies in 2011, when the exemption will be reduced to $1 million. If the husband disclaimed $3 million in 2011, $2 million would be subject to estate tax. To avoid paying any estate tax, he could disclaim only $1 million, and receive the other $2 million directly. By contrast, with a standard AB trust, the husband would have to put all of the wife's trust property, the full $3 million, into Trust A.

Given the uncertainty over the future of the estate tax law, you may sensibly decide you want an AB trust that doesn't force the surviving spouse to split your AB trust into Trust A and Trust B.

An AB disclaimer trust also allows the surviving spouse to best plan for his or her financial and tax situation after the first spouse dies.

EXAMPLE:

Vanita and Steve have assets worth roughly $3.8 million. They create an AB disclaimer trust.

Vanita dies in 2009 with an estate worth $1.9 million. Steve could disclaim the entire amount and no estate tax would be due on Vanita's estate because it does not exceed the estate tax threshold for 2009 ($3.5 million). However, because Steve lost his job and the couple had some investment losses, Steve decides that he wants to inherit some of her

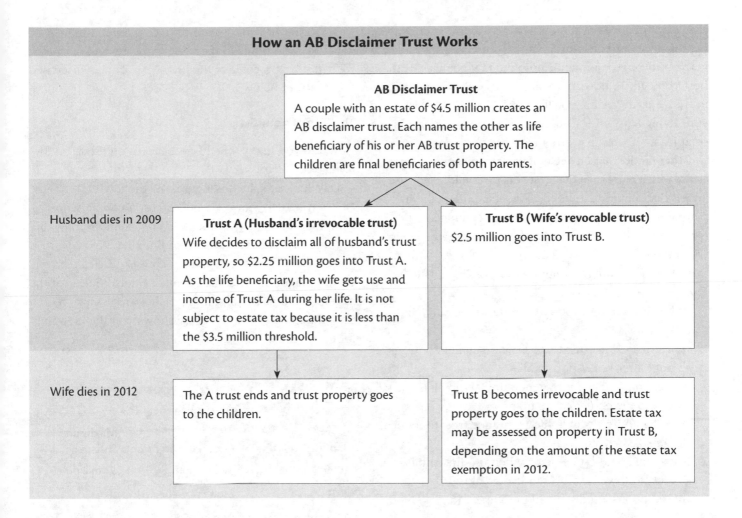

How an AB Disclaimer Trust Works

AB Disclaimer Trust
A couple with an estate of $4.5 million creates an AB disclaimer trust. Each names the other as life beneficiary of his or her AB trust property. The children are final beneficiaries of both parents.

Husband dies in 2009

Trust A (Husband's irrevocable trust)
Wife decides to disclaim all of husband's trust property, so $2.25 million goes into Trust A. As the life beneficiary, the wife gets use and income of Trust A during her life. It is not subject to estate tax because it is less than the $3.5 million threshold.

Trust B (Wife's revocable trust)
$2.5 million goes into Trust B.

Wife dies in 2012

The A trust ends and trust property goes to the children.

Trust B becomes irrevocable and trust property goes to the children. Estate tax may be assessed on property in Trust B, depending on the amount of the estate tax exemption in 2012.

money directly. So he disclaims $1 million of her property, which goes to trust A, and he directly inherits the other $0.9 million.

Risks of an AB Disclaimer Trust

A disclaimer trust isn't without potential drawbacks. Here are some you should think about.

A disclaimer trust gives the surviving spouse total control over trust assets left to the survivor. The surviving spouse can to choose to inherit the deceased spouse's property outright, even if that's not the wisest tax decision.

EXAMPLE:

Peter and Wanda, an elderly couple, have a combined estate worth $5 million. They create an AB disclaimer trust. Wanda dies in 2009, leaving her $2.5 million to Peter. If Peter takes Wanda's property outright and dies in 2011 or afterward, $4 million (under current tax law) of his estate would

be subject to tax. So creating a Trust A is an astute tax move.

However, Peter has secretly lusted after a house in the Hamptons for years. So he does not disclaim any of Wanda's property, and instead inherits it all. He uses it for a down payment on the house. Peter also now has the right to leave all of his property, including what once was Wanda's share, to whomever he wants. If a Trust A had been established, that trust's property would, after Peter died, have gone to the final beneficiaries Wanda named.

You still have to keep up with the estate tax law. As you know, current law provides that the estate tax exemption will be reduced to $1 million in 2011. But Congress will likely revise the estate tax law—somehow—before that date. If you're wealthy enough to concern yourself with estate tax, you need to keep abreast of changes in the tax law and revise your estate plan if necessary. Relying on an AB disclaimer trust to get you through, no matter how the law changes, is the best you can do now. But still, unless one of you dies in the next few years, you'll probably need to revise your living trust after Congress settles on a permanent, or at least apparently permanent, estate tax law.

Other tactics may be better if you or your spouse has an estate worth more than the estate tax threshold. Don't use an AB disclaimer trust without understanding other tax planning options. For instance, if your combined estate is over $7 million, estate tax will be assessed no matter when the surviving spouse dies (except for 2010). In this situation, you have a number of possible estate tax-saving strategies, including:

- leaving some property outright to the surviving spouse
- using a QTIP trust to postpone payment of taxes until after both spouses die
- creating one or more generation-skipping trusts to save on eventual estate taxes
- using an irrevocable life insurance trust to reduce the size of your estate, or
- paying some estate taxes when the first spouse dies, to lower the overall taxes paid.

These options are discussed in Chapter 15.

SEE AN EXPERT

See an expert. Advanced estate tax planning is a province of specialists. Talk with an accomplished lawyer before deciding on your wisest plan.

Choosing One of Nolo's AB Trusts

Here we'll look in detail at Nolo's AB trusts, to help you decide if one of them might work for you.

Is a Nolo AB Trust Right for You?

One of Nolo's AB trusts can work well for you meet all three of the following criteria:

- you and your spouse have a combined estate that may be subject to estate tax
- you want to leave all or the bulk of your estate to your spouse (if that's desirable tax-wise), and

- you want your spouse to have the maximum possible rights to the trust property, without being the legal owner of the property. (This is discussed further below.)

The Size of Your Estate

How can you know whether you'll save on estate tax by using an AB trust?

Let's look at some tax figures. At the low end, one of Nolo's AB trusts can be beneficial for a couple whose combined estate is over the personal exemption for the year the first spouse dies. Second, with a Nolo AB trust, you can shield from estate tax a combined estate worth up to double the personal exemption for the year of the first spouse's death (assuming each spouse owns half the property). The table below shows you the amounts for each year.

How Much a Nolo AB Trust Can Shield From Estate Tax		
Year of First Spouse's Death	Personal Exemption	Maximum Shielded
2009	$3.5 million	$7 million
2010	Estate tax repealed	
2011 and thereafter	$1 million	$2 million

From the table above, we can see that a combined estate worth over $2 million could benefit from an AB trust if both spouses were to die in 2011 or thereafter.

EXAMPLE:

Thalia and Tyrone, an elderly couple, prepare a Nolo AB disclaimer trust. Their combined estate is worth $2.8 million. Each spouse owns half. Tyrone dies in July 2011, and Thalia dies in 2013. If they had not used an AB trust, but each left their property outright to each other, Thalia would have wound up with an estate of $2.8 million. The personal exemption for 2013 is $1 million. So $1.8 million would be subject to tax. Surely, Thalia and Tyrone would prefer that this money go to their final inheritors rather than the U.S. Treasury.

Life is unpredictable—if you're old enough to investigate estate planning, you've certainly learned that. Since you can't predict how long you or you spouse will live, how can you determine whether your estate is within the guidelines for using Nolo's AB trust? The conservative approach is to assume that your AB trust will become operational in the year of the lowest estate tax exemption—which is $1 million.

So the most cautious approach would be for a couple to prepare an AB trust if their combined estate is over $1 million. That way, if the estate tax is not revised by Congress, and the estate tax exemption for 2011 and thereafter remains at $1 million (unlikely, but possible), they would obtain the tax benefits an AB trust provides.

Estimating the Value of Your Estate

To decide whether you want to use one of Nolo's AB trusts, you'll need a rough estimate of the net value of your estate. You don't need to obtain precise appraisals. You simply want a ballpark figure to see if your estate is likely to be over the estate tax threshold when you die.

You can use the Property Worksheet described in Chapter 6 if you want to itemize your property and make written estimates of its worth.

Your Personal Situation

From a personal point of view, Nolo's AB trusts work best when all involved—both spouses and all final beneficiaries—understand and agree on the purposes of the trust, which is to save on estate taxes and, at the same time, give the surviving spouse maximum rights to use Trust A money and property if Trust A becomes operational. Without this understanding, serious conflicts between the surviving spouse and the final beneficiaries may develop.

Nolo's AB trusts are designed for families where:

- The final beneficiaries understand that all property in any Trust A morally, albeit not legally, belongs to the surviving spouse. It is available for her or his basic needs, such as to pay for health care or to support her or his accustomed manner of living.

- The final beneficiaries understand that taking the trouble to create Nolo's AB trust is a generous act by parents, who do this not to benefit themselves, but their inheritors. After all, the estate tax savings benefit only the final beneficiaries, who receive more (usually much more) of the couple's combined estate than they would if the spouses had left property outright to the other.

- Family members are sufficiently trusting of each other, so that it's reasonable to believe they can resolve any inheritance conflicts without lawsuits (or bloodshed).

- The final beneficiaries can be trusted to support the surviving spouse if he or she (as trustee) decides he or she needs to spend trust principal for reasons authorized by the IRS and listed in the trust document—that is, "support, health, education, or maintenance in his or her accustomed manner of living." They won't question these expenditures (if there are any) in an effort to preserve the largest possible amount for themselves.

If there is any potential for conflict between the surviving spouse and the final beneficiaries of the trust (often the couple's children), an AB trust may provoke or aggravate it. After all, in theory at least, there is an inherent possibility of conflict of interest between the life estate beneficiary and the final beneficiaries. These final beneficiaries may want all the trust principal conserved, no matter what the needs or wishes of the surviving spouse.

Similarly, with an AB disclaimer trust, the surviving spouse can inherit outright all of the deceased spouse's trust property. If this happens, the final beneficiaries named by the deceased spouse lose all their legal rights to that property. The surviving spouse could amend her or his Trust B and name new beneficiaries for what was once the deceased spouse's property.

Another problem can arise if the surviving spouse becomes ill and can no longer serve as trustee. If a child who stands to eventually receive trust assets takes over as successor trustee, it's possible the child might be more concerned with preserving principal than with a parent's medical or other needs. I've heard of instances where it seemed to other family members and friends that a child, acting as trustee of Trust A, disregarded his parent's basic needs to protect the trust principal for himself.

Conflicts can also occur if the final beneficiaries believe the surviving spouse, as trustee, is not managing the trust property sensibly—for example, he is investing in very speculative stocks or real estate. If this situation arises, there can be real trouble, possibly even a lawsuit.

SEE AN EXPERT

Having doubts? See a lawyer. If you have doubts about these personal matters, one of Nolo's AB trusts is not for you. See a lawyer to work out a more individualized trust.

The Surviving Spouse's Rights Over Trust A Property

If a Trust A becomes operational, the surviving spouse's rights over that trust property are defined by the trust document. There is no one legal standard that must be used when defining the rights a surviving spouse has over the property in Trust A. The spectrum runs from the maximum permitted by the IRS (any more and the surviving spouse would become the legal owner of the trust property—exactly what you don't want) to fairly rigid restrictions and controls placed on how the surviving spouse can use the property.

Both of Nolo's AB trusts give the surviving spouse the maximum rights IRS regulations allow over Trust A property. The survivor:

- receives all interest or other income from the trust property
- is entitled to use and control the property—for example, he or she can live in a house that's owned by the trust, or sell it and buy another house or do other things with the profits of the sale, such as buy a retirement condo or conserve the profits in a trust account, and
- can spend (invade) any amount of Trust A property (principal) for his or her health, education, support, or maintenance in his or her accustomed manner of living.

EXAMPLE:

Mabel and Anthony, who together own property worth $1.8 million, create an AB disclaimer trust. Each names the other as the life beneficiary and trustee of Trust A. They have one child, Walter, who has two grown children, Rose and Tim. Mabel and Anthony each name all three as final beneficiaries: Walter to receive 60%, and Tim and Rose each 20%.

Mabel dies in 2012. Her estate is worth $900,000. Anthony disclaims all of her property so it goes to Trust A. Her estate is below the estate tax threshold. Anthony's same-sized estate goes into his revocable Trust B.

During 2013, Anthony suffers both major financial disasters and grave health problems. To continue his style of living, and pay medical bills, Anthony spends a total of $160,000 of Trust A principal. He also spends all the income from Trust A property. He does not become legal owner of the Trust A property even though he's spent a portion of the principal on himself. When Anthony dies, the amount remaining in Trust A is $740,000, which is turned over to the final beneficiaries.

With either of Nolo's AB trusts, the surviving spouse has the right to spend part or all of the Trust A principal for what really concerns most couples, particularly older ones—the surviving spouse's health care and other basic needs. (The rights of the surviving spouse are discussed in more detail in Chapter 5.)

The surviving spouse has no power to change the final beneficiaries of Trust A. (The surviving spouse can change the beneficiaries of his or her own, revocable trust.) The final beneficiaries of Trust A were named by the deceased spouse when the AB trust was originally prepared.

Couples Who Are Unlikely to Want Either of Nolo's AB Trusts

Should all married couples who might face estate taxes use an AB trust? No. Aside from couples whose estate is too large to safely use one of Nolo's AB trusts, it is generally not advisable for:

- Younger middle-aged couples—roughly, couples in their 40s, perhaps 50s. In this age group, you probably won't want to tie up assets in a trust, which may last for many years or decades, if one spouse dies prematurely. The surviving spouse could live for decades and be seriously burdened by the hassles and restrictions of the trust. (See "Drawbacks of an AB Trust," below.)

Many younger couples create a basic shared living trust to leave each other all or most of their property. Then, once they're older—say in their late 50s or 60s—they revoke their old trust and create an AB trust. (After all, for married couples, if one spouse unexpectedly dies, the survivor will inherit everything estate-tax free, no matter what the amount, because of the marital deduction.) The surviving spouse will probably have years to use the money—and years to arrange for other methods of reducing any possible estate tax. (See Chapter 15.)

- Couples where one spouse is considerably younger than the other and presumably will live much longer. Again, generally there's no need to burden the surviving spouse with a trust designed to save estate taxes when he or she is likely to live for many years. (Of course, such couples may well sensibly decide to use a basic shared living trust, to avoid probate.)
- Couples who don't want to leave the bulk of their property for use of the surviving spouse, but want instead to leave substantial amounts of property directly to other beneficiaries. If you want to make many specific gifts outside the AB trust property that add up to a substantial amount of money—as a rough rule, over $50,000 to $100,000—you can simply use a basic shared living trust. After all, if you won't leave most of your property for the benefit of your spouse, there's little reason to bother with an AB trust.
- Many couples in second or subsequent marriages. If a Trust A is established (under a standard or disclaimer trust), the surviving spouse can use that trust's principal for basic needs. Many people in second marriages do not want the other spouse to have this broad right. Spouses with children from prior marriages commonly want to be certain that these children will inherit some, or even most, of their property.

Further, one or both spouses may want a child from a former marriage to serve as trustee or cotrustee. Other concerns can include: Does the surviving spouse have the authority to sell Trust A property? What reports and accountings of Trust A must be given to the children, the final beneficiaries?

In sum, there are often worries about conflicts between the surviving spouse and the deceased spouse's children—how best to allocate rights and powers between them? If relations could become strained between your children and your spouse, you may very well not want to set things up so that they essentially share ownership of property for many years.

SEE AN EXPERT

Resolving personal issues. Many individual family concerns must be dealt with when setting up an AB trust for couples in second or subsequent marriages. You need to see an experienced estate planning lawyer to draft a trust specifically geared to your situation and desires. (These issues are discussed further in Chapter 15.)

Drawbacks of an AB Trust

Before deciding whether to use either of Nolo's AB trusts, both spouses should understand what they're getting into. Risks of an AB disclaimer trust—particularly, the power of the surviving spouse to inherit the deceased spouse's property and not set up the tax-saving Trust A—have already been discussed. Other drawbacks may arise when a Trust A becomes irrevocable and operational. Trust A imposes limits and burdens on the surviving spouse that cannot be changed.

Restrictions on the Surviving Spouse's Use of the Property in Trust A

The surviving spouse has the right to any income generated by Trust A property and fairly broad rights to use the property for health, education, and support. But he or she cannot spend trust property freely on whatever he or she feels like. Except for legally permitted expenditures, that property must be held in trust for the final beneficiaries.

Administrative Expenses

For either type of AB trust, when one spouse dies, an estate lawyer or accountant will usually be needed to determine how to best divide the couple's assets between the irrevocable Trust A and Trust B. Each item of the couple's shared property does not have to be divided 50-50 between the two trusts. The only requirement is that the shared property in both trusts must be of equal total value. There can be considerable flexibility in allocating assets between the two trusts. It usually takes an expert to decide on the best division. (See Chapter 14.)

Trust Tax Returns

The surviving spouse, as trustee of Trust A, must obtain a taxpayer ID number for this trust. Also, the surviving spouse must file an annual trust income tax return for that trust. This usually isn't a momentous hassle, but like any tax return, it'll require work.

Record Keeping

The surviving spouse must keep two sets of books and records: one for his or her own property (which remains in the surviving spouse's revocable living trust) and one for the property in Trust A (which is legally separate from property owned by the surviving spouse).

No Gifts From Trust A Principal

The surviving spouse has no rights, either as trustee of Trust A or as that trust's beneficiary, to make gifts of the Trust A principal to any other person. For instance, a surviving spouse may sensibly want to give some of the Trust A principal to a child, to help him or her purchase a home, or for other needs. But such a gift is not legal under IRS rules. The principal can be spent only for the surviving spouse's needs for "health, education, support, or maintenance."

More Complex Simultaneous Death Provisions

Here's an unlikely scenario, but one that could possibly occur. A couple creates an AB disclaimer trust. Then they're in a car crash. The husband dies instantly; the wife lingers for several weeks before succumbing. During those weeks she did not disclaim any of her husband's trust property. So no Trust A was established, and a higher estate tax bill results.

Trusts can include provisions to authorize someone else to make the disclaimer, if the surviving spouse in unable to. But do you want to bother with this? Most people don't. The chances of it occurring seem very low. However, if you want to be sure you've handled all possible contingencies regarding use of the disclaimer, you should see a knowledgeable estate planning lawyer, because state law determines who can have authority to exercise a disclaimer on behalf of an incapacitated principal.

To end this chapter on a note of optimism, despite the possible drawbacks and limitations, Nolo's AB trusts have worked very well for many thousands of couples and families. If it fits your situation and needs, it will work just fine for you and save your children or other final inheritors a bundle. For most surviving spouses, the drawbacks amount to no more than relatively minor accounting and record-keeping hassles. These hassles may be well worth conserving tens or even hundreds of thousands of dollars for the final beneficiaries.

Nolo's Tax-Saving AB Trusts

C ouples use one of Nolo's AB trusts for three primary purposes:

1. To save on estate taxes, increasing the amount that can be conserved for their children or other final beneficiaries.
2. To make the deceased spouse's property available for use by the surviving spouse to the extent legally permitted.
3. To avoid probate.

SEE AN EXPERT

Do not use either of Nolo's AB trusts if you want to restrict the surviving spouse's rights. Nolo's Trust A allows the surviving spouse to have as much right to the deceased spouse's trust property as IRS regulations permit. You may want to limit the surviving spouse's rights. For instance, some couples in second or subsequent marriages decide that the surviving spouse will have no right to spend the deceased spouse's trust principal, no matter what his or her needs. The desire is to make sure the principal remains intact for the deceased spouse's final inheritors, often including children from prior marriages. To prepare an AB trust with restrictions over the surviving spouse's rights in Trust A property, many individual questions must be resolved, and you will need a lawyer's help.

This chapter takes a deeper look at how Nolo's AB trusts work. First, let's review the tax rules.

The Size of Your Estate

As discussed in Chapter 4, AB trusts make sense for couples who have a combined estate that may trigger estate tax. As you now know, the estate tax exemption varies by year, so the conservative approach would be use an AB trust if your combined estate is larger than the smallest possible estate tax exemption—$1 million. The table below shows the current estate tax exemptions and the amounts that Nolo's AB trusts can currently shield from estate tax.

However, as discussed, the federal estate tax exemptions will likely be revised by Congress soon. You can get the latest information on the exempt amounts at Nolo's website, www.nolo.com.

How Much a Nolo AB Trust Can Shield From Estate Tax		
Year of First Spouse's Death	Personal Exemption	Maximum Shielded
2009	$3.5 million	$7 million
2010	Estate tax repealed	
2011 and thereafter	$1 million	$2 million

Should You Do It Yourself?

Before we plunge into details of how Nolo's AB trusts work, I want to repeat a serious warning: AB trusts come in a variety of forms, having different tax, legal, and practical consequences. This book presents two types of AB trusts, useful for many couples. As long as one of these trusts is right for you, don't hesitate to use it. But if you conclude that your family and monetary situations are different than those discussed below, this trust is not advisable for you.

Here's a summary of the basic requirements you should meet to use one of Nolo's AB trusts:

- You have a combined estate that's large enough to trigger concern about estate tax.
- You want to leave the bulk of your property for the use of your spouse during her or his lifetime, if that spouse survives you.
- You and your spouse want to eventually leave your property to your children (or other people or institutions) in a way that avoids estate tax.
- Key family members understand and approve of the fact that Nolo's AB trust allows the surviving spouse broad powers over Trust A property.
- You are confident that there will be no conflict between your spouse and your final beneficiaries over your trust property.

The comforting truth is that Nolo's AB trusts work fine for many couples. If you're among this group, you'll find that the technical aspects of preparing your trust (covered in Chapters 10 and 11) are not onerous, and you can safely prepare this trust yourself, saving yourself at least $1,000—and probably a good deal more—in attorney fees.

How Nolo's AB Trusts Work

Here we'll focus on how Nolo's AB trusts function in the real world. You have two options: the standard AB trust, or an AB disclaimer trust.

Creating the Trust

To create a standard AB trust, use Form 3. To create an AB disclaimer trust, use Form 4. You can find both forms in Appendix B or on the CD-ROM. (Step-by-step instructions for completing these forms are in Chapter 10.) In general, the process for either type of trust is as follows:

- Both spouses together create one overall living trust and transfer their property to it.
- Within this living trust, each spouse creates an AB trust. This part of the trust document provides that when the first spouse dies, the living trust property will be split into Trust A and Trust B. Trust A is an irrevocable trust that will contain some or all of the deceased spouse's property. Trust B contains the property that is owned by the surviving spouse.
- Each spouse names the other as the life beneficiary and trustee of his or her Trust A. Each spouse names his or her final beneficiaries (and alternates) to receive his or her trust property after both spouses have died. Spouses can name different final beneficiaries, but couples in a first marriage generally name the same final beneficiaries—their children.
- The spouses name a successor trustee to take over and distribute the Trust A and Trust B property after both spouses have died.
- With a standard AB trust, when the first spouse dies, all of that spouse's trust property goes into Trust A, which becomes irrevocable.
- With an AB disclaimer trust, the surviving spouse (acting as trustee) decides whether to disclaim any of the deceased spouse's trust property. All disclaimed property goes to Trust A. Property not disclaimed goes to Trust B, the surviving spouse's ongoing living trust.

That's basically all there is to it. (That's enough, no?) All the terms and phrases necessary to create a legal AB trust, following the IRS rules to ensure estate tax savings, are in the trust document.

EXAMPLE:

Meredith and Gary have a total estate (all shared property owned equally) of roughly $1,820,000. They use Form 3 to create a standard AB trust in which:

- Both transfer all property into the living trust.
- Meredith leaves her share of the property in her Trust A. Gary is the life beneficiary, and their children are her final beneficiaries in equal shares.
- Gary leaves his share of the property in his Trust A. Meredith is the life beneficiary, and their children are his final beneficiaries in equal shares.
- Gary and Meredith name their daughter Alice to serve as successor trustee after both spouses die.

In practical, day-to-day terms, so long as Meredith and Gary live, nothing really changes after they've created their AB trust. They can still revoke or amend their living trust, and all trust transactions (such as any sale of trust property, or other income from trust property) are reported on the couple's regular income tax return. But when one spouse dies, the trust really becomes operational.

How an AB Trust Becomes Operational

When a couple creates either of Nolo's AB trusts, they cannot know which spouse will be the first to die. So each spouse must create a separate Trust A and Trust B. Only the Trust A of the first spouse to die can ever become operational.

When one spouse dies, what happens next depends on which type of trust was used. With a standard AB trust, Trust A immediately goes into effect. With an AB disclaimer trust, the surviving spouse decides whether a Trust A becomes operational or not. In either case, the surviving spouse's Trust A now cannot become operative, because he or she does not have a spouse to survive him or her. (However, if he or she remarries, the surviving spouse can create a new AB trust with the new spouse.)

EXAMPLE:

Continuing with our example of Meredith and Gary, above, Gary dies in 2011. His half of their property is worth $910,000 and goes into his Trust A. Meredith's half of the property goes into her Trust B. Meredith is the life beneficiary of Trust A, with all rights of the surviving spouse. Meredith dies in 2013, and Alice becomes successor trustee. She transfers the property in Trust A and Trust B to the final beneficiaries.

With Nolo's AB disclaimer trust, the trust document provides that when the first spouse dies, the trustee (that is, the surviving spouse) divides the living trust assets into three shares:

- The survivor's share. Basically, this is all trust property owned by the surviving spouse before the other spouse died; it stays in the survivor's revocable trust.

- The marital deduction share. This is all trust assets of the deceased spouse (excluding any specific gifts) that are not disclaimed by the surviving spouse; these assets also go into the survivor's trust.
- The bypass trust share. This consists of assets disclaimed by the surviving spouse; these assets go to Trust A.

If the surviving spouse does not disclaim any assets, the bypass trust share is zero. So no Trust A would be created, because there would be nothing to put in it.

When you create a disclaimer trust, you can't know whether or not a Trust A will eventually be created and become operational. If a Trust A is created, it functions exactly the same as a Trust A in a standard AB trust.

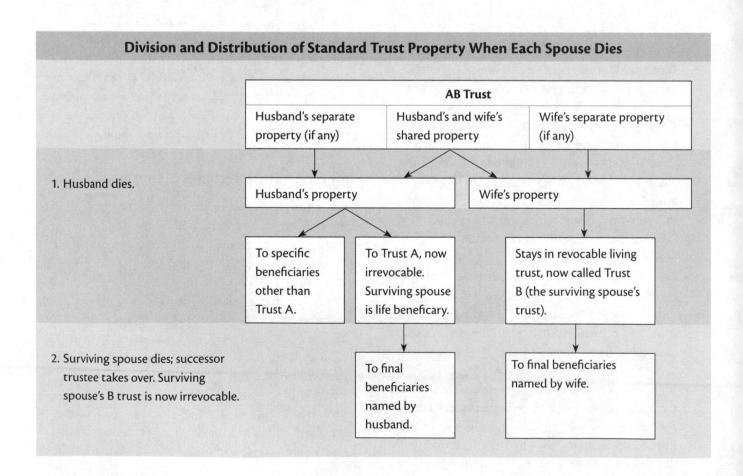

EXAMPLE:

Brigit and Tyrell, an unmarried couple, create a Nolo AB disclaimer trust. They have shared assets worth $3.8 million. Brigit also individually owns property worth $600,000. Tyrell dies in 2009, with an estate worth $1.9 million. Brigit owns the other $1.9 million and her $600,000, for a total of $2.5 million. Brigit could choose to inherit all of Tyrell's property free of estate tax. However, that would make her estate worth $4.5 million, and subject to tax if she died in any year except 2010. So Brigit decides to disclaim all of Tyrell's property, which goes into Trust A. Because the amount placed in Trust A is under the $3.5 million exemption for 2009, Tyrell's property will never be subject to estate tax.

The Surviving Spouse's Rights to Property in Trust A

Because this subject is a matter of such vital concern to many couples, I want to stress here, at the risk of some repetition, the rights of the surviving spouse. Nolo's AB trusts allow the surviving spouse the maximum legally permitted rights overall property in Trust A. The trust uses the specific language required by the IRS so that Trust A property is never legally owned by the surviving spouse. At the same time, the surviving spouse has all of the following rights to Trust A property:

- The right to income from the trust property. The trust specifically states that the trustee "shall pay to or spend for the benefit of the surviving spouse the net income of Trust A in quarter-annual or more frequent installments."
- The right to use trust property—for example, to live in a house owned, or partially owned, by the trust.
- The right to sell trust property, reinvest trust funds, or buy new property in the name of the trust, as long as principal is not used up. For example, the surviving spouse, as trustee, can sell a house owned or co-owned by the trust and buy a condo in Florida or North Carolina, but cannot use the proceeds to gamble at Las Vegas.
- The right to use the trust principal for any amount necessary for the surviving spouse's "health,

education, support, or maintenance in accord with his or her accustomed manner of living." (IRS Reg. 20.2041-1(c)(2).)

The only practical effect of the IRS limitations is that the surviving spouse cannot spend trust principal any way he or she wants, say for a painting by Elmer Bischoff or a six-month vacation in Europe.

How would the IRS find out if the surviving spouse were improperly spending money from Trust A? (Please realize that this is mostly a lawyer's theoretical question. Surely the overwhelming majority of couples who create and use an AB trust do so in good faith and want to conserve the trust principal for their final beneficiaries.) Improper spending of Trust A principal might be detected by an IRS audit of the annual trust tax return, or perhaps one of the final beneficiaries would learn of these improper expenses and oppose them. (It might take a lawsuit, though, to actually prevent the spouse from continuing to abuse his or her position.) But even if the final beneficiaries had no objection to the surviving spouse spending the money, if the IRS decided it had been spent for an improper purpose, it could conclude that there was never any intention of creating a bona fide AB trust. In that case, the trust is disallowed, for tax purposes, and all Trust A property is treated as owned by the surviving spouse—exactly what you don't want.

> **CAUTION**
>
> **Don't change a word.** The language permitting the surviving spouse to spend Trust A principal for "health, education, support, or maintenance in accord with his or her accustomed manner of living" is crucial. If you add a word like "well-being" or "comfort" to the list, under IRS rules the standard for spending principal becomes "subjective"—a fatal mistake. If a subjective standard is used, the Trust A property is legally owned by the surviving spouse and would be included in the surviving spouse's estate. As you know, the whole point of setting up an AB trust is to prevent both estates from being lumped together for estate tax purposes.

The right of the surviving spouse to invade Trust A principal for any amount needed for "support, health, education, or maintenance in his or her accustomed manner of living" could be of great importance. If the surviving spouse faces any grave financial need—a costly medical emergency, housing crisis, or other necessity of life—and doesn't have enough other funds or assets to pay them, he or she is legally authorized, as trustee, to spend any amount needed of Trust A principal to pay for these needs. If a surviving spouse couldn't use Trust A principal for these needs, AB trusts would be far less popular.

The surviving spouse is not required to use up all of his or her assets before using trust principal to pay for, or help pay for, such costs. For example, a survivor doesn't have to sell his or her house and spend all the proceeds on medical care before using Trust A property for medical needs. The IRS regulations specifically provide that he or she is entitled to continue to live in his or her "accustomed manner of living." What's required here is simply that the surviving spouse's use of trust principal be reasonable, under the circumstances, and for one of the IRS-authorized purposes.

EXAMPLE:

A couple, Kumar and Hari, has assets of $2.6 million —a house worth $600,000 (equity), investments, stocks, and money market funds worth $2 million. They establish an AB trust, with each spouse having the maximum legal rights over the trust's property.

Kumar dies in 2009. His half (worth $1.3 million) goes into Trust A. (Hari's property goes into Trust B.) Hari is both the life beneficiary and trustee of Trust A. The couple's children are the final beneficiaries.

Hari remains in the house. She also receives all the income from the $2 million in investments, stocks, and money market funds—half because she owns half the stocks and money market funds directly, half as Trust A income.

Hari has some major health problems over the next years. The costs of the illness are mostly covered by her insurance and Medicare. But one immense medical bill is not covered, and Hari's income, including income from Trust A, is not sufficient to pay it. Hari, as trustee, can spend some of the Trust A principal to pay this bill.

Property Left to Specific Beneficiaries

With Nolo's AB trusts each spouse can leave specific gifts, in addition to any property left in Trust A or retained in Trust B. (Of course, you don't have to leave any specific gifts. In that case, all the deceased spouse's trust property goes to and is held in Trust A.) Any specific gifts left by the deceased spouse go to the named beneficiaries when that spouse dies. Similarly, specific gifts left by the surviving spouse go to the beneficiaries when that spouse dies.

Legally, with either type of AB trust you can leave as many specific gifts as you want. However, in my experience, it's rare for someone to want to both leave a number of specific gifts while simultaneously leaving the bulk of property for use of the surviving spouse. Nolo's AB trust forms contain provisions to leave up to three specific gifts. However, if you want to leave more than three, you can do so. When preparing your trust document with Forms 3 or 4, simply copy the specific gift clause and repeat it for each additional gift you want to leave.

You can leave separate gifts from your separate property (if you have any), from your half of shared property, or some combination of both. If you choose to leave specific gifts, they should be relatively minor. After all, a central purpose of an AB trust is to leave the bulk, or all, of one spouse's property for the use of the other spouse during his or her lifetime.

EXAMPLE:

Shauna is married and has an estate worth $916,000. Although she wants to leave the bulk of her estate in a disclaimer AB trust, she decides to leave some of her separate property heirlooms to her sister and nieces: an old music box to her sister, Bernice, an antique clock to her niece Danielle, and several lace dresses to her niece Moira. Shauna can sensibly use Nolo's AB disclaimer trust.

Division of AB Trust Property When One Spouse Dies

Eventually, one spouse dies. At this point, the property in the AB trust is divided. With a standard AB Trust, Trust A is automatically created. However, with an AB disclaimer trust, the surviving spouse can decide not to create Trust A. Whether or not Trust A is created, the surviving spouse must determine how much the trust property is worth and how much each spouse owned of it. If a Trust A is created, either because a standard AB trust was used or because a surviving spouse disclaimed property to Trust A, any gifts the deceased spouse left to specific beneficiaries are distributed. If a surviving spouse chooses not to disclaim any of the deceased spouse's trust property, any specific gifts will be made from the deceased spouse's trust property. The surviving spouse will inherit all that is left after these specific gifts are made.

The property in Trust B includes:

- The surviving spouse's 50% share of co-owned trust property. (Each item does not have to be divided 50-50, but the total value of the deceased spouse's share of co-owned property must be the same as the value of the surviving spouse's share.)
- All separate trust property of the surviving spouse.
- If an AB disclaimer trust was used, all of the deceased spouse's trust property not disclaimed by the surviving spouse (or left by specific gifts).

Dividing the property between Trust A and Trust B is the responsibility of the surviving spouse, as trustee of both trusts. With a standard AB trust, the surviving spouse must decide which property will be placed in the (irrevocable) Trust A, and which will be retained in the surviving spouse's (revocable) Trust B. All that is legally required is that the total dollar value of equally shared ownership property in each trust be equal. Ownership of each individual item of property does not have to be split in half.

With an AB disclaimer trust, the surviving spouse first decides on the worth of property to be placed in Trust A. If property is to be placed in Trust A, the surviving spouse must decide what part of the deceased spouse's trust property to use for that purpose.

If your goals include maximum future income tax savings and estate tax savings, deciding which property goes where is often neither clear nor simple.

Suppose a couple shares ownership of a house worth $800,000, and stocks, money market accounts, and other investments totalling $1 million, and the husband has separate property worth $100,000. With a standard AB trust, what's the wisest way to divide up this property when the first spouse dies? It depends on the couple's needs and circumstances, as well as on trying to see into the future.

First, let's look at the house. If the entire $800,000 value of the house is put in Trust A, it will not be subject to estate tax (even if the husband's $100,000 of separate property is added as well), because the total in Trust A is less than the estate tax threshold, no matter what the year of death. If, over the years, the value of the house rises to $7 million before the surviving spouse dies, this increase is never subject to estate tax. (This property was subject to estate tax only once, when the deceased spouse died and Trust A became operational and irrevocable.) If the house weren't in Trust A, it could be assessed at $7 million for estate tax purposes when the second spouse died.

But, as we've seen recently, it's not a law of nature that house prices always rise. House prices are set by a free market, and the only thing we really know about a free market is that (as Bernard Baruch said of the stock market) "prices will fluctuate." If real estate prices go down or even remain flat, maybe the couple (and the children, as the final inheritors) would be better off if the money market funds were all put in Trust A. Or maybe splitting both the house and the money market funds between Trust A and Trust B will prove wisest.

Further, you can sell your home (once every two years) and not pay capital gains tax on the first $250,000 of profit. (For a couple, $500,000 is exempt from capital gains tax.) But this right is available only to a person, not to an irrevocable trust. How does this play into the decision of where to place the house? Would it be better if the house all went into Trust B, so the surviving spouse retained the option to sell it during her lifetime and obtain the capital gains tax break?

Dividing property between Trust A and Trust B is discussed in more detail in Chapter 14.

SEE AN EXPERT

Hiring an expert to determine the wisest property division. Most spouses faced with dividing property between the two trusts decide to hire a good accountant or estate tax lawyer to determine the most advantageous division. This should cost a few hundred dollars—but not thousands—and it's wise to spend the money. An expert can discuss your situation with you and help you understand the possible tax effects of different allocation decisions.

Some paperwork is required to officially allocate property between the two trusts. All property with documents of title that is placed in Trust A must have new title documents prepared (and recorded, if need be, as with real estate deeds), listing Trust A as owner. Technically, the property is transferred from the trustee of the living trust to the trustee of Trust A of the living trust. Yes, this sounds mushy, but it's important.

EXAMPLE:

Mike and Samantha Corbin-Pawlowski establish an AB disclaimer trust. Samantha dies. Mike decides to transfer some of her real estate to Trust A. Mike prepares a deed, transferring the real estate from "The Mike and Samantha Corbin-Pawlowski Trust," to "The Mike and Samantha Corbin-Pawlowski Trust, Trust A." He signs the deed as "Mike Corbin-Pawlowski, as trustee of the Mike and Samantha Corbin-Pawlowski Trust."

Property without title must be listed on a schedule attached to the Trust A document.

Usually, no new paperwork is required to establish Trust B, the surviving spouse's trust, except that a list of the property in it should be separate and kept with the original trust document. No other paperwork is required. Because Trust B is a revocable trust, no separate tax records need be kept.

The IRS will learn of the existence of Trust A when the first trust income tax return is filed. The IRS insists that there be a clear, legally valid record of what property is in each trust. Because the IRS is familiar with the Trust A and Trust B terminology, captioning ownership documents in those terms removes one source of potential tax hassles.

Managing the Property in Trust A

When or if the deceased spouse's Trust A becomes operational, it exists as a distinct taxable entity. The surviving spouse, as trustee, manages Trust A. The minimum required here is to:

- obtain a federal taxpayer ID number for the trust (this can be done by sending the IRS a simple form)
- keep separate, clear tax records of all Trust A transactions (a checkbook will usually suffice), and
- file a separate trust tax return for Trust A each year.

While all of this requires energy and involves some paperwork hassles, few spouses find it truly onerous, at least not in light of the tax savings they're achieving for their inheritors.

If the gross value of the property in Trust A turns out to exceed the personal exemption for the year of the deceased spouse's death, the surviving spouse, as trustee, is responsible for filing a federal estate tax return and paying any taxes due, within nine months of death. Using an AB disclaimer trust can reduce or eliminate this possibility.

Once Trust A is legally established, the surviving spouse, as trustee, must manage the trust property responsibly. For example, any property taxes due on real estate in Trust A should be paid from funds or property of that trust. If there are no liquid assets—cash, or property that can be turned into cash—in Trust A, the surviving spouse is stuck and must pay them from some other source. But remember, she could always refinance the house, assuming there was some equity in it, to obtain cash.

Legally, as trustee, the surviving spouse has what is called a "fiduciary duty" to the final beneficiaries. That means she must manage the trust property reasonably and protect the final beneficiaries' interest in the trust property (principal), except as otherwise authorized in the Trust A document. With Nolo's Trust A, the surviving spouse has the authority to hire financial advisers or consultants, paid for from trust funds (including principal), if need be. Realistically, the surviving spouse has only to use common sense in managing the trust property; he or she should not make risky investments or spend principal in reckless or rash ways.

With either of Nolo's AB trusts, the surviving spouse has no obligation to provide reports about the property in Trust A to any of the final beneficiaries, except to provide them with copies of the annual trust income tax return. This is a compromise between allowing the final beneficiaries no rights at all to know what is going on in Trust A and allowing them extensive rights or controls. Since the surviving spouse must prepare and file an annual trust income tax return for Trust A, it does not seem unduly burdensome or intrusive to give copies of it to the trust's final beneficiaries.

Amending Trust B

Trust B, the surviving spouse's living trust, remains revocable while the survivor lives. Nolo's trust forms specifically provide that the surviving spouse retains all rights in Trust B property until his or her death. The survivor can amend the terms of Trust B, or revoke it entirely, as long as he or she is mentally competent.

Many surviving spouses don't need to name new beneficiaries for some or all of their Trust B property. Commonly, both spouses want to leave their property to their children, who were originally named as both spouses' final beneficiaries. This desire usually doesn't change after one spouse dies.

EXAMPLE:

Zora and Glenway create an AB disclaimer trust. Each name their two children as final beneficiaries. Glenway dies. Zora disclaims some of his property. So Trust A is created and becomes irrevocable. Zora's Trust B is revocable, but that doesn't mean she wants to change who she wants her property to go to. She continues to want to it go to her children, so she leaves the designation of her final beneficiaries unchanged.

Normally, it's inadvisable for the surviving spouse to change the successor trustee of her trust, unless there are compelling reasons. That's because when the surviving spouse dies, there would be two trustees involved in transferring the property of the two trusts—Trust A, the marital life estate trust, and Trust B, the surviving spouse's trust—to the same final beneficiaries (assuming the final beneficiaries are the same for both trusts). Risks of conflict and tension could arise when two different trustees work to protect "family" money in two different trusts.

However, if the surviving spouse amends the trust to name new final beneficiaries, it may well make sense to also name a new successor trustee for this trust. When the surviving spouse dies, this new successor trustee will distribute trust property to the new beneficiaries. And the successor trustee for Trust A will distribute that trust's property to the final beneficiaries named by the deceased spouse in the original living trust document.

After the Surviving Spouse Dies

After the death of the surviving spouse, the successor trustee distributes any Trust A property to that trust's final beneficiaries. In addition, the surviving spouse's own living trust, Trust B, becomes irrevocable on his or her death, and the successor trustee distributes that trust's property as the trust document directs.

This usually involves some paperwork and dealing with financial institutions such as stock brokerage companies and title companies. (See Chapter 14 for a full discussion of this process.) In addition, the successor trustee manages any children's trusts created by either spouse's trust. Finally, the successor trustee is responsible for handling any other trust-related matters. For example, if the gross value of the surviving spouse's estate exceeded the personal exemption in the year of death, the successor trustee must file a federal estate tax return and pay any tax due from the estate.

EXAMPLE:

Lamont and Iola create an AB disclaimer trust, with their three children as the final beneficiaries to share equally. Lamont leaves some of his separate-property artworks to his sister, Coreen. He leaves everything else to his wife, with the right to disclaim. They name their daughter Thelma as the successor trustee.

When Lamont dies, Iola disclaims to Trust A all of the property that Lamont left to her. She is the trustee and life estate beneficiary of this trust. She receives all income from that trust property and has the right to use it and manage it (as trustee) for the rest of her life.

When Iola dies, Thelma, the successor trustee, transfers the property in Trust A to the three children; they own it together, in equal shares. One child, Willie, is only 20 years old, so his property stays in a child's trust, managed by Thelma, until Willie becomes 35. (See Chapter 9.) Thelma also transfers Iola's Trust B property equally among the three children. Again, Willie's share of Iola's trust property is placed in the child's trust, with Thelma as the trustee.

Alternatives to Nolo's AB Trusts

If you are quite wealthy and can't safely use one of Nolo's AB trusts, there are a number of methods and devices you can consider to achieve tax savings and other estate planning goals. To use any of these, you'll need to hire a lawyer. Yes, estate planning lawyers are expensive, but remember:

- By studying this book, you'll be better prepared to deal with a lawyer, and can suggest ways to keep fees reasonable. For example, you can transfer assets to your trust rather than paying an attorney $250 or more per hour for what is basically clerical work.
- You are seeing a lawyer to save on overall estate taxes on a combined estate that is worth millions. You can afford to spend some money on legal help.
- Estate tax-saving trusts (including more sophisti- cated versions of an AB trust) can become exceedingly complex and technical. If you don't fully comply with IRS regulations, estate tax savings will be lost.
- Even if your trust qualifies under IRS rules, if it isn't properly geared to your situation, you may not achieve your goals and desires. If you or your spouse has children from a prior marriage, for example, you may need a carefully prepared trust to minimize possibilities of family conflict. This can be doubly true if one spouse has far more money than the other, and if you remarried late in life. An AB trust that is technically and legally correct can nevertheless lead to disastrous conflicts if the personal concerns of all involved haven't been addressed and resolved as thoroughly as possible.

Now let's look briefly at some of the more widely used sophisticated estate tax-saving trusts and devices.

An AB Formula Trust

An AB formula trust defines and limits the value of the property placed in Trust A when the first spouse dies. The formula (a series of clauses) specifies that no more than the amount of the personal estate tax exemption in the year of death is placed into the A trust. An AB formula trust is used to ensure that the trust property of the first spouse to die is not subject to estate tax. However, all trust property of the deceased spouse must be placed in Trust A, up to the exempt amount for the year of death. The surviving spouse/trustee does not have the option of placing a lesser amount in Trust A, even if that might be desirable for long-range financial planning. An AB disclaimer trust allows more flexibility in deciding how much, if any, property to place in Trust A.

In an AB formula trust any surplus is dealt with by other methods, to avoid estate tax at this point. It can be left outright to the surviving spouse, exempt under the marital deduction, or it can be left to what is called a "QTIP" trust. (QTIP is jargon for "Qualified Terminal Interest Property." That clears it all up, right?) A QTIP trust allows the surviving spouse to postpone taxes that would otherwise be due on the deceased's estate, while not leaving this property outright to the surviving spouse. (If it sounds tricky, that's because it is.)

EXAMPLE:

Damian and Victoria have a combined estate worth $7 million. Damian's separate property is worth $400,000. Victoria's separate property is worth $850,000. Damian has one child from a prior marriage; Victoria has two children from her prior marriages. Ultimately, each wants his or her property to go to the children. To achieve this, they create an AB formula trust and a QTIP trust for any overage. Damian dies in 2009. His estate is worth $3.9 million. The estate tax exemption for 2009 is $3.5 million. $400,000 is placed in the QTIP trust, with Damian's child as the final beneficiary.

An AB formula trust makes sense only where there could be an overage in the deceased spouse's estate— that is, more money than the estate tax exemption in the year of death. If your estate is that large, you have several choices for dealing with the matter. You can:

- make tax-free gifts from your property while you live, reducing the size of your taxable estate
- if you are married, leave any overage outright to the surviving spouse—that gift is exempt from estate tax because of the marital deduction (this only works for opposite-sex married couples because the federal marital deduction does not apply to same-sex married couples)

- leave all your property in Trust A, understanding that some estate tax will likely be paid at the death of the first spouse (this may result in a lower overall tax than if the surplus had been left to the surviving spouse)
- if one spouse's estate is much larger than the other's, equalize the size of the estate by transferring some property while you both live to the spouse who owns less, or
- leave the surplus in a QTIP trust, avoiding any tax until the death of the surviving spouse.

 SEE AN EXPERT

If you are concerned about a possible overage. For the rich, estate planning involves many complexities, including (1) understanding how your various options work, both generally and in your particular case, (2) evaluating the effects of the changes in the annual exemption amounts, and the uncertainty of current estate tax law, on your planning regarding the surplus, (3) choosing which option, or combination of options, you want to use, and (4) drafting the technical legal language to accomplish your goals. All this is far beyond what this book can offer—see an expert lawyer.

Limiting the Rights of the Surviving Spouse

As discussed, an AB trust does not have to grant the surviving spouse the broadest powers allowed by law over the deceased spouse's Trust A property. It's possible to limit, or prohibit altogether, the surviving spouse's right to spend (invade) the Trust A principal. Some AB trusts impose other restrictions on the surviving spouse, such as requiring regular trust reports to trust beneficiaries, or requiring the consent of a specific final beneficiary before spending principal.

Desiring these types of restrictions commonly occurs in second or subsequent marriages, where each spouse wants to ensure that his or her children from a prior marriage are protected and will actually receive the

principal of Trust A. Because these trusts raise many concerns related to the couple's personal needs and financial circumstances, people who want them should consult a lawyer.

The goal of imposing limits and controls on the property left to the surviving spouse can be combined with estate tax savings, or it can be independent. Even if a couple has no estate tax problems—their combined estate is less than the exempt amount—they may want to create an AB trust to control property left to a surviving spouse. For example, such a trust may be useful if a husband in a second marriage wants to leave his property for the use of his wife during her lifetime, but wants to be certain that the property eventually goes to his children from his first marriage. (Limiting the rights of a surviving spouse is discussed further in Chapter 15.)

The "5 and 5" Power Trust

Under present IRS rules, the surviving spouse of an AB trust can be given the right to obtain annually, for any reason whatsoever, up to a maximum of 5% of the Trust A principal or $5,000, whichever is greater. Estate planners call this the "5 and 5" power. There can be drawbacks to including this in an AB trust, including adverse tax consequences if the money isn't actually taken annually by the surviving spouse. This "5 and 5" power is not included in this book's AB trust because the surviving spouse already has authority to obtain trust principal in any amount for "health, education, support, or maintenance." In my view, an additional general power for the spouse to use the principal for any reason is unnecessary and possibly unwise.

Other Options

There are other high-end devices you may want to consider that are beyond the scope of this book. These devices are discussed briefly in Chapter 15.

Choosing What Property to Put in Your Living Trust

Okay, it's time to begin hands-on work. In this chapter, you'll make your initial decisions about what property to put in your trust.

You can place any amount of property in your trust. However, some types of property are better suited for living trusts than other types. This chapter explains which types of property are best for your living trust, and which types of property should be distributed in another way. (Chapter 15 explains some of those other methods.)

For many people, deciding what property to transfer to a living trust is not a difficult matter. They have one, or a few, "big ticket" items—for example, a house, some stocks, and a money market account—and they know they want to avoid probate of this property. But for many other people, matters aren't quite so simple. Some have questions about different types of property—say, about personal checking accounts, retirement accounts, or more unusual items such as copyrights or patents. And if you're married, you may need to determine which property is shared in equal amounts and which is the separate property of one spouse.

This chapter:

- discusses types of property you'll probably want to put into your trust
- reviews state marital property laws that can require you to leave property to your spouse, and
- provides a property worksheet you can use to make a thorough inventory of what you own and estimate the net value of your property. You can use this estimate of your net worth to see if your individual, or combined (if you are a couple), estate exceeds the federal estate tax threshold.

Even if you think you know what property you want to put in your trust, read these materials carefully to be sure your decisions pose no potential problems. Of course, you can always revise your decisions before preparing your actual trust document. The point isn't to lock you in now, but to get you started.

Listing the Property to Be Put in Your Trust

You must list, as part of your trust document, each item of property held in trust. Any property you don't list will not go into your living trust and will not pass under the terms of the trust. It may instead have to go through probate.

A list of trust property is called a "schedule" and is attached to the trust document. (This is explained in detail in Chapter 10.) A trust for one person has only one schedule. A trust for a married couple (either a basic shared trust or an AB trust) has three schedules: one for shared-ownership property, one for any separate property of one spouse, and another for any separate property of other spouse. If a spouse doesn't have any separate property, you can simply eliminate the appropriate schedule.

> **CAUTION**
>
> **Transferring title to the trustee.** You must also prepare separate documents formally transferring property ownership to the trust. Property with a document of title—like a deed to a house, or a stock account—must be transferred by preparing and signing a new document of title. You do that by placing title in the trustee's or trustees' name(s), "as trustee(s) for the _____[name]_____ Trust." Property without a document of title—such as household goods, jewelry, and clothes—can be transferred simply by listing them on a trust schedule. Preparing these documents is vital, and is explained in detail in Chapter 11. But for right now, your concern is simply to decide which property you want in the trusts and to write down how you'll list that property.

Many people instinctively think of their trust beneficiaries and property together: The antique dresser goes to Mary, the house will be divided between the kids, and so on. But to be thorough and sure you do the job right, I suggest that you separate these two key elements. Here, list your trust property. Then, in the next chapter, you'll learn about naming your trust beneficiaries.

Adding Property to the Living Trust Later

If you acquire valuable property in your name after you create your living trust, you can easily add it to the trust. Also, once you've set up the trust, if you're buying property you intend to keep for a while, you can simply acquire it in the name of the trustee(s) of your trust. Finally, if you mistakenly leave something out of your trust, you can add it later by amending your trust. (See Chapter 13.)

Property You Should Not Put in Your Living Trust

You don't need to put everything you own into a living trust to save money on probate. Property that is of relatively low value (the amount depends on state law) may be exempt from probate or qualify for a streamlined probate procedure that's relatively fast and cheap. And in some states, at least some of the property left to a surviving spouse can probably be transferred without a full-blown probate court proceeding.

Generally, it's better not to include the following types of property in your trust:

- **Your personal checking account,** unless you want to pay your bills in the name of the trust. A checking account in the name of a trust can cause raised eyebrows—even refusal to accept the check—by people or institutions who wonder, "Why can't she write the check in her own name? What's this trust business?"

- **Individual retirement accounts.** Retirement accounts such as IRAs, 401(k)s, 403(b)s, and profit-sharing plans should not be put in your trust. Indeed, for some individual retirement accounts, it's not legal to do so. With a retirement account, you name a beneficiary or beneficiaries to receive any money left in the account at your death, without probate. While you could name your trust as beneficiary of these accounts, there's generally no reason to do so unless you'll use an AB trust. If you are preparing an AB trust, consider whether you want to name that trust to receive funds left in the accounts when you die. (See below.)

- **Automobiles.** Some insurance companies won't insure a vehicle owned by a trust. They worry that an unknown number of people could be entitled, under the terms of the trust, to drive the vehicle. Anyway, the value of many people's car or cars isn't so high that they need to worry about transferring them by living trust. Also, most state motor vehicles departments have special forms that conveniently allow cars to be registered in joint tenancy, a handy way to avoid probate for an auto. And five states—California, Connecticut, Kansas, Missouri, and Ohio—allow "transfer-on-death" vehicle registration, where you name, on your vehicle registration, the person who will receive the vehicle upon your death. No probate is necessary.

  But if you own a valuable vehicle, or several, it can be worth your while to seek out an insurance company that will allow you to own and transfer them by living trust. Some insurance companies will insure a vehicle owned by a trust. Indeed, some insurance companies simply list the trust as an "additional insured," with no additional fee or premium.

- **Property you buy or sell frequently.** If you don't expect to own the property at your death, there's no compelling reason to transfer it to your living trust. (Remember, the probate process you want to avoid doesn't happen until after your death.)

- **Cash.** You can't put actual cash, hard currency, in a living trust— you can't put a stack of bills into a document. You can, however, transfer a cash money *account* into a trust, and then you can make cash gifts from that trust.

- **Life insurance.** When you buy an insurance policy, you name beneficiaries to receive the proceeds of the policy outside of probate. However, if you want a minor or young adult to be the beneficiary of an insurance policy, you need to name an adult to manage the proceeds in case the insurance is paid out before the beneficiary is a legal adult. One way to accomplish this is to create a child's trust as part of your living trust and then name the trustee as the beneficiary of your life insurance. If the trustee receives the proceeds while the young beneficiary is still a minor, the trustee manages that money for him

Naming Your AB Living Trust as Beneficiary of Your Retirement Account

If you have substantial assets in an individual retirement account, you may want any funds remaining in that account when you die to help fund Trust A of your AB trust. You can legally do this. However, you need to remember that, except for a Roth IRA, an individual retirement account is a "wasting asset." Once you reach age 70½, you must withdraw a certain percentage of your account each year. The withdrawal percentage is calculated on the basis of your statistical life expectancy. (The IRS determines the withdrawal percentage by using what it calls the "Uniform Lifetime Table.") So, if you live a long life, much or all of the funds in your account will have been withdrawn.

Withdrawal amounts are different if your spouse is the sole beneficiary and more than ten years younger than you. In this case, distribution rules are more favorable, meaning you are required to withdraw a lower percentage each year. Withdrawal percentages here are calculated on the life expectancies of both you and your spouse. (The IRS determines this withdrawal percentage by use of what it calls the "Joint Life and Last Survivor Tables.")

Still, you may understandably be concerned with what happens to your retirement account if you die prematurely, or if, for whatever reason, significant funds remain in the account at your death. You can leave these funds to your AB trust by naming your successor trustee as beneficiary of your account.

However, if you do this and your spouse is more than ten years younger than you, you lose the ability to make withdrawals based on both your life expectancies. If you named your living trust as your retirement account beneficiary, your surviving spouse (if there is one) loses valuable rights to roll over your retirement account fund into his or her own account without penalties.

SEE AN EXPERT

Get expert help before naming your AB trust as beneficiary of your retirement account. There are significant financial risks if you name your AB trust as beneficiary of your retirement account. If you're wrestling with this issue, get the help of a knowledgeable lawyer or accountant.

There may be additional paperwork or hassle to complete to validly name your AB trust as beneficiary of your retirement plan. For example:

- Federal law requires that all funds in a 401(k) or 403(b) plan be left outright to a surviving spouse unless that spouse has given a written waiver of that right.
- 401(k) and some other retirement plans must adopt an amendment allowing life expectancy, for withdrawal purposes, to be calculated on the basis of the plan owner and the oldest trust beneficiary. The IRS can supply you with a model amendment form.
- Retirement accounts purchased with community property are co-owned equally by both spouses. If you want all funds in such an account to go to your Trust A, you need a written declaration of gift from your spouse.

A thorough explanation of the applicable laws and rules can be found in *IRAs, 401(k)s & Other Retirement Plans: Taking Your Money Out,* by Twila Slesnick and John C. Suttle (Nolo).

or her through the trust. If the young beneficiary is old enough to be entitled to receive trust property outright, the trustee can simply give him or her the money. (This is covered in detail in Chapter 9.)

- **Joint tenancy property.** Property held in joint tenancy does not go through probate, as is explained in Chapter 15. So generally there is no need to worry about transferring jointly owned property, including joint bank accounts, into your living trust. However, one possible reason for transferring jointly owned property to the trust is that you cannot name alternate beneficiaries for joint tenancy property. If all owners die simultaneously, each owner's share of the joint tenancy property passes under their will. While you could eliminate this remote possibility by transferring your share to your living trust, making the transfer requires a couple of paper steps that are at least a bit of a hassle (See "Paperwork" in Chapter 11.) Most people understandably don't bother with this level of contingency planning.

- **Pay-on-death bank accounts.** With these accounts, you name a beneficiary or beneficiaries to receive directly, without probate, all funds in the accounts when you die. (See Chapter 15.)

- **Transfer-on-death real estate deeds.** In a few states, you can use a deed to name a beneficiary for real estate. Upon your death, the real estate will be transferred to the beneficiary free of probate. States which allow this are: Arizona, Arkansas, Colorado, Kansas, Missouri, Montana, Nevada, New Mexico, Ohio, and Wisconsin.

- **Community property with right of survivorship.** Alaska, Arizona, California, Nevada, Texas, and Wisconsin expressly authorize spouses to own community property in this manner. Thus, married spouses in these states can retain the benefits of community property (see "Marital Property Laws," below) and simultaneously obtain the probate avoidance plus of joint tenancy.

- **Employee stock options.** Some businesses give, or allow employees to purchase, options to buy stock of the company for a set price. Often the company imposes restrictions or prohibitions on employee transfers of the options. Even if the

company allows transfer to a living trust, complex IRS rules govern the exercise of this type of stock option and subsequent sale of the stock. Because of these rules, it is normally not a good idea to transfer employee stock options to your living trust. By contrast, you can transfer stock options bought on a recognized stock exchange—for instance, the right to buy 1,000 shares of Apple Computer for a set price. This contractual right may be transferred to your living trust by Notice of Assignment. (See "Securities" in Chapter 11.) Indeed, if you trade frequently in publicly traded options, you can open an option account in the trust's name.

SEE AN EXPERT

If you decide you must transfer employee stock options to your trust. If you want to transfer employee stock options to your living trust, you'll need a lawyer who's up to date on the complex tax rules, including capital gains tax, that govern the transaction.

- **Contaminated real estate.** Do not transfer to your trust any real estate you know, or suspect, has been chemically polluted. (See Chapter 3.)

- **Income or principal from a trust.** If you are the beneficiary of an established trust and have the right to leave any of your interest in this trust to someone else, you cannot do that in your own living trust. The reason is that you cannot transfer title of the trust that benefits you into your own living trust, because you are not the owner of the trust. Your trust cannot give away what it doesn't technically own. You can leave your rights to this type of trust income property by your will. (See Chapter 16.)

- **Annuities.** Generally you name a beneficiary or beneficiaries in the annuity policy contract. These beneficiaries receive any money in the account when you die, outside of probate.

Property You Can Put in Your Living Trust

Whatever type of trust you create with this book, a primary goal is avoiding probate fees. As a general rule, the more an item is worth, the more it will cost to probate it. That means you should transfer at least your most valuable property items to your living trust—or use some other probate-avoidance device to leave them at your death. Think about including:

- houses and other real estate
- small business interests, including stock in closely held corporations
- money market accounts
- other financial accounts
- stocks, bonds, and other security accounts held by brokers
- royalties, patents, and copyrights
- valuable jewelry, antiques, furs, and furniture
- precious metals
- valuable works of art, and
- valuable collections of stamps, coins, or other objects.

SEE AN EXPERT

Property on which you owe money. Some items of property are commonly not owned free and clear. The most obvious example is a house with a mortgage. When you use your living trust to leave that house to a beneficiary, he or she will receive it subject to the mortgage. Similarly, if you give someone a car subject to a loan and lien, those debts go with the car.

If you have sufficient assets, it's legally possible to use your trust to provide that these debts be paid off. That way, the beneficiary receives a house, car, or other previously debt-encumbered property free and clear. See a lawyer to arrange this.

Real Estate

The most valuable thing most people own is their real estate: their house, condominium, or land. Other types of real estate include property such as a boat marina dock space or a time-share interest in a piece of property, like a vacation house or apartment used twice a year. You can save your family substantial probate costs by transferring your real estate through a living trust.

If you own real estate in joint tenancy or tenancy by the entirety, however, you've already arranged to avoid probate for that property, so there's much less reason to transfer it to a living trust. (See Chapter 15.) One

advantage of owning real estate in a living trust is that, in a living trust, you can provide for who will receive the real estate in the event that both owners die at the same time. You cannot provide for this with real estate owned in joint tenancy. Another reason for transferring joint tenancy real estate into a living trust is if you use an AB living trust and want part of the real estate to be part of the Trust A property.

If You're Not Sure How You Hold Title

If you own real estate with someone else but aren't sure how the title is held, look at the deed. It should say how title is held:

- in joint tenancy (sometimes abbreviated JT or JTWROS, for "joint tenancy with right of survivorship")
- tenancy in common
- community property (in community property states; in a community property state, if the deed says the property is owned "as husband and wife," that means community property)
- community property with right of survivorship, or
- tenancy by the entirety.

If you own real estate with someone else, you can transfer just your interest in it to your living trust.

Co-op apartments. If you own shares in a co-op corporation that owns your apartment, you'll have to transfer your shares to your living trust. You may run into difficulties with the corporation; some are reluctant to let a trust—even a revocable living trust completely controlled by the grantor—own shares. Check the co-op corporation's laws and rules, then do some good lobbying, if necessary.

CAUTION

Retirement co-ops. Occasionally, an unfortunate technicality is used to deny transfer to a living trust. For instance, some co-op retirement units restrict ownership to people over a certain age, say 65 or 70. In a few instances, co-op boards have interpreted these rules to prohibit transfer to a trustee of a living trust, claiming that the trust doesn't have an age. While correct, this should be irrelevant. As you know by now, it is not the trust that is the technical owner, but the trustee of the trust. Here, that's the grantor, the person over 65 or 70 who lives in the co-op. If the IRS can understand that the living trust has no independent legal existence as long as the person who created it is alive, co-op officials should be able to comprehend that, too.

Mobile homes. The rules on when an attached mobile home becomes "real estate" vary in different states. If this matters to you, see a lawyer or look up your state's law. (Legal research is discussed in Chapter 17.)

Time-shares. A time-share is usually an interest in a vacation property, often a condominium. The time-share gives the owner the exclusive right to stay in the property for specific time periods. Technically, ownership of a time-share may be held by deed, contract, or lease. (Sometimes terms such as "vacation license" or "time-share ownership" are used.) If the ownership is by deed, a new deed needs to be prepared transferring the interest to your trust. (If ownership is listed as "vacation license" or "time-share ownership" you'll need to find out if that type of ownership is considered an interest in real estate under state law. If it is, you need to make the transfer by deed.) If ownership of the time-share is held by contract or lease, that contract or lease should be assigned to the trust.

Leases on real estate. If you're the owner of a lease on real estate (you've leased a store for five years, say, and the lease has two years to run), that lease is generally considered an interest in real estate. You can transfer it to your living trust if you wish.

Homeowner's Insurance

Don't bother notifying your homeowner's insurance company that you have placed your home in your living trust. As I've explained, as long as you live, you personally are, for all real-world purposes including the IRS and homestead rights, the owner of your home. Your homeowner's policy will still cover your home. But if you tell your insurance company about the transfer, they might raise problems and questions that you'll have to waste time answering. Don't risk the hassles.

Small Business Interests

The delay, expense, and court intrusion of probate can be especially detrimental to an ongoing small business. Using your living trust to transfer business interests to beneficiaries quickly after your death is almost essential if you want the beneficiaries to be able to keep the business running, or even to be able to sell it for a fair price.

SEE AN EXPERT

Controlling management of a business. If you want to impose controls on the long-term management of your business, a revocable living trust is not the right device. See an estate planning lawyer to draft a different kind of trust, with provisions tailored to your situation.

Different kinds of business organizations present different issues when you want to transfer your interest to your living trust.

Sole proprietorships. If you operate your business as a sole proprietorship, with all business assets held in your own name, you can simply transfer your business property to your living trust as you would any other property. You should also list the business's name itself on a trust schedule; that transfers the customer goodwill associated with the name.

Partnership interests. If you operate your business as a partnership with other people, you can probably transfer your partnership share to your living trust. If there is a partnership certificate, it must be changed to show the trust as owner of your share.

Some partnership agreements require the people who inherit a deceased partner's share of the business to sell that share to the other partners if they want it. But that happens after death, so it shouldn't affect your ability to transfer the property through a living trust.

It's not common, but a partnership agreement may limit or forbid transfers to a living trust. If yours does, you and your partners may want to see a lawyer before you make any changes. If the other partners won't agree to revise your partnership agreement to allow this transfer, you're stuck.

Solely owned corporations. If you own all the stock of a corporation, you should have no difficulty transferring it to your living trust. All you need do is prepare the appropriate corporate papers—for example,

Notice of Meeting of Shareholders, and Resolution of Shareholders (there's only one, remember)—authorizing the transfer of the shares of stock to the living trust. The precise corporate paperwork needed depends on what's required by your articles of incorporation and the bylaws of your corporation.

Closely held corporations, including limited liability companies (LLCs). A closely held corporation is a corporation that doesn't sell shares to the public. A limited liability company is akin to the closely held corporation, except that it is treated as a partnership for tax purposes. All shares or ownership interests are owned by a few people who are usually actively involved in running the business. Normally, you can use a living trust to transfer your interest in an LLC or shares in a closely held corporation by listing the interest or stock in the trust document. With the stock, the certificates must be reissued in the trustee's name.

You'll want to check the corporation's bylaws and articles of incorporation to be sure that if you transfer the shares to a living trust, you will still have voting rights in your capacity as trustee of the living trust; usually, this is not a problem. If it is, you and the other shareholders should be able to amend the corporation's bylaws to allow it.

There may, however, be legal restrictions on your freedom to transfer your shares to a living trust. Check the corporation's bylaws and articles of incorporation, as well as any separate shareholders' agreements or, for LLCs, the operating agreement.

One fairly common rule is that surviving shareholders or LLC owners have the right to buy the shares of a deceased shareholder or owner. In that case, you can still use a living trust to transfer the shares or LLC interest, but the people who inherit them may have to sell them to the other shareholders or owners.

SEE AN EXPERT

Subchapter S or professional corporations. Special IRS rules apply if you want to transfer shares in a Subchapter S corporation to a living trust. The trust must contain special provisions that make it a "Qualified Subchapter S Trust" under the IRS regulations. You must see a lawyer to draft the appropriate provisions for your trust. Also see a lawyer if your business is a professional corporation, such as one for lawyers, doctors, or architects.

Money Market and Bank Accounts

Money market funds can be readily transferred into your trust. Often, these money market funds contain substantial amounts of cash, so it's wise to place them in your living trust.

It's not difficult to hold bank accounts or credit union accounts (aside from your personal checking account) in your living trust. But you may well decide that you don't need to, because there's another easy way to avoid probate of the funds. With a "pay-on-death" account (sometimes called a Totten Trust, or a "revocable trust account"), you can designate a beneficiary for the funds in a bank account. The beneficiary receives whatever is in your account at your death, without probate.

A living trust, however, offers one advantage that most pay-on-death arrangements do not: If you transfer an account to a living trust, you can always name an alternate beneficiary to receive the account if your first choice as beneficiary isn't alive at your death. The lack of an alternate may not be a problem if you use a pay-on-death account and name more than one beneficiary to inherit the funds; however, if one of the beneficiaries isn't alive, the other(s) will inherit the money.

Certificates of Deposit

Before you put a CD in your trust, check with the issuing bank to see if it will allow the transfer. Some will, and many will not. Your bank may refuse the transfer by claiming that for even technical ownership of a CD to change, it must have matured, and that an early transfer will cost you a penalty. In that case, you can only wait until the CD matures, and change title to it when or if you roll it over.

Stocks and Securities

Stocks and stock accounts are commonly held by living trusts. Brokerage companies are familiar with living trusts; you can readily transfer an existing stock brokerage account into your living trust, or create a new trust account. Once your account is in your trust's name (technically, in your name as trustee for your trust), all stocks in that account become owned by the trust, so you can trade as often as you want without additional trust paperwork.

In your living trust, you can leave your brokerage accounts however you desire—all to one person, divided by percentage between several people, or specific stocks to specific people.

If you have personal possession of individual stock certificates, you need to get new certificates issued, listing the new owner as trustee of your trust. (See Chapter 11.)

> ## An Alternative: Transfer-on-Death Registration
>
> Every state except Texas allows ownership of securities to be registered in a "transfer-on-death" form. This allows you to designate someone to receive the securities, including mutual funds and brokerage accounts, after your death. No probate will be necessary.

Cash Accounts

It's common for people to want to leave cash to beneficiaries—for example, to leave $5,000 to a relative, friend, or charity. To acomplish this, you can transfer ownership of a cash account—a savings account, money market account, or certificate of deposit, for example—to your living trust. (Don't transfer a pay-on-death account, since the beneficiary for it is already named.) Then, in the trust document you can name a beneficiary to receive the contents of the account or any specified sum from it. So if you want to leave $5,000 to cousin Fred, you can put this amount in a bank or money market account, transfer it to your living trust, and name Fred, in the trust document, as the beneficiary. Or you could put an account with a larger amount in your trust, and leave $5,000 from it to Fred and the balance to another beneficiary.

EXAMPLE:

Michael would like to leave some modest cash gifts to his two grown nephews, Warren and Brian, whom he's always been fond of. He puts $25,000 into a money market account and then transfers the account into his living trust. In his trust document, he names Warren and Brian as beneficiaries of $5,000 each from that, with whatever is left to go to Michael's wife. After Michael's death, the two nephews will each receive $5,000 from the trust.

If you don't want to set up an account to leave a modest amount of cash to a beneficiary, think about buying a savings bond and leaving it to the beneficiary.

U.S. Treasury Notes or Bonds

You can place U.S. Treasury notes or bonds—such as series EE/E or I bonds—in your living trust. There are no adverse tax consequences. The federal government requires that a specific form be used to make the transfer into the trust. (See Chapter 11.)

Royalties, Copyrights, and Patents

You can transfer your right to future royalties, or copyrights and patents you own, to your living trust. Simply list the royalty, copyright, or patent in your trust property schedule and then transfer your interest in a copyright, patent, or royalty to the trust using the proper legal form. (Instructions are in Chapter 11.)

SEE AN EXPERT

Oil, gas, or mineral interests. If you want to transfer one or more of these interests to your living trust, see a lawyer. Complicated matters, such as possible assignment of leases or handling depletion allowances, can arise that require professional attention.

Other Valuable Property

You need special forms to transfer some types of valuable property to your trust. For example, because all airplanes must be registered with the FAA, you transfer an airplane to your trust by complying with appropriate FAA regulations and forms. Similarly, for large boats registered with the Coast Guard, you need to complete that agency's forms. And for powerboats registered with a state agency, you need the appropriate state form. Less valuable boats—unregistered ones, like a rowboat or canoe—do not have documents of title and can simply be assigned to your trust. (See Chapter 11.)

Many other types of valuable property can also be placed in your trust, including jewelry, antiques, furs, furniture, precious metals, works of art, and collectibles—from Depression china to antique soldiers to old dolls to stamps to whatever objects people will pay money for.

The common denominator of all these types of property is that none of them has any formal ownership papers, like a deed for real estate. Some may have papers authenticating them, but these are not documents of title and don't need to be changed. So you can transfer any of these valuables to your trust simply by listing them on the trust schedule. You may also want to prepare an "assignment" form for this property, as is explained in "Paperwork" in Chapter 11.

Marital Property Laws

If you are married, you need to know what property is owned by each spouse separately and what property is held in shared ownership to properly complete your trust. Whether you make separate trusts (because most or all of each spouse's property is owned separately) or a shared trust (either the basic shared trust or AB trust), you need to clarify which spouse owns what to know which schedule—shared or individual—to list the property on. Each spouse controls, in the trust document, who will inherit his or her own trust property.

To figure out who owns what, you need to know a little about the law of the state where you live (and of any other state in which you own property) regarding marital property. Marital property laws can be divided into two basic groups: community property states and common law states.

Community Property States

Alaska (if spouses prepare a written community property agreement)

Arizona	Louisiana	Texas
California	Nevada	Washington
Idaho	New Mexico	Wisconsin

Same-Sex Couples

Property laws that have always governed married couples' property now apply to some same-sex couples in some states.

- In California, same-sex couples can register as domestic partners. Married couples and registered domestic partners are covered by the state's community property laws.
- In Hawaii, couples who register as reciprocal beneficiaries can own property in tenancy by the entirety. Such property is automatically inherited, without probate, by the surviving spouse when one spouse dies.
- Connecticut and Massachusetts allow same-sex couples to marry. Married couples may own property in tenancy by the entirety.
- In Connecticut, New Hampshire, New Jersey, and Vermont, couples joined in a civil union are also entitled to own property in tenancy by the entirety.
- Similarly, in Oregon, registered domestic partners can own tenancy by the entirety property.

In these states, the general rule is that spouses own everything acquired during the marriage 50-50 unless the spouses agree otherwise. It doesn't matter whose name is on the title slip.

There are a few important exceptions to the general rule. Property acquired before marriage is not community property; it is the separate property of that spouse. Likewise, property given to one spouse, by gift or inheritance, is separate property.

Community Property Basics

Community property includes:	Separate property includes:
• money either spouse earns during marriage	• property owned by one spouse before marriage
• things bought with that money, and	• property given to just one spouse, and
• separate property that has become so mixed (commingled) with community property that it can't be identified.	• property inherited by just one spouse.

Married couples don't have to accept these rules. They can sign a written agreement that makes some or all community property the separate property of one spouse or has separate property become community property.

Typically, most property owned by spouses is community property, especially if the couple have been married for a number of years. For example, if while married you bought real estate with money you earned during marriage, your spouse legally owns a half interest in it unless you both signed an agreement keeping it separate.

Sometimes it's not obvious who owns what. For example, are life insurance proceeds shared property or the separate property of the deceased spouse? The answer depends on the source of the funds used to pay for the insurance and the intention of the couple. If the insurance was paid for with shared marital property, the proceeds are co-owned. Similarly, if the couple agreed (in writing) that the proceeds were shared property, no matter who paid for them, that agreement controls. But if the policy was paid for from the separate property of the deceased, with no agreement that it was a shared ownership policy, the proceeds are the separate property of the deceased.

SEE AN EXPERT

Marital property agreements. If you and your spouse have complex property holdings, and there's any question whether any of your property is community or separate, it's wise to prepare a written marital property agreement, defining the nature of each major item of your property. Of course, to prepare the document, you two have to agree how your property should be classified. If you need help with that, see a lawyer or an accountant.

Special Wisconsin Rules

Wisconsin law allows a married couple to include, in a marital property agreement, binding provisions directing how each spouse's property is to be distributed upon that spouse's death. This property is transferred without probate. A spouse can direct that his or her property be transferred upon death to that spouse's living trust. The trust document defines how the property will be distributed to named beneficiaries. The benefit of using a marital property agreement for this purpose is that while you live you don't have to bother transferring property into a living trust. (See Chapter 11.)

If you move from a common law state to California, Idaho, Washington, or Wisconsin, some of your property may be reclassified as community property. In these states, the rule is that property acquired by a couple during marriage, no matter who owned it in a common law state, is treated as community property, owned equally by each spouse, if it would have been community property had the couple acquired it in one of these states. The legal term for such property is "quasi-community property." This means each spouse owns half of this property and can leave only that share at death. Wisconsin has a similar concept, called "deferred marital property." When one spouse dies, the survivor is entitled to half the value of deferred marital property owned by both spouses.

EXAMPLE:

Cora and Eric Gustafson live in Florida, a common law state. Cora buys some stocks with money she earned while married. She owns the stocks in her own name and is free to leave them by will or trust to whomever she pleases, subject to state law on the inheritance rights of spouses.

Later, Cora and Eric move to California. Because the stocks would have been Cora and Eric's community property if they had been bought in California, they are now "quasi-community property." At death or divorce, the stocks will be treated as community property, owned 50-50 by each spouse. Cora now owns only half and can leave only half in her trust or will.

However, if you move from a community property state to a common law state, your ownership rights in the property already acquired stay the same. The new state's law applies only to property acquired in the new state.

In community property states, separate property may turn into community property if it is mixed ("commingled") with community property. For example, if you deposit separate property funds into a joint bank account and then make more deposits and withdrawals, making it impossible to tell what part of the account is separate money, it's all considered community property.

EXAMPLE:

Roberto and Celia live in Nevada, a community property state. They have been married for 20 years. Except for some bonds that Celia inherited from her parents, virtually all their valuable property—house, stocks, car—is owned together. The money they brought to the marriage in separate bank accounts has long since been mixed with community property, making it community property too.

In community property states, there are restrictions on one spouse's freedom to transfer community property. Especially in the case of real estate, the consent of both spouses is necessary for either to sell or give away his or her half-interest in the property. Each spouse can, however, leave his or her half-interest in the property through a will or living trust.

If you live in a community property state, and you and your spouse create a living trust together, property you transfer to the trust will stay community property, even though it is technically owned by the living trust. Separately owned property (property of only one spouse) will also remain separate property. That means that community property transferred to a living trust is still eligible for the favorable tax treatment given community property at one spouse's death. (Both halves of community property left to the surviving

spouse get a "stepped-up basis" for income tax purposes; see Chapter 15.)

It also means that if either spouse revokes the living trust, ownership of the property will go back to the spouses as it was before the property was transferred to the living trust. Community property goes back to both spouses equally, and separate property goes to the spouse who owned it before ownership was transferred to the trust.

Common Law Property States

Alabama	Kentucky	North Dakota
Alaska	Maine	Ohio
Arkansas	Maryland	Oklahoma
Colorado	Massachusetts	Oregon
Connecticut	Michigan	Pennsylvania
Delaware	Minnesota	Rhode Island
District of Columbia	Mississippi	South Carolina
Florida	Missouri	South Dakota
Georgia	Montana	Tennessee
Hawaii	Nebraska	Utah
Illinois	New Hampshire	Vermont
Indiana	New Jersey	Virginia
Iowa	New York	West Virginia
Kansas	North Carolina	Wyoming

In these states, it's usually fairly easy for spouses to keep track of who owns what. The spouse whose name is on the title document—for example, the deed, brokerage account paper, or title slip—owns it. In these states, if the property doesn't have a title document, it belongs to the spouse who paid for it or received it as a gift. It's possible, though, that if there were a dispute about ownership, a judge could determine, based on the circumstances, that a spouse whose name is not on the title document might own an interest in the property.

It's increasingly common for couples, especially if they are older and have children from a prior marriage, to sign an agreement (before or during the marriage) to own property separately. Or they may not make a formal agreement, but carefully avoid mixing their property together.

If You're Unsure of Your Marital Status

Most people are quite certain whether or not they're married. If you're not sure, here's what you need to know.

The divorce decree. You're not divorced until you have a final decree of divorce (or dissolution, as it's called in some states) issued by a state court in the United States.

If you think you're divorced but never saw the final decree, contact the court clerk in the county where you think the divorce was granted. Give the clerk your name, your ex-spouse's name, and the date, as close as you know it, of the divorce.

Legal separation. Even if a court has declared you and your spouse legally separated, and you plan to divorce, you are still married until you get the divorce decree.

Foreign divorces. Divorces issued to U.S. citizens by courts in Mexico, the Dominican Republic, or another country may not be valid if challenged, especially if all the paperwork was handled by mail. In other words, if you or your spouse got a quickie foreign divorce, you may well be still married under the laws of your state. If you think that someone might make a claim to some of your property after your death based on the invalidity of a foreign divorce, see a lawyer.

Common law marriages. In some states, a couple can become legally married by living together, intending to be married, and presenting themselves to the world as a married couple. Even in states that allow such common law marriages, most couples who live together don't have common law marriages. If you really do have a valid common law marriage, you must go to court and get a divorce to end it—there's no such thing as a common law divorce.

Common law marriages can be created in Alabama, Colorado, District of Columbia, Georgia (only before January 1, 1997), Idaho (only before January 1, 1996), Iowa, Kansas, Montana, New Hampshire (for inheritance purposes only), Ohio (only before October 10, 1991), Oklahoma, Pennsylvania (only before January 1, 2005), Rhode Island, South Carolina, Texas, and Utah. If a common law marriage is created in one of these states, and the couple moves to another state, they are still legally married.

Gay or lesbian couples. Massachusetts and Connecticut currently allow marriage between two people of the same sex. In California, Connecticut, Hawaii, Maine, New Jersey, and Vermont, lesbian or gay couples can register with the state and obtain many of the rights of married couples.

If you want to co-own property equally, you can do that simply by taking title to property in both names for new property, or preparing a new ownership deed for previously owned property, listing the new owners as both of you. You should also state you own the property "equally, as tenants in common" if you intend to place the property in your living trusts. (For married couples, no state taxes will be assessed because of any transfer of title, because any transfer of property between spouses is free of tax.)

SEE AN EXPERT

In common law states, see a lawyer if you don't want to leave at least half of your living trust property to your spouse. This matter is discussed further in "Disinheritance" in Chapter 8.

Completing the Property Worksheet

On the worksheet in this section, you can list all of your property. This groundwork should make preparing your actual trust document easier. But completing it is not mandatory; use it if you think it will help you.

Even if you plan to leave everything to your spouse or children, you need to describe your property sufficiently on a trust schedule so that it is readily identifiable. In other words, every item (or group of items, in some circumstances) must be specifically described and listed as part of the trust document. (Examples are given in Chapter 10.)

You can list assets that will not be transferred to your living trust, such as retirement accounts, cars, and life insurance policies. Listing all of your property here will help you estimate your net worth, to see if your estate could be subject to estate taxes.

Remember, this worksheet is purely for your convenience. It can be as messy or as neat as you care to make it. Pencil is recommended (unless you're the type who does the *New York Times* crossword puzzle in ink).

You can find an electronic version of the property worksheet on this book's CD-ROM.

Section I: Assets

Column 1—Property Description

Here you write out what you own. How specific you should be depends in part on how you plan to leave your property (who your beneficiaries are), which you'll pin down in Chapter 8. For example, if you're going to leave all of your books to your daughter, there's no need to list them individually. But if you own several rare first editions that you'll leave to separate beneficiaries, list each book.

Column 2—Net Value of Your Ownership

In Column 2, estimate the net value of each item listed. "Net value" means your equity in your share of the property—the market value of your share, less your share of any debts on that share, such as a mortgage on a house or the loan amount due on a car.

If you're a couple, "your share" means the value of both of your interests. For estate tax purposes, it's the value of what you both own that really counts.

Obviously, listing net values for your property means making estimates. That's fine; there's no need to burden yourself with seeking precise figures. After all, your death taxes, if any, will be based on the net value of your property when you die, not its current worth. For example, if you think the net worth of your house, after you subtract the mortgage, is about $200,000, your car $5,000, and your stamp collection would fetch $2,000 if you put an ad in a philatelists' journal, use those numbers.

If you own property with someone other than a spouse or mate, simply estimate the worth of your share of that property.

EXAMPLE:

Paul owns a house with a market value of $380,000 as a tenant in common with his sister Ava; each owns half. Paul computes the net value of his share by first subtracting the amount of mortgages, liens, and past due taxes from the market value to arrive at the total equity in the property. There's a $100,000 mortgage and a $20,000 lien against the property.

The total equity, then, is $380,000 minus $120,000, or $260,000. The net worth of Paul's half of the property is $130,000.

With some common sense, you can probably safely make sensible estimates yourself. Only with more complex types of property, such as business interests, might you want expert help.

EXAMPLE:

Stacey is sole owner of the Maltese Falcon Restaurant, a successful business she has run for 20 years. She has only a vague notion of its market value, since she has never been interested in selling it. Making a reasonable estimate of the worth of the business is difficult, since the market value of her restaurant includes the intangible of "goodwill." Stacey talks to an accountant to help her arrive at a sensible estimate of the worth of the restaurant.

Column 3—Who Owns It

Because you need to identify which property is shared and which is separate, indicate that here. Use whatever symbols you want to identify the ownership—for example, O (ours); H (Husband); W (Wife); S (shared); M (Mary); N (Neil).

Column 4—Transfer to Trust

In Column 4, indicate whether you want to transfer this item of property to the trust. For each item you'll put in the trust, put a "T."

Section II: Liabilities

Here, list any liabilities (debts) you haven't already taken into account in Section I. For example, list any significant personal debts—the $10,000 loan from a friend or the $5,000 unsecured advance on a line of credit. Also list all other liabilities, such as tax liens or court judgments, and add up all these liabilities.

Section III: Net Worth

Here's where you calculate your net worth by subtracting your total liabilities (Section II.D) from the total net value of your assets (Section I.E).

Property Worksheet

I. Assets

Description of Your Property	Net Value of Your Ownership	Who Owns It	Transfer to Trust?

A. Liquid Assets

1. cash (dividends, etc.)

2. savings accounts

3. checking accounts

4. money market accounts

5. certificates of deposit

6. Treasury bills or notes

7. promissory notes (owed to you)

Description of Your Property	Net Value of Your Ownership	Who Owns It	Transfer to Trust?

B. Other Personal Property
   (all your property except liquid assets, business interests, and real estate)

1. listed (private corporation) stocks and bonds

2. unlisted stocks and bonds

3. government bonds and securities

4. automobiles and other vehicles, including planes, boats, and recreational vehicles

5. precious metals

6. household goods

7. clothing

Description of Your Property	Net Value of Your Ownership	Who Owns It	Transfer to Trust?
8. jewelry and furs			
9. artworks, collectibles, and antiques			
10. tools and equipment			
11. valuable livestock/animals			
12. life insurance proceeds			
13. money owed you (personal loans, etc.)			
14. retirement accounts, including IRAs, 401(k)s, and profit-sharing plans			
15. life insurance (proceeds payable on death)			no

Description of Your Property	Net Value of Your Ownership	Who Owns It	Transfer to Trust?
16. other valuable personal property			
_____	_____	____	____
_____	_____	____	____
_____	_____	____	____
_____	_____	____	____

C. Miscellaneous Receivables

(mortgages, deeds of trust, or promissory notes held by you; any rents due from income property owned by you; and any payments due for professional or personal services, or property sold by you that are not fully paid by the purchaser)

_____	_____	____	____
_____	_____	____	____
_____	_____	____	____
_____	_____	____	____

D. Real Estate

1. address

_____	_____	____	____
_____	_____	____	____
_____	_____	____	____
_____	_____	____	____

2. address

_____	_____	____	____
_____	_____	____	____
_____	_____	____	____
_____	_____	____	____

3. address

_____	_____	____	____
_____	_____	____	____
_____	_____	____	____
_____	_____	____	____

4. address

_____	_____	____	____
_____	_____	____	____
_____	_____	____	____
_____	_____	____	____

5. address

_____	_____	____	____
_____	_____	____	____
_____	_____	____	____
_____	_____	____	____

E. Total Net Value of Your Assets $ _____

II. Liabilities

To Whom Debt Is Owed   **Amount**

A. Personal Property Debts

1. personal loans (banks, major credit cards, etc.)

_____   _____

_____   _____

_____   _____

_____   _____

_____   _____

_____   _____

_____   _____

2. other personal debts

_____   _____

_____   _____

_____   _____

_____   _____

_____   _____

_____   _____

_____   _____

_____   _____

_____   _____

B. Taxes (include only taxes past and currently due; do not include taxes due in the future or estimated estate taxes)

_____   _____

_____   _____

_____   _____

_____   _____

_____   _____

C. Any Other Liabilities (legal judgments, accrued child support, etc.)

_____   _____

_____   _____

_____   _____

D. Total Liabilities (excluding those liabilities already deducted in Section I) $ _____

III. Net Worth (Total Net Value of Your Assets, from Section I.E, above, minus Total Liabilities, from Section II.D, above) $ _____

Trustees

To be legally valid, your living trust must have a trustee—someone responsible for managing the property in the trust. The trust property is actually held in the trustee's name. When you create a trust from this book, you are the initial trustee. If you create a basic shared living trust or an AB trust, you and your spouse are cotrustees.

When the initial trustee, or both trustees, have died, the "successor trustee" takes over. This person is responsible for transferring trust property to the beneficiaries and handling any other matters required by the trust—such as managing a child's trust, or filing federal tax returns. Technically, the executor of your will is responsible for filing tax returns, but normally, the executor and successor trustee are the same person. If not, the executor and successor trustee will have to work together.

For many people, the decision of who to name as successor trustee is clear, but for others, complexities and uncertainties can arise.

The Initial Trustee

A key to how a living trust works is that you, or you and your spouse, are the initial trustees. Grasping this point is essential to understanding what a living trust is—a device that allows you to absolutely control your own property while you are alive, and at the same time avoid probate of the property after you die.

SEE AN EXPERT

Naming someone else as initial trustee. If you want to name someone besides yourself to be your initial trustee because you don't want to, or cannot, continue to manage your own assets, see a lawyer; don't use the trust forms in this book. When you make somebody else your initial trustee, you create a more complicated trust, often necessitating much more detailed controls on the trustee's powers to act. In addition, under IRS rules, if you aren't a trustee of your own living trust, separate trust records must be maintained, and a fiduciary trust tax return (Form 1041) filed each year.

Your Responsibilities as Trustee

You won't have any special duties as trustee of your trust. As a day-to-day, practical matter, it makes no difference that you now manage your property as trustee, rather than in your own name. You do not need to file a separate income tax return for the living trust. As long as you are trustee, any income the trust property generates must be reported on your personal income tax return, as if the trust did not exist. (IRS Reg. § 1.671-4.) Likewise, you don't have to obtain a trust taxpayer ID number or keep separate trust records.

You have the same freedom to sell, mortgage, or give away trust property as you did before you put that property into the living trust. (Thus, one spouse does not have rights over the other spouse's separate property.) Normally, the only difference is that you must now sign documents in your capacity as trustee. It's that easy.

EXAMPLE:

Celeste and Angelo want to sell a piece of land that is owned in the name of their living trust. They prepare a deed transferring ownership of the land from the trustees of the trust to the new owner. They sign the deed as "Celeste Tornetti and Angelo Tornetti, trustees of the Celeste Tornetti and Angelo Tornetti Living Trust dated February 4, 20xx."

If you make a shared living trust (either a basic shared trust or an AB trust), it's important to realize that once shared property belongs to the trust, either trustee (spouse) has authority over it. Legally, either spouse can sell or give away any of the shared trust property. In practice, however, both spouses will probably have to consent (in writing) to transfer shared real estate out of the living trust. Especially in community property states, buyers and title insurance companies usually insist on both spouses' signatures on transfer documents.

SEE AN EXPERT

Naming only one spouse as trustee. If you want only one spouse to be the original trustee of a basic shared living trust or an AB trust, there's an unusual—and unequal—distribution of authority over shared property, and you should see a lawyer.

Naming a Cotrustee

If you think you'll want or need someone else to manage your trust property for you, but don't want the hassles of having a separate trustee, you can consider naming yourself and another person to both be the initial trustees of your trust. Both of you would have authority to act on the trust's behalf. No fiduciary trust tax return is required, since *one* of the trustees is the original grantor.

EXAMPLE:

Beatrice is in her 80s. She doesn't want to abandon control over her property but has difficulty managing things—keeping track of bills and payments, for example. So she creates a living trust, naming herself and her daughter Polly as initial cotrustees. Either trustee can act for the trust. Because Beatrice is one of the initial trustees, she does not have to keep separate records or file a trust tax return. And as a practical matter, Polly can handle most trust transactions on her own.

SEE AN EXPERT

Get help if you want initial cotrustees. If you want to have a cotrustee to serve with you, it's best to see a lawyer, so the authority of the trustees is clearly defined and specifically geared to your situation. Don't rely on the forms in this book.

The Trustee After One Spouse's Death or Incapacity

If you create a basic shared living trust or either type of AB trust, when one spouse dies or becomes incapacitated and unable to manage his or her affairs, the other becomes sole trustee.

Using the trust forms in this book, a spouse's physical or mental incapacity is determined by the vote of people you've chosen to make that decision (discussed below). If one spouse is incapacitated, the other spouse, as sole trustee, takes over management of both spouses' trust property. As trustee, that's the extent of his or her authority; the living trust does not give the surviving spouse power over property of the incapacitated spouse not owned by the living trust, and

it does not give the surviving spouse authority to make health care decisions for the incapacitated spouse. For this reason, it's also wise for each spouse to create documents called durable powers of attorney and health care directives, giving the other spouse authority to manage property not owned in the name of the trust and to make health care decisions for an incapacitated spouse. (See "Planning for Incapacity" in Chapter 15.)

The duties of a surviving spouse as trustee under a trust prepared with this book are summarized below. They are discussed in more detail in Chapters 4 and 5.

The Successor Trustee

Your trust document must name a successor trustee. The successor trustee takes over after you have died, or, for a basic shared trust or an AB trust, after both members of the couple have died. The successor trustee also takes over if you, or both you and your spouse, become incapacitated and are unable to manage the trust property.

Incapacity means the inability to manage your affairs. For a basic shared trust or an AB trust, the successor trustee has no authority to act if one spouse is alive and capable of managing trust property.

Picking your successor trustee is an important decision. Not only must you pick someone you trust who can do the job and is willing to do it, you also probably don't want to ruffle any family feathers when making your choice. You can name successor cotrustees, if this fits your needs.

When you decide on your successor trustee, your job isn't done. You should also name an alternate successor trustee, in case the successor trustee dies before you do or can't serve for some other reason. If you named two or more successor trustees, the alternate won't become trustee unless none of your original choices can serve.

The Job of the Successor Trustee

Obviously, when you choose your successor trustee, it helps for you both to understand what he or she will need to do. The primary job of the successor trustee is to turn trust property over to the beneficiaries you named in the trust document. This is normally not difficult if the property and beneficiaries are clearly identified. Still, some effort is required.

The Surviving Spouse's Trustee Duties

With a basic shared trust:

- The surviving spouse, as trustee, is responsible for distributing the trust property of the deceased spouse as the trust document directs. Trust property left by the deceased spouse to the surviving spouse does not require any actual distribution, since the trust form specifies that such property remains in the revocable living trust. So no further steps need to be taken to legally transfer this property to the surviving spouse.
- The surviving spouse manages, as sole trustee, the ongoing revocable trust that contains his or her property, including trust property inherited from the deceased spouse.

With a standard AB trust:

- The surviving spouse, with the help of an expert, divides the living trust property between the Trust A, containing the deceased spouse's property, and the Trust B, the surviving spouse's trust.
- The surviving spouse distributes any specific gifts made by the deceased spouse.
- The surviving spouse leaves all remaining trust property of the deceased spouse in the Trust A.
- As trustee, the surviving spouse legally establishes and manages the Trust A (obtains a federal taxpayer ID number, keeps trust records, etc.).
- The surviving spouse manages the Trust B, as an ongoing revocable trust that contains his or her property.

With an AB disclaimer trust:

- The surviving spouse, as trustee, must decide how much, if any, of the deceased spouse's trust property to disclaim to Trust A.
- The surviving spouse distributes any specific gifts left by the deceased spouse.
- If Trust A is established, the surviving spouse, with the help of an expert, divides the property between Trust A and Trust B.
- The surviving spouse operates and manages Trust A.
- The surviving spouse manages the ongoing Trust B, that spouse's living trust.

With any one of these types of trusts, the surviving spouse may have long-term duties if the trust document creates a child's trust for trust property inherited by a young beneficiary, because the surviving spouse may have to manage this property for many years.

Usually, the successor trustee obtains several certified copies of the death certificate of the grantor. Then he or she presents a copy of the death certificate and a copy of the living trust document, along with proof of his or her own identity, to financial institutions, brokers, and other organizations that have possession of the trust assets. They will then release the property to the beneficiary. If any documents of title (ownership) must be prepared to transfer trust property to the beneficiaries, the successor trustee prepares them. For example, to transfer real estate owned by a living trust to the beneficiaries after the death of the grantor, the successor trustee prepares, signs, and records (in the local land records office) a deed from himself or herself, as trustee of the living trust, to the specified beneficiaries. No court or agency approval is required.

What happens if an institution won't cooperate with the successor trustee? Happily, such problems are unlikely. Institutions that deal with financial assets—from title companies to county land records offices to stock brokers—are familiar with living trusts and how they work.

No Government Filing Required

A successor trustee who takes over because the original grantor(s) have died doesn't need to file any documents to establish his or her authority with any court or governmental agency. However, if a trust is an ongoing entity, such as Trust A of an AB trust or child's trust, the successor trustee must contact the IRS and maintain proper tax records.

It's even easier for the trustee to distribute trust assets that don't have documents of title—household furnishings, jewelry, heirlooms, collectibles—to the appropriate beneficiaries. The trustee just turns the property over to the beneficiaries.

When all beneficiaries have received the trust property left to them in the trust document, the successor trustee's job is over, and the trust ends.

In some situations, additional tasks may be required of the successor trustee.

- **Managing trust property if the trust grantor or grantors become incapacitated.** With all Nolo living trusts, if the grantor (or grantors) become incapacitated and can no longer manage the trust property, the successor trustee manages the trust until the grantor dies or regains capacity. The term "incapacity" is not defined in the trust document. In commonsense terms, it means that the grantor has become mentally or physically unable to handle his or her financial affairs.

In this book's trust forms, you name three people who can determine, by majority vote, whether or not you have become incapacitated, if the issue ever arises. Name any three persons you trust and who are likely to be around (both alive and accessible) longer than you.

Don't, however, name as your successor trustee a person who may determine incapacity. You don't want your successor trustee wearing two hats—participating in the decision about control, and then taking over. This could create at least the appearance of a conflict of interest, which might mean that financial institutions would be hesitant to accept your successor trustee's authority.

SEE AN EXPERT

Keep track of the people you've named to make incapacity decisions. If one or more of the people you've chosen to make a decision about your (possible) incapacity become unavailable, for whatever reason, you should amend your trust to name a new person. (See Chapter 13 for more on amending your living trust.) If the need for a determination ever arises (hopefully it will not), you want three people involved in making that decision. Not only are three heads better than two or one, but you also want to avoid the risk of having only two people, who might disagree. A tie vote over whether you have become incapacitated would not be good.

Having a Doctor Make the Determination

In our culture, doctors are often called upon to determine someone's mental capacity, even though this is not strictly a medical determination. With living trusts, one possible method for determining incapacity is by a doctor's statement. But there are possible problems with this. As anyone who has visited a doctor's office in the last few years has learned, federal law (the Health Insurance Portability and Accountability Act, commonly referred to as HIPAA, 42 U.S.C. § 1320(d)) gives patients the right to privacy when it comes to medical information. HIPAA severely restricts the release of a patient's medical information.

This creates a catch-22 when it comes to getting a doctor to issue a statement about someone's capacity to handle his or her affairs. If your successor trustee goes to a doctor and asks for a statement saying you are incapacitated and can no longer manage the trust, the doctor could well be precluded, by HIPAA, from giving it.

SEE AN EXPERT

If you want a doctor to be able to determine your capacity—and thus when your successor trustee is entitled to take over—your trust document must specifically authorize doctors to use and release any of your medical records needed or used in making that determination. Granting that authorization isn't simple; you'll need a lawyer to prepare the correct release forms. HIPAA is a federal law, but some states have their own, even more stringent, patient privacy laws. For example, California law requires a medical release to be in 14-point type and cover several matters not required under federal law. (Civ. Code §§ 56.10–56.16.) Be sure to find a lawyer who's knowledgeable about both federal law and your state's requirements.

With Nolo's marital trusts, either a shared trust or one of the AB trusts, the successor trustee could wind up managing both spouses' trusts if both spouses are alive but incapacitated. Further, with an AB trust, if one spouse has died, the successor trustee could be called upon to manage two trusts—Trust A of the deceased spouse and Trust B of the surviving, incapacitated spouse.

When a successor trustee takes over for an incapacitated grantor, the job is basically financial. The successor trustee must become (rapidly) familiar with the grantor's financial resources and needs, and handle all money matters and problems as they arise.

- **Preparing and filing estate tax returns.** If a federal estate tax return must be filed after a grantor's death, and taxes paid, the successor trustee is responsible for these tasks. Also, a final income tax return must be filed for the deceased grantor. The successor trustee must also file a state inheritance tax return if one is required. The executor you name in your backup will (see Chapter 16) shares legal responsibility for filing these tax returns. Usually, the same person is appointed as the successor trustee and executor.
- **Managing children's trusts.** The trust forms in this book allow you to leave trust property to young beneficiaries (under 35 when you die) in simple child's trusts. (See Chapter 9.) If you die before any child reaches the age you've specified, your successor trustee will manage trust property left for the benefit of that child until he or she reaches that age. Thus, the successor trustee can have ongoing management responsibilities for a child's trust. Annual trust income tax returns are required for each operational child's trust and are the responsibility of the successor trustee.
- **Amending an AB trust if both spouses are incapacitated.** If—or when—Congress revises the estate tax law during the next few years, it could be desirable to amend an existing AB trust to take best advantage of the new law. If both spouses are alive but incapacitated when a new law takes effect, it could be very important to the trust's final beneficiaries that the successor trustee be allowed to amend the trust. The AB trust forms in this book provide that the successor trustee

can amend the trust to take best advantage of the current estate tax law. The successor trustee has this power only if both spouses are incapacitated when the need arises. You do not have to grant your successor this power; you can eliminate the provision if you want to. (See Step 5A in Chapter 10.)

The tasks required of a successor trustee are discussed at more depth in Chapter 14. Specific, state-by-state instructions for trustee tasks are provided in *The Executor's Guide: Settling a Loved One's Estate or Trust*, by Mary Randolph (Nolo).

The Successor Trustee's Authority

The trust forms in this book spell out the specific powers granted to the successor trustee.

The Successor Trustee's Powers

The living trust forms in this book give the successor trustee all powers permitted under state law. The forms also define certain specific powers—for example, that the trustee has authority to buy and sell real estate and stocks. Some banks, title companies, stock brokerage companies, or other financial institutions demand this level of detail before approving a trust transaction, even though such authority is clearly included in a general grant of power under state law.

The living trust forms also give the successor trustee broad authority to manage any child's trust, including the power to spend any amount of each child's trust income or principal for that child's "health, support, maintenance, or education." As long as you trust your successor trustee, defining the power to manage young beneficiaries' trust property in this broad way is the best approach.

Once in a while, a financial institution gets quirky and demands that a trust specifically authorize some relatively unusual transaction the trustee wants to engage in. For example, a brokerage company may claim that some very sophisticated maneuver isn't authorized by the trustee's powers clause in your trust. The general trustee powers clause should give you all the authorization you need. But if a financial institution proves recalcitrant, find out the exact wording the institution wants, and then include those words in the trustee powers clause of the trust document.

The Successor Trustee's Duty to Act Responsibly

The successor trustee must manage any trust property, including any property in a child's trust, in a "prudent manner." This means the trustee must always act honestly and in the best interests of the beneficiary. For example, the trustee must not make risky investments with trust property.

Legally, the trustee cannot personally profit or benefit from a transaction (this is called "self-dealing"). Basically, this means personally profiting or benefiting from a transaction involving trust property, such as buying a house from the trust. But remember, legal restrictions can be enforced only by a lawsuit. Be sure you have someone you trust as successor trustee, to minimize the possibility of litigation.

The successor trustee has authority to get professional assistance if necessary and pay for it with trust money. For example, the successor trustee might want to pay a tax preparer for help with the child's trust income tax return, or to consult a financial planner for investment advice.

Payment of the Successor Trustee

Typically, the successor trustee of a basic probate-avoidance living trust isn't paid. This is because the successor trustee's duty is simply to distribute the deceased grantor's trust property, which is not normally an arduous job. Also, the successor trustee is usually a major beneficiary of the trust. For these reasons, the trust forms in this book provide that no compensation be paid to the successor trustee, with two exceptions:

- managing any trust when the grantor or grantors have become incapacitated, and
- managing an ongoing child's trust.

The trust forms provide that in these situations a successor trustee is entitled, without court approval, to "reasonable" compensation for services. The successor trustee decides what is reasonable and takes it from the appropriate trust property, in either the child's trust or the Trust A.

In these situations, the successor trustee might have to actively manage the trust property for some time, so some pay for that work seems fair. The duties and burdens of a successor trustee who manages a child's trust can be substantial. The trust can last for decades and entail extensive financial responsibilities. If you

have more than one trust, the job can become even more demanding.

Similarly, a successor trustee who takes over a Trust A for an incapacitated spouse will be required to do all the paperwork and other chores needed to keep the trust valid in the eyes of the IRS. Again, it seems fair to provide for reasonable compensation for this work.

Notifying Trust Beneficiaries

In a number of states, a successor trustee of a living trust is specifically required by statute to provide basic information about the trust to trust beneficiaries. This duty includes notifying trust beneficiaries that the trust has become irrevocable and possibly providing a copy of the trust document. In all states, it's wise for the successor trustee to give this information to beneficiaries, even if a specific statute does not compel it. A successor trustee should understand and accept this responsibility. The good news is that it shouldn't be hard to do—a simple letter setting out basic trust information should suffice.

RESOURCE

Get state-by-state details about the successor trustee's duties. *The Executor's Guide: Settling a Loved One's Estate or Trust*, by Mary Randolph (Nolo), lists every state's rules regarding a successor trustee's duties. If a state imposes specific duties, the citation to that state's statute is provided.

SEE AN EXPERT

See a lawyer to restrict the trustee's authority. Consult a lawyer if you are uneasy about:

- the broad grant of powers to the successor trustee
- the successor trustee's authority to sell trust property, regardless of the desires of other beneficiaries
- the lack of specific restrictions on the successor trustee
- the successor trustee's authority to manage and invest trust funds, or
- allowing open-ended compensation for managing a child's trust or Trust A.

Such a concern may well indicate potential serious problems, which require careful professional attention.

Also, if you decide that you want your successor trustee to be compensated for tasks entailed in transferring trust property to adult beneficiaries, see a lawyer. Compensation might be appropriate if your estate is a large one and federal estate tax returns will have to be filed.

Choosing Your Successor Trustee

Your successor trustee will play a vital role in carrying out the aims of your living trust.

In most situations, the successor trustee does not need extensive experience in financial management; common sense, dependability, and complete honesty are usually enough. A successor trustee who may have long-term responsibility over a young beneficiary's trust property probably needs more management and financial skills than a successor trustee whose only job is to distribute trust property. But as I've said, the successor trustee does have authority, under the terms of the trust document, to get any reasonably necessary professional help—from an accountant, lawyer, or tax preparer, perhaps—and pay for it out of trust assets.

Your successor trustee should be whoever you feel is most trustworthy to do the job, who's willing to do it, and can actually do it. Often a major beneficiary, such as a spouse or adult child, is named as successor trustee. However, you don't have to name a beneficiary as trustee. If you believe the beneficiary (much as you love him or her) will be troubled by having to handle the practical details and paperwork, it is preferable to name someone else, often another family member. Or as a last resort, consider naming an institution as trustee.

If you are married and create a basic shared trust, keep in mind that the successor trustee does not take over until both spouses have died (or become incapacitated). That means that after one spouse's death, the surviving spouse may have time to amend the trust document and name a different successor trustee if he or she wishes.

The situation is different with an AB trust. Trust A becomes irrevocable upon the death of the first spouse. Therefore, the successor trustee for the Trust A cannot be changed by the surviving spouse, so your choice here is particularly important. The surviving spouse remains free, of course, to amend or revoke her own Trust B and name a new successor trustee for it.

Avoiding Conflicts Between Your Trust, Your Will, and Other Documents

Your living trust, will, and durable power of attorney for finances all give someone the authority to make decisions about your property if you can't. If you choose different people to act for you in these different documents, each will become involved in case of your incapacity, and when you die. You don't need three heads here. Pick the same person for all three tasks.

See Chapter 15 for details about wills and durable powers of attorney.

SEE AN EXPERT

If for some reason you want to name different people to be your successor trustee, executor of your will, and to act for you in your durable power of attorney for finances, see a lawyer.

Obviously, you should confer with the person you've chosen to be your successor trustee to be sure your choice is willing to serve. If you don't, you risk creating problems down the line. No one can be drafted to serve as a successor trustee. The person you've chosen may not want to serve, for a variety of reasons. And even if the person would be willing, if he or she doesn't know of his or her responsibilities, transfer of trust property after your death could be delayed.

Naming More Than One Successor Trustee

Legally, you can name as many successor cotrustees as you want, to serve together with power divided among them as you specify. However, as a general rule, because of coordination problems and possible conflicts among multiple trustees, it's generally best to name just one successor trustee. This isn't invariably true, however. For example, a parent may not want to be seen to favor one child over others, and to avoid this could name two or more children as successor cotrustees. This can be especially appropriate if the children are equal beneficiaries of the trust. If the children all get along, it rarely causes a problem.

When appointing cotrustees, you must decide how authority is shared among them—whether each can act separately for the trust, or all must agree in writing to act for the trust. Consider giving each the power to act for the trust without the formal written consent of the others. Especially if they live far away from one another or travel often, this could speed up the eventual property transfer process, avoiding delays that might otherwise be caused if one cotrustee were temporarily unavailable.

But what is most important is that you have complete confidence that all your successor trustees will get along. Do be cautious here. Power and property can lead to unexpected results (ask King Lear). If the cotrustees are prone to conflict, you may well create serious problems (and are doing none of them a favor) by having them share power as trustees.

If the cotrustees can't agree, it could hold up the distribution of trust property to your beneficiaries. In extreme situations, the other trustees might even have to go to court to get a recalcitrant trustee removed so that your instructions can be carried out. The result might be much worse, and generate much more bad feeling, than if you had just picked one person to be trustee in the first place.

Having more than one successor trustee is especially risky if the successor trustees may be in charge of property you have left to a young beneficiary in a child's trust. The trustees may have to manage a young beneficiary's property for many years, and will have many decisions to make about how to spend the money—greatly increasing the potential for conflict. (Children's trusts are discussed in Chapter 9.)

If you name more than one successor trustee, and one of them can't serve, the others will serve. Only if none of them can serve will the alternate successor trustee you name take over.

SEE AN EXPERT

Handling conflicts between successor cotrustees. If you're naming successor cotrustees and fear potential conflicts, see a lawyer. Such situations are too touchy to resolve without careful individual analysis. For this reason, the trust forms in this book don't contain clauses for resolving conflicts between successor cotrustees. A lawyer may recommend requiring the trustees to submit disputes to arbitration or mediation, or

providing that if there is a dispute, one identified trustee gets to make the call.

Naming a Sole Beneficiary as Successor Trustee

It's perfectly legal to name a beneficiary of the trust as successor trustee. In fact, it's common.

EXAMPLE:

Santiago names his only child, Jaime, to be his sole trust beneficiary. Santiago also names Jaime as successor trustee. So when Santiago dies, Jaime's only task is to turn the trust property over to himself.

Naming an Out-of-State Trustee

Your successor trustee does not have to live in the same state as you do. But someone close by will probably have an easier job, especially with real estate transfers. For transfers of property such as securities and bank accounts, it usually won't make much difference where the successor trustee lives.

Naming a Bank or Trust Company as Successor Trustee

In my experience, it is almost always a bad idea to name a bank as successor trustee. I've heard some horror stories involving the indifference or downright rapaciousness of banks acting as trustees of family living trusts. Institutional trustees also charge hefty fees, which come out of the trust property and leave less for your family and friends. And banks probably won't even be interested in "small" living trusts—ones that contain less than several hundred thousand dollars' worth of property.

Your successor trustee is your link with the ongoing lives of your loved ones. You want that link to be a human being you trust, not a corporation dedicated to the enhancement of its bottom line. However, if there is no person you believe will act honestly and competently as your successor trustee, you'll need to select some financial institution to do the job. Of course, you must obtain the agreement of a financial institutional to serve as your successor trustee, which may prove difficult, or very expensive, or both. Probably the best choice here is a private trust company. These companies generally offer more humane and personal attention to a trust than a bank or other large financial institution. Also, they can be more reasonable about fees charged to wind up a living trust.

For a very large living trust, another possibility is to name a person and an institution as successor cotrustees. The bank or trust company can do most of the paperwork, and the person can keep an eye on things and approve all transactions. ●

Choosing Your Beneficiaries

After deciding what property you'll put in your trust and who will be your successor trustee, your next step is to decide who will be your trust's beneficiaries. Who gets what? This is the heart of preparing your living trust.

This chapter raises some important concerns about choosing beneficiaries and provides a worksheet on which you can list each beneficiary and what property you want to leave him, her, or it. You can name any person or institution you want as a beneficiary. A beneficiary does not have to be a U.S. citizen or resident. An institution does not have to be located in the United States.

Even if you believe your beneficiary decisions are cut-and-dried, please do not be tempted to skip this chapter. It contains important information you should take into account even if you have already decided who will inherit your property. For instance, you may initially think you don't want to bother naming alternate beneficiaries. But to make that decision sensibly, you should understand how alternate beneficiaries are used in living trusts, and why it's often wise to name them.

Kinds of Trust Beneficiaries

Several different classes of trust beneficiaries are used in trusts in this book.

Individual or Basic Shared Trusts

When you make a basic probate-avoidance living trust, you can name three kinds of beneficiaries:

- **Primary beneficiaries,** whom you name to receive specific property. Primary beneficiaries include individuals, institutions, and groups who receive property together.
- **Alternate beneficiaries,** whom you name to receive property left to a primary beneficiary if that primary beneficiary predeceases (dies before) you.
- **Residuary beneficiaries (and alternate residuary beneficiaries),** who receive all trust property not left to primary or alternate beneficiaries (including when both predecease you). You can, if you choose, leave all trust property to your residuary beneficiary, and not name any primary or alternate beneficiaries.

Keep It Simple

Some living trust books argue that:

- you cannot be trusted to choose your beneficiaries without professional help, and
- you need to create all sorts of complex beneficiary provisions to cover all sorts of contingencies, such as providing for what happens if a child's needs change long after you die, or a spouse remarries.

It's not hard to dream up remote possibilities about beneficiaries. While this certainly makes work for lawyers, it isn't what most people want. Most folks realize that it's rarely sensible to try to impose post-death controls over property given to beneficiaries.

"My life has been full of misfortunes, most of which never happened." —Mark Twain

This book assumes you'll leave property outright, with no strings attached (except for gifts to minors or young adults, discussed in Chapter 9, or property in an AB trust, discussed in Chapter 5).

> **CAUTION**
>
> **Conditions on gifts.** If you do want to impose conditions on gifts—for instance, distributing money in three installments, or varying the amount left to a beneficiary depending on future needs—see a lawyer.

Unmarried Couples

Because most couples who use shared living trusts are married—and to simplify the instructions—throughout this chapter I use the term "spouse." However, the instructions apply equally to unmarried couples. If you are part of an unmarried couple, simply replace the term "spouse" with "partner" or whatever term you prefer.

AB Living Trusts

If you and your spouse create a Nolo AB trust to save on estate taxes, you each will name:

- **The life beneficiary.** This beneficiary is always the surviving spouse.
- **Final beneficiaries.** Each spouse names these for his or her trust property. Eventually, the final beneficiaries are those (1) named by the deceased spouse to receive the property in Trust A when the surviving spouse dies, and (2) named by the surviving spouse to receive the property in the surviving spouse's Trust B.
- **Specific beneficiaries.** If you wish, you can name beneficiaries who will inherit specific gifts left by the deceased spouse. You do not have to name any specific beneficiaries.

Naming Your Primary Beneficiaries

For single people, or couples using a basic shared living trust, choosing your primary beneficiaries is often the heart of making your trust. Deciding on your primary beneficiaries is entirely up to you. Your beneficiaries can include a spouse, mate, friends, young adults, children, or charitable or other institutions.

> **CAUTION**
>
> **Disinheriting a spouse or child.** If you are married and live in a common law state and you don't plan to leave at least half of what you own to your spouse, consult a lawyer experienced in estate planning. (See list of common law states below.) Whatever your wishes, state law entitles your spouse to some of your estate, possibly including some of the property in your living trust. In most circumstances, you don't have to leave anything to your children. But if you want to disinherit a child, you should state that expressly in your will. See "Disinheritance," below.

Property Received by Beneficiaries Is Not Subject to Income Tax

Beneficiaries who inherit property are not liable for any federal income tax on that property. Of course, large estates may have had to pay estate taxes, but once they've been paid, the recipient of a gift is not subject to income tax on its value. If that gift generates income in the future, the beneficiary is responsible for paying income tax on that.

Individual Trust

Naming beneficiaries here is simple. Just list on the worksheet, and later on Form 1, whomever you want to receive your trust property. That's it!

EXAMPLE:

Ruth has three grown children and two grand-children. She also has a brother she is close to, and she's been a long-time contributor to Doctors Without Borders. She names the following primary beneficiaries for her trust property:
- Each child receives 21%.
- Each grandchild receives 7%.
- Her brother receives 14%.
- Doctors Without Borders receives 9%.

Basic Shared Living Trust

Each spouse names beneficiaries separately, because each spouse's share of trust property is distributed when that spouse dies. When the first spouse dies, that spouse's trust property is distributed to the beneficiaries he or she named in the trust document. Property left to the other spouse stays in the ongoing revocable trust of the surviving spouse. When the second spouse dies, all the property in his or her trust is distributed to the second spouse's beneficiaries.

EXAMPLE 1:

Roger and Marilyn Foster create a basic shared living trust. Each puts shared, equally owned property and separately owned property in the trust. When Roger dies, Marilyn takes over as sole trustee. The property Roger left to Marilyn stays in the trust. Marilyn distributes the trust property Roger left to other beneficiaries. When Marilyn dies, her trust property will be distributed by her successor trustee to her beneficiaries.

EXAMPLE 2:

Marcia and Perry transfer all the property they own together into their basic shared living trust. Marcia names Perry as the beneficiary of all her interest in the trust property. Perry names Marcia to inherit all of his half except his half-interest in their vacation cabin, which he leaves to his son from a previous marriage, Eric. If Perry dies first, Perry's half-interest in the cabin will go to Eric, who will co-own it with Marcia.

AB Trust

If you use either type of AB trust, you have much less concern with specific beneficiaries. The bulk of your property is left in Trust A, or to your surviving spouse. While with this book's AB trust forms each spouse can name specific beneficiaries to receive gifts outside of the trust property, such individual gifts are relatively minor. (See Chapter 5.) Each spouse can also name alternate beneficiaries for any specific beneficiaries.

As discussed in Chapter 5, the property in Trust A is left for the surviving spouse for use during his or her lifetime. Each spouse names final beneficiaries—the people who will eventually inherit the trust property when the second spouse dies. However, if you use an AB disclaimer trust, the final beneficiaries named by the deceased spouse may not inherit that spouse's trust property if the surviving spouse does not disclaim trust property and create Trust A.

Commonly, both spouses name the same final beneficiaries. This is usually the case when the couple are in their first marriage and both want their property eventually to go to their children. When each member of a couple wants to name different final beneficiaries, that's usually because each has children from prior marriages.

Each spouse can name different final beneficiaries using either of Nolo's AB trusts. However, as I've urged, be cautious when doing this. As a general rule, there's likely to be less tension and conflict if a surviving spouse and final beneficiaries have a parent-child relationship than if they do not. But if you feel secure that all people involved trust each other and will cooperate and get along, you can name different final beneficiaries.

You can also name alternate final beneficiaries, in case a final beneficiary predeceases you.

Both spouses create a Trust A on paper, since you can't know which spouse will die first—or, with an AB disclaimer trust, if a Trust A will be needed. (Remember that the surviving spouse's Trust A never goes into effect because there's no spouse for the surviving spouse to leave property to.) Both spouses also need to name final beneficiaries for their trust property, because, again, they can't know which one will die first. (See Chapter 10.)

Some Thoughts About Gifts

Before plunging into technical concerns about how to name beneficiaries or shared gifts, let's pull back for a moment and consider what gifts are. In our predominantly commercial culture, gifts are special, whether they are made during life or at death. Gifts are free, voluntary transfers of property, made without any requirement or expectation of receiving anything in return. The essence of gift-giving is generosity, an open spirit. To say one makes gifts "with strings attached" is not a compliment.

Much of the real pleasure of estate planning comes from contemplating the positive effects that your gifts will have on those you love. Sometimes, these pleasures are focused—you know how much Judith has always liked your mahogany table, and now she'll get to enjoy it. Others are more general—your son will be able to buy a house with the money you leave him, which will relieve some of the financial pressure that has been weighing on him.

I mention the spirit of giving here because it's easy to get bogged down by the mechanics of preparing a living trust and lose sight of your real purpose. So, if technicalities and legalities start to get to you, take a break and remember to whom you're giving your property, and why. And if you wish to explore in profound depth what gift-giving is or can mean, read Lewis Hyde's *The Gift* (Vintage/Random House), a brilliant exploration of how gifts work in many cultures.

Simultaneous Death Clauses

The statistical probability of simultaneous death is very low, but still it's one of the first things many couples ask about when preparing a shared living trust or an AB trust: "What happens if we're both killed in a plane crash?"

If you leave all your trust property directly to your spouse or in an AB trust, and your trust document doesn't have a clause to cover simultaneous death, and you and your spouse die in circumstances that make it difficult to tell who died first, your property could pass to your spouse, and then immediately to your spouse's inheritors. That might not be the result either of you wants.

Note: The forms in this book (the basic shared living trust or AB trust, and the will for a member of a couple) contain a simultaneous death clause to prevent this. These clauses are worded slightly differently depending on the form, because the trust is a joint form used by both spouses and the will is a separate form for each spouse. But each clause achieves the same result: If both spouses die simultaneously, or if it's difficult or impossible to tell who died first, the property of each spouse is disposed of as if he or she had survived the other.

EXAMPLE:

In their shared living trust, Edith and Archie leave much of their property to each other. However, Archie wants his property to go to his daughter from his first marriage if Edith dies before he does. Edith wants her property to go to her sister if Archie dies before she does. Edith and Archie are killed in a car crash. Under the living trust's simultaneous death clause, Archie's property would go to his daughter, and Edith's to her sister.

Because each spouse's trust property is distributed as if the other spouse died first, both spouses' estate tax exemptions are used.

EXAMPLE:

Josh and Linda are killed in a boating accident in 2009. They have a shared estate worth $4.2 million. Linda also owns separate property worth $300,000. Josh's estate of $2.1 million is under the estate tax exemption of $3.5 million, so no tax is assessed. Linda's estate, totaling $2.4 million is also under the estate tax exemption. In contrast, if their estates had been combined, $1 million would have been taxed.

You may ask, "How, logically, can simultaneous death clauses work? How can I be presumed to have outlived my spouse when she's also presumed to have outlived me?" Yes, it is a paradox, but it does work. Under the law, each person's trust and will property is handled independently of the other. This allows both spouses to achieve the results each wants in the event of simultaneous death. (As Oliver Wendell Holmes put it, "The life of the law has not been logic, it has been experience.")

Shared Gifts

You can name more than one beneficiary (primary, alternate, residuary, or final) to inherit any item of trust property. People frequently want to make shared gifts to their children, for example.

When making a gift to be shared by two or more beneficiaries, always use the beneficiaries' actual names; don't use collective terms such as "my children." It's not always clear who is included in such descriptions. And there can be serious confusion if one of the people originally included as a beneficiary dies before you do; the law may give the beneficiary's children the right to inherit their parent's share, which may not be the result you intend.

Obviously, if you name shared beneficiaries for a piece of property that can't be physically divided—a house, for example—give some thought to whether or not the beneficiaries are likely to get along. If they are incompatible, disagreements could arise over taking care of property or deciding whether or not to sell it.

You need to resolve these important questions before naming cobeneficiaries:

1. What percentage of ownership will each beneficiary receive?
2. What happens down the line if the beneficiaries can't agree on how to use the property?
3. What happens if one beneficiary dies before you do?

The rest of this section discusses these concerns.

Percentage of Ownership

The key here is to say in your living trust document how ownership is to be shared between the beneficiaries. If you don't specify shares of ownership, it's generally presumed that you intended equal shares, but this rule isn't ironclad, so if you want a gift shared equally, say so.

Here are two examples of what the language in your trust document might look like:

> The grantor's three children, Anne Pasquez, Rob Pasquez, and Tony Pasquez, shall be given the house at 1123 Elm St., Centerville, Iowa, in equal shares.
>
> The grantor's granddaughters, Maxine Jones and Simone Beal, shall be given all stock accounts, in equal shares.

The beneficiaries can share ownership any way you want. For instance:

> The grantor's spouse and children shall be given all the grantor's interest in the grantor's house and real estate known as 111 57th St., Muncy, Iowa, in the following shares:
> 50% to the grantor's spouse, Mary
> 25% to the grantor's son, Jon
> 25% to the grantor's daughter, Mildred.

You can also leave beneficiaries different percentages of different trust assets. Here's an example:

> The grantor's grandchildren shall be given the house at 65 Swan Lane, Springfield, Iowa, in the following shares:
> 40% to Brandon Otto
> 30% to Elaine Otto Rubenstein
> 30% to Martha Otto.
>
> All jewelry held in the trust shall be given as follows:
> 50% to Elaine Otto Rubenstein
> 50% to Martha Otto.

Notice that the beneficiaries' shares are defined by percentages, not dollar amounts. When you prepare your living trust, you can't know precisely how much your house, stocks, jewelry, or other property will be worth at your death. So if you leave each beneficiary a dollar amount, it creates inevitable problems. At your death, the property may not be worth enough to pay all the dollar amounts. Or there may be money left over after the dollar amounts are paid. If you want to leave someone a set dollar amount, do it from a trust liquid asset, like a bank account or money market fund—and make sure there's always enough in the account to cover it.

Conflict

Shared ownership creates the risk of conflict between beneficiaries. Suppose the people to whom you've left property disagree about how to use it. In most states, any co-owner can go to court and force a partition and sale, with the net proceeds divided by percentage of ownership. Let's say, for example, you leave your house to your three children. Suppose two want to sell it, and one doesn't. The house would be sold even if one child wanted to live in it.

If you are apprehensive, discuss it with the proposed beneficiaries. If there's genuine agreement among them, potential problems are less likely to become real ones. If you conclude there's no risk of conflict, you can simply make the shared gift without any conditions or directions, leaving it up to the beneficiaries to resolve any problems.

It's possible to put provisions governing what the shared owners can do in your trust document. For instance, you could state, "The house cannot be sold unless all three of my children agree on it." But often other problems follow. If two want to sell the house, but one doesn't, who manages the house? Does it have to be rented at market value? Can the child who wants to keep the house live in it? If so, must that child pay the others rent? And what happens if one child dies? The difficulties of dealing with these types of complications are why it's usually more sensible not to specify details of long-term control of property you leave beneficiaries. Let them work it out. If you don't think the beneficiaries can work out any such problems, a shared gift probably isn't appropriate.

 SEE AN EXPERT

Imposing controls on cobeneficiaries. If you fear conflict between cobeneficiaries and want to impose controls on the use of the property you leave them, see a lawyer.

One solution would be to allow the trustee to sell a shared gift if the beneficiaries can't agree how to dispose of it. The trustee would then divide the sale profits to beneficiaries, as defined by the trust grantor. But even this apparently simple solution can raise problems. How and when does it become clear that the beneficiaries can't agree? Suppose all beneficiaries agree property should be sold, but don't agree on the timing of the sale? Or the minimum price required? If you are concerned about a conflict between a shared gift left to beneficiaries, you need the attention and expertise of an experienced estate-planning lawyer.

What Happens If a Beneficiary Dies Before You Do

You can name alternate beneficiaries for each primary beneficiary. If the primary beneficiary dies before you do, the alternate will get the share of your property that would have gone to the primary beneficiary. See "Naming Alternate Beneficiaries," below.

Some Common Concerns About Beneficiaries

Here are some common concerns and choices you may face when choosing your beneficiaries.

One Primary Beneficiary

With an individual trust you can name as many primary beneficiaries as you want. Similarly, with a shared living trust, each spouse can name as many primary beneficiaries as she or he wants. With either type of trust, you can name one person as your sole primary beneficiary either by listing that person as the primary beneficiary or by leaving everything to him or her as your residuary beneficiary. See "Residuary Beneficiaries," below.

With either type of AB Trust, you must name only one primary beneficiary—your spouse.

Married Beneficiaries

When you leave property to someone who's married, the gift is that person's individual or separate property if you make the gift only in his or her name. For example, suppose your trust document says: "Mary Kestor shall be given the antique clock," or "Mary

Kestor shall be given the grantor's interest in the house at 279 18th Street, San Francisco." Mary would be entitled to the entire gift as separate property. As long as the gift is kept separate from, not commingled (mixed) with, her marital property, the gift would not be the property of her spouse.

If you want to emphasize your wishes, you could say: "Mary Kestor shall be given the grantor's antique clock as her separate property." But if Mary later commingles the gift with shared marital property, it may lose its separate property status. Proof once again that you have, at best, limited control over what happens to your property after your beneficiary receives it.

If you want to make a gift to a member of a couple and have it remain that person's separate property, note that on the beneficiary worksheet, to remind you that when you prepare your living trust in Chapter 10, you should expressly state that.

By contrast, if you wish to make a gift to a married couple, simply make it in both their names. For example: "Edna and Fred Whitman shall be given the grantor's silver bowl." Again, you can provide clarity by expressly stating your intent: "Edna and Fred Whitman shall be given the grantor's silver bowl as co-owners."

Children From Prior Marriages

If you or your spouse have children from a prior marriage, you have a number of alternatives for leaving gifts to them—and you also have the right to disinherit the children:

- You can leave them gifts outright, using either a basic shared living trust (Form 2) or a standard AB trust (Form 3) or an AB disclaimer trust (Form 4).
- You can use either of Nolo's AB trusts to create a life estate for your spouse, and name children from a prior marriage as final beneficiaries. Often each child is left a set percentage of the remaining trust property when your spouse dies.

 **SEE AN EXPERT**

See a lawyer if you anticipate a conflict between a surviving spouse and children. If there is a risk of conflict after your death between your surviving spouse and your children, see a lawyer.

- You can create a trust that imposes more restrictions on the power of the surviving spouse to use and spend trust principal than Nolo's standard AB trust does. Nolo's standard AB trust gives the surviving spouse the maximum powers over trust principal allowed by the IRS. (Review this in Chapter 5.) Some spouses in second or subsequent marriages want to limit the surviving spouse's power to use or spend trust principal, in order to be sure that the principal is preserved for their children.

EXAMPLE:

Marshall, age 67, and Lisa, age 71, marry. Lisa has a son, Nick, age 32, from a prior marriage. Lisa owns a paid-for house that she and Marshall will live in, and she has $280,000 worth of other assets. She creates a trust that allows Marshall to live in the house if she dies before he does, but doesn't allow him to sell it, rent it, or borrow against it. Nick will receive the house free and clear when Marshall dies.

 SEE AN EXPERT

See a lawyer to draft a trust restricting the rights of your spouse. Creating this kind of trust is discussed further in Chapter 15. As explained there, many individual questions need to be resolved to set up such a trust, which must be prepared by a knowledgeable lawyer.

Minors or Young Adults

If a beneficiary you name is a minor (under 18) or a young adult who can't yet manage property without responsible adult supervision, you can arrange for an adult to manage the trust property for the beneficiary. The management will take effect only if the beneficiary is still too young to sensibly manage property when he or she inherits it. (See Chapter 9.)

Your Successor Trustee as a Beneficiary

It's very common and perfectly legal to leave trust property to the person you named to be successor trustee—the person who will distribute trust property after you (or if you are making a trust with your spouse, you and your spouse) die.

EXAMPLE:

Nora and Sean name their son Liam as successor trustee of their basic shared living trust. Each spouse names the other as sole beneficiary of his or her trust property, and both name Liam as alternate beneficiary. When Nora dies, her trust property goes to Sean and stays in the trust. Unless Sean amends the trust document to name someone else as successor trustee, after Sean's death, Liam, acting as trustee, will transfer ownership of the trust property from the trust to himself.

Pets

As a part of their estate planning, many pet owners arrange informally for a friend or relative to care for a pet. But you can make more formal arrangements. Here are a few things to keep in mind:

- You can use your living trust (or will) to leave your pets, and perhaps some money for expenses, to someone you trust to look out for them. But don't make the gift of an animal a surprise— make sure the people you've chosen are really willing and able to care for your pets.
- You can't leave money or property outright to a pet. The law says animals are property, and one piece of property simply can't own another piece. In most states, if you do name a pet as a beneficiary in your will or living trust, whatever property you tried to leave it will probably go to the residuary beneficiary instead. If there's no residuary beneficiary, the property will be distributed according to state law.
- Consider making arrangements for emergency care for your animals in case you suddenly can't care for them.
- In about half of the states, you can establish a trust for your pet. A trustee you name will manage the trust. In the trust document, you direct how your pet is to be cared for. Pet trusts can be desirable if you'd prefer not to leave your pet outright to someone. But creating a pet trust is more costly and complicated than simply leaving your pet to someone as a gift.

SEE AN EXPERT

You'll need an attorney to prepare a pet trust. Laws about pet trusts are complicated and state-specific. You'll need to hire an attorney to draft one.

RESOURCE

Read more about pets and the law. These issues are discussed in detail in *Every Dog's Legal Guide*, by Mary Randolph (Nolo).

Naming Alternate Beneficiaries

You can name an alternate beneficiary, or beneficiaries, for each gift made to a primary beneficiary. The alternate beneficiary receives the gift if the primary beneficiary predeceases you (dies before you) and you haven't amended your trust to name a new primary beneficiary for that gift.

Naming alternate beneficiaries can be sensible, for a number of reasons. For example, you might name an alternate beneficiary if:

- you've left property to older people or to people in poor health
- you're a cautious person
- you don't want the bother of redoing your trust document if a beneficiary does die before you, or if
- you're concerned that you might not have time, before your own death, to revise your estate plan after a beneficiary dies.

On the other hand, some people decide they don't want to name alternative beneficiaries—maybe because they don't want the morbid bother of worrying about their beneficiaries dying before they do. These folks may leave their property to beneficiaries considerably younger than themselves, and they count on having time to modify the trust to name a new beneficiary if a beneficiary dies before they do.

Here are two examples of how alternate beneficiaries are named in a trust document:

> Mike McGowan shall be given the grantor's outboard motor and boat. If he doesn't survive the grantor, they shall be given to his son, Pat McGowan.

> The grantor's children, Bert Wemby and Cherrie Wemby, shall be given the grantor's interest in the house at 221 Maple Avenue, Winton, New York. If one beneficiary doesn't survive the grantor, the house shall be given to the other. If neither survives the grantor, the house shall be given to Kamal Abram.

You don't have to name an alternate for a charity or other institution you name as a beneficiary. If the institution is well established, it seems safe to assume that it will still exist at your death.

If You Don't Have Any Person You Want to Name as Alternate Beneficiary

Although it's not common, sometimes the maker of a living trust has only a single beneficiary, and does not want to name any anyone else as alternate beneficiary.

For example, a single mother has a one son, her beneficiary, and there is no one she wants to name as alternate if her son predeceases her. The problem in this situation is that if tragedy strikes and the son dies first, there is no alternate for her estate and it could end up with the state if there are no other relatives.

If you can't think of another person that you'd want to name as an alternate, consider naming a charity or a cause you like instead. That way, in the worst case scenario, your property will at least go to an institution you believe in.

Basic Shared Trust

With a basic shared living trust, each spouse makes his or her own separate gifts, and each spouse has the right to name his or her own alternate beneficiaries. They do not need to be the same as the other spouse's.

EXAMPLE:

Larry and Louisa create a basic shared trust. Each leaves a one-half interest in their house to the other. Larry names his two children from a previous marriage as alternate beneficiaries for his half-interest in the house. Louisa names her sister as her alternate beneficiary for her gift.

AB Trusts

Alternate beneficiaries play a different role with an AB trust. If you do make gifts to specific beneficiaries, outside of property left to Trust A or the surviving spouse, you can name alternates for those beneficiaries.

The surviving spouse is always the life beneficiary of the property that remains in Trust A when the first spouse dies. You do not name an alternate beneficiary for the surviving spouse. Instead, each spouse names final beneficiaries, and can name alternates for those final beneficiaries.

When both spouses die, the property in both Trust A (if one is established) and Trust B goes to each trust's final beneficiaries. If a beneficiary is deceased, the property goes to the deceased final beneficiary's alternate. Often, in a first marriage, both spouses name the same alternate final beneficiaries, commonly grandchildren.

EXAMPLE:

Vittorio and Sophia create an AB disclaimer trust. Each names their two children, Luigi and Anna, as final beneficiaries. Vittorio and Sophia also each name the same alternate final beneficiaries: for Luigi, the alternate beneficiary is his child, Alfonso; for Anna, the alternate beneficiaries are her children, Gina, Carmela, and Marcello, in equal shares.

The surviving spouse's Trust B remains revocable during his or her life. As long as he or she is competent, the surviving spouse can amend this trust to name new (final) beneficiaries, and alternates, disposing of the trust property any way he or she chooses. Only when he or she dies does Trust B become irrevocable.

Naming More Than One Alternate Beneficiary

You can name more than one person or institution as alternate beneficiaries. If you do, you must define how these co-alternate beneficiaries will share the property.

EXAMPLE 1:

Rosa names her husband, Ramon, as beneficiary of her interest in their house, which they have transferred to their basic shared living trust. As alternate beneficiaries, she names their three children, Miguel, Constanza, and Guillermo, to share equally.

Ramon dies just before she does, leaving his half of the house to Rosa. Under the terms of the trust document, it stays in the living trust. At Rosa's death, the house goes to the three children, because Ramon is not living. All three own equal shares in all of it. If they sell the property, each will be entitled to a third of the proceeds.

EXAMPLE 2:

Benjamin names Bela, his wife, as his primary beneficiary of his interest in their house. He names their children, Susan and Zelda, as alternate beneficiaries. However, Benjamin and Bela have paid many thousands of dollars to help Zelda through medical school. Susan has been self-supporting since she left college. So Benjamin and Bela decide to leave Susan 75% of the house and Zelda 25%, and state this in the trust document when naming them as alternate beneficiaries.

Naming Alternate Beneficiaries for Cobeneficiaries

Things become complicated if you decide to move on to the next level of contingencies—naming alternate beneficiaries for a shared gift. Say you want to leave your house to your three children. What are your options if you want to name alternate beneficiaries?

- You can specify that a deceased child's share is to be shared by the remaining beneficiaries.

    Here's a clause specifying that the other beneficiaries of a shared gift share the interest of a deceased beneficiary:

    Mollie Rainey, Allen Rainey, and Barbara Rainey Smithson shall be given the grantor's house at 1701 Clay St., Peoria, IL. If any of them fails to survive the grantor, his or her interest in the grantor's house shall be shared equally by the survivors.

- You can provide that a deceased child's share is to be shared equally by that beneficiary's own children, and, if there are none, then between the remaining beneficiaries.

- You can name an "outside" alternate beneficiary (a friend or other relative) to receive the interest of any child who dies before you do.
- You can name separate alternate beneficiaries, one for each child—for example, each of their spouses.

Before plunging into complexities about alternate beneficiary provisions for a shared gift, consider whether or not you really want to worry about this contingency. Some people don't like to consider the possibility of one of their children dying before them (and you can always revise your trust if that remote possibility occurs). And once you get started worrying about these kinds of possibilities, where do you stop? You could also worry about what happens if all your alternate beneficiaries, as well as your beneficiaries themselves, die before you. There's no total security, no matter how many levels of alternate beneficiaries you name.

Imposing a Survivorship Period

Some people want to impose what is called a "survivorship period" on gifts made to primary and/or alternate beneficiaries. This means that the beneficiary must outlive the grantor by a set period of time, defined in the living trust, to receive the gift. If the beneficiary doesn't live this long, the gift goes to the alternate beneficiary.

The trust forms in this book do not impose a survivorship period. Many people (including me) think they are unnecessarily cautious. And people who do want them differ widely as to how long the period should be.

If you decide you do want to impose a survivorship period on your primary beneficiaries, you can add one to the trust document. (I explain how to do this in Chapter 10.) I recommend a relatively short period, between 15 and 45 days. Imposing a longer period normally just unnecessarily delays distribution of gifts to the primary beneficiaries.

EXAMPLE:

In Laura's basic shared living trust, she imposes a 15-day survivorship requirement on all her beneficiaries.

Laura leaves all her trust property to her husband, Juan-Carlos, and names her daughter from a previous marriage as alternate beneficiary. Laura and Juan-Carlos are seriously injured in a car accident; Juan-Carlos dies four days after Laura does. Because Juan-Carlos did not survive Laura by at least 15 days, the trust property he would have inherited from Laura goes to Laura's daughter instead.

If there had been no survivorship requirement, Laura's trust property would have gone to Juan-Carlos. When he died four days later, it would have gone to beneficiaries he had named in the trust document.

Residuary Beneficiaries

Residuary beneficiaries are the person, persons, or institutions you name to receive trust property that isn't given, for whatever reason, to a primary beneficiary or an alternate. For example, if a primary beneficiary predeceases you or can't be located, and you didn't name an alternate, the property would go to the residuary beneficiary.

Individual or Basic Shared Living Trusts

With a living trust for one person, you should always name a residuary beneficiary and an alternate residuary beneficiary who will inherit if the residuary beneficiary dies before you.

With a basic shared living trust, each spouse names his or her own residuary beneficiary and alternate residuary beneficiary. They may name different people.

EXAMPLE:

Peter leaves a house to his wife, Jane, or, if Jane dies before him, to Jane's sister Carolyn. He names his sister Julie as residuary beneficiary. Jane and Carolyn are killed in a car crash three days before Peter dies. Because the primary and alternate beneficiaries are dead, the house goes to Julie. (Pretty cheerful example of how living trusts can work, huh?)

You can name coresiduary beneficiaries, and co-alternate residuary beneficiaries as well. But if you do, you must handle all the potential problems of naming cobeneficiaries (discussed above).

For instance, a person could split the bulk of her estate among her children by leaving it all to the children as residuary beneficiaries. For example, she could name as her residuary beneficiaries: "Henry McCormick, Aaron McCormick, and Joanne Guiliam, in equal shares."

Another approach is to make a few relatively minor gifts and leave the bulk of your property to your residuary beneficiary.

EXAMPLE 1:

Jennifer wants to leave her two Tiffany lamps to her friend Linda, $5,000 in a money market account to her niece Martha, and her car to her sister Joan. She wants to leave all the rest of her extensive estate— houses, stocks, limited partnerships—to her long-time partner, Paul. She can simply name Paul as her residuary beneficiary, after listing the three specific gifts. She names Joan as her alternate residuary beneficiary.

EXAMPLE 2:

Claudia and Hank are in their second marriage. They have no children together. Each has children from their first marriages—Claudia's are Wendy and Linus, Hank's are Krystin, Phil, and Gary. Claudia and Hank each name the other as residuary beneficiary. But as alternate residuary beneficiaries, Claudia names Wendy and Linus. Hank names Krystin, Phil, and Gary.

The residuary beneficiary of a living trust for a single person, or of one person's portion of a basic shared living trust, will receive:

- any trust property for which both the primary and alternate beneficiaries you named die before you do
- any trust property that you didn't leave to a named beneficiary (this could include property you transferred to the trust later but didn't name a beneficiary for, and trust property that was owned by your spouse, which he or she left you)
- any property you leave to your living trust through a "pour-over" will (because property left through a pour-over will doesn't avoid probate, there's usually no reason to use one; see Chapter 15), and

- any property that you actually transferred to your living trust but didn't list in the trust document.

AB Trusts

With an AB trust, residuary beneficiaries have no role. Aside from any specific gifts left to specific beneficiaries or alternates, all property of a deceased spouse goes into Trust A or to the surviving spouse. After the death of the surviving spouse, any Trust A property is distributed to the final beneficiaries. Likewise, property in Trust B goes to that trust's final beneficiaries. If both a specific beneficiary and alternate for a specific gift predecease a grantor, and the trust is not amended to name a new beneficiary for the gift, that gift becomes part of the deceased spouse's property, or part of the property in the surviving spouse's Trust B.

Disinheritance

You can disinherit most people simply by not leaving them anything in your living trust or will. If you don't leave someone any of your property, she or he has no rights to it, period. However, you can disinherit your spouse only if you live in one of the eight community property states. When it comes to your children, you should either leave them something or expressly disinherit them in your will.

Disinheriting a Spouse

Whether or not you can legally disinherit a spouse (not that many people want to) depends on whether you live in a community property state or common law state.

Community Property States

Alaska (if spouses prepare a written community property agreement)

Arizona	Louisiana	Texas
California	Nevada	Washington
Idaho	New Mexico	Wisconsin

In community property states (listed above), the general rule is that spouses together own all property that either acquires during the marriage, except property one spouse acquires by gift or inheritance. Each spouse owns a half-interest in this "community property."

You are free to leave your separate property and your half of the community property to anyone you choose. Your spouse—who already owns half of all the community property—has no right to inherit any of your half.

Unmarried Couples

Unmarried couples living together have no right to inherit any of each other's property (except lesbian and gay couples in California, Connecticut, Hawaii, New Jersey, and Vermont who register with the state). In short, each person can leave his or her property to anyone he or she wants to. However, if the couple has created a valid contract that gives each one the specific right to inherit specific property, that contract will normally be enforced if the person who feels cheated goes to court.

For detailed information about such contracts (and much more), see *Living Together: A Legal Guide for Unmarried Couples*, by Ralph Warner, Toni Ihara, and Fredrick Hertz (Nolo).

Common Law States

Alabama	Kentucky	North Dakota
Alaska	Maine	Ohio
Arkansas	Maryland	Oklahoma
Colorado	Massachusetts	Oregon
Connecticut	Michigan	Pennsylvania
Delaware	Minnesota	Rhode Island
District of Columbia	Mississippi	South Carolina
Florida	Missouri	South Dakota
Georgia	Montana	Tennessee
Hawaii	Nebraska	Utah
Illinois	New Hampshire	Vermont
Indiana	New Jersey	Virginia
Iowa	New York	West Virginia
Kansas	North Carolina	Wyoming

If you live in one of these states, your spouse always has the right to claim some of your property after your death.

In a common law state, a surviving spouse who doesn't receive a set portion of the deceased spouse's property (through a will, living trust, or other method) is entitled to insist upon that share of the property. The exact share depends on state law. So, a spouse who doesn't receive the minimum he or she is entitled to under state law (the "statutory share") may be able to claim some of the property in your living trust. To be safe, give your spouse at least half your property in your trust (except, of course, in an AB trust, where he or she receives only a life interest in the Trust A property).

Even property given away before death may legally belong to the surviving spouse under these laws. For example, take the case of a man who set up joint bank accounts with his children from a previous marriage. After his death, his widow sued to recover her interest in the accounts. She won; the Kentucky Supreme Court ruled that under Kentucky law, a spouse is entitled to a half-interest in the other spouse's personal property (everything but real estate). Her husband had not had the legal right to give away her interest in the money in the accounts. (*Harris v. Rock,* 799 S.W.2d 10 (Ky. 1990).) Most noncommunity property states have similar laws, called "dower" or "curtesy" laws.

State law may also give your spouse the right to inherit the family residence, or at least use it for his or her life. The Florida constitution, for example, gives a surviving spouse the deceased spouse's residence, no matter what the deceased spouse's will says. (Fla. Const. Art. 10, § 4.)

 **SEE AN EXPERT**

Get expert legal advice about disinheriting your spouse. If you live in a common law state and you want to leave your spouse less than half of your property from a basic shared trust, see a lawyer.

Disinheriting a Child

With rare exceptions, it is legal to disinherit a child. (The Florida constitution prohibits the head of a family from leaving his or her residence to anyone except his or her spouse or child, if he or she has either (Fla. Const. Art. 10, § 4).)

You do not have to leave your child anything in your living trust. But to completely disinherit a child (or the children of a deceased child), your state laws require you to do so in your will, even if you transfer all your property by a living trust.

There are two ways to disinherit a child in a will. One is to expressly disinherit the child in the will, by stating that you aren't leaving him or her anything. The other is to leave the child a minimal amount, which ensures the child cannot successfully claim to have been overlooked or accidentally omitted. If you don't mention a child in your will, state law may give him or her the right to a certain share of your property.

The will forms in this book require you to list all your children. The forms then state that if you haven't left any property to a listed child, that failure to do so is intentional. So, if you leave a child nothing (by will or otherwise), this functions as a disinheritance clause.

Children Born After a Will or Trust Is Prepared

Most state laws protect offspring who were born after a parent's will was prepared. Although these laws mention only wills, not living trusts, it's possible that a court could apply them to a living trust, reasoning that the living trust is serving the function of a will. And as living trusts become more widespread, state legislatures may expand their laws to include children not mentioned in living trusts.

These laws presume that the parent didn't mean to disinherit a child who is born after the parent's will has been signed, and thus is not mentioned in a parent's will. (Such children are called "pretermitted heirs," in legalese.) The law assumes that the parent simply hadn't yet gotten around to writing a new will. Such a child is legally entitled to a share (the size is determined by state law) of the deceased parent's estate, which may include property in a living trust.

The easy answer to this problem is to amend your living trust after a child is born. Most parents want to provide for a new child, so it's simply a matter of getting the work done. Amending your trust to provide for a new beneficiary is not difficult. (See Chapter 13.)

 SEE AN EXPERT

Posthumously conceived children. Medical technology now makes it possible for a child to be conceived after the biological mother or father has died. Inheritance rights for such children have already been litigated in a handful of states, with inconsistent results. California has adopted a statute specifically dealing with the rights of such children (Cal. Prob. Code § 249.5). Other states are likely to adopt similar laws. If your planning includes the possibility of a posthumously conceived child, you'll want to know your state's laws (if any) on this subject, as well as figuring out what you think is best. You'll need to discuss this matter with a knowledgeable estate-planning lawyer.

Grandchildren

Grandchildren have no right to inherit from their grandparents unless their parent has died. In that case, the grandchildren essentially take the place of the deceased child and are entitled to whatever he or she would have been legally entitled to.

General Disinheritance Clauses

You may have heard that some lawyers recommend leaving $1 to close relatives in your trust or will. This is not legally necessary—and it's a bad idea. There's no need to mention anyone but your spouse and perhaps your children in your trust. No one else has a legal right to any of your property. Moreover, your successor trustee must track down each beneficiary to whom you leave a dollar and procure an acknowledgment that the beneficiary received the dollar. That's a lot of work, especially when there's no point to it.

Lawsuits contesting a living trust are very rare. A relative could conceivably try to contest your trust by claiming that you, the grantor, were mentally incompetent when you prepared your trust, and were duped by someone to leaving most or all of your property to them while you really wanted to leave it to this relative.

SEE AN EXPERT

Head off contests by relatives. If you think a relative might try to contest your trust, you might leave that relative $1, to make it absolutely clear you did consider that person and wanted to give no more. But before you settle on that option, see a lawyer to determine the wisest course of action.

No-Contest Clauses

A "no-contest clause" in a living trust (or a will) is a device used to discourage beneficiaries of your trust or will from suing to void the trust or will and claiming they are entitled to more than you left them. Under a no-contest clause, a beneficiary who challenges a living trust or will and loses forfeits all his inheritance under that document. Without a no-contest clause, someone left property from a living trust can sue, lose, and still collect the amount given him or her in the trust.

EXAMPLE:

Pip leaves his daughter Estelle $10,000 in his living trust, and includes a no-contest clause in that document. If Estelle challenges the trust and loses, she does not receive the $10,000.

No-contest clauses can be sensible if there's a risk a beneficiary might challenge your estate plan. On the other hand, many people do not like to include a no-contest clause in their estate planning documents, because it seems to imply a suspicion of their beneficiaries that they don't actually feel. The trust and will forms in this book do not contain no-contest clauses.

SEE AN EXPERT

See a lawyer to add a no-contest clause. If you think you may need a no-contest clause, that's an indication of a potential serious problem. See a lawyer to discuss how to handle the risk of a court fight; often, a no-contest clause is just one part of a larger strategy.

Putting Conditions on Beneficiaries

Occasionally, a person wants to make a gift with restrictions or conditions on it. The trust forms in this book do not allow you to make conditional gifts. (You can, however, appoint someone to manage trust property inherited by a minor child or young adult. See Chapter 9.)

EXAMPLE:

Ravi wants to leave money to his nephew, Monir, if he goes to veterinary school but if he doesn't, to his niece Sheela. This sounds simple, but here are just a few problems inherent in this approach: How soon must Monir go to veterinary school? What happens if he applies in good faith but fails to get in? Who decides if he's really studying? What happens to the money before Monir goes to veterinary school? What happens if Monir goes to veterinary school but drops out after a year and says he'll go back eventually? What happens if he graduates but doesn't become a vet?

Imposing restrictions and controls on beneficiaries is sometimes called "dead-hand control." The obvious risk of dead-hand control is that circumstances can change, so you must try to anticipate what is likely—or even possible—to occur in the future, and provide for it. This, at best, is complex work, and helps to enrich estate planning lawyers.

SEE AN EXPERT

Get expert advice about long-term trusts. Except for an AB trust or child's trust, you cannot create long-term trusts using this book. Some major types of long-term trusts are discussed in Chapter 15. You'll need a lawyer's help if you want to prepare one.

Property That Is No Longer in Your Trust at Your Death

If you make a gift of specific property in your trust, but then remove that property from your trust before you die—that is, you sell it or give it to someone—the beneficiary for that gift will probably be out of luck, and is likely to be quite upset if he knew he was supposed to get it. So if you do transfer property from your trust, be sure to amend your trust document and formally delete the provision that left it to a beneficiary. (I explain how to amend your trust document in Chapter 13.)

Beneficiary Worksheets

On one of the following worksheets, list your beneficiaries and the property you want to leave to each.

- Use Worksheet 1 for an individual living trust.
- Use Worksheet 2 for a basic shared living trust. Each spouse names beneficiaries separately.
- Use Worksheet 3 for an AB trust. Each spouse can also name beneficiaries of specific gifts, in addition to the surviving spouse and final beneficiaries.

To get started, go back to the Property Worksheet, in Chapter 6, where you listed what items you will transfer to your trust. On these worksheets, you will name a beneficiary for each item. If you're making a gift to cobeneficiaries and naming alternate cobeneficiaries, you need to decide what share each cobeneficiary receives.

You can also find these worksheets in Appendix B and on the CD-ROM.

Beneficiary Worksheet 1: Individual Living Trust

1. Specific Gifts

_____
Item of Property

_____
Primary Beneficiary

_____
Alternate Beneficiary

_____
Item of Property

_____
Primary Beneficiary

_____
Alternate Beneficiary

_____
Item of Property

_____
Primary Beneficiary

_____
Alternate Beneficiary

_____
Item of Property

_____
Primary Beneficiary

_____
Alternate Beneficiary

_____
Item of Property

_____
Primary Beneficiary

_____
Alternate Beneficiary

_____
Item of Property

_____
Primary Beneficiary

_____
Alternate Beneficiary

_____
Item of Property

_____
Primary Beneficiary

_____
Alternate Beneficiary

_____
Item of Property

_____
Primary Beneficiary

_____
Alternate Beneficiary

_____
Item of Property

_____
Primary Beneficiary

_____
Alternate Beneficiary

_____
Item of Property

_____
Primary Beneficiary

_____
Alternate Beneficiary

2. Residuary Beneficiary or Beneficiaries

_____
Residuary Beneficiary(ies)

_____

_____

_____
Alternative Residuary Benficiary(ies)

_____

Beneficiary Worksheet 2: Basic Shared Living Trust

Wife's Beneficiaries

1. Specific Gifts

_____
Item of Property

_____
Primary Beneficiary

_____
Alternate Beneficiary

_____
Item of Property

_____
Primary Beneficiary

_____
Alternate Beneficiary

_____
Item of Property

_____
Primary Beneficiary

_____
Alternate Beneficiary

_____
Item of Property

_____
Primary Beneficiary

_____
Alternate Beneficiary

_____
Item of Property

_____
Primary Beneficiary

_____
Alternate Beneficiary

_____
Item of Property

_____
Primary Beneficiary

_____
Alternate Beneficiary

_____
Item of Property

_____
Primary Beneficiary

_____
Alternate Beneficiary

_____
Item of Property

_____
Primary Beneficiary

_____
Alternate Beneficiary

_____
Item of Property

_____
Primary Beneficiary

_____
Alternate Beneficiary

_____
Item of Property

_____
Primary Beneficiary

_____
Alternate Beneficiary

2. Residuary Beneficiary or Beneficiaries

_____
Residuary Beneficiary(ies)

_____

_____

_____
Alternative Residuary Benficiary(ies)

_____

Beneficiary Worksheet 2: Basic Shared Living Trust (cont'd)

Husband's Beneficiaries

1. Specific Gifts

Item of Property

Primary Beneficiary

Alternate Beneficiary

Item of Property

Primary Beneficiary

Alternate Beneficiary

Item of Property

Primary Beneficiary

Alternate Beneficiary

Item of Property

Primary Beneficiary

Alternate Beneficiary

Item of Property

Primary Beneficiary

Alternate Beneficiary

Item of Property

Primary Beneficiary

Alternate Beneficiary

Item of Property

Primary Beneficiary

Alternate Beneficiary

Item of Property

Primary Beneficiary

Alternate Beneficiary

Item of Property

Primary Beneficiary

Alternate Beneficiary

Item of Property

Primary Beneficiary

Alternate Beneficiary

2. Residuary Beneficiary or Beneficiaries

Residuary Beneficiary(ies)

Alternative Residuary Benficiary(ies)

Beneficiary Worksheet 3: AB Trust

1. Wife's Specific Beneficiaries

Item of Property

Primary Beneficiary

Alternate Beneficiary

Item of Property

Primary Beneficiary

Alternate Beneficiary

Item of Property

Primary Beneficiary

Alternate Beneficiary

2. Wife's Final Beneficiaries

3. Wife's Alternate Final Beneficiaries

4. Husband's Specific Beneficiaries

Item of Property

Primary Beneficiary

Alternate Beneficiary

Item of Property

Primary Beneficiary

Alternate Beneficiary

Item of Property

Primary Beneficiary

Alternate Beneficiary

5. Husband's Final Beneficiaries

6. Husband's Alternate Final Beneficiaries

Property Left to Minor Children or Young Adults

f any of the beneficiaries you've named (including alternate, residuary, or final beneficiaries) might inherit trust property before they are able to manage it responsibly, you'll want to arrange for an adult to manage that beneficiary's property.

If your young beneficiaries won't inherit anything of great value—that is, if you're leaving them objects that have more sentimental than monetary value—you don't need to arrange for an adult to manage the property.

Here are the beneficiaries you should arrange management for:

- **Any beneficiary now under 18.** Children under 18 cannot, by law, directly manage substantial amounts of money—roughly, anything over $2,500 to $5,000, depending on state law.

    If a minor inherits valuable trust property, and you have not arranged for the property to be managed by an adult, a court-appointed guardian will have to manage the property. Contrary to what you might expect, a child's parent does not automatically have legal authority to manage any property the child inherits. A child's parent will have to ask the court to grant him or her that authority, and will be subject to the court's supervision. If neither of the beneficiary's parents are alive, there may be no obvious person for the court to appoint as property guardian. In that case, it may be even more important for you to name someone in your living trust.

TIP

Use your will to name a personal guardian. If you have a child under age 18, you must nominate a personal guardian—the adult responsible for raising the child—in your will. You can't do this in your living trust.

- **Any beneficiary over 18 you believe is not mature enough to responsibly handle your gift.** If a beneficiary is over 18 when he or she inherits trust property, you do not need, legally, to have anyone manage the property on the beneficiary's behalf. If you don't make any arrangements, the beneficiary will get the property with no strings attached. But with the forms in this book, you can arrange for property management to last until a young adult beneficiary turns any age up

to 35—that is, you can choose any age between 19 and 35 when the young adult receives the property outright.

Why 35?

We've created a rule that any beneficiary must receive a gift made from a Nolo living trust outright by age 35 at the latest. We've chosen 35 for the cutoff age because it seems reasonable to conclude that an adult who can't manage financial matters responsibly by that age may never be able to do so. If you want someone else to manage the trust property of a beneficiary who's over 35, you'll probably want to see a lawyer to create a special type of trust, usually called a "spendthrift trust," and resolve specific problems, such as who will be the trustee many years down the line if the beneficiary survives to old age.

Whether or not you want to provide for management of property inherited by a young adult beneficiary is a personal decision. Some young adults are fully capable of managing money at age 21, while others at the same age might indulge recklessly, even disastrously, if they received a large inheritance outright.

Property Management Options

If you want to provide for property management for a gift to a minor or young adult beneficiary, you have several options.

- **Leave the property directly to an adult to use for the child.** Many people don't leave property directly to a child. Instead, they leave it to the child's parent or to the person they expect to have care and custody of the child if neither parent is available. There's no formal legal arrangement, but they trust the adult to use the property for the child's benefit.
- **Create child's trusts.** You can establish one or more child's trusts in your living trust. Technically, a child's trust is a subtrust of the overall living trust. You create a separate child's trust for each young beneficiary. If you establish child's trusts, your

successor trustee will manage the trust property you left each child or young adult and spend it for that child's education, health, and other needs. If you create a shared living trust or an AB trust, the surviving spouse will manage property left to minors by the deceased spouse; the successor trustee will act only after both spouses die. Each child's trust ends at whatever age you designate for that child (between 18 and 35), and any remaining property is then turned over to the beneficiary outright.

- **Name a custodian under the Uniform Transfers to Minors Act (UTMA).** This is a model law written by a national panel of experts. All but two states (South Carolina and Vermont) have adopted this law, sometimes with minor modifications. In states with the UTMA, you can use your living trust to name a "custodian" to manage property you leave a child, until the child reaches 18 or 21, or up to 25 in some states, depending on state law. If you don't need management to last beyond the age your state law allows, a custodianship is often preferable to a child's trust.

RESOURCE

Children with special needs. These property management options are not designed to provide long-term property management for a child or young adult with serious disabilities. *Special Needs Trusts*, by Stephen Elias (Nolo), explains how you can create a trust that provides for your loved one without interfering with his or her eligibility for SSI or Medicaid benefits.

Which Method Is Better for You: Child's Trust or Custodianship?

Both a child's trust and a custodianship are safe, efficient ways of managing trust property that a young person inherits. Under either system, the person in charge of the young beneficiary's property has the same responsibility to use the property for the beneficiary's support, education, and health. For example, you can leave a gift of life insurance by using a child's trust or by naming a custodian under the UTMA, and in either case, the proceeds will be held in trust by an adult for benefit of the child you name

States That Have Adopted the UTMA			
State	Age at which minor gets property	**State**	Age at which minor gets property
Alabama	21	Missouri	21
Alaska	18–25	Montana	21
Arizona	21	Nebraska	21
Arkansas	18–21	Nevada	18–25
California	18–25	New Hampshire	21
Colorado	21	New Jersey	18–21
Connecticut	21	New Mexico	21
Delaware	21	New York	21
District of Columbia	18–21	North Carolina	18–21
Florida	21	North Dakota	21
Georgia	21	Ohio	21
Hawaii	21	Oklahoma	18–21
Idaho	21	Oregon	21–25
Illinois	21	Pennsylvania	21–25
Indiana	21	Rhode Island	21
Iowa	21	South Dakota	18
Kansas	21	Tennessee	21–25
Kentucky	18	Texas	21
Maine	18–21	Utah	21
Maryland	21	Virginia	18–21
Massachusetts	21	Washington	21
Michigan	18–21	West Virginia	21
Minnesota	21	Wisconsin	21
Mississippi	21	Wyoming	21

to be the beneficiary. So use whichever method works best for you, and don't get hung up worrying about technicalities or puzzling over possible legal intricacies.

The most significant difference between a child's trust and an UTMA gift is that a child's trust can last longer than a custodianship, which must end by age 21 in most states (or up to 25 in some states). For that reason, a child's trust is a good choice when it's conceivable that a young person could inherit a large amount of property, and you want the money handled by a more mature person, at least through the child's middle 20s.

An UTMA custodianship is usually preferable to a child's trust if the beneficiary will inherit between $50,000 and $100,000. That amount is likely to be used up for living expenses by the time the child reaches age 18 or 21—the ages when UTMA custodianship ends in most states. And if your state allows the UTMA gift to be kept in custodianship until the child is 21 or older, amounts up to $100,000 can surely be consumed by four years of college costs. In these situations, there's probably no need to create a child's trust to last beyond the UTMA cutoff age.

A custodianship can have other advantages as well:

- Handling a beneficiary's property can be easier with a custodianship than with a trust. A custodian's powers are written into state law, and most institutions, such as banks and insurance companies, are familiar with the rules. Trusts, on the other hand, vary in their terms. So before a bank lets a trustee act on behalf of a beneficiary, it may demand to see and analyze a copy of the trust document.

- You can name whomever you wish to be a custodian, and you can name different custodians for different beneficiaries. So if you want to arrange custodianships for grandchildren, for example, you could name each child's parent as custodian. A child's trust is not so flexible: The surviving spouse, or the successor trustee, will be the trustee of all child's trusts created for your young beneficiaries.

- A custodianship may offer better income tax rates than a trust. A trust is taxed at 15% on retained income up to $2,000 annually, with the top rate reaching 35% on income over $9,750. By contrast, property managed by an UTMA custodian is taxed as income paid directly to the child, often a lower rate than paid by a trust. (This can get complicated, because income paid to a child under 14 is taxed at the child's parents' tax rate.)

Tax-Saving Educational Investment Plans

Beyond leaving property to children, you should know that federal law provides two different plans you can use to save for the educational expenses of children.

These plans could affect your living trust planning because if you establish one of these plans for your own children, you should have less worry about future educational expenses draining your estate.

529 Plans

A 529 plan is an investment account established to pay for the higher education of a named beneficiary. The beneficiary must be a "family member," who can range from your own children to cousins. Income accumulates in a 529 plan free of taxes. More importantly, no income tax is assessed on money paid from a 529 plan for the beneficiary's tuition, books, fees, supplies, and equipment necessary to attend college, graduate school, or approved vocational institutions. Authorized expenses can also include special needs services for a student with disabilities.

There are two basic types of 529 plans:

- A savings plan. You make contributions to the plan, which are then invested as you, within the plan limits, decide. Whatever money has accumulated is available for the beneficiary when she or he goes to college.

- A prepaid plan. You can prepare all or part of the costs of in-state college education. You pay the money directly to the educational institution. There's also an Independent 529 plan, a prepaid plan for private colleges.

Generally, an individual can give each beneficiary up to $13,000 per year free from gift tax. (Contributions can be made only in cash.) Couples can combine their gifts to give each beneficiary up to $26,000 per year. However, 529 plans allow you to aggregate five years of gift tax allowance on a one-time gift. For example, you could make a one-time payment of $65,000 ($130,000 per couple). That gift would not be subject to tax, but you would not be able to make any additional tax-free gifts to the account for the next five years. Gifts made in excess of these limits are subject to federal gift tax. (See "Federal Gift and Estate Taxes" in Chapter 15.)

These plans are called "529" plans because they were created by that section of the Internal Revenue Code. (They are also sometimes called "qualified tuition programs.") Under federal law, you can invest only in a state-authorized plan. Each state now has its own separate plan, managed by an investment company or companies selected by that state. Managers range from TIAA-CREF to Vanguard to J.P. Morgan to various lesser-known financial institutions.

Some state plans allow you to invest only if you live in that state. Also, about half the states allow residents to deduct 529 contributions from their state income tax, which could be a major incentive to buy a home-grown 529 plan. On the other hand, the majority of 529 plans allow anyone to invest in them. Indeed, you could invest in more than one. If you're seeking the best plan for your investment needs and beliefs, you have a rather bewildering array of plans to choose from.

However you choose to invest in a 529 plan, you are basically investing in securities—stocks and bonds—that come with the stock market pitfalls we've all become aware of. But some state's 529 managers have a far more aggressive (risky) investment strategy than do managers of other state's plans. So you'll need to do quite a bit of homework before selecting a 529 plan that's right for you.

If a beneficiary does not attend college, you can name a new beneficiary from the eligible family group. But if you wind up taking money out of a 529 plan for non-educational purposes, taxes and penalties apply.

RESOURCE

Funds in a 529 plan are considered a parental asset, not a child's. For college financial aid purposes, having funds in a parent's 529 plan, rather than in the child's name, can be very desirable. The federal formula for college aid requires students to contribute 20% of their assets to their education. For parents, the figure is 5.6%.

Coverdell Accounts

With a Coverdell account (formerly called an Education IRA), you can contribute up to $2,000 per year, though contribution amounts phase out for folks with six-figure incomes. Further, this $2,000 limit is the total amount that can be set aside in any one year for any one beneficiary. In other words, different family members cannot each contribute $2,000 per year for one beneficiary. Combined, they can contribute no more than $2,000.

Contributions are not tax-deductible when you make them. But money in the account is not taxed when (or if) it grows, and no tax is due when you make qualified

withdrawal from the account to pay for a child's education expenses.

The $2,000 limit definitely decreases the appeal of a Coverdell account, and more parents use 529 plans to save for their children's education. But a Coverdell account can still be useful in the right circumstances. For example, a grandparent or other relation could establish Coverdell accounts for your children, while you invest in a 529 account or save in other ways for higher education costs.

Child's Trusts

As I've stressed, if you leave any trust property to minors or to young adults who cannot responsibly manage property, you can create, within your living trust, a separate child's trust for each such beneficiary. Your surviving spouse or successor trustee manages all child's trusts.

How a Child's Trust Is Created

The first step is to make your gifts in your living trust document, including gifts left to any children or young adults. One common example is life insurance proceeds made payable to your living trust. You name your child or children as beneficiaries for all proceeds turned over to the trust. Then you complete another clause in your trust document, the child's trust clause, where you list each child's name and the age (from 19 to 35) at which this beneficiary is to receive his or her trust property outright. If at your death the beneficiary is younger than the age you specified, a trust will be created for that beneficiary. If the beneficiary is older, he or she gets the trust property with no strings attached, and no trust is created. (Leaving life insurance through your trust is discussed in more detail below.)

EXAMPLE:

In their basic shared living trust, Roger and Victoria each leave their trust property to the other. They name their daughters, who are 22 and 25, as alternate beneficiaries, and arrange for any trust property they may inherit, including their life insurance proceeds, to stay in children's trusts until each daughter reaches 30. They name Victoria's sister, Antoinette, as successor trustee.

Roger and Victoria die in a car accident when one daughter is 28 and the other is 31. The 28-year-old's half of the trust property stays in a children's trust, managed by Antoinette, until she turns 30. The 31-year-old gets her half outright; no trust is created for her.

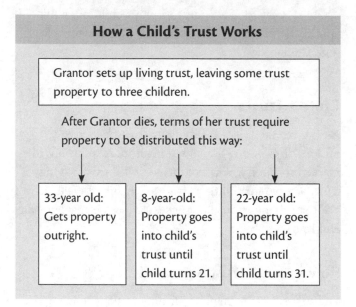

How a Child's Trust Works

Grantor sets up living trust, leaving some trust property to three children.

After Grantor dies, terms of her trust require property to be distributed this way:

| 33-year old: Gets property outright. | 8-year-old: Property goes into child's trust until child turns 21. | 22-year old: Property goes into child's trust until child turns 31. |

If a child's trust becomes operational, your successor trustee (or surviving spouse, if you made a trust together) must obtain a separate trust taxpayer ID number for each child's trust, file separate tax returns, and keep separate accountings and records for each trust. The successor trustee must manage each trust individually. So an operational child's trust is both a component of the overall living trust and a distinct entity. If light can be both a wave and a particle, surely this kind of duality is acceptable. And indeed it is, in the real world of the IRS, banks, and trust beneficiaries.

EXAMPLE:

In his individual living trust, Stanley names his 14-year-old son Michael as beneficiary of $75,000 worth of stock. He specifies that any stock Michael inherits when Stanley dies should be kept in a trust until Michael is 28, subject to the trustee's right to spend it on Michael's behalf.

Stanley dies when Michael is 19. The stock goes into a child's trust for him, managed by the successor trustee of Stanley's living trust. The trustee is free to use the stock (and the income it produces)

to pay for Michael's education and support. Michael will receive what's left of the stock when he turns 28.

You can create a separate child's trust for each young beneficiary you list. If these trusts ever become operational, Nolo's living trust forms provide that each one is given the name of its particular beneficiary. This allows each child's trust to be readily identified and managed in the real world.

EXAMPLE:

Leo Goldstein's living trust creates child's trusts for his grandchildren, Janet and John Ronninger, which are to last until each is 30. Leo dies while Janet and John are minors. Leo's successor trustee manages the children's trusts, one of which is called "The Leo Goldstein Living Trust, The Janet Ronninger Child's Trust" and the other of which is called "The Leo Goldstein Living Trust, The John Ronninger Child's Trust." Thus these trusts are identified as independent entities, while technically they are part of the original living trust as well.

With an AB trust, child's trusts are also possible. You can use your AB trust to make specific gifts and name alternate beneficiaries for each gift. If any of these beneficiaries is a minor or young adult, you can create a child's trust. Also, if any of the final beneficiaries are minors or young adults, you can set up child's trusts for them.

Who Serves as the Trustee

The trustee for each child's trust is your successor trustee or, if you made a shared or AB trust with your spouse, then your spouse. After both spouses are deceased, the successor trustee takes over any operational child's trusts. The trust forms in this book do not allow you to name another person to be a trustee for a child's trust.

The reason is that naming separate trustees creates serious paperwork and practical problems. Which trustee gets the original of your living trust document? Do you create several originals? Besides, it's usually hard enough to find one competent person who'll serve as trustee for all child's trusts. If you really want to name someone other than your successor trustee to be custodian for a gift to a minor, you can use the UTMA (in all states except South Carolina and Vermont). (See "Custodianships," below.)

SEE AN EXPERT

See an expert if you want to name someone else to be trustee of a child's trust. If you want to have child's trusts managed by someone other than your surviving spouse or your successor trustee, see a lawyer.

The Trustee's Duties

The trustee's powers and responsibilities are spelled out in the trust document. The trust trustee must:

- Manage each child's trust's property until that trust's beneficiary reaches the age set out in the trust document—which can take years.
- Use each trust's property or income to pay for that trust beneficiary's expenses, such as support, education, and health care.
- Keep separate records of trust transactions and file income tax returns for each trust.
- A very few states require periodic reports to the beneficiary of a child's trust. However, in most cases, it doesn't matter whether or not it's done, since everything is within the family.

A trustee who needs to hire an accountant, tax lawyer, or other expert to help manage a trust can use that trust's assets to pay a reasonable amount for the help.

The trust document also provides that the trustee of a child's trust is entitled to reasonable compensation for his or her work as trustee. The trustee decides what is a reasonable amount without court approval; the compensation is paid from the assets of the particular trust involved.

When the beneficiary reaches the age designated by the trust document, up to 35, the trustee must give the beneficiary what remains of that child's trust property.

Leaving Life Insurance Proceeds Through a Child's Trust

If you name minor children as beneficiaries, or alternate beneficiaries, of your life insurance, you need to create some type of adult management for the proceeds. You may also want mature adult management while the children are younger adults.

One sensible way to accomplish this is to name your living trust as the beneficiary of your life insurance. Technically, you name the trustee of your trust as the beneficiary. Then in the trust document, you name each child as a beneficiary of the proceeds, specifying the percentage or amount each child is to receive. Finally, within your living trust, you create a separate child's trust for each child.

Your living trust does not become the owner of the life insurance policy. You remain the owner. If you die while the child or children are under the age you specified in your living trust, the money will be managed for the child by your successor trustee until the child is old enough to receive the money outright.

Another possible approach for life insurance with child beneficiaries is to create a custodianship for each child, and name each child's custodian as beneficiary in specified portions for the insurance. (See "Custodianships," below.) A problem with this approach is that in most states, the custodian must turn over all property to the child when he or she reaches 21; in a number of states, the age is 18. With a child's trust, you can extend the age the child must reach before gaining unfettered control of the property.

Technically, passing the proceeds of a life insurance policy through your living trust is a bit more complicated than leaving other property this way. You must take two steps:

1. Name the trustee, as trustee of the child's trust of the living trust, as the beneficiary of your life insurance policy. Your insurance agent will have a form that lets you change the beneficiary of the policy. Tell the agent what you want to do and make sure you have forms that are acceptable to the insurance company.
2. When you list property items in the living trust document (that is, property owned by the trust), list the proceeds of the policy, not the policy itself. (Chapter 10 contains an example of how to list beneficiaries for insurance proceeds left to your trust.)

Custodianships

Creating a custodianship for a gift under your state's Uniform Transfers to Minors Act (UTMA) may be a preferable alternative to creating children's trusts.

You can create an UTMA custodianship in all but two states: South Carolina and Vermont.

How a Custodianship Is Created

After you make all your gifts in your living trust, in a separate section of the trust form you can create as many custodianships as you want for minor or young adult beneficiaries. You do this by identifying the property and the beneficiary it is left to, and appointing a custodian to be responsible for supervising that property. The form provides that the custodian is to act "under the [*your state*] Uniform Transfers to Minors Act." You can also name an alternate custodian in case your first choice can't do the job. Finally, you list the age at which the minor is to receive the property outright, using the list above as your guide. In most states, you have no choice and must list the age that state's UTMA decrees. In a few states, you can choose an age in a set range.

The custodian manages any trust property the young beneficiary inherits until the beneficiary reaches the age at which state law says the custodianship must end. (See the chart that shows when UTMA ends in each state, above.)

EXAMPLE:

Sandra and Don make a basic shared living trust. Sandra leaves 100 shares of Starbucks stock to her niece Jennifer. She names Hazel, Jennifer's mother, as custodian under the Illinois Uniform Transfers to Minors Act. At Sandra's death, Jennifer is 13. So Don, as trustee of the living trust, turns the stock over to the custodian, Hazel. She will manage it for Jennifer until Jennifer turns 21, the age Illinois law says she must be given the property outright.

As discussed, in some states, you can specify—within limits—the age at which custodianship will end. If your state allows this, you must state the age at which the custodianship will terminate.

Other Types of Trusts for Minors or Young Adult Beneficiaries

In some situations, you may want a different type of child's trust than the individual trusts you can create with this book's living trust forms. Consult a lawyer if you want to:

- place extensive controls over the use of property in the trust—for example, if you place real estate in the trust and you want it managed in a specific way
- provide for special care for a child with disabilities
- create a trust for any beneficiary who is already over age 35, or
- combine property for different children into a single trust (often called a "family pot" trust). In this type of trust, the trustee doles out money to different children as he or she sees fit, according to their needs. Establishing this sort of trust may not be a good idea. The trust doesn't end until the youngest child reaches the designated age (the older ones can't get their share outright before this), and the trustee may prefer one child's needs over another's, setting up the possibility of conflict, or at least resentment. On the other hand, for young children in a family group, this sort of trust may be sensible, so that the trustee can spend, as a parent would, according to the children's needs.

EXAMPLE:

Alexis and Jonathan, who live in New Jersey, make a basic shared living trust. They leave most of their trust property to each other and leave some property to their young children, Ian and Noel. They both specify, in the trust document, that any trust property the children inherit should be managed by the other spouse as custodian, under the New Jersey Uniform Transfers to Minors Act, until the boys turn 21. Under New Jersey law, they could have specified any age from 18 to 21. As alternate custodian, both name Jonathan's mother.

Alexis and Jonathan die simultaneously in an accident. Jonathan's mother, as custodian, takes over management of the trust property left to her grandchildren. When each boy turns 21, he will receive whatever of his property hasn't been used for his support or education.

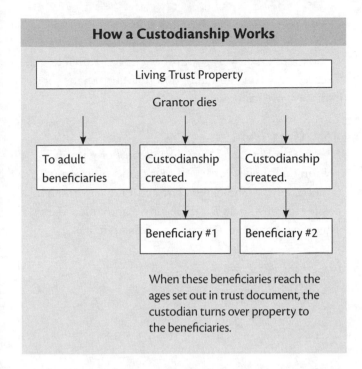

How a Custodianship Works

Living Trust Property

Grantor dies

To adult beneficiaries

Custodianship created.

Custodianship created.

Beneficiary #1

Beneficiary #2

When these beneficiaries reach the ages set out in trust document, the custodian turns over property to the beneficiaries.

Changes in State Law

States are free to change their rules about the age at which custodianships terminate. If your state does this after you make your living trust, it could affect any custodianships you have set up, though not in any drastic way.

- If your state raises the age at which custodianships terminate, the new age will determine when your beneficiary's custodianship ends.
- If your state adopts a flexible scheme allowing you to choose the age at which the custodianship ends, you can amend your living trust document to designate an age. If you don't amend it, the custodianship will end when the beneficiary reaches the youngest age allowed under the law.

If You Move

If you move to South Carolina or Vermont, states that haven't adopted the UTMA, it may be necessary to revise your living trust by creating children's trusts for any gifts previously made using a custodian. However, if the beneficiary of the gift, or the custodian for it, remains in a state that has an UTMA, you can still use that law for your gift.

If you move from one UTMA state to another, you can keep your UTMA clause as it is, unless you've moved to a state that has a lower age for turning over the gift to the minor than the age allowed in your old state. If this is the case, you'll have to amend your trust to establish a new age for the gift to be turned over to the child.

See Chapter 13 for a discussion on how to amend your living trust.

The Custodian's Responsibilities

A custodian has roughly the same responsibility as the trustee of a child's trust: to manage the beneficiary's property wisely and honestly. The custodian's authority and duties are clearly set out by the Uniform Transfers to Minors Act, as enacted by your state. No court directly supervises the custodian.

The custodian must:

- Manage the property until the beneficiary reaches the age at which, by law, he or she gets the property outright. If the child is quite young at your death, this can be a number of years.
- Use the property or income to pay for the young beneficiary's support, education, and health care.
- Keep the property separate from his or her own property.
- Keep separate records of trust transactions. The custodian does not have to file a separate income tax return; income from the property can be reported on the young beneficiary's return. (By comparison, the trustee of a child's trust must file a separate tax return for the subtrust.)

A custodian who needs to hire an accountant, tax lawyer, or other expert can use the property to pay a reasonable amount for the help.

If state law allows it, the custodian is entitled to reasonable compensation and reimbursement for reasonable expenses. The payment, if any is taken, comes from the property the custodian manages for the beneficiary. If this concerns you, check out your state's laws or see a lawyer. (See Chapter 17.)

Choosing a Custodian

In most cases, you should name as custodian the person who will have physical custody of the minor child. That's almost always one of the child's parents. If the beneficiary is your child, name the child's other parent, unless you have serious reservations about that person's ability to handle the property for the child.

Only one person can be named as custodian for one beneficiary. You can, however, name an alternate custodian to take over if your first choice is unable to serve. And you can name different custodians for different beneficiaries.

EXAMPLE:

Elaine, in her living trust, leaves property to two young nephews, Jerry and Mark, and one young niece, Reyna. She names Jerry and Reyna's mother, Alice, as custodian for their gifts. She names Mark's mother, Angela, as custodian for his gift.

Preparing Your Living Trust Document

Now it's time to actually prepare your living trust document. This chapter explains how to do it, step-by-step, when you use one of the trust forms in this book.

Please read this entire chapter carefully so you understand the choices you will make. Take your time and reread as much as you need to.

Checklist for Preparing Your Living Trust Document

1. ☐ **Decide which trust form to use.**

2. ☐ **Prepare your trust document.**

   A. Using a tear-out form in Appendix B

   ☐ Remove the form you need from Appendix B.

   ☐ Fill in the form by following the step-by-step instructions in this chapter.

   ☐ Type and proofread a final version of the completed form using a computer or typewriter.

   B. Using a form on the CD-ROM

   For instructions on how to use the forms CD that comes with this book, see Appendix A. Then:

   ☐ Open the form file you need.

   ☐ Fill in the form by following the step-by-step instructions in this chapter.

   ☐ Use your word processor's "Save As" command to rename and save your completed document.

   ☐ Print out and proofread your final document.

3. **Finalize your document.**

   ☐ Sign your trust document in front of a notary public in the state where you live.

   ☐ Store your trust document in a safe place. (See Chapter 12.)

Choosing the Right Trust Form

Appendix B and the CD-ROM contain four fill-in-the-blanks living trust forms:

- **Form 1:** Basic probate-avoidance living trust for one person.

- **Form 2:** Basic probate-avoidance shared living trust for a couple (married or not) with shared ownership property.

- **Form 3:** Nolo's standard AB living trust for a couple (married or not) that wants to avoid probate and save on overall estate taxes.

- **Form 4:** Nolo's AB disclaimer living trust for a couple that wants to avoid probate and have maximum flexibility for possible savings on overall estate taxes.

Generally, you should use only one trust. However, in a few special situations you may decide it's preferable to use more than one. (See Chapter 4 for a discussion.)

TIP

Make a few copies if you use the tear-out form. Many people need to make only one draft before they type up their final document. But having extra copies of the form certainly can't hurt, and may be useful if you need to prepare more than one draft. Use a pencil to make corrections easier, and go through the form slowly and carefully.

Making Changes to a Trust Form

These Nolo trusts are intended to be used with the language we give to you, except for minor, common-sense variations, or where the directions specifically allow you a choice of what to include. Generally, it's risky to make changes to the trust forms, particularly Form 3, Nolo's standard AB trust, and Form 4, Nolo's AB disclaimer trust. Changes in the language create the possibility of confusion and contradiction regarding what you intend with your trust. If you are inclined to make many changes to the form language, this may indicate that our form does not suit you, and you need to see a lawyer.

That said, most people who use these forms may need to make minor word changes. For example, if you want to name cosuccessor trustees, you'll need to change the word "trustee" to "trustees" at various places in the form.

⊘ **CAUTION**

Be very cautious about making changes. You will have to use your common sense to decide whether or not minor changes in the form are needed. But do be very careful. Don't stray far from the language of the form, especially with either AB trust. You certainly don't want to risk making a change that could cost you your estate tax savings. Be sure you understand the effect of any changes you make.

Step-by-Step Instructions

Important: These instructions are keyed to numbers on the trust forms. For example, Step 1 tells you how to fill in your name(s) and how to name your living trust. On the trust form, each time your name, or names, are called for, you'll see a ①. (If you prepare your trust using the CD-ROM, the numbers will appear in parentheses rather than in a circle.)

The steps are set out in the most logical order. However, the circled numbers on the forms do not always proceed sequentially; for example, number ①, the name of your trust, appears at the beginning of the form and also later, after other circled numbers. This is because the information called for is needed in more than one place in your trust form. Other numbers appear out of sequence because the information called for is necessary only for that one form, so the number given comes after the numbers and information common to all forms. Just remember the basic principle: *The circled number refers you to the specific step in this section that explains how to fill in this blank.*

Some simple information you must fill in is not keyed to a circled number because no instructions seem necessary. For instance, where you see a blank and "he/she" printed underneath, put in either "he" or "she," depending on whether the person referred to (which will be clear in the context) is male or female. Similarly, where you see a blank with "your state" printed underneath, fill in the state where you live.

When you have completed the form, proofread it carefully. Then proceed, as explained in the last three sections of the chapter, to finalize your trust document.

For couples. For the most part, the same decisions must be made whether you're preparing a living trust for one person or for a couple, so the instructions are just about the same. However, some instructions apply only to the two shared living trusts. They are identified by this symbol:

Special Instructions for Unmarried Couples

Forms 2, 3, and 4 are written in terms of a married couple. Therefore, an unmarried couple will need to change some wording in these forms. For example, the printed forms use the terms "spouse" or "surviving spouse" and, in Forms 3 and 4, "surviving spouse's trust." You can use "mate," "partner," or whatever words seem most suitable to you. Once you have selected a word or words, stick with them throughout the trust. And, of course, be sure you've read the trust document carefully, to make all the necessary substitutions.

Aside from words like "spouse" in the text, you'll see a number of blank lines to be filled in, with words below the line, such as

_____
wife's name

or

_____
husband's name

You will delete the words that appear below the lines from your final trust. But of course, you need to fill in the appropriate member of the couple's name.

Though making these word changes does require some extra work, it's really just a matter of cross-outs and substitutions, which hopefully you won't find onerous.

Step ① : Name Your Living Trust

You must give your living trust a name. Normally, you simply use your own name—for example, "The Denis Clifford Living Trust." It's legal to use more inventive names, for reasons ranging from a desire for privacy to nostalgia. (I once had a client who created the "Rue de Rivoli Trust.") Also, if you create more than one trust, you will want to distinguish them. One way to do this is to use numbers, particularly Roman numerals, to prevent any confusion in a basic shared trust, which splits into Trust #1 and Trust #2 on the death of a spouse. For example, "The Denis Clifford Living

Trust #I," "The Denis Clifford Living Trust #II," and so on. Generally, however, it's preferable to sign the trusts on different days and identify each trust by the date signed—for example, "The Denis Clifford Living Trust, 3/19/20xx"; "The Denis Clifford Living Trust, 4/7/20xx."

Use only one name per person; don't enter various versions of your name joined by "aka" (also known as).

If you go by more than one name, be sure that the name you use for your living trust is the one that appears on the ownership documents for property you plan to transfer to the trust. If it isn't, it could cause confusion later, and you should change the name on your ownership documents before you transfer the property to the trust.

EXAMPLE:

You use the name William Dix for your trust, but own real estate in your former name of William Geicherwitz. You should prepare and sign a new deed, changing the name of the real estate owner to William Dix before you prepare another deed to transfer the property from you (William Dix) to your living trust.

COUPLES

Couples who make a basic shared living trust or an AB trust normally use both their names to identify their trust—for example, "The Kay and Ornette Lewison Living Trust" or "The Cynthia Duffy and Mike O'Mally Living Trust." As with a trust for an individual, a couple can give their shared trust a fanciful name.

If you use your name or names for your trust, insert it every time there is a ① on the living trust form.

If you don't use your own name, you'll need to determine, each time you see a ①, whether your own name or the trust's name is required. For example, when naming the original trustees, you'll put in your own name(s), not the trust's name.

Step ② : Decide How Many Property Schedules Your Trust Needs

By this time, you should have decided which items of your property you will place in your living trust and which you will leave by other means. (See Chapter 6.)

Now you need to list all property that you will transfer to the trust on a "schedule" or "schedules," which will be attached to your trust document. How to list the property on a trust schedule is explained in Step 3.

As you can see by looking at the trust forms, a trust schedule is nothing more than a blank sheet of paper.

First, you must decide how many trust schedules you want to use. If you're creating a trust for one person (Form 1), you will use only one schedule, "Schedule A," even if several—or many—different types of property will be transferred to the trust.

EXAMPLE:

Mrs. Johnson wants to transfer her house, stock accounts, jewelry, and household possessions to her living trust. She lists all this property on one trust schedule, Schedule A.

For a couple, there are these:
- Schedule A, Shared Property Placed in Trust
- Schedule B, Wife's Separate Property Placed in Trust, and
- Schedule C, Husband's Separate Property Placed in Trust.

COUPLES

The shared trust form (Form 2), Nolo's standard AB trust (Form 3), and Nolo's AB disclaimer trust (Form 4) have three schedules, A, B, and C. Schedule A is for the couple's shared ownership property. On Schedule A, you need to identify the character of shared ownership property such as "community property" or "tenants in common." (This is discussed in detail in Step 4, below.) Schedule B is for the wife's separate property, and C is for the husband's separate property. If you have shared property and each spouse has separate property, you will use all three schedules.

EXAMPLE:

Mrs. and Mr. Andrezly, in their 60s, have been married for 15 years. Each has children from a former marriage. When they got married, each owned property that they agreed would remain each one's separate property. Since they married, they have acquired shared property, including a home. In their basic shared living trust, each wants his or her separate property to go to the children from his or her first marriage; their shared property goes to the surviving spouse.

They list their property in the basic shared living trust by using three schedules: Schedule A for the shared property, Schedule B for Mrs. Andrezly's separate property, and Schedule C for Mr. Andrezly's separate property.

If the Andrezlys created three separate trusts—a basic shared living trust for the shared marital property and two individual living trusts for each spouse's separate property—they would use only Schedule A of the shared trust for their shared marital property.

If one or both spouses do not have separate property, you won't use Schedule B, Schedule C, or both of them. You'll also need to delete references in the trust document to that spouse's (or both spouses') separate property. The paragraphs you may need to change are listed below.

EXAMPLE:

Tau and Lien Yu prepare a basic shared living trust. They own shared property. Lien has separate property; Tau does not. So they omit Schedule C from their draft trust and using draft Form 2, they edit Sections II(D)1 and II(D)2 as shown below.

---

1. Shared Property

All trust property listed on Schedule A was shared property:

4 ~~owned as community property of the grantors and shall retain that character after~~
~~identify the character of shared property listed in Schedule A~~

being transferred to this trust. If the trust is revoked, this property shall be returned to

the grantors as their community property.

.

2. Separate Property

The trust property listed on Schedule B shall retain its character as the separate property of

_____ Lien Yu _____ . ~~The trust property listed on Schedule C~~
wife's name

~~shall retain its character as the separate property of~~ _____ .
husband's name

Changes to Trust Forms 2, 3, or 4 If Separate Property Is Not Included

If either spouse doesn't transfer separate property to the trust, you'll need to make appropriate changes on Form 2, 3, or 4 by deleting the irrelevant material from the following sections:

- Section II, Paragraph A, refers to Schedules A, B, and C. Thus, if neither spouse has separate property, delete "B and C." If a wife has separate property and her husband does not, this would become "Schedules A and B."
- Section II, Paragraph B(1), refers to the wife's separate property.
- Section II, Paragraph B(2), refers to the husband's separate property.
- In Section II, Paragraph D(2), the first sentence refers first to the wife's separate property on Schedule B. The second sentence refers to the husband's separate property on Schedule C.
- Section IV(A) of Form 2 refers to Schedules A and C; Section IV(B) refers to schedules A and B.
- Section V(B) of Form 2 refers to Schedules A, B, and C.

Step 3 : List Your Trust Property on the Trust Schedule(s)

After you've decided how many schedules to use, list your trust property on them. Listing the trust property on a schedule does not give that property to beneficiaries. You list the property to make clear what property you have transferred to the trust and is owned by the trust. Then, in your trust document, you name your beneficiaries—that is, specify who will inherit the trust property after your death (Step 7, below).

CAUTION

Transferring property to the trust. To complete the transfer of property to the trust, you also must reregister title to that property in the trustee's or trustees' name(s). This absolutely essential process is explained in detail in Chapter 11.

When listing trust property on a trust schedule, generally you can use the same wording you used on the worksheet in Chapter 6. Just describe each item clearly enough so that the surviving spouse or successor trustee can identify it and transfer it to the right person. No magic legal words are required. Remember, this isn't a document that will be picked over by lawyers and courts. It's a document for the real world; what's important is that your successor trustee, family, and other beneficiaries are clear on what you've done and what you want.

Identifying Ownership of Trust Property

Don't use "my" or "our" when listing trust property on a schedule. For example, don't enter "my books" or "my stereo system." That's because once the property is in the living trust, technically it doesn't belong to you anymore—it belongs to the living trust, and is held in the name of the trustee.

If you need to refer to yourself or your property in a trust schedule, do so in the third person, by calling yourself "the grantor" or "grantors" rather than using "I" or "we." Sometimes, to clarify what property is owned by the trust, it helps to state on the schedule that identified property was "formerly" or "previously" owned by the grantor.

For example, on a trust schedule, you list: "The ¾-carat diamond bracelet formerly owned by the grantor."

A variation of this is to identify and list property "in the possession of the grantor," for example, "All compact discs and videos in the possession of the grantor."

Think about who will ultimately inherit the property. If you're leaving everything to one person, or a few major items to be parceled out among a few people, there's less need to list property in great detail. But if there will be a number of trust beneficiaries, and objects could be confused, be more precise about each one. When in doubt, err on the side of including more information.

When you name the beneficiaries for the trust property in your trust document (Step 7), your gifts must, of course, be consistent with the property listed on the trust schedule(s). You can't leave someone something that isn't listed on a trust property schedule. But the schedule does not have to be as detailed as your gifts. For example, on a schedule you could list "the house, furnishings, and personal possessions at [*street address*]." You can leave all this property to one beneficiary, or you could divide it, naming one beneficiary for the house and another for the furnishings and possessions, or break it down still further into many separate gifts.

Real Estate

A house can be listed by its street address—for example, "The house and real estate at 10001 Lakeway Drive, Seaview, Florida." Similarly, unimproved property can usually be listed by its common name: "The lots previously owned by the grantor on 50 to 80 Alligator Road, Seaview, Florida."

Usually, the street address is enough. It's not necessary to use the "legal description" found on the deed, which gives a subdivision plat number or a metes-and-bounds description. But if the property has no street address or common name—for example, if it is undeveloped land, off-road, out in the country—you need to designate exactly what land you're referring to. So carefully copy the full legal description, word for word, from your deed.

If you own a house and several adjacent lots, it's a good idea to indicate that you are transferring the entire parcel to your living trust by describing the land as well as the house.

EXAMPLE:

> The house at 390 Normal Road, Montclair, New Jersey, and all unimproved land between 390 Normal Road and 320 Normal Road.

Real estate often contains items that are properly classified as personal property. For instance, farms are often sold with tools and animals. If you intend to leave both real estate and personal property together to a beneficiary, make clear what this "together" consists of.

It's best to specify the large-ticket items (tractor, cattle) and refer generally to the rest of the items as "personal property." For example:

- 240-acre truck farm on Route 11, in Whitman County, Iowa, with all tools, animals, tractors, threshers, and other machines and all other personal property located there.
- Fishing cabin on the Wild River in Washington County, Maine, with all the fishing gear, furniture, tools, and other personal property found there.
- The house at 442 Wanaha Bay Road, Island of Hawaii, Hawaii, and all personal possessions and household furnishings in the house.
- The mobile home permanently located at E-Z motor camp, Kalispell, Montana, and all possessions and furnishings contained in it.

If you own real estate with someone else and are transferring only your share to the trust, you don't need to specify how big a share you own. Just describe the property. The trust schedules then state that you are transferring all your interest in the property, whatever share that is, to the living trust.

EXAMPLE:

Rhea owns a one-fifth interest in an apartment house located in Atlanta, Georgia. She prepares a deed transferring her one-fifth interest to her living trust's name. On the trust schedule, she simply writes:

> The interest in the apartment house at 434 Madison Street, Atlanta, Georgia, previously owned by the grantor.

Time-shares. A time-share in a house or apartment can be transferred to the trust. You can describe your interest as "the grantor's share in ____(*address*)____," or "the grantor's right to three weeks per year use of ____(*address*)____."

You also need to formally reregister title to a time-share in the trust. Depending on your state law, the time-share may be considered real estate, and so must be transferred by recorded deed. Otherwise, the time-share may be transferred with a simple notice of assignment. (See Chapter 11.)

Furnishings and Household Items

Household furnishings can be listed generally:

- The house and real estate at 12 High St., Chicago, Illinois, and all household furnishings and personal possessions in it.
- All the grantor's household goods and personal possessions located at 82 West Ave., Chicago, Illinois.

Or you can get more specific:

- All the furniture normally kept in the house at 44123 Derby Ave., Ross, Kentucky.
- All furniture and household items normally kept in the house at 869 Hopkins St., Great Falls, Montana.

You can also list individual items, if you plan to leave them separately. For example:

- The antique brass bed in the master bedroom in the house at 33 Walker Ave., Fort Lee, New Jersey.
- Daumier print captioned "Les beaux jours de la vie."
- Two Victorian rocking chairs in the living room at 75 Washington Street, Jefferson, Montana.

Bank and Money Market Accounts

You can list bank accounts by any means sufficient to identify them. Generally, it makes sense to list the account number:

- Bank account # 78-144212-8068 at Oceanside Savings, Miami, Florida, Market St. Branch.
- Savings Account No. 9384-387, Arlington Bank, Arlington, Minnesota.
- Money Market Account 47-223 at Charles Schwab & Co., Inc., San Francisco, California.

Cash

You cannot transfer cash to a living trust simply by stating a dollar figure on the schedule. For example, if you list "$25,000" on Schedule A, this doesn't transfer that amount of cash to the trust, because no source for these funds is given. Instead, list a specific source of cash. You can then make specific cash gifts from this source when you name your trust beneficiaries. Here are some examples:

- Bank account #33-931007-6214 at Bonanza Thrift, Miami, Florida.
- $25,000 from the grantor's stash in his desk. (This is obviously risky. If the money is removed from the desk, technically it is no longer owned by the trust.)

Securities

Securities, including mutual fund accounts, need to be listed clearly so there is no question what property is referred to:

- Mutual fund account #6D-32 2240001, at International Monetary Inc., Chicago, Illinois.
- All stock and any other assets in account #144-16-4124, at Smith Barney & Co., New York City, branch at 58th St./6th Ave.
- 100 shares of General Motors common stock.
- Mutual funds in account # 55-144-2001-7, Calvert Social Responsibility Fund, Boston, Massachusetts.

Sole Proprietorship Business Property

With a sole proprietorship business that has not been incorporated, the proprietor is the legal owner of all assets of the business, including the business name and any "goodwill." So you can simply list all assets of that business as a single item of trust property. For example:

- All assets of the grantor doing business as Mulligan's Fish Market, 44 Wellington St., Wymouth, Kentucky.
- All assets of the grantor doing business as Fourth Street Records and CDs, 10 Piper's Lane, Hoboken, New Jersey.
- All assets of the grantor doing business as Jim Pine Plumbing, 477 Market Street, Fort Lauderdale, Florida.

You can also divide up the business assets if you're leaving different parts to different people. For example:

- All accounts receivable of the business known as Garcia's Restaurant, 988 17th St., Atlanta, Georgia.
- The business name, goodwill, lease, and all food and food preparation and storage equipment, including refrigerator, freezer, hand mixers, and slicer, used at Garcia's Restaurant, 988 17th St., Atlanta, Georgia.

Shares in a Closely Held Corporation

- The stock of ABC Hardware, Inc., formerly owned by the grantors.

Partnership Interest

Because a partnership is a legal entity that can own property, you don't need to list items of property owned by the partnership. Just list your partnership interest:

- All the grantor's interest in Don and Dan's Bait Shop, a Partnership, Belmore, Oregon.

Shares in a Solely Owned Corporation

- All shares in XYZ Corporation.
- All stock in Fern's Olde Antique Shoppe, Inc., 23 Turnbridge Court, Danbury, Connecticut.

Membership Interest in a Limited Liability Company

- The grantor's membership interest in the Goat-Cheese-and-Wine LLC.

Miscellaneous Items of Personal Property

There are various ways you can list items of personal property on a trust schedule, depending primarily on whether you want to leave separate items to different beneficiaries, or all of one type of item to a sole (or group of) beneficiaries.

For items of significant monetary or sentimental value, you may want to list them individually. For example:

- The Apple computer (serial number 129311) with keyboard (serial number 165895).
- The medical textbooks in the grantor's office at 1702 Parker Towers, San Francisco, California.
- The photograph collection usually kept at 321 Glen St., Omaha, Nebraska.
- The collection of European stamps, usually kept at 440 Loma Prieta Blvd., #450, San Jose, California. (Describe any particularly valuable stamps.)

- The Martin D-35 acoustic guitar, serial number 477597.
- The signed 1960 Ernie Banks baseball card kept in safe deposit box 234, First National Bank of Augusta, Augusta, Illinois.
- The Baldwin upright piano kept at 985 Dawson Court, South Brenly, Massachusetts.
- Gold earrings with small rubies in them, purchased from Charles Shreve and Co. in 1971.

If you are like most people, you have all sorts of minor personal possessions you don't want to bother itemizing. To deal with them, you can group a number of items in one category, such as:

- all carpenter's tools, including power saws, in possession of the grantor
- all dolls
- baseball cards
- records, tapes, and compact discs, or
- machines and equipment.

Of course, some items without large monetary value can have great emotional worth to you and your family: a photo album, an old music box, a treasured chair. These can be separately listed as you desire.

If you're leaving all these groups of personal items to one beneficiary, there's no need to separately list them, even as groups. You can simply conclude your list with one catch-all item, such as "all personal property previously owned by the grantor."

Sample Schedule A for Shared Property

Below is a sample of a draft Schedule A for shared property for Form 2, a basic shared trust. When the final trust form is typed, the schedule is likewise typed, eliminating the printed instructions on the form. The final typed schedule is attached to the trust document.

Sample

Schedule A

Shared property placed in trust:

The house and real estate at 428 Dubuque Drive, Alameda, California.

All shares of stock in the Mo-To Corporation, Alameda, California.

The grand piano located at 428 Dubuque Drive, Alameda, California.

The Diebenkorn painting located at 428 Dubuque Drive, Alameda, California.

All other household possessions and furnishings located at 428 Dubuque Drive, Alameda, California.

Money market account #7033372, Working Assets, Boston, Massachusetts.

Certificate of Deposit No. 10235, Lighthouse Savings and Loan Association, Oakland, California.

All copyrights and rights to royalties previously owned by the grantors in these books, currently published by Fly High Press, Berkeley, California:

Dunk It: You Can Learn to Dunk a Basketball
Winning Through Whining, a Self-Help Guide
Watch It! How to Survive Urban Life

Step 4 : Identify the Nature of Shared Trust Property (Forms 2, 3, and 4 Only)

If you and your spouse are creating a trust together, you should state in the trust document that all shared property transferred to the trust (listed on Schedule A) retains the legal character it had before. That means that it stays community property if you live in a community property state. If you live in a common law state, all shared property transferred to the trust should be owned equally by the couple as tenants in common, not as joint tenants or tenants by the entirety. (See "Paperwork" in Chapter 11. Also see Chapter 6 for a discussion of community property states and common law states.)

If you don't share ownership 50-50, be sure to list each person's percentage of ownership.

If you are an unmarried couple that owns property together, you can likewise state that shared ownership property on Schedule A be returned to you two in the percentages of ownership you define in the schedule, and in this clause, if the trust is ever revoked.

To define the nature of shared trust property, insert one of the following clauses directly after the words, "All trust property listed on Schedule A was shared property":

- **If you live in a common law state:**
  co-owned equally by the grantors as tenants in common and shall retain that character after being transferred to this trust. If the trust is revoked, this property shall be returned to the grantors as co-owned equally by them as tenants in common.

- **If you live in a community property state:**
  owned as community property of the grantors and shall retain that character after being transferred to this trust. If the trust is revoked, this property shall be returned to grantors as their community property.

- **If you are an unmarried couple:**
  co-owned equally by the grantors as tenants in common. Any power reserved to the grantors to alter, amend, modify, or revoke this trust, as to the property listed in Schedule A, must be exercised by both grantors, in writing, to be effective. If this trust is revoked, this property shall be returned to the grantors as co-owned equally by them as tenants in common.

If you are married, you can change ownership of trust property without any possible gift tax consequences—for example, to convert one spouse's separately owned property to shared or community property or vice versa.

Step 5A : Decide Whether You Want Management of Trust Property If You Become Incapacitated (All Forms)

Form 1 provides that the successor trustee takes over management of the trust if you (the grantor) become incapacitated and unable to manage trust property. These provisions eliminate any need for court proceedings to appoint a guardian or custodian for trust property if you become incapacitated.

COUPLES

The basic shared trust (Form 2), the standard AB trust (Form 3), and the AB disclaimer trust (Form 4) provide that if both spouses become incapacitated, or if the survivor becomes incapacitated after one spouse dies, the trust property is managed by the successor trustee for the grantor's benefit.

Specifically, each trust form provides that if the grantor or grantors become incapacitated, the successor trustee "shall pay trust income at least annually to, or for the benefit of, the grantor(s) and may also spend any amount of trust principal necessary in the trustee's discretion for the needs of the grantor(s)." In other words, the successor trustee has a duty to make sure the incapacitated grantor(s) are properly cared for. If the annual income from the trust is higher than the expenses of the incapacitated grantor(s), the trustee can simply put the surplus in the grantors' bank account, thus using this money "for the benefit of the grantor(s)."

It's sensible and standard to provide for management of trust property if you become incapacitated. This book's trust forms ask you to name three people whom you want to determine your capacity to manage the trust if the question ever arises. If at least two of the three you named determine that you're not able to manage the trust—for example, because you're ill and hospitalized—they can authorize the successor trustee to take over. This way, there will be someone with power to make sure your trust affairs are taken care of.

Pick three people you trust, and who are likely to remain available throughout your life. If one or more of them later becomes unable to do this task, you can amend your trust to name a new person.

If the successor trustee ever asks them, the three should sign a single document recording their decision about your capacity. The successor trustee will likely need such a document to validate his or her authority with financial or other institutions. There is no standard legal form for this document. Below is a sample of what it might look like.

Allowing your successor trustee to step in and manage trust property doesn't give your successor trustee legal authority over property that's not in your living trust. To give someone that power, you need a document called a "durable power of attorney for finances."

Sample Determination of Incapacity

Determination of Incapacity

Each of the signers below has determined that Lois H. Fulbright, grantor of the Lois H. Fulbright Revocable Living Trust dated June 5, 20xx, has become incapacitated and is no longer reasonably able to manage the trust.

Each signer's determination was made on the basis of his or her knowledge of the grantor's/grantors' circumstances and condition.

Under the terms of the trust document, this determination allows the successor trustee named in that document to serve as trustee.

_____ Date: _____

_____ Date: _____

_____ Date: _____

If you don't prepare a durable power of attorney for finances and you become incapacitated, property not transferred to your living trust will need to be managed by a court-appointed conservator or guardian.

For this reason (and because you may receive other property or income in the future that doesn't make it into the trust), I strongly suggest that you also create a durable power of attorney for finances. See "Planning for Incapacity" in Chapter 15.

Step 5B: Decide Whether Your Spouse or Successor Trustee May Amend Your AB Trust If You Are Incapacitated and the Estate Tax Law Changes (Forms 3 and 4 Only)

The trust forms in the book do not allow either spouse to amend a trust if one spouse is incapacitated. Nor do the forms allow a successor trustee to amend a trust (though you can change this; see "Who Can Amend a Living Trust Document" in Chapter 13). If you prepare either type of AB trust and the estate tax law changes, it may become desirable to amend the trust to take full advantage of the new tax law. (See Chapter 4 for a discussion.) It's wise to consider what will happen if you are incapacitated and this need arises. Here you can give your spouse, or the successor trustee, the authority to amend your AB trust for the narrow and specific purpose of taking advantage of any new estate tax law.

Realistically, this situation is unlikely to occur. The provision would take effect only if both of the following things happen:

- Both spouses are still alive and one or both are incapacitated. If one spouse has died and a trust has become operational, that trust has become irrevocable. It was subject to tax under the estate tax law that existed when the spouse died, and so cannot be affected by subsequent changes in that tax. If an AB disclaimer trust was used, and no Trust A was created because the surviving spouse did not disclaim any of the deceased spouse's property, all the remaining trust property is now in Trust B, the surviving spouse's trust. Trust B is revocable as long as the surviving spouse remains alive and competent.
- Congress changes the estate tax law in ways that make it desirable to change the existing AB trust.

If you want your spouse or successor trustee to have authority to amend your AB trust if these two criteria are met, simply leave the provision found in Section VII (B) of Form 3, or Form 4 where you see the **5B**. This provision reads:

> If both grantors are alive and one is incapacitated, and Congress changes the estate tax law, the competent spouse shall have authority to amend this AB trust in order to take best advantage of the new tax law. If both grantors are alive and both are incapacitated, and Congress changes the estate tax law, the successor trustee shall have authority to amend this AB trust in order to take best advantage of the new tax law.

If you include this provision in your AB trust, it is absolutely essential that you fully trust your successor trustee. If you have any worries that your successor trustee might somehow abuse this power, do not use this provision. It's understandable that you might not want to risk letting anyone else alter your AB trust. You could sensibly decide that the risk of undesired change outweighs the possibility of need for change if the estate tax law is revised. If you feel this way, simply delete the provision from your final trust document.

SEE AN EXPERT

See a lawyer if you want more control. You could try to pin down more precisely what circumstances would authorize your successor trustee to amend your trust. For instance, you could speculate on changes Congress might make, and provide rules for each possibility. Or you could require that the successor trustee get the agreement of another key beneficiary before being able to make the changes. If you want to try for this kind of control, see a lawyer for help with drafting your provision. But be advised that it may turn out to be both complicated and costly. Also, the very fact that you want more control means you have some doubt about your successor trustee, at least in this situation. That alone suggests you'd be wise to talk with an attorney about your concerns.

Step 6: Name Your Successor Trustee

In the blanks with the **6** on the trust forms, name your successor trustee and your alternate successor trustee. (Choosing your successor trustee is discussed in Chapter 7.) You've already named yourself as the original trustee, or trustees.

EXAMPLE:

Using Form 4, the AB disclaimer trust, a couple completes Section III(E), Successor Trustee, as follows:

> Upon the death or incapacity of the surviving spouse, or the incapacity of both spouses, the successor trustee shall be Vicki J. Benoit. If she is unable to serve or to continue serving as successor trustee, the next successor trustee shall be B. J. Benoit.

Listing Specific Trustee Powers

The trust forms give the trustee "all authority and powers" your state's laws allow. But the trust forms also list specific powers, including the power to sell trust real estate, buy or sell stocks, and several other detailed powers. All of these specific powers are normally included in the general authority conferred on a trustee under state law. But banks, title companies, stock brokerage companies, and other financial institutions have been known to insist that a trustee be specifically authorized by the trust document to engage in a transaction involving their institution. So often spelling out these powers makes the successor trustee's work much easier in the real world.

Naming More Than One Successor Trustee

If you name more than one successor trustee or more than one alternate successor trustee, you need to specify in your trust document how the authority of the cotrustees is to be shared. Clearly, this is your personal decision, depending on how well the cotrustees get along and whether or not you think it's safe to let any of them act individually for the trust. So, depending on your needs, immediately after you name your successor trustees and alternate successor trustees, you'll insert one of the following clauses from the form:

> Any of the successor trustees has full and independent authority to act for and represent the trust.

or

> All the successor trustees must agree in writing to any transaction involving the trust or trust property.

If you have only one successor trustee, you'll need to delete all this material from the form.

Bond

The forms provide that no trustee has to post a bond. A bond is basically an insurance policy guaranteeing that a person will honestly carry out his or her duties; it pays off up to a stated amount if he or she doesn't. Bonding companies, which are normally divisions of insurance companies, issue a bond in exchange for a premium, usually about 10% of the face amount of the bond.

If you select a trustworthy successor trustee, there's no reason for a bond. In almost all situations, the question never comes up. Since the successor trustee handles the trust outside any court system, there's no forum where a demand for a bond could be raised. But just in case the question is somehow raised in a lawsuit (very unlikely), it's sensible to have waived any bond requirement. The cost of a bond would have to be paid for by your estate, and your beneficiaries would then receive less. Also, it's difficult for an individual to even get a bond in many states.

 SEE AN EXPERT

See a lawyer to require a bond. If you do want your successor trustee to post a bond, see a lawyer.

Step 7 : Name the Primary and Alternate Trust Beneficiaries

Now you enter the names of your trust beneficiaries, naming who gets what.

With a trust for an individual (Form 1) or a basic shared living trust (Form 2), insert their names and descriptions of property given them in the blanks where you see 7 . You can make as many separate gifts as you need to. The forms have spaces for five; if you have more, use another sheet of paper.

Reminder for unmarried couples: If you are an unmarried couple and use Form 2, 3, or 4, you'll need to change the printed form's references to spouses. Thus "Husband's Beneficiaries" or "Wife's Beneficiaries" must be changed to the appropriate individual's name. Example: "Al Smith's Beneficiaries" instead of "Husband's Beneficiaries."

138 | MAKE YOUR OWN LIVING TRUST

COUPLES

With a standard AB trust (Form 3) or an AB disclaimer trust (Form 4), each spouse can also make separate gifts to specific beneficiaries, outside of the AB trust property, and can list alternates for these gifts. Of course, it isn't required that you make such gifts; many couples simply leave everything to each other. (See Chapter 5.)

With Forms 3 and 4, each spouse will also name his or her final beneficiaries, and alternate final beneficiaries. See Step 8B, below.

Changing Forms 1, 2, 3, or 4 If You Don't Leave Specific Gifts

If you, your spouse, or both of you choose not to leave any specific gifts, but instead leave all trust property to each other, you'll need to eliminate the provisions in Form 2, 3, or 4 for making specific gifts, and also make any necessary revisions to the beneficiaries section.

Similarly, if you use Form 1 and don't make any specific gifts but leave all property to your residuary beneficiary, you'll need to eliminate the specific gift provisions from your trust.

CAUTION

The example below shows only how to revise a trust form if you do not want to leave specific gifts. Some portions of the trust forms in the back of this book have been omitted from the following example.

With Form 2, this may involve deleting Section IV(A)1 and/or Section IV(B)2.

EXAMPLE 1, FORM 2:

Lola and Malcolm Decamp use Form 2. Lola leaves two specific gifts, Malcolm leaves none. They revise the Beneficiaries section of the form as shown below.

IV. Beneficiaries

(A) Husband's Primary and Alternate Beneficiaries

Upon the death of _____ husband's name,

trust property owned by _____ husband's name,

as his share of the trust property listed on Schedule A and any separate property listed on Schedule C,

shall be distributed as specified to the beneficiaries named in this section.

1. Husband's Specific Beneficiaries

a. 7 _____ beneficiary shall be given _____ property identified.

If _____ beneficiary does not survive _____ husband's name,

that property shall be given to _____ alternate beneficiary.

[All specific husband's beneficiary provisions deleted]

(A) ~~2.~~ Husband's Residuary Beneficiary

The ~~residuary~~ beneficiary of any trust property owned by _____ Malcolm Decamp _____

husband's name

_____ as his share of the trust property listed on Schedule A or any separate property

listed on Schedule C, ~~and not specifically and validly disposed of by Section IV, Paragraph (A)1~~, shall be

8A _____ Lola Decamp _____ . If _____ Lola Decamp _____

residuary beneficiary   *residuary beneficiary*

_____ does not survive _____ Malcom Decamp _____

husband's name

that property shall be given to **8A** _____ Ted and Linda Decamp _____ .

alternate residuary beneficiary

(B) Wife's Primary and Alternate Beneficiaries

Upon the death of _____ Lola Decamp _____ ,

wife's name

trust property owned by _____ Lola Decamp _____ ,

wife's name

as her share of the trust property listed on Schedule A and any separate property listed on Schedule B,

shall be distributed as specified to the beneficiaries named in this section.

1. Wife's Specific Beneficiaries

a. **7** _____ Susan Fergis _____ shall be given

beneficiary

_____ all trust gold jewelry formerly owned by Lola Decamp _____ .

property identified

If _____ Susan Fergis _____ does not survive _____ Lola Decamp _____ ,

beneficiary   *wife's name*

that property shall be given to _____ Jean Fergis _____ .

alternate beneficiary

b. **7** _____ John Fergis _____ shall be given

beneficiary

_____ the autographed photo of Willie Mays _____ .

property identified

If _____ John Fergis _____ does not survive _____ Lola Decamp _____ ,

beneficiary   *wife's name*

that property shall be given to _____ the residuary beneficiary _____ .

alternate beneficiary

c. **7** _____ shall be given

beneficiary

_____ .

property identified

If _____ does not survive _____ ,

beneficiary   *wife's name*

that property shall be given to _____ .

alternate beneficiary

2. Wife's Residuary Beneficiary

The residuary beneficiary of any trust property owned by ___Lola Decamp___
wife's name

_____ as her share of the trust property listed on Schedule A or any separate property

listed on Schedule B, and not specifically and validly disposed of by Section IV, Paragraph (A)1, shall be

8A___Malcolm Decamp_____. If _____Malcolm Decamp_____
residuary beneficiary   residuary beneficiary

_____ does not survive ____Lola Decamp____
wife's name

that property shall be given to **8A**___Ted and Linda Decamp, in equal shares_____.
alternate residuary beneficiary

If you use Form 3 or Form 4, you may need to delete Section IV(A) and/or Section IV(B) and make selective deletions in Section V(B)2 and Section VI (C)2.

EXAMPLE 2, FORM 3:

Scott and Margie Vasquez create an AB trust using Form 3. Neither makes any specific gifts. Each leaves all their trust property to the other. They revise Form 3 as shown below.

IV. Specific Beneficiaries

(A) Wife's Specific and Alternate Beneficiaries

Upon the death of _____, the following gifts
wife's name

shall be made from trust property owned by _____.
wife's name

1. **7** _____ shall be given
beneficiary

_____.
property identified

If _____ does not survive _____,
beneficiary   wife's name

that property shall be given to _____.
alternate beneficiary

[All specific wife's beneficiary provisions deleted]

(B) Husband's Specific and Alternate Beneficiaries

Upon the death of _____, the following gifts
husband's name

shall be made from trust property owned by _____.
husband's name

1. **7** _____ shall be given
beneficiary

If _____ does not survive _____ ,
                              property identified
         beneficiary   husband's name

that property shall be given to _____ .
                                              alternate beneficiary

[All specific husband's beneficiary provisions deleted]

(C) Remaining Trust Property

~~Except as provided by Section IV, Paragraph (A) or (B), all other~~ All trust property of the deceased spouse

shall be transferred to, and administered as part of, Trust A, defined in Section V.

V. Creation of Trust A on Death of Deceased Spouse

[Section (A) not shown]

(B) Division of Trust Property on Death of Deceased Spouse

1. Upon the death of the deceased spouse, the trustee shall divide the property of The

①   Scott and Margie Vasquez _____ Living Trust
                              your names (or name of trust, if different)

listed on Schedules A, B, and C into two separate trusts, Trust A and Trust B.

2. All trust assets of the deceased spouse, as defined in Section V, Paragraph (A)2, shall be placed in

a trust known as Trust A ~~after making any specific gifts provided for in Section IV, Paragraph (A) or (B),~~

~~subject to any provision in this Declaration of Trust that creates child's trusts or creates custodianship under~~

~~the Uniform Transfers to Minors Act.~~

[Sections (B)3-4 and (C) not shown]

VI. Trust B: The Surviving Spouse's Trust

[Sections (A) and (B) not shown]

(C) Distribution of Property in Trust B

1. Upon the death of the surviving spouse, Trust B becomes irrevocable.

2. ~~The trustee shall first distribute any specific gifts of the surviving spouse to the beneficiaries named~~

~~in Section IV, Paragraph (A) or (B).~~ The trustee shall ~~then~~ distribute all ~~remaining~~ property of Trust B to ~~his~~

the
~~or her~~ final, or alternate final, beneficiaries, as named in Section V, Paragraph (C)3 or (C)4.

How to Enter Beneficiaries' Names

Many people worry that some precise, technical language must be used in living trusts to identify their beneficiaries, or their gifts won't be legally binding. Fortunately, this isn't true. You simply need to give the name that clearly identifies a beneficiary, so that your successor trustee understands to whom the gift is to be made. You don't have to worry about using a person's "legal" name, such as the full name on his or her birth certificate. Nor do you need to list the beneficiary's address or Social Security number.

If you name an institution (charitable or not) to inherit property from your trust, enter its complete name. It may be commonly known by a shortened version, which could cause confusion if there are similarly named organizations. Call to ask if you're unsure. (An institution that stands to inherit some of your money will be more than happy to help you.) Also, be sure to specify if you want a specific branch or part of a national organization to receive your gift—for example, a local chapter of the Sierra Club.

Identifying Property Left to Beneficiaries

There are three basic approaches to identifying property in a beneficiary clause:

1. Use exactly the same words you used on your property schedule. For example, if you listed "Money Market Account #60-32 2240001 at International Money Inc., Boston, MA" on your schedule, use exactly the same words in the beneficiary clause.

2. Group items left to a certain beneficiary. If you listed and specifically identified a number of similar items on a schedule (for example, five bank accounts, ten valuable paintings, four automobiles) and you wish to leave all items in a particular group to the same beneficiary, it's sufficient to say "all bank accounts listed on Schedule A" or "all paintings listed on Schedule A."

3. Be more specific in the body of your trust than in your trust schedule. For example, suppose on Schedule A you listed "all books in possession of the grantor" to indicate that ownership of all your books is transferred to your living trust. However, you don't wish to leave all these books to one beneficiary. When making gifts, you could state:

Beth Ruveen shall be given all books by F. Scott Fitzgerald in the possession of the grantor.

John Advale shall be given all books in French in the possession of the grantor.

Jim Horton shall be given all books in the possession of the grantor, except those left or given by this trust document to Beth Ruveen and John Advale.

COUPLES

Shared property. On Forms 2, 3, and 4, each spouse can give away only his or her half-interest in shared property, not all of it. So, when naming a beneficiary or beneficiaries for property listed on Schedule A of a shared living trust, it must be clear that each spouse is giving away only his or her share of the co-owned property. To accomplish this, when you leave a gift from property on Schedule A, add an identifying phrase to the beneficiary clause. Here are two examples; the language you must add is underlined:

If property left to one beneficiary:

Karen Zombanski shall be given all Lonnie Zombanski's
beneficiary

interest in the house listed on Schedule A.
property identified

If property left to more than one beneficiary:

Charles Berry shall be given 50%, and
beneficiary

Le Petit Richard and B. Diddly each shall
beneficiary   beneficiary

be given 25% of all Jackson Marquez's interest in

the stock account at Smith Barney, NYC,

#177-4N-2044, as listed on Schedule A.
property identified

Naming Children or Young Adults as Beneficiaries

You name a child or a young adult as a beneficiary exactly as you do an adult beneficiary, entering the child's name and identifying the trust property left to him or her.

Later in the trust document, you can arrange for an adult to manage property left to a young beneficiary. (See Steps 10 and 11.)

Leaving All Trust Property to One Beneficiary or Group of Beneficiaries

If you are using Form 1 or 2 and you want to leave all of your trust property to one person or to be shared by several, you can use just one beneficiary clause. Here are some examples:

For a basic shared trust, all property to your spouse:

> John Andrews shall be given all grantor Mary Andrews' interest in the property listed on Schedule A and Schedule B.

For an individual trust, all property equally to children:

> Steve Cronin, Elizabeth Cronin, and Roarke Cronin shall be given all property listed on Schedule A in equal shares.

Leaving Property to Several Beneficiaries to Share

You may want to leave an item of trust property to be shared among several beneficiaries. This is fine, as long as you use language that clearly identifies what share each beneficiary is to receive. This is best done by using percentages. If you use one of the marital trusts (Form 2, 3, or 4), be sure you are clear that you're giving away only your own interest in any property you share with your spouse. (Shared gifts are discussed in detail in Chapter 8.)

EXAMPLE:

From a stock account transferred to his shared living trust (Form 2), Jim Denniston makes the following gifts:

> Melinda Denniston shall be given 20% of Jim Denniston's interest in the trust's stock account #660134-N, Dean Witter Co.

> Mike Denniston shall be given 30% of Jim Denniston's interest in the trust's stock account #660134-N, Dean Witter Co.

> Roger Denniston shall be given 5% of Jim Denniston's interest in the trust's stock account #660134-N, Dean Witter Co.

> Margo Denniston shall be given 35% of Jim Denniston's interest in the trust's stock account #660134-N, Dean Witter Co.

> Cerrita Gibbs shall be given 10% of Jim Denniston's interest in the trust's stock account #660134-N, Dean Witter Co.

Naming Beneficiaries of Proceeds From a Life Insurance Policy

If you have named your living trust as the beneficiary or alternate beneficiary of a life insurance policy, you can simply name, within the trust, a beneficiary, or beneficiaries, for any insurance proceeds payable to the trust. The usual reason for doing this is that the life insurance beneficiaries are minors. (See "Child's Trusts" in Chapter 9.) In your trust, you arrange for an adult to manage property, including insurance proceeds that minors or young adults may inherit. (See Steps 10 and 11.) Remember, you don't need to list the policy on a trust schedule, because the trust never owns the policy; it is simply the beneficiary of it.

EXAMPLE:

> The grantor's children, Zack Philson and Zelda Philson, shall be given, in equal shares, all life insurance proceeds on the grantor's life paid to the trust.

Explanations and Commentary Accompanying a Gift

There are times, particularly in family situations, when explaining the reasons for your gifts can help avoid hurt feelings or family fights. If you wish, you can provide a brief commentary when making a gift. There are two ways to do it: in the trust document itself, or in a separate letter.

In the trust document. You'll need extra space for your comments. If you're using the tear-out form for your rough draft, you can simply write out your comments on a separate piece of paper and attach it to the trust form, with a note about where they should be inserted in the trust document. When you prepare your trust, you can integrate your comments into the trust form.

EXAMPLE:

- The grantor's business associate, Mildred Parker, who worked honestly and competently with her over the years, and cheerfully put up with her occasional depressions, shall be given $40,000 from the Money Market Fund #166-SJ-4111, Parnassus Mutual Funds, San Francisco, California.

- The grantor's best friend, Hank Salmon, whom the grantor enjoyed fishing with for so many years, shall be given the cabin and boathouse on Lake Serene, and the boat and outboard motor in the boathouse.

- Theodore Stein shall be given 40% of Alfred Stein's interest in the house at 465 Merchant St., Miami, Florida.

- Sandra Stein Rosen shall be given 40% of Alfred Stein's interest in the house at 465 Merchant St., Miami, Florida.

- Howard Stein shall be given 20% of Alfred Stein's interest in the house at 465 Merchant St., Miami, Florida.

- I love all my children deeply and equally. I give 20% to Howard because he received substantial family funds to go through medical school, so it's fair that my other two children receive more of my property now.

- Matt Jackson shall be given the bank account #41-6621-9403 at First Maple Bank.

- I love all my children deeply and equally. I leave more of my property to Matt than my other children because Matt is physically disadvantaged and is likely to need special care and attendants throughout his life.

Notice that in your explanations, you can refer to yourself in the first person, as "I," not "the grantor." It just sounds too awkward to express deep feelings as "the grantor." Besides, this type of wording isn't making a gift, but explaining it, so it's hard to imagine that any trouble could possibly arise from referring to yourself as "I" when speaking of your love for your kids.

In an accompanying letter. Another approach is to write a letter stating your views and feelings and attach it to your living trust document. Many people prefer this approach because it allows personal sentiments to be kept private. The living trust will have to be shown to people in various institutions, from banks to title companies to brokerage offices to county records offices. Many people don't want their personal feelings exposed to strangers in the business world. A letter can simply be removed from the trust document when showing the trust to any outsider. Also, if you have a lot to say, a letter is generally better than trying to express all your sentiments in the trust document itself.

Your letter isn't a legal part of your trust document, and it has no legal effect. It is prudent for you to state in your letter that you understand this, to eliminate any possibility someone could claim you intended the letter to somehow modify the terms of your trust.

The scope of your remarks is limited only by your imagination, short of libel. (If you write something so malicious (and false) that you libel someone, your estate could be liable for damages.) Some writers have expressed, at length and in their own chosen words, their love for a mate, children, or friend. By contrast, Benjamin Franklin's will left his son William, who was sympathetic to England during our Revolution, only some land in Nova Scotia and stated, "The fact he acted against me in the late war, which is of public notoriety, will account for my leaving him no more of an estate that he endeavored to deprive me of."

Imposing a Survivorship Period

When you leave property to a primary beneficiary, you can specify that if the beneficiary doesn't survive you by some specified period of time, the gift will go to the alternate beneficiary, if you name one, or the residuary beneficiary if you don't name an alternate. The pros and cons of survivorship periods are discussed in Chapter 8.

If you want to add a survivorship period, simply insert a specific time period before naming the alternate beneficiary.

EXAMPLE:

Hester Dinsdale (beneficiary) shall be given Herbert Grant's interest in the antique doll collection (property identified) located at 61 Hawthorn Lane, Gabels, Massachusetts.

If Hester Dinsdale (beneficiary) doesn't survive Herbert Grant by 30 days (husband's name), that property shall be given to Pearl Dinsdale (alternate beneficiary).

Naming Alternate Beneficiaries

As discussed, you are not required to name an alternate beneficiary for a gift. Some people don't wish to contemplate the chance of an inheritor, usually someone younger, dying before they do. But most people name an alternate beneficiary for each gift to a primary beneficiary. After all, there is always the chance that the primary beneficiary may not survive you, and you won't be able to amend your trust in time to leave the gift to someone else.

If you want to name alternate beneficiaries for a shared gift, be sure you read the discussion of this subject in Chapter 8.

With Form 1 or Form 2, if you don't name an alternate, the property that beneficiary would have received will be distributed to the person or institution you name as your "residuary beneficiary." (See Step 8A, below.)

With either AB trust (Forms 3 or 4), you can name alternate beneficiaries only for any specific gifts you make. If the primary beneficiary and alternate predecease you, that gift becomes part of the Trust A or Trust B property.

You can name more than one person or institution as alternate beneficiaries. These beneficiaries will share the property equally, unless you specify otherwise.

EXAMPLE:

Sherry names her husband as beneficiary of her interest in their house, which they have transferred to their basic shared living trust. As alternate beneficiaries, she names their three children, Sean, Colleen, and Tim, to share equally.

Sherry's husband dies just before she does, leaving his half of the house to Sherry. Under the terms of the trust document, it stays in the living trust. At Sherry's death, because her husband (the primary beneficiary) is no longer alive, the house goes to the three children. All three own equal shares in all of it.

For shared gifts, it's easiest to name the other surviving beneficiaries to receive a deceased beneficiary's share. You can accomplish this by using or adapting the following language, which may require some minor changes in the printed portion of a beneficiary clause:

If __Gwen Riordan, Richard Riordan, and Martha__
beneficiary
__Riordan Ling__ shall be given __Jack Riordan's__
property identified
__interest in the house at 41 Sussex Road,__
__Needles, Arizona, in equal shares__ .

If __any of these beneficiaries__ does not survive
beneficiary
__Jack Riordan__ , ~~that property shall be given to~~
husband's name
__the deceased beneficiary's interest shall be__
alternate beneficiary
__shared equally by the surviving beneficiaries__ .

You can also name different alternates for each beneficiary of a shared gift. For example, an older person who leaves a shared gift to his children may list each child's children (or spouse) as alternate beneficiaries for that child's share of the gift.

__Gwen Riordan, Richard Riordan, and Martha__
beneficiary
__Riordan Ling__ shall be given __all Jack Riordan's__
property identified
__interest in the house at 41 Sussex Road,__
__Needles, Arizona__ .

If __Gwen Riordan__ does not survive __Jack Riordan__ ,
husband's name
~~that property shall be given to~~ __her children, Mike__
__Riordan James and Tracy Riordan James, shall__
__be given the interest in the property she would__
__have received__ .

If __Richard Riordan__ does not survive __Jack Riordan__ ,
husband's name
~~that property shall be given to~~ __Richard's child,__
__Sean Riordan, shall be given the interest in the__
__property he would have received__ .

If __Martha Riordan Ling__ does not survive __Jack__
husband's name
__Riordan__ , ~~that property shall be given to~~ __her__
__husband, Patrick Ling, shall be given the interest__
__in the property she would have received__ .

Step 8A : Name Your Residuary Beneficiary (Forms 1 and 2 Only)

If you are preparing an AB trust (Form 3 or Form 4), skip to Step 8B. If you are preparing a trust for one person (Form 1) or a basic shared living trust (Form 2), the next step is to name your residuary beneficiary or beneficiaries.

You must name one or more residuary beneficiaries for your living trust, where you see the **8A** .

The residuary beneficiary of your living trust is the person or organization who will receive:

- any trust property designated for primary and alternate beneficiaries who die before you do
- any trust property that you didn't leave to a named beneficiary (this could include property you transferred to the trust later but didn't name a beneficiary for)
- any property you leave to your living trust through a pour-over will (because property left through a pour-over will doesn't avoid probate, there's usually no reason to use one; see Chapter 16), and
- any property that you actually transferred to your living trust but didn't list in the trust document.

Sometimes the residuary beneficiary of a basic living trust doesn't inherit anything from the trust, because all trust property is left to primary beneficiaries, with alternates. In this situation, naming a residuary beneficiary can be just a backup measure, to guard against the extremely small chance that both a primary and alternate trust beneficiary do not survive you.

You may, however, deliberately leave the residuary beneficiary trust property by:

- Not naming specific beneficiaries for most trust property. Everything not left to a specific beneficiary will go to your residuary beneficiary. It's common, for example, for a grantor to leave much of his estate to his children as residuary beneficiaries.
- Adding property to the trust later and not amending your trust document to name a specific beneficiary to receive it after your death.
- Using a pour-over will to leave property to your living trust and not naming a specific beneficiary in the trust document to receive property that passes through the will. (Wills are discussed in Chapter 16.)

More than one residuary beneficiary. If you name more than one residuary beneficiary (or alternate residuary beneficiary), you need to state, in the clause, what portion or percentage each residuary beneficiary will receive. It's common, especially if one's children are the residuary beneficiaries, to state that they each receive an equal share.

EXAMPLE:

The residuary beneficiaries ... shall be Rachel Weinstock and Alan Weinstock, each to receive 50% of all trust property not specifically and validly disposed of by earlier gifts....

Of course, you can also specify that residuary beneficiaries receive unequal shares. In that case, you must specify what percentage of the property each residuary beneficiary will receive.

EXAMPLE:

Zane Jilconty names three siblings—Lucy, Jill, and Warren—as his residuary beneficiaries. For several reasons, he wants to leave them unequal amounts. So he provides, in his residuary clause, that his residuaries are:

Lucy Jilconty, 50% of the residuary property; Jill Jilconty Jackson, 30% of the residuary property; and Warren Jilconty, 20% of residuary property.

Alternate residuary beneficiaries. You should also name an alternate residuary beneficiary, or beneficiaries, to be sure you have one final backup to receive trust property if all other beneficiaries, including your residuary beneficiary, predecease you and you can't amend your trust in time. (True, this is a remote possibility, but remote possibilities are lawyers' stock-in-trade, and even we at Nolo can't bring ourselves to completely jettison concern for such unlikely contingencies.)

Step 8B : Name Your Final Beneficiaries (Forms 3 and 4 Only)

If you are preparing either type of AB trust, it's vital that each spouse name a final beneficiary or beneficiaries, and normally alternate final beneficiaries, where you see 8B . Each spouse names his or her own final beneficiary or beneficiaries. Often these are the same people for both spouses, most commonly their children. But spouses can name different final beneficiaries if they want to. (See Chapter 5.)

EXAMPLE:

Cara and Hugh O'Neill create an AB trust. Each wants to name their four children as final beneficiaries. They complete Section V(C)3 and V(C)4 of Form 3 as follows:

> If Cara O'Neill is the deceased spouse, the final beneficiaries shall be: Paula O'Neill, Patrick O'Neill, Olivia O'Neill, and Moira O'Neill.

> If Hugh O'Neill is the deceased spouse, the final beneficiaries shall be: Paula O'Neill, Patrick O'Neill, Olivia O'Neill, and Moira O'Neill.

If there is more than one final beneficiary, each spouse should define what property each of final beneficiaries or alternate final beneficiaries will inherit. Often a spouse simply provides that all final beneficiaries share equally. But more complex divisions of property are certainly possible.

EXAMPLE:

Rebecca Gerhorst names her three children as her final beneficiaries. In her trust document, she provides:

> Will Gerhorst shall receive 25% of the property in Trust A; Brunehilde Gerhorst Smith shall receive 35% of the property in Trust A; Ulga Gerhorst shall receive 40% of the property in Trust A.

With a standard AB trust, the final Trust A beneficiaries will receive all property remaining in that trust after the surviving spouse (the life beneficiary) dies. (See Chapter 5.) The final beneficiaries might also receive any of the specific gifts the deceased spouse made, if both the specific beneficiary and the alternate beneficiary for a specific gift predecease that spouse (a remote possibility, surely, but not unheard of). In that case, the specific gift becomes part of the Trust A property.

Each spouse's final beneficiaries are also the primary beneficiaries of Trust B, the surviving spouse's trust. After one spouse dies, the surviving spouse's trust remains revocable. But if he or she does not amend that trust and name new beneficiaries, the property in that trust (again, except for any specific gifts) will go to the final beneficiaries he or she named in the original trust document.

As you know by now, if you use an AB disclaimer trust, it is not mandatory that a Trust A be established after the first spouse's death. That decision is made by the surviving spouse after the first spouse dies. If the surviving spouse does not disclaim any trust property, there is no property to go into Trust A. This means that the Trust A final beneficiaries named by the deceased spouse will not inherit unless the surviving spouse names them as beneficiaries of his or her trust (Trust B). The surviving spouse can now decide how much, if any, property those beneficiaries will inherit.

 SEE AN EXPERT

Get help if you want to name a charity as a final beneficiary. If you name a charity as a final beneficiary, and federal estate taxes are due, the IRS will take all the taxes from other gifts you've made. This may diminish the value of these gifts substantially, or even wipe some out. To avoid this, you can specify that any proportion of taxes on your estate be paid out of property left for the charity. Then the charity gets whatever is left. The math calculations here can get complex and confusing because the size of the charitable contribution depends on the amount of estate taxes, and vice versa. If you want to work out the exact figures, see a knowledgeable estate tax accountant or lawyer.

Step 9 : Provide for Payment of Debts and Taxes

There are two ways to handle payment of debts and taxes after your death:

- leave it up to the successor trustee, or
- designate that certain trust assets be used.

For many people, payment of debts and taxes is not a serious concern. Their estates are now well under the minimum estate tax threshold, so they don't expect that federal taxes will be due, and their debts are relatively minor—perhaps a few personal bills, credit card charges, household utilities, and any unpaid bills from the last illness or funeral/burial costs.

SEE AN EXPERT

See a lawyer if you have complex debt or tax problems. If your estate is likely to face difficult debt or tax problems, see an attorney to discuss how to handle this. A good lawyer can help you draft specific provisions for payment of these obligations. Similarly, if much of the value of your estate will be transferred by methods other than your living trust, do not rely on the debt and tax payment options presented here, which do not apportion payment between trust and nontrust assets.

Leave the Decision to the Trustee

You do not have to decide what assets will be used to pay your debts and taxes. Many people prefer to leave this decision to their successor trustee, who will know what the real financial situation is when these debts must be paid. You can, at best, make only a reasonable guess now. If you direct that a specific asset or assets be used to pay any debts or estate taxes, it can cause problems later on. If you've also left the asset to a specific beneficiary, the provision for payment of debts and taxes takes priority, so that beneficiary may receive little or nothing from your gift. Also, if the property you identified isn't sufficient to pay all your debts and taxes, your successor trustee will still have to decide how to pay any balance due.

If allowing the trustee to make the decision makes sense to you, for an individual trust, where you see the **9** , delete all language after the first sentence of this section, as shown in the example below.

With a basic shared living trust (Form 2) or Nolo's AB trust (Form 3 or 4), each spouse can choose how his or her debts are to be paid. If both spouses want their successor trustee to decide this, there's a little more crossing out to do. With Form 2, make deletions like those shown above for "Wife's Debts and Taxes," Section VIII C (1), and "Husband's Debts and Taxes,"

Section VIII C (2). Then delete all of the next provision, "If Specified Property Insufficient," Section VIII C (3). With an AB trust, make these same deletions. The section numbers for the AB trust are IX C (1), IX C (2), and IX C (3). Finally, if for some unusual reason one spouse wants to choose how debts and taxes are paid but the other does not, simply make deletions like those shown in the below example for the spouse leaving the decision to the trustee.

Designate Specific Assets

If you decide you want to make specific provisions for payment of your debts and taxes from trust property, write in the specific items you want used to pay them in the blank where you see the **9** on the trust forms. And do your best to be sure these assets will actually be sufficient to pay all your debts and taxes.

EXAMPLE:

> The grantor's debts and death taxes shall be paid by the trustee from the following trust property:
> - First, from the bank account #99-8062144, Wells Fargo Bank, Berkeley, California.
> - Second, from stock account #82-304, Smith Barney & Co., San Francisco, California.

Remember that any property you specify to pay your debts and taxes must be owned by your trust. That means you must list it on a property schedule and transfer title into the trustee's name. (That process is explained in Chapter 11.)

(C) Payment by Trustee of the Grantor's Debts and Taxes

The grantor's debts and death taxes shall be paid by the trustee. ~~The trustee shall pay these from the following trust property:~~

9 _____

_____

_____.

If the property specified above is insufficient to pay all the grantor's debts and death taxes, the trustee shall determine how such debts and death taxes shall be paid from trust property.

COUPLES

In a basic shared living trust or an AB trust, each spouse can specify the property to be used to pay his or her debts and death taxes.

EXAMPLE: Sid and Ellen Wall want each one's debts and taxes paid from a shared stock account. In their basic shared living trust, they provide:

1. Wife's Debts
   Ellen Wall's debts and death taxes shall be paid by the trustee from the following trust property: her interest in stock account #0014463, Smith Barney & Co.

2. Husband's Debts
   Sid Wall's debts and death taxes shall be paid by the trustee from the following trust property: his interest in stock account #0014463, Smith Barney & Co.

With an AB trust, the property a spouse specifies to be used to pay debts and taxes will normally be part of Trust A. So primarily what's accomplished by specifying assets to pay debts is to protect the specific gifts from being used to pay any debts and taxes.

Step 10 : Provide Property Management for Young Beneficiaries (Optional)

Next, you can provide property management for any young beneficiaries who you've named to receive trust property. You can use either a child's trust or the UTMA for each beneficiary. You can use a child's trust for one beneficiary and the UTMA for another, but you cannot set up a child's trust and the UTMA for the same beneficiary—you must choose one method for each beneficiary.

Create Children's Trusts (Optional) 10A

In the blank with the 10A on the trust forms, list each person (minor or young adult) you want to name as beneficiary of a child's trust. This may include minors and young adults you've named as alternate beneficiaries.

Children as Beneficiaries of Life Insurance

As discussed in Chapter 9, you can make minor children beneficiaries of life insurance policies in three steps:

1. Register the policy beneficiary in the name of the trustee(s).
2. In your trust, name the minor children as beneficiaries of the policy.
3. In your trust, create a child's trust for each minor child who will receive proceeds from the policy.

Be sure not to list as child's trust beneficiaries any persons you want to make gifts to using the Uniform Transfers to Minors Act (UTMA). You'll do that in Step 11. You cannot leave a gift to a minor by both the UTMA and a child's trust.

For each trust beneficiary you list where you see the 10A, you also state the age at which you want that beneficiary to receive his or her trust property. If you die before the beneficiary reaches the age you specify, the beneficiary's property will be retained in a child's trust until the age is reached. (See Chapter 9.) If you don't specify an age, each listed beneficiary will receive the trust property outright at the age of 35.

Create Custodianships Under the Uniform Transfers to Minors Act (Optional) 10B

If you want to make a gift to a child using your state's Uniform Transfers to Minors Act (UTMA), complete the custodianship clause where you see a 10B . The form contains three blank clauses for individual beneficiaries, but you can add as many additional clauses as you want.

To complete the UTMA clause, begin by listing the state where you live (after double checking the list in Chapter 9 to be sure your state has adopted the UTMA). Then, fill in the beneficiary's name, the custodian's name, and the age the beneficiary will receive the property outright. You can also use an UTMA clause to leave gifts to any minors, such as grandchildren, if they live in a state that has an UTMA law.

The age a child will receive the gift outright depends on state law; Chapter 9 lists each state's termination age. In some states, you are given a limited choice of when the custodianship ends. For example, you can choose any age from 18 to 21 in Maine, and 18 to 25 in California. But most states allow you no choice. The gift must end at the age set by the state. In those states, all you need do is fill in the age from the list in Chapter 9.

EXAMPLE:

In California, where you can choose an age between 18 and 25:

All property <u>Ned Clark</u> becomes entitled to under this trust document shall be given to <u>Mary Clark</u> as custodian for <u>Ned Clark</u> under the <u>California</u> Uniform Transfers to Minors Act until <u>Ned Clark</u> reaches age <u>24</u>.

In New Hampshire, where a custodianship must end at age 21:

All property <u>Luisa Brookside</u> shall become entitled to under this document shall be given to <u>Nancy Curtis</u> as custodian for <u>Luisa Brookside</u> under the <u>New Hampshire</u> Uniform Transfers to Minors Act until Luisa Brookside reaches age <u>21</u>.

If You Do Not Create a Child's Trust or Make Gifts Using the Uniform Transfers to Minors Act

If you do not create a child's trust or make any gifts under the Uniform Transfers to Minors Act, simply delete the blank section(s) before your final trust is typed. These clauses are at the end of the trust form so that you do not have to renumber other trust clauses if you delete both of them.

If you create children's trusts but do not make gifts under the Uniform Transfers to Minors Act, simply delete that later clause. Again, no renumbering of clauses is required.

However, if you do not create any children's trusts but do make gifts under the Uniform Transfers to Minors Act, you must delete the child's trust clause and renumber the Uniform Transfers clause. To do this, simply change the clause number for gifts under the Uniform Transfers to Minors Act:

- From "X" to "IX" in the Living Trust for One Person
- From "XI" to "X" in the Basic Shared Living Trust, and
- From "XII" to "XI" in the AB trust.

Step 11 : Decide About Reports to Final Beneficiaries (Forms 3 and 4 Only)

You have a choice regarding reports the surviving spouse (as trustee) must give the final beneficiaries about an operational Trust A.

The trust forms provide, where you see the 11 (in Section V(C)6), that the surviving spouse doesn't have to provide any accountings, except that the spouse must give the final beneficiaries copies of the trust's annual federal income tax return.

Some couples, understandably, feel that even providing tax returns is an intrusion into their financial privacy—that just because they've established a trust to save on estate taxes for their children is no reason they must reveal details of their finances to them yearly. If you feel this way, simply delete the final portion of this accounting clause, so that it reads:

No accounting of the Trust A shall be required of the trustee.

Another version is to provide that no accounting is required as long as the surviving spouse serves as trustee, but when the successor trustee takes over, accountings are required. If you decide on this approach, here is the clause to use when you see the 11 (Part V(C)6):

No accounting of Trust A shall be required as long as the surviving spouse serves as trustee. When any successor trustee serves as trustee of Trust A, the final beneficiaries shall be provided with copies of the annual trust income tax return.

Unless the surviving spouse becomes incapacitated and cannot serve as trustee for a while, the successor trustee will take over only when the surviving spouse dies. So usually, this last clause will require the successor trustee to provide only the one final trust income tax return to the beneficiaries. The trust property should be rapidly transferred to the final beneficiaries, and the last trust income tax return is just one part of closing down the trust.

Prepare Your Final Trust Document

When you have completely filled in the trust form, proofread it carefully. Check to be sure you have:

- included all property you want to leave through the trust
- clearly and accurately identified all property (double-check account and serial numbers, for example)
- included all beneficiaries to whom you want to leave property
- spelled beneficiaries' (including alternate and residuary beneficiaries) names correctly and consistently, and
- made adequate arrangements for management of trust property that young beneficiaries might inherit.

When preparing the final trust, you want a document that looks as much like a conventional lawyer's living trust as possible. **So in your final version, be sure you have deleted:**

- the top caption of the form, such as "Form 2, Basic Shared Living Trust." You can leave the heading of the trust schedules as printed. For example, if you use a Schedule C, "Schedule C, Husband's Separate Property Placed in Trust," this does not need to be crossed out or changed.
- instructions
- circled numbers
- any printed material on the form that doesn't apply to you, including:
  - blank beneficiary clauses, if you don't have as many beneficiaries as the forms provide space for
  - the alternate beneficiary provision of a beneficiary clause, if you decided not to name alternates for a specific gift
  - all material relating to trusts for minor beneficiaries, if you didn't create any, and
  - all material relating to the Uniform Transfers to Minors Act, if you didn't make any gifts using it.

Delete all material you want to eliminate before the final trust document is typed or printed.

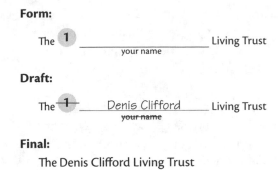

Form:

The ① _____ Living Trust
               your name

Draft:

The ~~①~~ _Denis Clifford_ Living Trust
            ~~your name~~

Final:

The Denis Clifford Living Trust

If you used the tear-out forms, once you're satisfied that your trust form is fully completed, type the final document from your draft, including all trust schedules. The final version should be typed or printed out on good quality (bond) 8½" x 11" typing paper. Although not required by law, obviously it makes sense to use nonerasable paper.

Be sure the pages of the final document are consecutively numbered correctly. You may have to change the numbering from that on the form. For instance, if you add material (such as commentary about gifts) or have quite a number of primary beneficiaries—say 16—you'll have to renumber the pages of your final document. Similarly, if you delete material (such as the sections on children's trusts or gifts under the Uniform Transfers to Minors Act), you'll need to renumber the pages of your final document.

If you used the forms on the CD-ROM, make sure page numbers print out with your document, use at least 12-point font (so that it's easier to read), and print your final document single-sided. Proofread the final trust document carefully and make corrections, if needed.

Consider Having Your Work Checked by a Lawyer

Once you are sure your final trust document is clear and correct, consider whether or not you want to look for a lawyer who can review your work. This can sound like a good idea that shouldn't cost much, but the reality is that it is often difficult to find a lawyer willing to do the job; most want a full fee for preparing a trust from scratch and won't accept review work. (Read more about finding a lawyer in Chapter 17.)

Before setting off to try to find a lawyer, take stock of whether you are really likely to benefit by employing one. If your desires are clear and straightforward, and you've followed the forms and instructions in this book, your trust should work just fine. On the other hand, if you have an estate large enough to be liable for estate taxes, or have other complex property or beneficiary concerns, this book has surely referred you to a lawyer already.

Sign Your Living Trust in Front of a Notary

It is essential that you sign your trust document and have your signature notarized by a notary public in the state where you live, even if you work in another state. Normally, no witnesses watch you sign a living trust. Because of this, it's always possible that after your death someone could claim that the signature wasn't genuine. As you won't be around to verify it then, you should do it now. The best way to remove any question of whether or not the signature on the document is authentic is to sign it in front of a notary.

The signature line on the trust form is preceded by a provision entitled "Certification by Grantor(s)." Here you state that you've read the trust document and approve of it. This is a bit of legalese, included to make your trust look more like ones with which most financial institutions are familiar.

A notarization form is included with each living trust form in Appendix B. If your notary prefers to use a different form, fine—the important thing is to get the notarization done.

Hopefully, finding a notary shouldn't be a problem; many advertise online and in the yellow pages. Or check with your bank, which may provide notarization as a service to customers. Real estate offices and title companies also have notaries.

No Lawyer Required

There is no legal requirement that a lawyer must review or approve your living trust before it can be notarized. Anyone, including a notary, who tells you that a lawyer must be involved is wrong.

! CAUTION

Special Florida requirements. In Florida, you must sign your living trust in front of two witnesses. Since the notary counts as one, you must have at least one other. Use the special Florida Witness Statement, Form 5, in Appendix B.

State-Specific Notarization Language

A few states have special requirements for notarization language. For example, Montana requires notaries to include their place of residence when they acknowledge a document. In this book, the Notary Acknowledgement forms use the required language for California, which will work in most states. If your state has different requirements, your notary will know the rules and can provide the correct certificate.

COUPLES

Both spouses must sign a basic shared trust, a standard AB trust, or an AB disclaimer trust, and both spouses must appear before a notary.

! CAUTION

Don't rely on a bank guarantee for your signature. Some banks provide guarantees for customers' signatures on bank and other important documents. Some readers have asked whether they can use a bank guarantee for their living trust, in place of notarization. The answer is no. After your death, it's vital that your living trust be accepted by many institutions, from title companies to county land records offices to stockbrokers. These institutions are not used to seeing living trust signatures validated by a bank guarantee. If any institution refuses to accept your living trust for this reason, there is little or nothing your successor trustee will be able to do about it. Getting a bank guarantee may, for some people, be easier than locating a notary. Unfortunately, this convenience is irrelevant. You must have your signature notarized.

! CAUTION

Don't stop now. Even after your trust document is signed and notarized, you're not done. You must transfer the property you listed in the trust schedules into the name of the trust. Do it as soon as possible. Chapter 11 shows you how.

Transferring Property to Your Trust

After you sign your living trust document, you have a valid living trust. But the trust is of absolutely no use to you until the property you listed in the trust document (on the property schedules) is actually transferred into the trust. Lawyers call this "funding" the trust.

Transferring your property to your living trust is crucial, and takes some time and paperwork, but it's not difficult. You should be able to do it yourself, without a lawyer.

We're Counting on You: Make Sure You Do It Right

Many lawyers who prepare living trusts insist on doing all the property transfer work themselves, because they claim their clients cannot be trusted to do this work themselves. In other words, lawyers get paid hundreds of dollars per hour to do paperwork and won't allow their clients to do it.

Both this book and Nolo rest on the belief that people can be trusted to understand basic legal forms and do the work required to make the forms work. It is absolutely essential that you do the work necessary to formally transfer your property to your trust. If you don't, your trust will not work and, perhaps worse, you'll be proving that those lawyers who say people just can't be trusted to do basic tasks correctly are, sadly, sometimes correct. So, study this chapter carefully and be absolutely sure you've properly transferred all trust property into the trust's name.

Paperwork

Each item of property listed on your trust schedule(s) must be transferred to the trust. How much paperwork is required depends on whether or not the property has a document of title—a formal ownership paper—such as a real estate deed, securities account registration form, or boat registration.

Property Without a Document of Title

Property without a document of title includes most furniture, clothing, books, appliances, and other household goods, as well as some more valuable items, like jewelry, artworks, furs, promissory notes, loans owed to you, precious metals, electronic and computer equipment, and most farm equipment and livestock. For property without a document of title (ownership document), in almost all states you don't need to do anything but prepare your trust document and list the property on a trust schedule.

You can prepare a written "Assignment of Property" of these kinds of property to your trust by using Form 6 or 7. Form 6 is an assignment form for a one-person trust. It is also for a member of a couple who assigns separately owned property to a shared trust or an AB trust. Form 7 is for a couple to assign shared ownership property to a shared trust or an AB trust.

In most all states, a written notice of assignment for property without documents of title is not required. However, many lawyers use it to provide additional written proof that these items of property have been transferred. Certainly it can't hurt.

> **CAUTION**
>
> **New York residents must prepare a notice of assignment for property without documents of title.** New York law requires you to prepare a separate Notice of Assignment for property without documents of title transferred to your trust (N.Y. Est. Powers and Trusts Law § 7-1.18). Simply listing such property on a trust schedule is not sufficient. If there's no Notice of Assignment, the property is not validly placed in the trust. However, the Notice can simply repeat the listing of such property as used in a trust schedule. (Use Form 6 or 7 from Appendix B or the CD-ROM.)

Property With a Document of Title

For items that have a title document that shows ownership, you will have to prepare new documents to establish that the trust owns the property. This chapter shows you how to accomplish this.

Technically, you transfer your property to yourself, as trustee of your living trust. You'll see how this works when you come to actually preparing title transfer documents below.

Some types of property without a title document may seem to require formal transfer because they are owned in paper form—such as promissory notes or deeds of trust. You can use an assignment form to make absolutely clear that this type of property is transferred to the trust. Find assignment forms (Forms 6 and 7) in Appendix B.

Finally, trademarks, patents, and copyrights have special transfer forms and are discussed below.

> **CAUTION**
>
> **Don't delay.** Formally transferring property to your trust is so vital, I'll give you one more warning, at the risk of redundancy. Failing to transfer property to the trust is the most serious mistake people can make when creating a living trust. If you don't get around to preparing, signing, and filing (where required) these new documents, your trust document will have no effect on what happens to any of your property after your death. Instead, that property will go to the residuary beneficiary named in your backup will. (See Chapter 16.) If you don't have a will, that property will go to certain close relatives, according to state law. Either way, it will probably go through probate.

Transferring Joint Tenancy Property If You Live in a Common Law State or Are Not Married

If you are a couple and live in a common law state—that is, any state except Arizona, California, Idaho, Louisiana, Nevada, New Mexico, Texas, Washington, Wisconsin, or Alaska (if agreed to in writing by both spouses)—transfers of property held in "joint tenancy" or "tenancy by the entirety" often require one more step than do transfers of other shared property. Also, if you are an unmarried couple in any state, you must go through the additional step described here to transfer joint tenancy property into a shared or AB living trust. If your deed or title document lists you as "tenants-in-common owners" (or lists ownership as "tenants in common"), you can safely go ahead and prepare a deed or title document transferring the property from you to the trust. But if you are listed as "joint tenants" or as holding the property "in joint tenancy" or "tenancy by the entirety," you'll likely have to do more work. Also, if your deed simply lists your names and makes no mention of what type of ownership you two share, you need to either take this extra step or check with a local lawyer regarding real estate ownership rules for your state. In some states, any deed to a husband and wife by itself creates a tenancy in the entirety, even if the document does not specifically state that.

Normally, before you transfer joint tenancy property to your trust, you'll need to prepare and execute an additional deed or title document transferring that property from you as "joint tenants" (or tenants by the entirety) to you as "tenants in common, in equal shares." This breaks the joint tenancy. Then you prepare a second deed or document of title transferring the property from you as "tenants in common" into the trust.

Why is this rigmarole necessary? Because some lawyers argue that joint tenancy property transferred to a living trust in common law states (somehow) retains its character as joint tenancy property, even if the trust declares otherwise. Worse, the IRS could argue the same. You do not want any risk of having joint tenancy property in your trust. Joint tenancy property must go to the surviving joint tenant. This may be what you want; indeed, if it is, consider leaving the property in joint tenancy rather than putting it in your trust. (See Chapter 15.) But if you want to leave some of that property to someone other than the other joint tenant(s), or you want to name alternate beneficiaries for your share of the property, you should be sure no one can assert, after you die, that the trust property is, in legal reality, still joint tenancy property.

With an AB trust, you could face even worse problems. If the joint tenancy property had to go to the surviving joint tenant, Trust A might have relatively little money or property in it. Most property of the deceased spouse would be owned outright by the surviving owner—exactly what you don't want.

So, to be absolutely safe, prepare the extra deed or document of title wherever your present ones list you as owning the property as "joint tenants" or as "tenants by the entirety," or simply lists your two names.

Technical Ownership

To transfer ownership of property with a document of title to your living trust, list the new owner(s) as your name, or names, followed by "as trustee(s) for the [your name(s)] Trust." It's common to include the date the trust was signed and notarized; however, including the date is optional, not mandatory.

EXAMPLE 1:

Denis Clifford creates a living trust and transfers real estate to it. On a new real estate deed, he lists the new owner as "Denis Clifford, as trustee of the Denis Clifford Living Trust, dated July 10, 20xx."

EXAMPLE 2:

Denise and Fred Gulekston create an AB disclaimer living trust and transfer their home, a money market account, and a stock brokerage account to the trust. On each title document, they name the new owners as "Denise and Fred Gulekston, as trustees of the Denise and Fred Gulekston Living Trust."

While including the date your living trust was signed and notarized isn't necessary, it may make your documents appear more lawyer-like, and, therefore, more acceptable to banks, title companies, and other financial institutions. It also avoids confusion over subsequent trusts with the same name, if there are any.

Another form of dating a living trust is to include the letters "UTD" (for Under Trust Dated) and then give the date. For example, "Denis Clifford, as trustee of the Denis Clifford Living Trust, UTD July 10, 20xx."

Formally, the property is owned by the trustee(s), not the trust itself. (There's one exception, which affects real estate in Colorado. See "Real Estate," below.)

Property You Acquire Later

If, after your trust has been created, you acquire property you want to hold in trust, you can simply take ownership in the trustee's name directly. There's no reason to buy the property in your personal name and then transfer it to you as trustee.

EXAMPLE:

Mr. and Mrs. Siqueiros buy a new house. They take title in their names, listing the new owners as "Juan and Luisa Siqueiros, as trustees of The Juan and Luisa Siqueiros Living Trust, dated September 20, 20xx."

Problems With Financial Institutions

I've received a few reports, from readers of other Nolo books and from lawyers, that some banks, mutual funds, or other financial institutions (usually in more remote parts of the country) have balked at reregistering trust property in the trustee's name. People have been told, "You can't do that. Only our trust department does that," or "You need a federal tax ID number."

If this happens to you, simply insist that it is absolutely legal, and essential, for you to reregister your property in the trustee's name, and that this can be done without a new taxpayer ID. If you have to, go higher up in the institution's bureaucracy until you find someone who understands what the law is now, not what it may have been 30 years ago (when a federal tax ID number was required).

Certifications of Trust

A certification of trust, sometimes called an "abstract of trust," is a kind of shorthand version of the trust document. You may find one useful when actually transferring property to your trust. County records offices, banks, or other institutions may require proof that the trust exists. The purpose of a certification of trust is to establish that the trust exists, without revealing the heart of it—that is, what property is in it and who will inherit. Some people do not want to reveal this core information to institutions that require proof of the trust's existence, so they submit a certification of trust rather than a copy of the entire trust.

In most states, there's no one set form for a certification of trust. Ask first, to see what's wanted. Some institutions accept a copy of the first and last (signature) pages of the trust. Another method is simply to remove the property and beneficiaries provisions from a copy of the trust and call what's left an abstract. You do not need to resign or renotarize this document. A photocopy of the original signature(s) and notarization suffices. Or, you can sign a statement swearing you created the trust. However a certification of trust is prepared, the following points are usually shown:

- that the trust was created (the first page of the trust document will do)
- who the original trustees are
- the date the trust was created (the date the trust document was signed)
- what the trustees' powers are (this can be quite a bit of verbiage)
- the signature of the grantor(s), and
- the notarization of the trust document.

You will find an example of a general form for a certification of trust on the next page. The signature and notarization are simply copies from the original trust.

CAUTION

Some states have their own certification forms. The states listed below have adopted statutes that certain basic information be included in a certification of trust. (More legislative tinkering, more work for lawyers.) If you live in one of these states, do not use or adapt the general form shown on the next pages. You can always choose not to bother with a certification and submit a copy of the entire trust, or you can do any of the following instead:

- Check with the financial institution involved to see what they'll accept.
- Look up your state's law and get the precise form for your state.
- See a lawyer to get your state's form.

If you want to look up your state's statute, go to www.nolo. com and click on the site map to access the legal research section. You can also find it in a local law library.

State	Statute Sections on Certification of Trust
Alaska	Alaska Stat. § 13.36.079
Arkansas	Ark. Code Ann. § 28-73-1013
California	Cal. Prob. Code § 18100.5
Delaware	Del. Code Ann. § 3591
District of Columbia	D. C. Code Ann. § 19-1310.13
Idaho	Idaho Code § 68-115
Indiana	Ind. Code Ann. § 30-4-4-5
Iowa	Iowa Code § 633.4604
Kansas	Kan. Stat. § 58a-1013
Maine	Maine Rev. Stat. Ann.18-B § 1013
Michigan	Mich. Comp. Laws Ann. § 565.432
Minnesota	Minn. Stat. Ann. § 501B.56
Mississippi	Miss. Code Ann. § 91-9-7
Missouri	Mo. Rev. Stat. § 456.10-1013
Nevada	Nev. Rev. Stat. Ann. § 164.410
New Hampshire	N.H. Rev. Stat. Ann. § 564-A:7
New Mexico	N.M. Stat. Ann. § 46A-10-1013
North Carolina	N.C. Stat. Ann. § 36C-10-1013
North Dakota	N.D. Cent. Code § 59-18-13
Ohio	Ohio Rev. Code § 5301.01
Oklahoma	Okla. Stat. tit. 60, § 175.6
Oregon	Or. Rev. Stat. § 128.236
Rhode Island	R.I. Gen. Laws § 34-4-27
South Carolina	S.C. Code § 62-7-1013
South Dakota	S.D. Codified Laws § 55-4-42
Texas	Texas Property Code § 114.086
Utah	Utah Code Ann. 75-7-1013
Virginia	Va. Code Ann. § 55-550.13
West Virginia	W. Va. Code § 36-1-4a
Wyoming	Wyo. Statutes Ann. § 4-10-1014

Certification of Trust
The Norine and Paul Lombardi
Declaration and Instrument of Trust

I. Trust Name

This trust shall be known as The Norine and Paul Lombardi Trust.

II. Trust Property

(A) Norine and Paul Lombardi, wife and husband, called the "grantors" or the "trustees," declare that they have set aside and hold in The Norine and Paul Lombardi Trust all their interest in that property listed in attached Schedules A and B. The trust property shall be used for the benefit of the trust beneficiaries, and shall be administered and distributed by the trustees in accordance with this trust document.

...

IX. Trustee's Powers and Duties

(A) Powers Under State Law

To carry out the provisions of this Declaration of Trust and to manage the trust property of The Norine and Paul Lombardi Living Trust, The Marital Life Estate Trust, and The Surviving Spouse's Trust, and any child's trust created under this Declaration of Trust, the trustee shall have all authority and power allowed or conferred under New York law, subject to the trustee's fiduciary duty to the grantors and the beneficiaries.

(B) Specified Powers

The trustee's powers include, but are not limited to:

1. The power to sell trust property, and to borrow money and to encumber property, specifically including trust real estate, by mortgage, deed of trust, or other method.

2. The power to manage trust real estate as if the trustee were the absolute owner of it, including the power to lease (even if the lease term may extend beyond the period of any trust) or grant options to lease the property, to make repairs or alterations, and to insure against loss.

3. The power to sell or grant options for the sale or exchange of any trust property, including stocks, bonds, debentures, and any other form of security or security account, at public or private sale for cash or on credit.

4. The power to invest trust property in property of any kind, including but not limited to bonds, debentures, notes, mortgages, and stocks.

5. The power to receive additional property from any source and add to any trust created by this Declaration of Trust.

6. The power to employ and pay reasonable fees to accountants, lawyers, or investment experts for information or advice relating to the trust.

7. The power to deposit and hold trust funds in both interest-bearing and non-interest-bearing accounts.

8. The power to deposit funds in bank or other accounts uninsured by FDIC coverage.

9. The power to enter into electronic fund transfer or safe deposit arrangements with financial institutions.

10. The power to continue any business of either grantor.

11. The power to institute or defend legal actions concerning the trust or the grantors' affairs.

12. The power to execute any documents necessary to administer any trust created in this Declaration of Trust.

13. The power to diversify investments, including authority to decide that some or all of the trust property need not produce income.

. . . .

Certification by Grantors

We certify that we have read this Declaration of Trust and that it correctly states the terms and conditions under which the trust property is to be held, managed, and disposed of by the trustee, and we approve the Declaration of Trust.

Dated: July 6, 20xx

Norine Lombardi
Norine Lombardi

Paul Lombardi
Paul Lombardi
Grantors and Trustees

State of New York

County of Dutchess

On July 6, 20xx, before me, _____Ilana Weinstock_____, a notary public for the State of New York, personally appeared Norine Lombardi and Paul Lombardi, known to me to be, or proved to me on the basis of satisfactory evidence, to be the trustees and grantors of the trust created by the above Declaration of Trust, and to be the persons whose names are subscribed to the Declaration of Trust, and acknowledged that they executed it as grantors and trustees.

IN WITNESS WHEREOF, I have set my hand and affixed my official seal the day and year first above written.

/s/ _____*Ilana Weinstock*_____
NOTARY PUBLIC

Real Estate

The term "real estate" includes land, houses, condominiums, cooperatives, many time-shares, and any other interest in what lawyers call "real property." To transfer title of a piece of real estate to a living trust, you prepare and sign a deed listing the trustee or trustees of the trust as the new owner. You can fill out the new deed yourself; it's not difficult. Then you sign the deed in front of a notary public and record a copy of it with the county land records office. You don't have to prepare a second document transferring your mortgage; that liability follows the asset, the real estate. Nor do you need to notify the mortgage holder (the bank) of the transfer. (See Chapter 3.)

Co-op apartments. If you own a co-op apartment, you can't simply use a deed to transfer your shares in the co-op. You will have to check the co-op corporation's rules to see if the transfer is allowed. Some co-ops resist such transfers because they are afraid a living trust isn't a proper shareholder in the corporation. You can probably overcome any resistance you encounter by reminding the powers that be that, for all practical purposes, you and the trust are the same—you have the same tax identification number, for example.

Mobile or manufactured homes. Whether or not a mobile home is treated as real estate depends upon the law of the state where it is located, and, in some states, whether it is permanently affixed to land or not. You'll have to check with the state agency that handles mobile home registrations to learn how to transfer title to your trust.

Time-shares. A time-share is an ownership interest in a vacation property. Each owner has the right to exclusive use of the property for set time periods. Ownership can be held by real estate deed, lease, or contract, depending on your state's law. If a deed is used, the time-share must be transferred to your living trust by a deed. If ownership is by lease or contract, you can use a simple assignment form.

Colorado Real Estate

If you want to transfer Colorado real estate to your living trust, transfer title into the name of the trust itself, not the trustee. Although Colorado law does not mandate that real estate be held in the trust's name, a state statute encourages it, and it is becoming the expected way to proceed. (Colo. Rev. Stat. § 38-30-108.5.)

Preparing the Deed

First, locate your existing deed. Then get a deed form in common use in the state where the real estate is located. Many office supply stores carry deed forms. The technical requirements for real estate deed forms vary from state to state, so it is essential that you get one from the appropriate state.

Finding Deed Forms and Instructions

If you're in California, you can find deed forms and instructions for filling them out in *Deeds for California Real Estate*, by Mary Randolph (Nolo). Much of the book's information is valid in other states as well, but it's best to use a deed form that's in common use in your area.

In many places, you can find blank deed forms in office supply stores. If you can't find a deed in a local store, go online or call an office supply store in a nearby city—deed forms are the same throughout a state. Or go to a local law library; look for books on "real property" that have deed forms you can photocopy. Finally, you could ask a local title company for deed forms, especially if you've used that company before.

Except in Texas, you can use either a quitclaim or warranty deed form. (Technically, a quitclaim deed doesn't make the promises of full and clear ownership that a grant or warranty deed does.) In Texas, it appears that a warranty deed is required. In other states you can use any deed form; after all, you are merely transferring the property from yourself under one hat to yourself under another.

Although deed forms vary somewhat, they all require the same basic information. Using a typewriter or word processor, fill out your deed like the sample shown below. Type in:

- **The recording information, at the top left of the document.**
- **The date.**
- **The current owners' names.** If you are the sole owner, or if you and someone else co-own the property and you are transferring just your share, only your name goes here. If you are transferring only a portion of ownership, you can specify what portion (for example, "⅓ ownership of …" or simply state "all his/her interest in …"). If you and your spouse own the property together and are transferring it to a shared marital trust or an AB trust, type in both of your names. Use exactly the same form of your name as is used on the deed that transferred the property to you and you used in your living trust document.

As you can see from the sample completed document, you may have to type in the correct ending of some printed words, like "part…." If you are a couple, you add "ies" to make this "parties." If you are a single person, you add a "y" to make it "party."

If Your Name Has Changed

If your name has changed since you bought real estate, how do you sign the transfer deed? Simply sign using both names: the name you used when you originally bought the property and the name you use now.

- **The new owner's name.** Fill in the trustee's name or trustees' names, and add the date of notarization of the trust if you wish. (See "Technical Ownership," above.) Remember that for Colorado real estate, the new owner is the trust, not the trustee.
- **The "legal description" of the property.** This is usually something like, "From a point 12 degrees South of… Map 4, Book 6," etc. Copy the description exactly as it appears on the previous deed.

Depending on the form you use, you may need to cross out inappropriate printed language, such as words stating the transfer is "forever," or that the property is also transferred to the second party's (here, the trust's) "assigns, etc."

By the way, if you see "SS" on the previous deed form—some readers have, and were baffled by it—it means "Solemnly Sworn" (not Social Security).

After everything is filled in, sign and date the deed in front of a notary public for the state in which the property is located. Everyone listed as a current owner who is transferring his or her interest in the property to the trust must sign the deed.

On the next page is an example of a quitclaim deed that could be used to transfer a home to a living trust.

Out-of-State Real Estate

If you own real estate located in another state, you face a few problems transferring that property to your trust:

- Tracking down the deed form for that state, and getting a blank deed. Often the easiest way to get the correct deed is to call a title company in the state where the real estate is located.
- Making sure your notarization of the deed is acceptable in the other state. Generally, deeds can be notarized in the state you live in, even for out-of-state real estate.
- Learning whether any other paperwork is required for a valid transfer. One example of this is California's Preliminary Change of Title Report, discussed in "California Property Taxes," below.
- Properly recording the deed.

SEE AN EXPERT

Transferring out-of-state real estate. Transferring out-of-state real estate located in the United States. can be a real hassle. If it becomes one for you, you might decide to hire a lawyer to do just this one task.

Recording requested by

Jane and Gordon McCann
47 Greene Street
Chicago, Illinois, 606xx

and when recorded mail
this deed and tax statements to

Jane and Gordon McCann
47 Greene Street
Chicago, Illinois, 606xx

For recorder's use

Quitclaim Deed

~~For valuable consideration, receipt of which is hereby acknowleged,~~ _Jane and Gordon McCann_ _____ hereby quitclaim(s) to

Jane and Gordon McCann, as trustees of the Jane and Godon McCann Living Trust ,

the following real property in the City of _Chicago_ , County of

Cook , _Illinois_ :

Commonly known as 47 Greene Street, and more particularly described as:

[Legal description, exactly as given in previous deed]

Date: _4/21/xx_ _____   _Jane McCann_

Date: _4/21/xx_ _____   _Gordon McCann_

Date: _____

State of _Illinois_ _____ }

County of _Cook_ _____

On _____, before me, _____

_____, a notary public in and for said state, personally appeared

_____,

personally known to me (or proved to me on the basis of satisfactory evidence) to be the person(s) whose name(s) is/are subscribed to the within instrument, and acknowledged to me that he/she/they executed the same in his/her/their authorized capacity(ies) and that by his/her/their signature(s) on the instrument the person(s), or entity upon behalf of which the person(s) acted, executed the instrument.

_____   [SEAL]
Signature of Notary

Recording the Deed

After the deed is signed and notarized, you must "record" it—that is, put a copy of the notarized deed on file in the county office that keeps local property records. Depending on the state, the land records office is called the county recorder's office, land registry office, or county clerk's office.

Just take the original, signed deed to the land records office. (You can probably mail it in, if you wish. Call the land records office to find out the correct procedure.) For a small fee, a clerk will make a copy and put it in the public records. You'll get your original back, stamped with a reference number to show where the copy can be found in the public records.

Transfer Taxes

Very rarely, if ever, will you have to pay a state or local transfer tax when you transfer real estate to a revocable living trust. Most real estate transfer taxes are based on the sale price of the property and do not apply when no money changes hands. Others specifically exempt transfers where the real owners don't change—as is the case when you transfer property to a revocable living trust you control.

To be safe, before you record your deed, get information on any possible transfer tax from the county tax assessor, county recorder, or state tax officials.

> ! **CAUTION**
>
> **Check with your county recorder.** Before you record your deed, check with your County Recorder's office to see if there are any local requirements that must be included on that deed. For instance, some California County Recorder's offices now require that a specific statute be cited and summarized on the deed form to establish that a deed transferring property to a living trust is exempt from transfer tax. For example: "The undersigned grantors declare that the transfer is to a living trust for the benefit of the grantors and is not pursuant to a sale and is exempt from the documentary transfer tax pursuant to Revenue and Taxation Code Section 11911."

California Property Taxes

In California, transferring real estate to a revocable living trust does not trigger a reassessment for property tax purposes. Similarly, transfers from the trustee back to the original owner don't cause reassessments. (Cal. Rev. & Tax. Code § 62(d).) You will, however, have to file a form called a Preliminary Change of Title Report with the county tax assessor. If you do, you sign this form with your name, as trustee for your trust.

EXAMPLE: Erin Quake signs a Preliminary Change of Title Report as "Erin Quake, Trustee, the Erin Quake Living Trust dated November 7, 20xx."

Due-on-Sale Mortgage Clauses

Many mortgages contain a clause that allows the bank to call ("accelerate") the loan—that is, demand that you pay the whole thing off immediately—if you transfer the mortgaged property. Fortunately, in most instances lenders are forbidden by federal law to invoke a due-on-sale clause when property is transferred to a living trust. The lender can't call the loan if the borrower is a trust beneficiary and the transfer is "unrelated to occupancy" of the premises. (Garn-St. Germain Act, 12 U.S.C. §§ 1464, 1701.) Also, it's doubtful that the transfer of any real estate to your trust is the type of transfer that would legally permit a bank to call a loan. (See Chapter 3.)

Insurance

Your insurance policies should not be changed simply because your home has been placed in your living trust. You do not need to notify your insurance company (or any title company) of the transfer of real estate property. (Why disturb a bureaucracy if you don't have to?)

Transferring Deeds of Trust

One type of real estate asset is called a "deed of trust." It is similar to a mortgage. If you lend money to someone, you may receive a deed of trust, making real estate collateral for a loan—that is, if the borrower defaults, you can foreclose on the real estate to collect what's owed you. Because a deed of trust is an interest in real estate, it should be recorded.

To transfer a deed of trust to your living trust, you can prepare a "Notice of Assignment" transferring it from you to your trust. You then record that document. Use Form 6 or 7 in Appendix B.

Real Estate Outside the United States

There is no reason to transfer foreign real estate to a U.S. living trust. That property wouldn't go through U.S. probate anyway, and U.S. courts don't have authority to order transfer of real estate in another country. Each country has its own rules and laws regarding real estate. (When I lived in Ireland, I had to visit a lawyer—a "solicitor"—and sign a fancy legal document to rent an apartment.)

SEE AN EXPERT

Transferring foreign real estate. If you own property in another country, consider hiring someone in that other country to learn what you need to do. After all, if you own real estate in a foreign country, that's fortunate, so spending a little money to learn how to transfer that property after your death isn't a disaster.

Bank Accounts and Safe Deposit Boxes

It should be simple to reregister ownership of a bank account in your name(s) as trustee(s) of your living trust or open a new account in the trustee's name. Just ask the bank what paperwork you need to submit.

The bank will be concerned with the authority granted to the trustees to act on behalf of the trust. Depending on the kind of account, the bank may want to know whether the trustees have the power to borrow money, put funds in a non-interest-bearing account, or engage in electronic transfers. (The trust forms in this book include all these powers.)

To verify your authority, the bank may want to see a copy of your trust document or a certification of trust, or it may have you fill out its own form.

If you want to transfer title to a safe deposit box to your trust, you'll have to reregister its ownership, too. The bank will have a form for you to fill out.

Estate planning note. Instead of transferring a bank account to a living trust, you may want to turn the account into a pay-on-death account. It's another, even easier, way to avoid probate of the money in the account. (See Chapter 15.)

Securities

How you transfer stocks, bonds, mutual funds, and other securities to your living trust depends on how you hold them.

Brokerage Accounts

If, like most people, you hold your stocks, bonds, or other securities in a brokerage account, either change the account to the trustee's name or open a new account in the trustee's name. Simply ask your broker for instructions. The brokerage company may have a straightforward form that you can fill out, giving information about the trustees and their authority.

Tell them you want the account to keep the same account number as when it was in your name. If they don't want to, insist (politely). If they still refuse, you've got a technical problem, because the account number listed in your trust document isn't the same as the new number of that account in the trustee's name. You'd have to revise a trust schedule to get the new account number in it. So, you can see why you want to insist the account keep your original number.

If the brokerage company doesn't have its own form, you will probably need to send the broker:

- a copy of the trust document or certification of trust, and
- a letter instructing the holder to transfer the brokerage account to the trustee's name or open a new account in the trustee's name.

After you've submitted your request, get written confirmation that the account's ownership has in fact been put in the trustee's name.

Stock Certificates

If you have the actual stock certificates or bonds in your possession—most people don't—you must get new certificates issued, showing the trustee as owner. Ask your broker for help. If the broker is unwilling or unable to help, write to the "transfer agent" of the corporation that issued the stock. You can get the address from your broker or the investor relations office of the corporation. The transfer agent will give you simple instructions.

You will probably have to send in:

- your certificates or bonds
- a form called a "stock or bond power," which you must fill out and sign
- a copy of the trust document or a "certification of trust," showing your notarized signature, and
- a letter requesting that the certificates be reissued in the trustee's name.

The stock or bond power may be printed on the back of the certificates; if not, you can probably find a copy at an office supply store.

Government Bonds

To transfer U.S. government bonds, you need to complete Form PD 1851 and mail it to the U.S. Treasury. You can get the form through your stockbroker if you have one, or you can contact the local Federal Reserve Bank. Also, local banks may have the necessary transfer forms.

Mutual Fund Accounts

Mutual funds should be reregistered in the name of the trustee of your living trust by communicating with the company and meeting its requirements. You'll probably just need to send a letter of instructions (or a form the company provides) and a copy of the trust document.

Stock Options

You can transfer publicly traded stock options by using a Notice of Assignment (Form 6 or 7 in Appendix B). Private, employee stock options often cannot be transferred to a living trust. (See Chapter 6.)

Vehicles, Boats, and Planes

Most people don't transfer vehicles such as cars or trailers to a living trust, for reasons discussed in Chapter 6. (A mobile home may be considered real estate rather than a vehicle. See "Real Estate," above.)

If you want to put a vehicle in trust, you must fill out a change of ownership document and have title to the vehicle reissued in the trustee's name. The title certificate to your vehicle may contain instructions. If you have questions, call your state's motor vehicles department.

Transferring a large boat to your living trust requires you to reregister title with the Coast Guard. The paperwork is handled by the U.S. Department of Transportation's National Vessel Documentation Center (800-799-8362). The forms and information needed to transfer a boat into a trust are contained in the "Exchange Packet," available without charge. You need to complete Form CG-1340 (a "Bill of Sale") and Form CG-1258 and pay the appropriate fee.

To transfer larger, motorized boats registered with a state agency, you must prepare a new state registration form, listing the trust—that is, you as trustee—as the new owner. Transferring small boats, such as rowboats or canoes, can be done simply by listing them on a trust schedule, and, if you wish, by preparing a Notice of Assignment for them.

If you own an airplane, you must contact the FAA to obtain a new certificate of registration in the trustee's name.

Business Interests

How you transfer small business interests to your living trust depends on the way the business is owned.

Trademarks and Service Marks

If you have a registered trademark or service mark, you must reregister ownership in the name of the trustee of the living trust. For sample forms, see *Trademark: Legal Care for Your Business & Product Name*, by Stephen Elias (Nolo).

Sole Proprietorships

An unincorporated business that you own by yourself is the easiest to transfer to a trust. First, you list the business, by name, as an item of property on a trust schedule—for example, "De Tach Restaurant." That transfers the name and whatever customer goodwill that goes with it, to your living trust.

Because you own the business assets in your own name (a sole proprietorship, unlike a corporation, is not an independent entity that can own property), you transfer them to your living trust like you would any other valuable property. For many businesses, this simply means listing those business assets on the appropriate trust schedule—for example, "… all property and assets used in the grantor's business, Jim Dimes Hardware." Because there is no ownership document for the business, nothing further is required.

Solely Owned Corporations

If you own all the stock of a corporation, you shouldn't have any problem transferring it to your living trust. Follow these steps:

Step 1. Fill out the stock transfer section on the back of the stock certificate.

Step 2. Mark the certificate "canceled" and place it in your corporate records book.

Step 3. Reissue a new certificate in the name of the trustee of the living trust.

Step 4. Show the cancellation of the old certificate and the issuance of the new certificate on the stock ledger pages in your corporate records book.

Closely Held Corporations and Limited Liability Companies

Normally, you can transfer your shares in a closely held corporation or interest in a limited liability company (LLC) to your living trust by following corporate bylaws or an LLC operating agreement and having the ownership document reissued in the name of the trustee of the trust. But first, check the corporation's bylaws and articles of incorporation, as well as any separate shareholders' agreements or the LLC operating agreement, to see if there are any restrictions on such transfers. If an agreement limits or forbids transfers, it will have to be changed before you can put your shares in your living trust.

Partnership Interests

To transfer your partnership interest to your living trust, you must notify your business partners and modify the partnership agreement to show that your partnership interest is now owned by the trustee of your living trust. If there is a partnership certificate, it must be changed to substitute the trustee as owner of your share.

RESOURCE

Revising a partnership agreement. You can revise your partnership agreement by using *Form a Partnership*, by Denis Clifford and Ralph Warner (Nolo).

Limited Partnerships

Limited partnerships are a form of investment, governed by securities laws. Contact the partnership's general partner to find out what paperwork is necessary to transfer your interest to a living trust.

Copyrights

If you want to transfer your interest in a copyright to your living trust, list the copyright on a trust schedule. Then sign and file, with the U.S. Copyright Office, a document transferring all your rights in the copyright to the trustee of the living trust. Sample transfer forms are in *The Copyright Handbook*, by Stephen Fishman (Nolo).

Patents

If you own a patent and want to transfer it to your living trust, you should prepare a document called an "assignment" and record it with the U.S. Patent and Trademark Office in Washington, DC. There is a small fee for recording. Assignment forms and instructions are in *Patent It Yourself*, by David Pressman (Nolo).

Royalties

Your rights to receive royalties—from sales of a book, copies of photos, residuals for TV ads, whatever—can be transferred to your trust, with technical ownership held by the trustee. It's best to transfer any royalty rights by preparing an Assignment of Property (Form 6 or 7), although legally, just listing these rights on a trust schedule would suffice. But with an assignment form, you can clearly specify, in a separate, distinct document, exactly what royalty rights are transferred to the trust.

It is sensible to give a copy of the assignment form to whatever company pays you the royalty rights. Let them know, of course, that they are to keep making payments to you while you live. It can help get these payments to your beneficiaries without great hassles if you give the company some warning that your royalty rights will be transferred by your successor trustee out of your living trust when you die.

Copying, Storing, and Registering Your Trust Document

After you've completed your living trust and signed all documents necessary to transfer property to the trust, you're almost done. There are just a couple of minor tasks left to accomplish.

Making Copies

You will probably need some copies of your completed trust document. Some lawyers advise stamping or writing the word "COPY" on each duplicate, so none can ever be mistaken for an original. While you can certainly do this, it seems a bit overcautious to me. Photocopies of your original trust are different from the original—your signature is not in ink on the copy, nor is the notary stamp original. But then again, that's not always so easy to determine these days, with better and better quality photocopying, so if you want maximum security, go ahead and write or stamp "COPY" on each copy, or even on each page of each copy.

You may well need copies to transfer certain types of property—stocks, for example—to your trust. (See Chapter 11.) If a broker, bank, or other institution wants to see your trust document, use a photocopy of the original.

You may want to give a copy of your trust document to your successor trustee so that person knows what is in your trust well in advance of actually serving as trustee. Keep the original where your successor trustee can readily find it.

Finally, you should instruct your successor trustee to give copies after your death to any custodian you named for trust property inherited by a young beneficiary.

There's no requirement that you give copies to any beneficiaries. Indeed, there can be drawbacks to this. If you later revoke or amend the trust but don't collect all the old copies, there will be outdated copies of your trust document floating around. Someone who is given less (or nothing) in the new document may cause trouble later on. Also, the property in the trust may substantially change later if the trustee must dip into or even deplete the trust because of a grantor's illness or other unexpected expenses. Why set up expectations that may not be fulfilled even with the best of intentions?

On the other hand, if you doubt the trust property will change much, and if there are only a few beneficiaries and you trust them all—as is true for many families—why not let your beneficiaries know now what they'll receive? What's wrong with revealing your generosity?

In addition, some states require that, when a successor trustee takes over, he or she provide information about the trust to all beneficiaries. Even when this is not legally required, it's wise policy. (See Chapter 14.)

> **CAUTION**
>
> **Sign only one trust document.** It is important not to prepare another "original" document—that is, to sign a second copy of your living trust form. This is because each trust document you actually sign becomes, legally, a distinct trust document (even if it isn't notarized). If you revoke or change one original, that does not revoke or change other originals. Clearly, you don't want any duplicate original trust documents floating around.

Storing the Trust Document

Store your living trust document where you keep other important papers, such as your financial records, will, or durable power of attorney. A fireproof box in your home or office is fine. If you want to be extra careful, a safe deposit box is a good choice, but only if your successor trustee has access to it. Many people keep their living trust document in a locked drawer in a home desk or file cabinet. (After all, it's very unlikely anyone would steal a trust document, since it has no value to anyone but you. But this doesn't deal with the risk of fire or other disaster.)

Make sure your successor trustee (or spouse, if you made a basic shared living trust or an AB trust) knows where the original trust document is and can get hold of it soon after your death or incapacity. The new trustee will need it to manage or distribute trust property. (The new trustee's responsibilities are discussed in Chapter 14.)

Registering the Trust

States That Provide for Registration of Living Trusts		
Alaska	Idaho	Nebraska*
Colorado**	Maine	North Dakota
Florida*	Michigan	Ohio***
Hawaii	Missouri*	

* Not mandatory.

** Registration of a revocable living trust not required until the grantor's death; no registration required if all trust property is distributed to the beneficiaries then.

*** If a trust holds real estate, successor trustee must file an affidavit in the county where real estate is located.

Some states require that the trustee of a trust register the trust with the local court. But there are no legal consequences or penalties if you don't, which, in effect, means this is an optional requirement. (The only exception is that if a court demands that a trustee register a trust, and the trustee refuses, the trustee can be removed.)

If you register your trust, it is possible for others to have access to certain information about the trust. But only minimal information need be made public through registration—the name of the grantor, the date of the trust—not the key terms of the trust, such as the property in it, and who are the beneficiaries.

Registration of a living trust doesn't give the court any power over the administration of the trust, unless there's a dispute. Registration serves to give the court jurisdiction over any disputes involving the trust—for example, if after your death a beneficiary wants to object to the way your successor trustee distributed the trust property. But if you don't register your trust, the result is the same: The court still has jurisdiction if a disgruntled relative or creditor files suit.

To register a revocable living trust, the trustee must file a statement with the court where the trustee resides or keeps trust records. The statement must include at least the following:

- the name(s) of the grantor(s)
- the name(s) of the original trustee(s)
- an acknowledgment of the trusteeship (that is, a written acceptance by the trustees of their role), and
- the date of the trust document.

A trust can be registered in only one state at a time.

Living With Your Living Trust

This chapter discusses what you need to know after you have established your living trust, including how to change your trust document if your circumstances change.

By now, you know that as a day-to-day, practical matter, it makes no difference that your property is now owned by your revocable living trust. You have no special paperwork to prepare, tax forms to file, or other duties to perform as the trustee of your own revocable living trust. Nor do you have any legal responsibilities to any of the beneficiaries you named in the trust document. They have no rights over any trust property while you are alive.

Some lawyers urge you to have your trust reviewed and updated by a lawyer every year. There's no need for this. Indeed, there's no need for you to review your trust yourself every year. Review your trust if something major has changed, or you want to make a major change. But for many, probably most, people who create a living trust, there's very little or no change that affects the trust from the time they create it to the time it goes into effect at their death.

Adding Property to Your Living Trust

The living trust forms in this book specifically give you the right to add property to your trust. If you acquire valuable items of property after you create your living trust, you should promptly add them to the trust so that they won't have to go through probate at your death.

There are four steps to adding property to your trust:

Step 1. Type a revised Property Schedule A, B, or C of your trust document, adding the new property. (If you made an individual trust, you have only one schedule, Schedule A. If you and your spouse made a basic shared living trust or an AB trust, Schedule A lists your co-owned property, Schedule B lists the wife's separate property, if any, and Schedule C lists the husband's separate property, if any.)

Step 2. Remove the old schedule from your trust document and attach the new one.

Step 3. Place title of the property in the trustee's name. If, acting in your capacity as trustee, you originally purchased the property in the trustee's name, you don't need to bother about this, because, obviously, you've already done it. But if you acquire the property in your own name—for example, an inheritance—you need to prepare the appropriate title document. (See Chapter 11.)

EXAMPLE:

Rose and Michael prepare an AB trust. Later on, they buy a new house, and they want it to be in their living trust. So, on the deed, they take title in the name of "Rose Morris and Michael Morris, trustees of the Rose Morris and Michael Morris Living Trust, dated January 13, 20xx." They then type a revised Schedule A (which lists shared property) of their trust document and replace the old Schedule A.

Step 4. Amend the trust document if you need to name a beneficiary for the new property. You won't need to amend the trust document if you've left all your trust property to one person or if you want the property to go to your residuary beneficiary.

EXAMPLE:

Mercedes adds a new money market account to her living trust. She wants to leave this account to her brother, Neil, who is not her residuary beneficiary. Mercedes must prepare an amendment of her trust, listing Neil as the beneficiary for this new property.

Usually, you won't need to amend the trust document of an AB trust if you put new property in the trust. That property will be subject to the trust provisions creating the AB trust. Only if you want the new property to go to someone other than Trust A, for the benefit of your spouse and then to your final beneficiaries, do you need to amend the trust.

Selling or Giving Away Trust Property

You have complete control over the property you have transferred to the living trust. If you want to sell or give away any of it, go ahead, using your authority as trustee. This means you (or you and your spouse, if you made a basic shared marital trust or either type of AB trust) sign ownership or transfer documents (the deed, bill of sale, or other document) in your capacity as trustee(s) of the living trust.

EXAMPLE:

Martin transfers ownership of his house to his living trust, but later decides to sell it. He transfers the house to the buyer by signing the new deed as "Martin Owens, trustee of the Martin Owens Living Trust dated June 18, 20xx."

If you and your spouse made a basic shared living trust or either type of AB trust, either trustee (spouse) has authority over shared-ownership trust property. That means that either spouse can sell or give away any of the shared trust property. However, one spouse cannot control what was the separate property of the other spouse before it was transferred to the trust. Also, even for shared property, both spouses will probably have to consent to transfer real estate out of the living trust. Especially in community property states, buyers and title insurance companies usually insist on both spouses' signatures on transfer documents.

If for any reason you want to take property out of the trust but keep ownership of it, you can transfer the property back to yourself. So if Martin, in the previous example, wanted to take his house out of his living trust but keep ownership in his own name, he would make the deed out from "The Martin Owens Living Trust dated June 18, 20xx, Martin Owens, trustee" to "Martin Owens." He would sign the deed "Martin Owens, trustee of the Martin Owens Living Trust dated June 18, 20xx."

Unless this change will be for a brief period (for example, only for the time necessary to obtain refinancing of your home loan), you should modify the property schedule of your trust document to reflect the change. If you don't, the schedules will still show that the property is owned by the trust. Legally, the trust no longer owns it, and the discrepancy could be confusing to the people who carry out your wishes after your death.

EXAMPLE:

Wendy and Brian, a married couple, made a basic shared living trust several years ago. Wendy transferred a valuable antique dresser, which she inherited from her grandfather before she was married, to the living trust. It's listed on Schedule B of the trust document. The trust document provides that the dresser will go to her son at her death. But she's changed her mind and decided while she's alive to give the dresser to her daughter.

After Wendy gives the dresser to her daughter, she prepares two documents. First, she prepares a new Schedule B, deleting the dresser from the list of property, and replacing the old Schedule B attached to her trust document. Second, she prepares a trust amendment, stating that the paragraph that left the dresser to her son is no longer in effect.

When to Amend Your Living Trust Document

One of the most attractive features of a revocable living trust is its flexibility: You can change its terms, or end it altogether, at any time. This section discusses several events that should be red flags alerting you that you may need to amend your living trust.

In most circumstances, you will want to amend your living trust document, not revoke it. At first glance, it might seem easier to revoke it and start again, as is usually done with a will. But if you revoke your living trust and create another one, you must transfer all the trust property out of the old living trust and into the new one. This means preparing new documents of title and all the other paperwork required to transfer property to your original trust. ("Revoking Your Living Trust," below, discusses when it is advisable to revoke your living trust and make another.)

As explained above, you may need to amend your trust document if you sell or give away property from your trust. Here are some other events that normally require amendment of a trust.

You Marry or Have a Child

If you get married or have a child, you'll almost certainly want to amend your trust document to provide for your new spouse or offspring. And remember that your spouse or minor child may be entitled, under state law, to a certain portion of your property. (See Chapter 8.)

You Move to Another State

Although your living trust is still valid if you move to another state, you may want to change your living trust in response to your new state's laws. Here are several aspects of your trust, and overall estate plan, that may be affected by a move to a new state.

Registering Your Trust

Your new state may authorize you to register your living trust document with a state agency or court. (See "Registering the Trust," in Chapter 12.)

Marital Property Laws: Who Owns What

If you are married and move from a common law state to California, Idaho, Washington, or Wisconsin, property you acquired during marriage may become "quasi-community property," and so owned by both spouses, however it was originally owned. Wisconsin has a similar rule. See "Marital Property Laws" in Chapter 6. You'll need to review your property disposition to make sure it complies with your new state's laws.

Property Management for Young Beneficiaries

Your state's law determines the choices you have when it comes to arranging for property management for young trust beneficiaries. In all states, you can create a child's trust for any beneficiary who might inherit trust property before he or she is 35. And in all states but South Carolina and Vermont, you can appoint an adult custodian to manage the child's property. The age at which the child receives the property outright can vary from state to state, between the ages of 18 to 25. (See Chapter 9.)

If you made a gift using your old state's version of the Uniform Transfers to Minors Act (UTMA) and you move to South Carolina or Vermont, you may need to amend your trust, deleting the UTMA gift and creating a child's trust for it. Or, if you move to a state that has a lower UTMA age for turning over the property to the minor, you'll have to amend your trust to set the new age for the child to receive the gift. (See Chapter 9.)

Rights of a Surviving Spouse to Inherit

Different states entitle surviving spouses to different shares of a deceased spouse's estate. If you prepare a shared basic living trust and you plan to leave at least one-half of your total estate to your spouse, you don't have to worry about this. And this doesn't apply to an AB trust. But if you want to leave your spouse less than one half, and you're concerned that your spouse might challenge your estate plan and demand the "statutory share" of your property after your death, you'll need to know what your new state's laws allow. (See "Disinheritance" in Chapter 8.)

State Inheritance Taxes

If you move to a new state, that state's laws, including its law on inheritance taxes, will govern all your property, except for out-of-state real estate. (See Chapter 15.)

You Change Your Name

If you legally change your name, for whatever reason—marriage, divorce, desire for a new identity—you should amend your trust to use your new name.

EXAMPLE:

Helen obtains a divorce, and resumes using her maiden name, Hickman, instead of her married name of Delouch. She amends her living trust, renaming it the Helen Hickman Living Trust. This amendment must be notarized. If Helen previously had a shared or AB trust with her now-ex-spouse, she would need to prepare a new trust for one person.

CAUTION

Changing the name of your trust. If you change the name of your trust, you also need to change the title to all property with documents of title in your trust. This is particularly true for real estate. While this requires some paperwork, it isn't a serious hassle.

EXAMPLE:

Helen Hickman had previously transferred real estate to her trust when she used the name Helen Delouch. Helen prepares and records a new quitclaim deed, transferring the property to herself as "Helen Hickman, trustee of the Helen Hickman Living Trust," from "Helen Delouch, trustee of the Helen Delouch Living Trust."

Your Spouse Dies

With a basic shared living trust, when one spouse dies the other will probably inherit some, if not all, of the deceased spouse's trust property. The surviving spouse may want to amend his or her trust to name beneficiaries for that property.

With an AB trust, the surviving spouse cannot amend Trust A, which is created when the first spouse dies. And there's often no reason for the surviving spouse to amend his or her trust, which remains revocable. (This is explained in Chapter 5.) The surviving spouse could amend her Trust B if she now wants to change it—for example, by revising her beneficiary plan or changing her successor trustee.

A Major Beneficiary Dies

If you left much or all of your trust property to one person, and that person dies before you do, you may well want to amend your trust document. If you named an alternate beneficiary for the deceased beneficiary, there's not an urgent need; the alternate will inherit the property. But it still makes sense to amend the trust so that you can name another alternate beneficiary, who will receive the property if the former alternate (now first in line) dies before you do.

EXAMPLE:

Maria and Carlos make a basic shared living trust together. Maria leaves all her trust property to Carlos, but he dies before she does. Because she named her daughter Teresa as alternate beneficiary for her husband, she has already planned for the possibility of Carlos's death. But it still makes sense for her to amend her trust to name Teresa as the beneficiary and then to name an alternate beneficiary for Teresa.

Remember that your trust document has another backup device built into it: the residuary beneficiary. If both the primary and alternate beneficiary die before you do, the residuary beneficiary will inherit the trust property.

With an AB trust, if a final beneficiary dies before either spouse dies, the spouses can amend their trust to name a new final beneficiary, or they can leave the trust as is, allowing the alternate(s) named for the deceased final beneficiary to inherit that beneficiary's share of the AB trust property. (If they were cautious, the couple might still amend the trust, to name new alternate final beneficiaries, since the previous alternates for the deceased final beneficiary have become the final beneficiaries themselves.)

Also with an AB trust, the surviving spouse can choose to amend the revocable surviving spouse's trust to name a new final beneficiary.

You Want to Change Ownership of Trust Property

Sometimes couples decide, for various reasons, to change shared property into property owned separately by one spouse or the other. Or a spouse may decide to change his or her separate property into shared ownership property. The legal term for this is "transmutation of property."

If after you've placed property in a trust you want to make this type of change, you'll need to:

- Prepare the appropriate transfer documents for a change of ownership. If real estate is involved, new deeds reflecting the changed ownership must be prepared. If it's property without documents of title, you need what's called a "reverse assignment." A reverse assignment is simply a document transferring property from the trust (technically, you as trustees back to yourself as a couple). There's no standard legal form for a reverse assignment. Any notice you prepare that's clear will do.
- Revise the appropriate trust schedules, so the changed property is deleted from the old schedule and placed on the correct one.

EXAMPLE:

Soon after they get married, Felicity and Russell Jones create a basic shared living trust. They live in a home in New Jersey that is Felicity's separate property, and is listed as such on Schedule B of their trust. After several happy years together, Felicity decides she wants to place the house in shared ownership with Russell. So she lists the house on Schedule A, the shared property schedule of their trust, removing it from Schedule B. As trustee, Felicity executes a deed transferring the house to herself, as her separate property. She then executes a second deed, identifying the property as co-owned equally between her and her husband. The house is now owned by the couple as trustees of their trust.

Since each spouse owns half the house, they'll need to revise their beneficiary provisions, unless each simply leaves all his or her property to the other spouse.

Who Can Amend a Living Trust Document

Who can amend the terms of a living trust document depends on the kind of trust you created.

Individual Living Trusts

If you created an individual living trust, you (the grantor) can amend any of its provisions at any time, as long as you are mentally competent.

Basic Shared Living Trusts and AB Trusts

While both spouses are alive, both must agree to any changes in the provisions of the trust documents—for example, to change a beneficiary, successor trustee, or the management set up for a young beneficiary.

After one spouse dies, a basic shared living trust is split into two trusts. The deceased spouse's trust can no longer be amended. The surviving spouse can, of course, amend his or her own revocable trust.

The same rules apply to Nolo's AB trusts. Both spouses must agree to any amendment unless it is a situation where one spouse is incompetent and the other is permitted to amend the trust if the estate tax rules change. When a spouse dies, the AB trust splits into two distinct new trusts. Trust A, containing property of the deceased spouse, becomes irrevocable. (If a disclaimer trust was used, however, there may not be a Trust A. See Chapter 5.) The surviving spouse cannot change it. He or she cannot, for example, name a new successor trustee for Trust A. But again, the surviving spouse can amend or revoke his or her own trust, Trust B.

Someone Acting on Your Behalf

A trust document created from a form in this book cannot be amended by someone acting on a grantor's behalf, except in a situation where you have permitted the successor trustee of an AB trust to amend the trust if both spouses are alive and incapacitated, and the federal estate tax law changes. If a successor trustee uses this authority to amend an AB trust, he or she would have to modify the appropriate trust amendment (Form 9) to specify that it is the successor trustee, and not the grantors, who amend the trust.

Granting someone else the power to amend your trust under other circumstances is inherently dangerous. You've gone to considerable trouble to set up your estate plan and living trust. Normally, those plans shouldn't change if you become incapacitated. Therefore, the trust forms in this book do not authorize amendment by others if you become incapacitated, with the sole exception of amending an AB trust to take advantage of any new tax law.

If you do want to allow your successor trustee to be able to amend your living trust if you become incapacitated, you need to do two things:

- **Expressly authorize amendments in your living trust.** To accomplish this, you would add a new provision to the trustee powers clause of your trust. The wording of this new provision would vary, depending on the type of trust. For a one-person trust, you'd need something like:

  If the original trustee of this trust becomes incapacitated, the acting successor trustee shall have authority to amend this trust.

  For a couple's trust, you might use something like the following:

  If one spouse becomes incapacitated, the other spouse can amend this trust. If both spouses become incapacitated, the successor trustee can amend this trust.

SEE AN EXPERT

Do not add these provisions yourself. The above provisions are only examples, not actual clauses for your trust. If you want to allow your successor to be able to amend your trust, see a lawyer. You could impose a variety of different limits on the power to amend.

- **Prepare a durable power of attorney for finances.** In this document, you name a person to handle your financial matters if you are incapacitated and cannot handle them yourself. This person is called your "attorney-in-fact" or your "agent." To avoid conflicts, you should name the same person to be both your attorney-in-fact under a durable power of attorney and your successor trustee under your living trust. And to make your intention absolutely clear, in your power of attorney you should expressly authorize your attorney-in-fact to amend your living trust. (See "Planning for Incapacity," in Chapter 15, for more information about durable powers of attorney.)

How to Amend Your Trust Document

It's simple to amend your trust document to change a beneficiary, successor trustee, or custodian named in it, or change any other provision. Simply complete Form 8 or Form 9 from Appendix B or the CD-ROM, sign it, have the form notarized, and then attach it to your original trust document. If you have an individual trust, use Form 8; if you have either a shared living trust or an AB trust, use Form 9.

You can subsequently refer to your trust by the date of the amendment. For example:

The Jane and Werner Kopf Trust, as amended
September 3, 20xx

With an AB trust, you can't change the life beneficiary (the other spouse) while both spouses are alive. To do so defeats the whole point of this kind of trust. Otherwise, any term of the trust can be changed while both spouses live.

A sample draft amendment of an AB living trust, ready for final typing, is shown below.

EXAMPLE:

Jim and Toni created their AB disclaimer trust three years ago. Jim named his sister Eileen as a specific beneficiary for some stock in the Wyche Co. that Jim transferred to the trust. He named no alternate beneficiary. But since then, Jim and his sister have had a falling out. He wants to amend the trust document to leave the stock to his brother Aaron.

All Jim and Toni need to do is use Form 9 to prepare a trust amendment. The amendment deletes the paragraph in the Declaration of Trust that left the stock to Eileen. It also adds a paragraph leaving the stock to Aaron and stating that if Aaron doesn't survive him, that it should go to Jim's nephew David.

If they eliminated Eileen as a beneficiary but didn't name a new beneficiary for the stock, it would eventually become part of Trust A or the surviving spouse's Trust B (if Toni predeceased Jim).

Their draft trust amendment form (before typing, with appropriate cross-outs in the form) is shown below.

Similarly, you can amend your trust document if you change your mind about who you want to serve as:

- **Successor trustee.** The person who handles the trust, and any children's trusts, after your death or after the surviving spouse's death if a shared trust was created.

CAUTION

Do not change the original trustees of your living trust. You (and your spouse, if you made a basic shared living trust or an AB trust) must be the original trustees of your living trust. If you aren't, the tax treatment of the trust changes. (See Chapter 7.)

- **Alternate successor trustee.** The person who takes over as trustee if your first choice can't serve.
- **Custodian of a child's property.** The person who manages a young beneficiary's property under the terms of the Uniform Transfers to Minors Act, if it's available in your state.
- **Alternate custodian.** The person who serves as custodian if your first choice can't serve.

Form 9: Amendment to Basic Shared Living Trust or AB Trust

Amendment to Living Trust

This Amendment to The **①** _____Jim and Toni Nance_____

your names (or name of trust, if different)

Living Trust dated _____July 1_____, 20XX, is made this __30th___ day of ____November_____,

date Declaration of Trust signed

20 XX , by _____Toni Nance and Jim Nance_____,

your names

_____ the grantors and trustees of the trust. Under the power of amendment reserved to

the grantors by Section II, Paragraph (F), of the Declaration of Trust, the grantors amend the trust as follows:

1. The following is added to the Declaration of Trust:

   in Section IV, Paragraph A(1), Aaron Nance shall be given all Jim Nance's interest in the Wyche

   Co. stock

2. The following is deleted from the Declaration of Trust:

   in Section IV, Paragaph A(1), Eileen Nance Jones shall be given all Jim Nance's interest in the

   Wyche Co. stock

[Repeat as needed]

In all other respects, the Declaration of Trust as executed on _____July 1_____, 20XX ,

date

by the grantors is affirmed.

Executed at ____Fairview_____, ____Ohio_____, on

city   state

____November 20_____, 20XX .

date

_____

Grantor and Trustee

_____

Grantor and Trustee

EXAMPLE:

Geoffrey creates a living trust and names his brother as successor trustee. His brother moves to Europe two years later, so Geoffrey prepares a trust amendment to his trust document, naming his friend Brad as successor trustee instead.

> ! **CAUTION**
>
> **If you have registered your trust.** If you live in a state where you can register your trust with a government agency, and have chosen to do so, you should file a copy of any amendment (or revocation) with that agency. (See "Registering the Trust" in Chapter 12 for a list of states that authorize registration of living trusts.)

Making Subsequent Amendments

If you've already amended your trust once, how do you do it again? It's vital that any later amendment clearly state which document(s) you are amending. So refer to both your original trust and all prior amendments. For example, say Cindy Dallis wants to amend her trust for the second time. The caption of her new amendment reads:

> This Second Amendment to the Cindy Dallis Living Trust dated January 23, 20xx and the First Amendment to the Cindy Dallis Living Trust dated August 2, 20xx is made this 18th day of February, 20xx.

Then, using Form 8, you set out whatever provisions you want to add to your trust. If any provisions are changed or deleted, identify them.

Finally, reaffirm the original declaration of trust and the prior amendment, like this:

> In all other aspects, the Declaration of Trust dated January 23, 20xx and the First Amendment to that trust dated August 2, 20xx are reaffirmed.

Revoking Your Living Trust

You can revoke your living trust at any time, but you probably won't want to. After all, the reasons you established a trust won't go away, and revoking a living trust (unlike revoking a will) requires some work. The revoked trust ceases to exist and cannot own property. That means you must transfer ownership of all the trust property out of the living trust, back into your own name (or names), or into the name of a new living trust.

Who Can Revoke a Living Trust

Who can revoke your living trust depends on the kind of trust you created.

Individual Living Trust

If you create an individual living trust, you (the grantor) can revoke it at any time. The trust document does not allow the trust to be revoked by someone acting on your behalf (your attorney-in-fact, for example) unless you have specifically granted that authority in another document. (See "Who Can Amend a Living Trust Document," above.)

Basic Shared Living Trust or an AB Trust

Either spouse can revoke either of these trusts, wiping out all terms of the trust. The trust property is returned to each spouse according to how they owned it before transferring it to the trust.

EXAMPLE:

Yvonne and André make a basic shared living trust. Each transfers separately owned property to the trust. They also transfer their house, which they own together equally, as tenants in common, to the trust. Later Yvonne, anticipating a divorce, transfers the trust property she owned back to herself, and the property her husband owned back to him. The co-owned house goes back to both of them, who own it as tenants in common as before. She then revokes the trust.

The reason either spouse can revoke either a basic shared or AB trust, but it takes both to amend one, is that revocation simply returns both spouses to the status quo. By contrast, in the event of divorce or bitter conflict, it's risky to allow one spouse to amend a trust that governs both spouse's property.

When to Revoke Your Living Trust

If you're like most people, amending your living trust will take care of your changing circumstances over the years, and you will never need to revoke your trust. But here are two situations in which you might need to revoke a living trust and start over.

You Want to Make Extensive Revisions

If you want to make very extensive revisions to the terms of the trust document, you should revoke it and start fresh with a new trust document. If you don't, you risk creating inconsistencies and confusion.

You Get Divorced

If you divorce, you should revoke your living trust, and you and your ex-spouse should make new, separate ones. In a few states, the provisions of your living trust that affect your spouse are automatically revoked by divorce, but you should definitely not rely solely on these laws. They might change. Your own revocation will not.

How to Revoke Your Living Trust

To revoke your living trust, you must do two things:

Step 1. Transfer ownership of trust property from the trust back to yourself. Basically, you must reverse the process you followed when you transferred ownership of the property to the trust's name. (See Chapter 11.) You can make the transfer because of your authority as trustee of the trust.

Step 2. Use Form 10 in Appendix B or on the CD-ROM to prepare a simple document called a Revocation of Living Trust. Type the form deleting all extraneous material from the final version. Sign the typed revocation in front of a notary. Then store the revocation in a safe place, with your other vital papers.

After a Grantor Dies

The benefit of a revocable living trust doesn't come until after a grantor's death, when trust property is transferred to beneficiaries or placed in an AB trust without probate. The all-important responsibility of handling that transfer falls to your surviving spouse if you made a basic shared living trust or an AB trust, or to your successor trustee if you made an individual living trust.

To transfer property outside of probate, the successor trustee or surviving spouse does not have to file any reports with, or be supervised by, any government agencies or court.

This chapter takes a look at the job of the successor trustee. It does not provide specific instructions, but rather offers an overview of the job to give you a sense of what your successor trustee will be expected to do.

RESOURCE

The trustee's duties. The responsibilities of a successor trustee are explained in detail in *The Executor's Guide: Settling a Loved One's Estate or Trust*, by Mary Randolph (Nolo). If you want specific instructions on what your successor trustee will or may have to do, read that book.

Who Serves as Trustee After the Grantor's Death

With a basic shared marital trust or either type of AB trust, the surviving spouse serves as sole trustee after one spouse's death. With an individual trust, or when the surviving spouse dies, the successor trustee is in charge.

Who Serves as Trustee After Grantor's Death?
Individual Living Trust
1. Successor trustee(s)
2. Alternate successor trustee(s)
Basic Shared Living Trust or Either AB Trust
1. Surviving spouse
2. Successor trustee(s)
3. Alternate successor trustee(s)

More Than One Successor Trustee

If more than one person is named in the trust document as successor trustee, they all serve together. Whether each must formally agree on any action taken with regard to the living trust property or they can act independently depends on the terms of the trust document.

If one of the trustees cannot serve, the others remain as trustees. The person named as alternate successor trustee does not take over unless all the people named as successor trustees cannot serve.

If a Trustee Resigns

A trustee can resign at any time using a resignation statement like the one shown below. The ex-trustee should prepare the notice, sign the notice in front of a notary public, and then deliver the notice to the person who is next in line to serve as trustee.

Notice of Resignation

I, Lucia Freni, current trustee of The Robert Ambruzzi Living Trust dated March 3, 20xx, resign my position as trustee, effective immediately.

Date: November 19, 20xx

Lucia Freni
_____

[Notarization]

Appointing a New Trustee

Under the terms of Nolo living trusts, any trustee, including the last acting trustee, can appoint someone else to take over if no one named in the trust document can serve.

Normally, it would be the last, or alternate, successor trustee who named someone else to act as trustee if the need arises. The appointment must be in writing, signed, and notarized. The trustee making the appointment can prepare a simple document like the one shown below.

Appointment of Trustee

I, Lucia Freni, Trustee of The Robert Ambruzzi Living Trust dated March 3, 20xx, appoint Clarence Ryan as trustee, effective immediately. This appointment is made under the authority granted in the Declaration of Trust.

Date: November 19, 20xx

Lucia Freni
_____

[Notarization]

Removing a Trustee

Very rarely, a beneficiary becomes seriously unhappy with the way a trustee handles trust property. For example, the beneficiary of a child's trust might complain that the trustee isn't spending enough of the trust property's income on the beneficiary's education. If the dispute can't be worked out, the beneficiary can file a lawsuit to try to force the removal of the trustee.

The Trustee's Duties

Every trustee must take two steps as soon as he or she assumes responsibility for your living trust: The trustee must execute and record a document establishing that he or she can act for the trust and must obtain at least a rough estimate of the value of major trust assets.

Beyond these basics, a trustee's job depends on whether your state imposes specific requirements on trustees and on what type of living trust you made: an individual living trust, a basic shared living trust with your spouse, or an AB trust.

 SEE AN EXPERT

The trustee may want expert help with tax returns. If the value of the grantor's estate is over the estate tax threshold (see Chapter 4), a federal estate tax return must be filed. The successor trustee (as well as the executor of the deceased's will) is responsible for filing this document. It is a complicated tax form, and an expert lawyer or tax accountant should be hired to do the work. Similarly, if a state inheritance tax return must be filed, the successor trustee or executor must handle that.

All Trustees

All successor trustees should take the following steps after assuming responsibility for a living trust.

Preparing an Affidavit of Successor Trustee

The trustee may need proof that he or she is entitled to act for the trust, particularly for transactions involving real estate, since there are no court proceedings to officially give the trustee authority. The accepted convention is to record a document called "Affidavit of Assumption of Duties by Successor Trustee" at the county land records office. (In some states, this document may also be defined by other words, such as "Acknowledgment of Trusteeship.") There is no set legal form for this affidavit. It should always include:

- the name of the trust
- the date the trust document was signed, and
- the name of the person becoming successor trustee.

A certified copy of the grantor's death certificate should be attached. Certified copies can be obtained from your county or state's vital records department.

A sample draft Affidavit of Assumption of Duties by Successor Trustee, ready for final typing, is shown below. A fill-in-the-blanks version is in Appendix B or on the CD-ROM, Form 13.

Appraising the Value of Significant Trust Assets

The successor trustee should prepare a written statement of the market value of major trust assets as of the date of the grantor's death. (The IRS also permits the trustee to value all the assets as of six months after death. This is an all-or-nothing proposition. The trustee cannot value some assets as of the date of death and others as of six months thereafter.)

Defining the market value of major trust assets can be important for two reasons. First, if the trust (the deceased's property) could be liable for federal estate (or state inheritance) taxes, accurate values for trust assets are crucial. Second, even if the trust property will not be subject to estate taxes, the beneficiaries need to know the value of trust property at the grantor's death in order to determine later profit or loss if that property is subsequently sold. All property of the deceased, including all living trust property, is entitled

Form 13: Affidavit of Successor Trustee

Affidavit of Assumption of Duties by Successor Trustee

State of ___Illinois_____, County of ___Cook_____.
                state   county of successor trustee

___Ida Bellengeur_____, of legal age, first being duly sworn, declares:
        successor trustee's name

On ___March 23_____, 20 _xx_ , ___Rosa and Vladimir Rostop_____
        date   name(s) of grantor(s)

_____ created The

___Rosa and Vladimir Rostop_____ Living Trust.
        name(s) of grantor(s) (or name of trust, if different)

On ___September 2,_____, 20 _xx_ , ___Vladimir Rostop_____
        date   grantor's name

died, as established in the attached certified copy of the Certificate of Death.

[For a shared or AB trust, add:]

On ___November 3_____, 20 _xx_ , ___Rosa Rostop_____
        date   second grantor's name

died, as established in the attached certified copy of the Certificate of Death.

The Declaration of Trust creating The ___Rosa and Vladimir Rostop_____
        name(s) of grantor(s) (or name of trust, if different)

_____ Living Trust provides that upon the death of the grantors, I,

___Ida Bellengeur_____ become the trustee of the trust.
        successor trustee's name

I hereby accept the office of trustee of the trust, and am now acting as trustee of the trust.

Dated: _____

_____

Successor Trustee

to a stepped-up basis under current estate tax laws (see Chapter 3). If the market value of living trust property is not obtained promptly after the grantor dies, it may be difficult or impossible to obtain reliable evaluations later. This may mean that the IRS will not allow any stepped-up basis when calculating profit, or loss, from any subsequent sale of the property.

EXAMPLE:

Marcello has a living trust with property worth $900,000, under the estate tax threshold. The most valuable item in his trust is a sculpture he bought more than 30 years ago for $10,000. When he dies, it is appraised at $550,000. That figure is the inheritors' tax basis. (The basis is stepped-up to the market value at death.) If they sell the sculpture a week later for $550,000, they have no taxable profit.

But if no appraisal had been done, the IRS could argue that the inheritors' basis was Marcello's original purchase price of $10,000. So if they sold the sculpture for $550,000, their taxable profit would be $540,000.

The lesson is clear: For any asset that's increased significantly in value since the grantor bought it, determine the market value of that property at the grantor's death.

Some valuations are easy to obtain. Stock and bond prices are, obviously, printed daily during the week. Other valuations may require more work. Real estate needs an appraisal, unless the property is promptly sold. In practice, a broker should be able to make a sensible estimate. Other valuable property, such as jewelry, collectibles, or artworks, requires appraisal by an expert in the field.

Providing Basic Information to Trust Beneficiaries

A successor trustee has a basic, if not always clearly defined, duty to provide essential trust information to trust beneficiaries. Doing so is also wise trustee policy—it's not hard to do and can eliminate conflicts or even lawsuits that could arise if a trustee works in secret.

State-Specific Duties

A number of states impose specific duties on the successor trustee. Usually, these duties involve a notice that must be given the trust beneficiaries. Upon taking over management of a living trust, the successor trustee should check state law to determine precisely what duties, if any, the state imposes.

RESOURCE

The successor trustee's specific legal duties. *The Executor's Guide: Settling a Loved One's Estate or Trust,* by Mary Randolph (Nolo), lists every state's rules regarding a successor trustee's duties. If a state imposes specific duties, the citation to that state's statute is provided.

Trust-Specific Duties

A successor trustee's job depends primarily on what type of living trust you made: an individual trust, a basic shared trust, or an AB trust.

Individual Trust

When the grantor, who is also the trustee, dies, the successor trustee named in the trust document takes over as trustee. The new trustee is responsible for distributing the trust property to the beneficiaries named by the grantor in the trust document.

EXAMPLE:

Jamie is Elliot's successor trustee. Elliot's trust leaves his house to his children, Clarence and Grace. Elliot dies. Jamie, as trustee, deeds the house from the trust to Clarence and Grace, who can do with it what they wish—live in it, rent it, or sell it. Jamie does not sell the house and divide the proceeds between the beneficiaries—that's not his decision to make.

Normally, the trust continues to exist only as long as it takes the successor trustee to distribute trust property to the beneficiaries. In many cases, a living trust can be wound up within a few weeks after a grantor's death. No formal termination document is required. Once the trust property has been distributed, the trust ends.

The successor trustee must manage trust property only during the (hopefully short) period between the death of the original trust grantor and the actual distribution of property, or title to property, to the trust beneficiaries. Pragmatically, it is not part of the successor trustee's job to sell any trust property. Technically, the successor trustee does have the power to sell trust property, as does any trustee. However, the authority to sell trust property is actually granted to the trustee for two reasons: (1) so that the original grantor(s) can sell trust property any time she, he, or they want; (2) so that a successor trustee managing the trust for an incapacitated grantor can sell trust property if that becomes necessary. When distributing trust property to the beneficiaries, the successor trustee should manage that property as little as possible. It is for the beneficiaries, not the successor trustee, to decide what will be done with trust property—whether it will be sold or held, mortgaged or rented, etc.

The successor trustee is also in charge of managing any property left to a young beneficiary in a child's trust. A child's trust will exist until the beneficiary reaches the age specified in the trust document, so if there's such a trust, the successor trustee may have years of work ahead. (See Chapter 9.)

If trust property inherited by a young beneficiary is to be managed by a custodian under the Uniform Transfers to Minors Act, instead of in a child's trust, the person named as custodian will receive that property and be responsible for it. The successor trustee may also have been named as the custodian for a young beneficiary's property.

The Successor Trustee's Duties: Individual Trust

- Distribute trust property to beneficiaries named in the trust document.
- Manage trust property left in a child's trust, if any.
- File federal estate and state inheritance tax returns, if necessary. This is also the responsibility of the executor of the estate, if there was a will. (See "Preparing and Filing Tax Returns," below.)

Basic Shared Living Trust

When a spouse dies, a basic shared living trust technically splits into two separate trusts:

- Trust 1 contains the deceased spouse's share of trust property, excluding any trust property he or she left to the surviving spouse. The terms of Trust 1 cannot be changed; it cannot be revoked.
- Trust 2 contains the surviving spouse's trust property, including any of the deceased spouse's share of the trust property that is left to the surviving spouse. The surviving spouse remains free to amend the terms of Trust 2, or even revoke it.

The survivor is sole trustee of Trust 1, Trust 2, and any child's trusts set up for the deceased spouse's young beneficiaries.

EXAMPLE:

Debra and Timothy Zeltzer create a basic shared living trust. Timothy dies in 2009. Debra can refer to her trust as "The Debra and Timothy Zeltzer Trust, Trust 2," and to her husband's trust, now irrevocable, as "The Debra and Timothy Zeltzer Trust, Trust 1."

It's the surviving spouse's job to distribute the property from Trust 1 to the beneficiaries the deceased spouse named in the trust document. If, as is common, much of the trust property is left to the surviving spouse, that spouse will have little to do. The trust property he or she inherits is already in the revocable trust (Trust 2), and remains there. The trust document provides that trust property left to the survivor does not go to the surviving spouse in a personal capacity but instead stays in the trust as part of the property in Trust 2. If it did not contain such a provision, the property would have to be transferred from the living trust to the spouse and then, if the surviving spouse wanted it to avoid probate, back to his or her living trust again.

When all the property in Trust 1 has been distributed to the beneficiaries, that trust ceases to exist. No formal termination document is required.

Trust 2 contains only the surviving spouse's property and remains revocable. The surviving spouse is free to change it as he or she wishes.

Few Formalities Required

Generally, the surviving spouse "creates" Trust 1 and Trust 2 for the purposes of property distribution only. The surviving spouse does not need to create formal new living trusts. He or she must simply figure out what property was owned by the deceased spouse, and what property was owned by the surviving spouse. Then the deceased spouse's property is distributed as the living trust directs.

The trust document provides that all trust property of the surviving spouse, including all trust property left to him or her by the deceased spouse, stays in the original living trust. The surviving spouse simply continues on with that trust, which remains revocable until his or her death.

The surviving spouse may want to change title of shared trust assets into his or her name alone, as sole trustee. Doing so will make it easier to sell or transfer trust assets. Transferring title requires preparation of the appropriate transfer document, plus a certified copy of the deceased spouse's death certificate, and perhaps a copy of the trust, depending on the type of asset.

EXAMPLE: After her husband, Ronald, dies, Linda decides to reregister title of their house in her name alone as trustee. So she prepares and records a new deed transferring ownership from "Linda and Ronald Lecleef, as trustees..." to "Linda Lecleef, as trustee..." She also records a copy of the death certificate.

EXAMPLE:

Edith and Jacques create a basic shared living trust. They transfer their house, which they own together, into the trust, and name each other as beneficiaries. Edith names her son as alternate beneficiary.

When Jacques dies, Edith inherits his half-interest in the house. Because of the way the trust document is worded, she doesn't have to change the trust document to name a beneficiary for the half-interest in the house that she inherited from her husband, nor does she have to prepare a new deed for the house. Both halves of the house will go to her son at her death. She may, however, want to amend the trust to make her son the primary beneficiary and name someone else to be alternate beneficiary.

When the second spouse dies, the successor trustee named in the trust document takes over as trustee. The process of winding up the living trust is the same as that for an individual trust.

EXAMPLE:

Harry and Maude, a married couple, set up a basic shared living trust to avoid probate. They appoint Maude's cousin Emily as successor trustee, to take over as trustee after they have both died. They transfer ownership of much of their co-owned property—their house, savings accounts, and stocks—to the trust. Maude also puts some of her family heirlooms, which are her separate property, in the living trust.

In the trust document, Maude leaves her heirlooms to her younger sister. She leaves her half of the trust property she and Harry own together to Harry.

When Maude dies, Harry becomes the sole trustee. Following the terms of the trust document, he distributes Maude's heirlooms (from Trust 1) to her sister, without probate. Maude's half of the property they had owned together stays in the trust (in Trust 2); no transfer is necessary. After Maude's death, Harry decides to amend the trust document to name his nephew, Burt, as successor trustee instead of Maude's cousin Emily. When Harry dies, Burt will become trustee and distribute the property in Trust 2 to Harry's beneficiaries. When all the property is given to Harry's beneficiaries, the trust ends.

The Surviving Spouse's Duties: Basic Shared Living Trust

- Distribute the deceased spouse's share of the trust property to beneficiaries named in the trust document.
- Manage property left in a child's trust, if any.
- File federal estate and state inheritance tax returns, if necessary (this is also the executor's responsibility, if there is a will).
- Amend Trust 2 to reflect changed circumstances, if necessary or desired.

Nolo's AB Trust and AB Disclaimer Trust

With either of Nolo's AB trusts, both spouses are the original trustees. When a spouse dies, the surviving spouse becomes sole trustee. With a standard AB trust, the living trust splits into two trusts: the irrevocable Trust A (of the deceased spouse) and Trust B, the revocable surviving spouse's trust. With an AB disclaimer trust, Trust A is created only if the surviving spouse disclaims trust property. When or if a Trust A is created, a new trust document is not needed, except that new schedules listing the property in Trust A and Trust B must be prepared.

With an operational Trust A, the surviving trustee prepares two new printed or typed schedules. On the first, the trustee lists all property which will be held and owned by Trust A. On the second, the trustee lists all property held in Trust B, property owned by the surviving spouse. The property needs to be described with sufficient clarity so that the IRS can tell what property belongs to Trust A. There is no legal requirement that the new schedules be notarized, but the trustee can have that done if desired. Attach the originals of the two schedules to the original trust document.

The surviving spouse, as trustee, must first distribute any trust property the deceased spouse left to specifically named beneficiaries. (Remember, each spouse can make specific gifts of trust property to beneficiaries other than the other spouse.) Then the trustee must maintain the rest of that property in the ongoing Trust A.

Determining the most financially desirable way to divide the living trust property between Trust A and the surviving spouse's Trust B is not a simple task. Any allocation of equally owned trust property is valid, as long as each trust gets 50% of the total worth. But each item of property does not have to be split, with half going to each trust. For example, stock worth $300,000 can be placed in Trust A, as long as other co-owned property with a total worth of $300,000 is placed in Trust B.

The Surviving Spouse's Duties If Trust A Is Established

- Create and maintain Trust A. Divide property between this trust and the surviving spouse's Trust B.
- In California and Tennessee, the trustee must notify the final beneficiaries of Trust A that this trust has now become irrevocable.
- Distribute any specific gifts of the Trust A property made by the deceased spouse.
- Administer Trust A. File a trust income tax return each year, and, if required by trust document, give copies to final beneficiaries.
- Manage property left in a child's trust, if any.
- File federal estate and state inheritance tax returns, if necessary. This is also the executor's responsibility if there is a will.
- Amend the surviving spouse's trust, Trust B, to reflect changed circumstances, if necessary or desired.

SEE AN EXPERT

Determining the wisest division of property between the Trusts A and B is difficult. Dividing trust assets after one spouse has died is the most complicated part of using an AB trust. The uncertainty surrounding the estate tax makes these decisions even thornier. The surviving spouse will need expert help from an experienced estate planning attorney to reap the greatest tax benefits. If state property ownership laws allow some flexibility with allocation of shared property, as is particularly true in community property states, you and your advisors can make tax-saving divisions. (For a discussion of some issues that can arise when allocating property between Trust A and Trust B, see Chapter 5.) Further complexities can arise if each spouse names different final beneficiaries for her or his portion of shared-ownership property. Does that mean that every item of the shared property must be divided 50-50? If not, how can the successor trustee ensure that all final beneficiaries will be treated equally? An expert can help to ensure that property will be divided and distributed as you wish.

Because the IRS might want to know, at some point, the value of the property placed in Trust A and in Trust B, the successor trustee should prepare a list stating the net value of each item of property as of the date of division.

Although the survivor does not need to create a new trust document, property must be clearly identified as being owned by Trust A or Trust B. This usually requires some reregistering of title of some of the living trust property in the name of Trust A. For example, if you decide that it is wisest to put all of a shared ownership house in Trust A, a new deed should be prepared to reflect this, listing the new owner as, for example, "The Moira and Joseph O'Sullivan Living Trust, Trust A." The deed is signed by the surviving spouse, as trustee.

In addition to a name, as just described, Trust A needs a federal taxpayer ID number. The surviving spouse must keep appropriate trust financial records and file a federal trust tax return every year. The IRS will want it clear which trust owns what. Annual state trust tax returns may also be required, in states with income taxes.

If the trust document requires it, the trustee is required to give copies of the trust's annual federal trust income tax return to the final beneficiaries.

As trustee, the surviving spouse manages the property in Trust A and, as life beneficiary, receives any income it generates.

The surviving spouse's trust, Trust B, goes on as before. Trust B remains revocable and can be changed at any time. No new property documents are required; any property the deceased spouse leaves to the surviving spouse is added to Trust B. No tax return needs to be filed for this trust.

After the death of the surviving spouse, the successor trustee winds up both A and B trusts by distributing all property (except for any specific gifts made by the surviving spouse) of both trusts to each trust's final beneficiaries. The successor trustee must file a final tax return for Trust A. The successor trustee also manages any property left in a child's trust and files a closing income tax return for the second spouse.

Transferring Property to Beneficiaries

The procedure for transferring trust property depends on who the beneficiaries are:

- Property of a basic shared living trust left by a deceased spouse to the surviving spouse remains in the trust, and no action is required.

- Property left to Trust A must be clearly identified as Trust A property.
- Property left to Trust B by the deceased spouse remains in the ongoing living trust, and no action is required.
- Trust property left to adult beneficiaries must be actually transferred to them.
- Property left to a young beneficiary in a child's trust stays in that trust until the child reaches the age to receive the trust property outright.
- Property left to a custodian under the Uniform Transfers to Minors Act must be given to the custodian named in the trust document.

To obtain the trust property, the trustee usually needs a copy of the grantor's death certificate (both grantors' death certificates, if both are dead and the trust property was originally co-owned) and a copy of the trust document. (The trustee should be prepared to show the original trust document in case anyone doubts the copy's authenticity.) Frequently, an Affidavit of Assumption of Duties by Successor Trustee will also be needed. And finally, in some cases, the trustee will need to prepare some other paperwork, such as a specific form of a brokerage company or a new deed for real estate.

Bureaucrats, Bureaucrats

In rare instances, the trustee can encounter odd and difficult problems, depending on the narrowness and obstinacy of the bureaucracy holding the property. For example, one successor trustee was told by two institutions that he must obtain a written statement or "certification" from a lawyer or bank that the trust hadn't been modified since it was signed. This was an irrational and unreasonable requirement. No law requires any "certification." The grantor was dead, and no lawyer or bank was involved in preparing his trust. Eventually, after considerable persistence, the trustee succeeded in persuading the institutions that he knew of no amendment to the trust, and it was ridiculous for them to demand impossible proof that no amendment existed. The transfers were allowed.

Moral: Be persevering if you must, and eventually you'll get the transfer approved by the transfer agent.

Specific requirements for transferring property vary slightly from place to place, and the trustee may have to make inquiries at banks, stock brokerages, and other institutions about current procedures, but here are the general rules. A trustee who runs into difficulties has the authority to get help—from a lawyer, accountant, or other expert—and pay for it from trust assets.

RESOURCE

Help for California residents. *How to Probate an Estate in California,* by Julia Nissley (Nolo), contains forms and instructions for transferring the property of a deceased person, including living trust property.

Terminology. This section refers to whoever takes over as trustee after a grantor's death as the "trustee." To remind you, if you made an individual trust, the trustee is the person you named as successor trustee. If you made a shared marital trust, or an AB trust, the trustee is the surviving spouse or, after both spouses have died, the successor trustee.

Property Without Title Documents

For trust property that doesn't have a title document—furniture, for example—the task of the trustee is quite simple. The trustee must promptly distribute the property to the beneficiaries named in the trust document. If the trustee thinks it's a good idea, it's appropriate to have the recipient sign a receipt. But in many family situations, where all trust each other, this formality isn't necessary.

Bank Accounts

It should be simple for the trustee to transfer the funds in a bank or savings and loan account, already held in the name of the living trust, to the beneficiary. Financial institutions are familiar with living trusts and how they work, and the bank probably has the trust document (or a bank form with information about the trust) already on file.

The trustee will need to show the bank or savings and loan:

- a certified copy of the trust grantor's death certificate

- a copy of the living trust document, if the bank doesn't already have one (again, being prepared to show the original trust document, if demanded), and
- proof of his or her own identity, perhaps including an Affidavit of Assumption of Duties by Successor Trustee.

Real Estate

The trustee needs to prepare and sign a deed transferring ownership of real estate from the trust to the beneficiary. The trustee signs the deed in her capacity as trustee.

EXAMPLE:

Jane Adanski, Trustee of The Robert Whilhite Living Trust, dated October 25, 20xx.

The signed and notarized deed should also be filed (recorded) with the county land records office. In most places, recording costs no more than a few dollars per page. It's unlikely, but depending on local and state law, there may be a transfer tax to pay. (Deeds, recording, and transfer taxes are discussed in "Real Estate" in Chapter 11.)

EXAMPLE:

The deed to Evelyn Crocker's house shows that it is owned by Evelyn Crocker, as trustee of her living trust. The living trust document states that Evelyn's daughter, Amanda, is to inherit the house when Evelyn dies. Amanda is also the successor trustee of the trust.

After Evelyn's death, Amanda prepares and signs a new deed, transferring ownership of the house from the trust to herself. She signs the deed in her capacity as trustee of the trust, and records the deed in the county land records office, along with an Affidavit of Assumption of Duties by Successor Trustee.

A title company, before it will issue title insurance to the new owners, will probably want a copy of the trust document and a certified copy of the death certificate of the trust grantor.

Stocks and Bonds

How to transfer stocks or bonds from a trust to the beneficiary depends on whether they were held in a brokerage account or separately. (For information about transferring stock in closely held corporations, see "Small Business Interests," below.)

Brokerage Accounts

The trustee should contact the broker and ask for instructions. The brokerage company will almost surely already have either a copy of the living trust document or a form that includes relevant information about the trust. (These are necessary to transfer the account to the living trust in the first place.)

If not, the trustee will probably need to send the broker:

- a copy of the trust document or an "abstract of trust" (the first, last, and other relevant pages of the trust document, showing the notarized signature—see Chapter 11 for a sample abstract of trust), and
- a letter instructing the holder to transfer the brokerage account to the beneficiary's name.

Stock Certificates

If the deceased grantor kept the stock certificates or bonds in his or her possession—most people don't—the trustee must get new certificates issued, showing the beneficiary as the new owner.

The trustee will have to send the securities' transfer agent several documents. It's a good idea to write the transfer agent and ask exactly what is needed. Usually, the name and address of the transfer agent appear on the face of the stock or bond certificate. But because transfer agents change occasionally, the first thing the trustee should do is write or call (or check with a stock brokerage firm) to verify the name and address of the current transfer agent.

The trustee will probably have to send in:

- a certified copy of the grantor's death certificate
- the certificates or bonds
- a document called a "stock or bond power," which the trustee must fill out and sign, with the signature guaranteed by an officer of a bank or brokerage firm (the stock or bond power may

be printed on the back of the certificates; if not, office supply stores carry them)

- a copy of the trust document or an abstract of trust if the transfer agent did not receive one when the securities were transferred into the trust
- an Affidavit of Domicile (a form available from banks and stockbrokers) signed by the trustee, showing what the trust grantor's state of residence was, and
- a letter of instructions requesting that the certificates be reissued in the beneficiary's name.

Also, the trustee may be required to have his or her signature "guaranteed" by a stockbroker. If neither the trustee nor the deceased grantor have, or had, a stock account with a brokerage company, this too may cause trouble. The trustee will have to locate a broker—maybe one who handles a friend's account—to guarantee your signature.

The trustee may be required to produce "certified copies" of the living trust, although the transfer agent isn't sure what agency "certifies" documents. Your best bet here is to file the original document with your local county records office and have them "certify" copies for you.

Government Securities

To transfer government securities—Treasury bills or U.S. bonds, for example—the trustee should ask the broker to contact the issuing government agency, or contact the government directly.

Mutual Funds or Money Market Accounts

For mutual funds or money market accounts owned in the trust's name, the trustee should ask the company what it requires to reregister ownership of the account in the beneficiary's name. Generally, the trustee must send the company proof of his or her own identity, a copy of the grantor's death certificate, a letter of instructions (or a form that the company provides), and a copy of the trust document.

Small Business Interests

How a trustee transfers small business interests owned by a living trust depends on the way the business was organized.

RESOURCE

Transferring trademarks. A registered trademark or service mark of a small business must be reregistered in the name of the beneficiary. See *Trademark: Legal Care for Your Business & Product Name,* by Stephen Elias and Richard Stim (Nolo).

Sole Proprietorships

The trustee must transfer business assets to the beneficiary as he or she would transfer any other trust property. The name of the business itself, if owned by the living trust, does not have a title document, so the trustee doesn't need to do anything to transfer it to the beneficiary.

Solely Owned Corporations

Corporation officers must prepare the appropriate corporate records to show that ownership has been transferred to the beneficiary. The specifics depend on the incorporation papers and company bylaws. Often a resolution by the board of directors is required. Additional paperwork may include such documents as "Notice of Special Meeting of Board of Directors" and "Waiver of Notice of Time Requirements to Hold Special Meeting of Board of Directors." Then the trustee must have the stock certificates reissued in the beneficiary's name.

Closely Held Corporations and Limited Liability Companies

The stock certificates or ownership interest owned by the trust will have to be reissued in the beneficiary's name. The trustee should contact the officers of the corporation or LLC; the other shareholders or owners may have the right, under the corporation's bylaws or a shareholders' agreement, to buy back the shares or interest. For LLC information, see *Form Your Own Limited Liability Company,* by Anthony Mancuso (Nolo).

Partnership Interests

The trustee should contact the deceased grantor's partners, who may have the right to buy out the grantor's share. If the beneficiary wants to enter into the partnership, the partnership agreement must be changed to add the beneficiary. See *Form a Partnership: The Complete Legal Guide,* by Denis Clifford and Ralph Warner (Nolo).

Copyrights

To transfer an interest in a copyright to a beneficiary, the trustee should sign and file, with the U.S. Copyright Office in Washington, DC, a document transferring all the trust's rights in the copyright to the beneficiary. Sample transfer forms are in *The Copyright Handbook: What Every Writer Needs to Know,* by Stephen Fishman (Nolo).

Patents

To transfer a patent from a living trust, the trustee should prepare a document called an "assignment" and record it with the U.S. Patent and Trademark Office in Washington, DC. There is a small fee for recording. Sample assignment forms and instructions are in *Patent It Yourself,* by David Pressman (Nolo).

Other Property With Title Documents

If an item of trust property has a title document that shows ownership in the name of the trust, the trustee must prepare and sign a new title document transferring ownership to the beneficiary. Usually, the trustee will need a copy of the trust document and of the trust grantor's death certificate if the property is in someone else's possession.

If a vehicle was owned by the trust, the trustee should contact the state department of motor vehicles to get the forms required to transfer it to the beneficiary.

Preparing and Filing Tax Returns

Depending on the circumstances, the successor trustee may have to file several tax returns:

- federal estate tax return for the deceased grantor, if the value of the estate is over the estate tax threshold for year of death
- state inheritance tax return for the deceased grantor, if state law requires it

- final federal income tax return (and state return, if there's a state income tax) for the deceased grantor, and
- final federal income tax return (and state return, if there's a state income tax) for Trust A after both spouses die.

Legally, filing these returns is the responsibility both of the successor trustee and of the executor named in the deceased grantor's will. The same person usually serves as both executor and successor trustee.

Generally, the state and federal income tax returns are due April 15 of the year following the grantor's death. The federal estate tax return is due nine months after the grantor's death.

The trustee is entitled, by the terms of the trust document, to pay for professional help out of the trust assets. And that help may well be necessary, because tax matters—particularly estate tax matters—can get quite tricky.

RESOURCE

Help with estate tax returns. The successor trustee can get a helpful set of instructions, "Instructions for Form 706," from the Internal Revenue Service. Another useful IRS publication is called *Introduction to Estate and Gift Taxes* (Publication 950). You can download these materials for free at the IRS website, www.irs.gov.

Administering a Child's Trust

If, in the trust document, the deceased grantor set up a child's trust, the trustee will have to manage that property if the beneficiary isn't old enough to receive it outright. A child's trust comes into being only if, at the grantor's death, the beneficiary has not yet reached the age the grantor specified.

EXAMPLE:

Carl sets up a living trust and names his two young children as beneficiaries. He specifies that if either child is younger than 30 when he dies, the property that child is to inherit from the trust should be kept in a separate child's trust.

When Carl dies, one child is 30; the other is 25. The 30-year-old receives her trust property with no strings attached. But a child's trust is created for the 25-year-old. The successor trustee is responsible for managing the property and turning it over to the child when he turns 30.

The trustee's duties when managing a child's trust are explained in Chapter 9.

Administering a Custodianship

Someone who is appointed in the trust document to be the custodian of trust property inherited by a young beneficiary has roughly the same management responsibilities as the trustee of a child's trust. (See Chapter 9.) The specifics of the custodian's duties are set out in the Uniform Transfers to Minors Act, as adopted by the particular state's legislature.

A Living Trust as Part of Your Estate Plan

A revocable living trust can accomplish most people's main estate planning goal: leaving their property to their loved ones while avoiding probate and perhaps saving on estate taxes as well. But it is not, by itself, a complete estate plan. For example, in most states, parents of young children can't use a living trust to appoint a personal guardian to care for their minor children. To do this, you need a will. A living trust also can't take care of property you buy or inherit shortly before you die and don't get around to transferring to the trust.

This chapter provides an overview of estate planning methods that you may want to explore in addition to a living trust. Basically, estate planning includes:

- deciding who will inherit your property when you die
- deciding who will take care of your children and their finances if you die while they are young
- setting up procedures and devices to minimize probate fees at your death
- if your estate is large, planning to reduce federal estate taxes and state death taxes, if your state has them (with the exception of an AB trust, the trust forms in this book don't afford any estate tax savings), and
- arranging for someone to make financial and health care decisions for you in case at some time you can no longer do so yourself.

Using a Backup Will

Even though you create a living trust, you need a simple backup will, too. Like a living trust, a will is a document in which you specify what is to be done with your property when you die.

Having a will is important for several reasons:

- A will is an essential backup device for property that you don't get around to transferring to your living trust.
- In a will you can name someone to be the personal guardian of your minor child, in case you and the child's other parent die while the child is still under 18. In most states, you can't do that in a living trust. (A few states' laws can be construed to permit appointing a child's personal guardian in a living trust, but it's prudent to be conventional and appoint the guardian in a will, the normal way.)
- If you want to disinherit your spouse or a child, you must make your wishes clear in a will. (State law may restrict your freedom to disinherit a spouse; see Chapter 8.)

Instructions for preparing a backup will are in Chapter 16, and sample will forms are in Appendix B and on the CD-ROM (Forms 11 and 12).

Other Probate-Avoidance Methods

A living trust is not the only way to transfer some kinds of assets without probate, and it's not the best in all circumstances. For example, it's usually cumbersome to have your personal checking account held in the name of your living trust, because businesses may be reluctant to accept your checks.

Fortunately, you can mix and match probate-avoidance techniques. Just put whatever property you want in your living trust, and choose other transfer methods—ones that also avoid probate—for the rest of your property.

You might, for example, want to put your checking account into joint tenancy with your spouse; at your death, your spouse would automatically take sole ownership of the account. Some helpful probate-avoidance methods are summarized below.

Pay-on-Death Financial Accounts

Setting up a pay-on-death account is an easy way to transfer cash at your death, quickly and without probate. All you do is designate, on a form provided by a financial institution, one or more persons you want to receive the money when you die.

Pay-on-death accounts are used primarily for bank accounts, including savings, checking, or certificate of deposit accounts. You can also register ownership of certain kinds of government securities, including bonds, Treasury bills, and Treasury notes, in a way that lets you name a beneficiary to receive them at your death.

Other Nolo Estate Planning Resources

Plan Your Estate, by Denis Clifford, covers all the estate planning methods briefly discussed in this chapter and more. It contains extensive discussion about probate avoidance methods and estate tax reduction techniques, from gift-giving to generation-skipping trusts, including estate and gift taxes, and ongoing trusts.

Estate Planning Basics, by Denis Clifford, provides concise, straightforward, and easy-to-read explanations of the major components of estate planning.

The Busy Family's Guide to Estate Planning, by Liza Weiman Hanks, shows parents what estate planning is crucial to do now, and what can wait for later. The book speaks to real-world concerns, and explains to readers how parents can prepare a complete estate plan, step by step.

Quicken WillMaker Plus (software for Windows) enables you to prepare a comprehensive will, including child's trusts for your minor children, allowing you to choose the age at which your children inherit property you leave them. It also helps you make a health care directive, a durable power of attorney for finances, and many other useful legal forms.

Nolo's Simple Will Book, by Denis Clifford, is an in-depth explanation of how to prepare a will that covers all normal needs, including child's trusts for your minor children.

Quick & Legal Will Book, by Denis Clifford, enables you to prepare a basic will easily and effectively.

8 Ways to Avoid Probate, by Mary Randolph, provides in-depth explanations of all major probate-avoidance methods.

How to Probate an Estate in California, by Julia Nissley, enables Californians to handle a normal probate without an attorney.

The Executor's Guide, by Mary Randolph, offers a thorough self-help explanation of what an executor/trustee must do after a will-writer or trust grantor dies. The book covers handling the legal and financial matters that arise after a death.

Deeds for California Real Estate, by Mary Randolph, explains how to use deeds to transfer real estate for estate planning.

Get It Together, by Melanie Cullen and Shae Irving, shows you how to organize and file important paperwork, so that you and your survivors can quickly locate vital documents and records.

Long-Term Care: How to Plan & Pay for It, by Joseph Matthews, discusses how to finance and choose long-term care.

Social Security, Medicare & Government Pensions, by Joseph Matthews and Dorothy Matthews Berman, is an excellent resource about rights and benefits of older Americans.

Get a Life: You Don't Need a Million to Retire Well, by Ralph Warner, shares sensible ways to create a fulfilling retirement. The book stresses the importance of nurturing family relationships, maintaining and creating friendships, improving health, keeping active, maintaining a robust curiosity about the world—and having sufficient financial resources so you don't become destitute.

EXAMPLE:

Terry opens a savings account in her name, and names Lynn Harris as the pay-on-death (P.O.D.) beneficiary. When Terry dies, whatever money is in the account will go to Lynn.

During your life, the beneficiary has absolutely no right to the money in the account. You can withdraw some or all of the money, close the account, or change the beneficiary, at any time. When you die, the beneficiary can claim the money simply by showing the bank the death certificate and personal identification.

CAUTION

Bank accounts may be frozen. Like other bank accounts, a pay-on-death account may be temporarily frozen at your death if your state levies inheritance taxes. The state will release the money to your beneficiaries when shown that your estate has sufficient funds to pay the taxes. If you live in a state that imposes inheritance taxes, you might want to check with your bank to learn if your accounts, including any pay-on-death accounts, may be frozen after you die. If so, it's sensible to warn your inheritors that they could face this hassle. (If you don't know if your state has inheritance taxes, ask the bank and see what they say.)

Most banks have forms for setting up this kind of account, and they don't charge more for keeping your money this way. Before you open a pay-on-death account, ask your bank if there are any special state law requirements about notifying the beneficiary. In a few states, a pay-on-death provision isn't effective unless you have notified the beneficiary that you've set up the account. Your bank should be able to fill you in on your state's rules.

Transfer-on-Death Registration for Stocks and Bonds

In every state but Texas, you can register securities (individual stocks or bonds or accounts, including mutual funds) in a transfer-on-death form. You simply designate a beneficiary or beneficiaries to receive the securities outside of probate. Your brokerage company should have a form for opening this kind of account.

Individual Retirement Accounts

Retirement accounts such as IRAs, Roth IRAs, SEP-IRAs, and 401(k) and 403(b) plans weren't designed to be probate-avoidance devices, but if you have any money left in such accounts when you die, they can function that way. All you have to do is name a beneficiary to receive the funds still in your pension plan or retirement account at your death, and the funds will not go through probate. If you are considering making your AB trust the beneficiary of your retirement account, see the discussion in "Property That You Should Not Put in Your Living Trust" in Chapter 6.

Except for a Roth IRA, after age 70½, federal law requires you to withdraw at least a certain amount of money every year from your individual retirement account or face a monetary penalty. The withdrawal amount is refigured every year, based on your current life expectancy and that of your beneficiary.

Life Insurance

As insurance agents will be delighted to explain, life insurance is a good way to provide surviving family members with quick cash for debts, living expenses, and, for larger estates, estate taxes. And because you name the beneficiary in the policy itself, not in your will, life insurance proceeds don't go through probate.

The only circumstance in which life insurance proceeds are subject to probate is if the beneficiary named in the policy is your estate. That's done occasionally if the estate will need immediate cash to pay debts and taxes. Still, it's almost always a better idea to name your spouse, children, or another beneficiary who can take the money free of probate and use it to pay debts and taxes.

Although the proceeds of a life insurance policy don't go through probate, they are included in your estate for federal estate tax purposes. If you think your estate will be liable for federal estate taxes, you can reduce the tax bill by giving away the policy to the beneficiary, another person, or an irrevocable life insurance trust (discussed later in this chapter).

Life Insurance to Provide for Your Children

If you have young children but not much money, consider buying a moderate amount of term life insurance, which would provide cash to support your children if you died while they were still young. Because term life insurance pays benefits only if you die during the covered period (often five or ten years), it's far cheaper than other types of life insurance. You can stop renewing the insurance when, by the end of the current term, the children will be on their own or your estate would be large enough to support them until they are.

Joint Tenancy

Joint tenancy is one of the more commonly used probate-avoidance devices. It's an efficient and practical way to transfer some kinds of property in some situations, but for most kinds of property, a living trust is usually a better choice. In many states, married couples can use a special type of joint tenancy called "tenancy by the entirety," described below.

How Joint Tenancy Works

Joint tenancy is a way two or more people can hold title to property they own together. It is available in almost all states. All joint tenants must, by law, own equal shares of the property, except unequal shares are allowed in Connecticut and Vermont.

Common Probate-Avoidance Methods

Method	Advantages	Disadvantages
Revocable living trust	Flexible, private. Easy to create. You keep control over property during your life.	Some paperwork involved. May need attorney if yours is a complicated estate.
Pay-on-death financial accounts	Easy to create, using a form provided by the bank or brokerage company.	Limited to bank accounts and securities.
Naming beneficiary of pension plan or retirement account	Easy to do. Beneficiary inherits all funds in the account at your death.	None, unless particular program imposes limits.
Life insurance	Good way to provide quick cash for beneficiaries or to pay estate taxes. Proceeds don't go through probate.	If family members won't need much immediate cash, expense of policy may not be justified.
Joint tenancy with right of survivorship	Easy to create.	Restricted in Alaska to husband and wife. If you already own property, you may not want to add another owner, who could sell his or her share. (For larger estates, there are negative gift tax consequences, too.) Can be a problem if a co-owner becomes incapacitated. No probate avoidance if all joint owners die at once.
Tenancy by the entirety	Easy to create.	Available in only about half the states; limited to married couples (or in a few states, to registered same-sex couples). Can be a problem if one spouse becomes incapacitated.
Community property with right of survivorship	All the benefits of community property ownership plus probate avoidance when one spouse dies.	Available only to married couples in Alaska, Arizona, California, Nevada, and Wisconsin. (In California, registered domestic partners may also own property this way.)
Gifts of property made while you're alive	Reduces amount of property in your estate, which avoids both probate and estate taxes.	You lose control over property given away. Large gifts use up part of your federal gift/estate tax exemption. Insurance policies must be given away at least three years before death, or proceeds are included in your taxable estate.
State laws that allow simplified probate proceedings	Exempts certain property from formal probate.	Applies only to small estates.
Transfer-on-death designation for motor vehicle	Easy to do. All you do is name, on your registration form, someone to inherit your vehicle.	Currently available only in California, Connecticut, Kansas, Missouri, and Ohio, but other states are considering it.
Transfer-on-death registration for securities	Easy to do. All you do is name, on the registration form, someone to inherit the securities at your death.	Not available in Texas.
Transfer-on-death real estate deeds	Easy to do. You prepare, sign, notarize, and file the deed form.	Available only in Arizona, Arkansas, Colorado, Kansas, Missouri, Montana, Nevada, New Mexico, Ohio, and Wisconsin.

For estate planning purposes, the most important characteristic of joint tenancy is that when one joint owner (called a joint tenant) dies, the surviving joint owners automatically get complete ownership of the property. This is called the "right of survivorship." The property doesn't go through probate court—there is only some simple paperwork to fill out to transfer the property into the name of the surviving owner.

EXAMPLE:

Evelyn and her daughter own a car in joint tenancy. When Evelyn dies, her half-interest in the car will go to her daughter without probate. Her daughter will need only to fill out a simple form to transfer ownership of the car into her own name.

Joint tenancy certainly has the virtue of simplicity. To create a joint tenancy, all the co-owners need to do is pay attention to the way they are listed on the document that shows ownership of property, such as a deed to real estate, a car's title slip, or a card establishing a bank account. In the great majority of states, by calling themselves "joint tenants with the right of survivorship," the owners create a joint tenancy. In a few states, additional specific words are necessary. If you want to set up a joint tenancy and aren't sure how to word a title document, ask a real estate lawyer or someone at a land title company.

A joint tenant cannot leave his or her share to anyone other than the surviving joint tenants. So even if Evelyn, in the preceding example, left a will giving her half-interest in the car to her son instead of her daughter, the daughter would still get the car.

This rule isn't as ironclad as it may sound. A joint tenant can, while still alive, break the joint tenancy by transferring his or her interest in the property to someone else (or, in most states, to himself, but not as a "joint tenant"). The new owner isn't a joint tenant with the other original owners.

EXAMPLE:

David, Jan, and Loren own property together in joint tenancy. David sells his one-third interest to Paul. Paul is not a joint tenant with Jan and Loren; he is a "tenant in common," free to leave his property to whomever he wants. Jan and Loren, however, are still joint tenants with respect to their two-thirds of the property; when one of them dies, the other will own the two-thirds.

Joint Bank Accounts

If you and someone else want to set up a joint tenancy account together so that the survivor will get all the funds, normally you can do it in a few minutes at the bank. Your bank should be able to tell you about any requirements. In a few states, you may need to comply with certain formalities. Texas law, for example, requires a written agreement—not just a signature card—to set up such an account. A dispute over such an account ended up in the Texas Supreme Court. Two sisters had set up an account together, using a signature card that allowed the survivor to withdraw the funds. When the surviving sister withdrew the funds, the estate of the deceased sister sued and won the funds.

When to Consider Joint Tenancy

Joint tenancy often works well when couples (married or not) acquire real estate or other valuable property together. If they take title in joint tenancy, probate is avoided when the first owner dies.

But there are advantages to transferring the property to your living trust, even if you already own it in joint tenancy. First, a living trust, unlike joint tenancy, allows you to name an alternate beneficiary—someone who will inherit the property if the first beneficiary (your spouse) doesn't survive you. If you own property in joint tenancy, and you and your spouse die at the same time, the property will go to the residuary beneficiary named in your will—but it will have to go through probate first.

Second, if you transfer joint tenancy property to a living trust, you will avoid probate both when the first spouse dies and when the second spouse dies. With joint tenancy, probate is avoided only when the first spouse dies. The second spouse, who owns the property alone after the first spouse's death, must take some other measure—such as transferring it to a living trust—to avoid probate.

Restrictions on Joint Tenancy

A few states limit joint tenancy. Here are the rules you should know.

- Alaska prohibits joint tenancy except between a wife and husband, who may own property as tenants by the entirety. (See "Tenancy by the Entirety," below.)
- Texas requires a separate written agreement to create a joint tenancy.
- In Oregon and Tennessee, a transfer to a husband and wife creates a tenancy by the entirety, not a joint tenancy.
- Wisconsin does not allow joint tenancy between spouses (after January 1, 1986). Any attempted joint tenancy between spouses is treated as community property with right of survivorship. (See "Community Property With Right of Survivorship," below.)

CAUTION

Transferring joint tenancy property in common law states. As discussed in Chapter 11, if you live in a common law state, when transferring joint tenancy property to a living trust you need first to transfer the property into "tenancy in common, in equal shares" by preparing a new deed, and then transfer the property to your trust.

When to Think Twice About Joint Tenancy

Joint tenancy is usually a poor estate planning device when an older person, seeking only to avoid probate, puts solely owned property into joint tenancy with someone else. Doing this creates several potential problems that don't occur with a living trust:

You can't change your mind. If you make someone else a co-owner, in joint tenancy, of property that you now own yourself, you give up half ownership of the property. The new owner has rights that you can't take back. For example, the new owner can sell or mortgage his or her share. And even if the other joint tenant's half isn't mortgaged, it could still be lost to creditors.

EXAMPLE:

Maureen, a widow, signs a deed that puts her house into joint tenancy with her son to avoid probate at her death. Later, the son's business fails, and he is sued by creditors. His half-interest in the house may be taken by the creditors to pay the court judgment, which means that the house might be sold. Maureen would get the value of her half in cash; her son's half of the proceeds would go to pay the creditors.

By contrast, if you put property in a revocable living trust, you don't give up any ownership now. You are always free to change your mind about who you want to get the property at your death.

There's no way to handle the incapacity of one joint tenant. If one joint tenant becomes incapacitated and cannot make decisions, the other owners must get legal authority to sell or mortgage the property. That may mean going to court to get someone (called a conservator, in most states) appointed to manage the incapacitated person's affairs. (This problem can be partially dealt with if the joint tenant has signed a document called a Durable Power of Attorney, giving someone authority to manage his or her affairs if he or she cannot. See below.)

With a living trust, if you (the grantor) become incapacitated, the successor trustee (or the other spouse, if it's a shared trust) takes over and has full authority to manage the trust property. No court proceedings are necessary.

Gift taxes may be assessed. If you create a joint tenancy by making another person a co-owner, federal gift tax may be assessed on the transfer. This probably isn't a reason not to transfer property; making a gift can be a sound estate planning strategy. But be aware that if gifts to one person (except your spouse) exceed $13,000 per year, you must file a gift tax return with the IRS. (See below.) There's one exception: If two or more people open a bank account in joint tenancy, but one person puts all or most of the money in, no gift tax is assessed against that person. A taxable gift may be made, however, when a joint tenant who has contributed little or nothing to the account withdraws money from it.

Surviving spouse misses an income tax break. If you make your spouse a joint tenant with you on property you own separately, the surviving spouse could miss out on a potentially big income tax break later, when the property is sold.

When it comes to property owned in joint tenancy, the Internal Revenue Service rule is that a surviving spouse gets a stepped-up tax basis only for the half of the property owned by the deceased spouse. The tax basis is the amount from which taxable profit is figured when property is sold. You may not face this problem if you live in a community property state. If property held in joint tenancy property is actually community property, it will still qualify for a stepped-up tax basis if the surviving spouse can show the IRS that it was in fact community property. But it's up to you to prove it; when one spouse dies, the IRS presumes that property held in joint tenancy is not community property. When the property is later sold, this means higher tax if the property has gone up in value after the joint tenancy was created but before the first spouse died.

If you leave your solely owned property to your spouse through your living trust, however, the entire property gets a stepped-up tax basis.

Tenancy by the Entirety

"Tenancy by the entirety" is a form of property ownership that is similar to joint tenancy, but is limited to married couples (and in Hawaii, New Jersey, Oregon, and Vermont, same-sex couples registered with the state). It is available only in the states listed below.

States That Allow Tenancy by the Entirety		
Alaska*	Maryland	Oklahoma
Arkansas	Massachusetts	Oregon*
Delaware*	Michigan	Pennsylvania
District of Columbia	Mississippi	Rhode Island*
Florida	Missouri	Tennessee
Hawaii	New Jersey	Utah*
Illinois*	New York*	Vermont
Indiana*	North Carolina*	Virginia
Kentucky*	Ohio**	Wyoming

*Allowed for real estate only.

**Only if created before April 4, 1985.

Tenancy by the entirety has almost the same advantages and disadvantages of joint tenancy and is most useful in the same kind of situation: when a couple acquires property together. When one spouse dies, the surviving spouse inherits the property. The property doesn't go through probate.

If property is held in tenancy by the entirety, neither spouse can transfer his or her half of the property alone, either while alive or by will or trust. A living spouse must get the other spouse's consent to transfer the property; at death, it must go to the surviving spouse. (This is different from joint tenancy; a joint tenant is free to transfer his or her share to someone else during his life.)

EXAMPLE:

Fred and Ethel hold title to their apartment building in tenancy by the entirety. If Fred wanted to sell or give away his half-interest in the building, he could not do so without Ethel's signature on the deed.

Community Property With Right of Survivorship

Married couples in one of the following community property states—Arizona, California, Nevada, Texas, Washington, or Wisconsin—have another option that may be useful.

Married couples in Arizona, California, Nevada, or Wisconsin can hold title to their community property "with right of survivorship"—meaning that when one spouse dies, the other automatically owns all the property. Several states, including Washington and Texas, let couples make a written agreement that some or all of their community property will have a right of survivorship.

These arrangements offer all the benefits of community property ownership, plus the important advantage that the property doesn't go through probate when one spouse dies. Instead, the surviving spouse owns it automatically.

Wisconsin law goes even further. It lets married couples avoid probate altogether for their marital property. In a "marital property agreement," they can name a beneficiary—a person, trust, or other entity—to inherit their marital property, without probate. And like an AB trust, the agreement can even provide for the disposition of property at the death of the second spouse (though that spouse can amend the agreement after the first spouse's death unless the agreement says otherwise).

Transfer-on-Death Deeds

In Arizona, Arkansa, Colorado, Kansas, Missouri, Montana, Nevada, New Mexico, Ohio, and Wisconsin, you can leave real estate using a special kind of deed that is effective only at death. The deed document should be clearly titled "transfer-on-death" or "T.O.D." The deed must clearly state that the transfer to the beneficiary you name is not to take effect until your death. Like any deed, a T.O.D. deed must be properly signed, notarized, and then recorded in with the property records office in the county where the real estate is located.

Gifts

If you give away property while you're alive, there will be less property in your estate to go through probate when you die. But if probate avoidance is your goal, usually it's better to use one of the other methods discussed above, which let you keep control over your property while you're alive, than it is to give away everything before you die.

Making tax-exempt gifts every year, however, may be a good strategy if you expect your estate to owe federal estate tax after your death and you want to reduce the eventual tax bite. (See below.)

Probate Shortcuts for Small Estates

Many states have begun, albeit slowly, to dismantle some of the more onerous aspects of probate. Who benefits? As you might guess, one big category comprises people who don't leave much of monetary value—and whose probate cases therefore aren't worth much to lawyers.

Because of the way the laws are written, however, not only small estates can benefit. Many larger estates—worth hundreds of thousands of dollars—legally qualify as "small estates," eligible for special transfer procedures that speed property to inheritors.

Here are the kinds of shortcuts available for small estates:

Claiming property with affidavits—no court required. If the total value of all the assets you leave behind is less than a certain amount, the people who inherit your personal property—that's anything except real estate—may be able to skip probate entirely. The exact amount varies tremendously. The limit in California or Hawaii is $100,000. The highest limit is $150,000 in Wyoming.

If the estate qualifies, an inheritor can prepare a short document stating that he or she is entitled to a certain item of property under a will or state law. This paper, signed under oath, is called an affidavit. When the person or institution holding the property—for example, a bank where the deceased person had an account—receives the affidavit and a copy of the death certificate, it releases the money or other property.

Leaving property to the surviving spouse—no court required. In some states, if a surviving spouse inherits less than a certain amount of property, no probate is necessary.

Simplified court procedures. Another option for small estates (again, as defined by state law) is a quicker, simpler version of probate. The probate court is still involved, but it exerts far less control over the settling of the estate. In many states, these procedures are straightforward enough to handle without a lawyer, so they save money as well as time.

Most people leave property that is worth more than can be passed through these probate shortcuts. In many states, if the value of your entire estate exceeds the maximum set by law for simplified procedures, you cannot use the procedures to pass any property.

EXAMPLE:

At her death, Jane has an estate worth $300,000. Her major asset is her home, worth $200,000, which she passes to her daughter through a living trust. She also passes $80,000 worth of other property through other probate-avoidance devices. That leaves $20,000 worth of property. In Jane's state, the maximum total estate (including all property transferred by all methods) for streamlined probate procedures is $25,000. So Jane's heirs can't use the simplified procedures for the last $20,000 because Jane's total estate exceeds the limit.

In some states, however, even if your total estate is too large, you can still make use of simplified procedures if the amount that actually goes through probate is under the limit. For example, in California, property worth less than $100,000 transferred by will is exempt from normal probate, no matter how large the total estate. So if Jane lived in California, the $20,000 worth of property left through Jane's will could be transferred out of court or through simplified court procedures.

RESOURCE

How to find out about your state's probate shortcuts. Some states have all the shortcuts discussed above; others have just one. You can learn the details of your state's law in *8 Ways to Avoid Probate* or *The Executor's Guide,* both by Mary Randolph (Nolo).

Federal Gift and Estate Taxes

We've already covered the basic federal estate tax rules in Chapters 4 and 5. Let's summarize them again, and then look a little deeper into taxes and estate planning.

- The personal exemption allows property worth between $1 million and $3.5 million, depending on the year of death, to be left free of tax. Further, the estate tax is scheduled to be repealed in 2010, but only for that year.
- The amount of the estate tax exemption is likely to be revised by Congress within the next couple of years.
- The marital deduction exempts from tax all property, no matter how large the dollar value, left by a deceased spouse to a surviving spouse. But if the surviving spouse is not a citizen of the United States, the marital deduction does not apply.
- The charitable exemption authorizes all property given or left to tax-exempt charities to pass tax-free.

Federal Estate and Gift Tax Exemptions

Year	Estate tax exemption	Gift tax exemption	Highest estate and gift tax rate
2009	$3.5 million	$1 million	45%
2010	Estate tax repealed	$1 million	Top individual income tax rate (gift tax only)
2011	$1 million unless Congress extends repeal	$1 million	55% unless Congress extends repeal

RESOURCE

Federal estate taxes. A comprehensive explanation of federal estate taxes is contained in *Plan Your Estate,* by Denis Clifford (Nolo).

A federal estate tax return must be filed if the gross value of the estate exceeds the exempt amount for the year of death. Estate taxes will be due if the net estate exceeds the amount of all applicable exemptions. The assets in the estate are valued as of the date of death or, as an optional alternative, six months later if it produces a lesser estate value. An exception is that any asset distributed to beneficiaries or sold at an earlier date must be valued when it is distributed or sold. Tax must be paid within nine months of death.

Federal Gift Taxes

As you can see from the above chart, the federal government also taxes substantial gifts made during life. Congress reasoned that if only property left at death were taxed, people would give away as much property as they could during their lives. Gift tax rates are the same as estate tax rates, to eliminate any tax incentive to gift making.

If you look closely at the chart, you will notice that the estate tax exemption now exceeds the gift tax exemption, which remains at $1 million. What does this mean? It means that before 2010, you can give away a total of up to $1 million in taxable gifts, but not pay any tax, because of the gift tax exemption. But if you give away more than $1 million, you are taxed.

EXAMPLE:

In 2009, Franklin makes taxable gifts of $2 million. When he dies later that year, his estate must pay tax on $1 million. But in 2009, the personal estate tax exemption is $3.5 million. If Franklin had left the $2 million at his death instead of as gifts during his lifetime, his taxable estate would have been $3 million and his estate would owe no taxes.

As this example demonstrates, the divergence of the gift and estate tax exemption matters mainly to those with very large estates.

More important for regular folks is the federal law that exempts from gift tax a set dollar amount of gifts per year. Currently, you can give up to $13,000 per person per year without owing gift tax. This gift tax exemption is indexed yearly to the cost of living. As the cost of living rises (assuming it does), the gift tax will also rise, in increments of $1,000. In other words, cost-of-living increases must cumulatively raise the current exemption by something more than $1,000 before the gift tax exemption will be raised to $14,000.

Normally, if gift tax is assessed, no tax is actually paid on gifts until your death, when your combined gift and estate tax liability is calculated. However, if you've made nonexempt gifts that total more than the estate tax threshold, gift tax must be paid on an annual basis.

EXAMPLE:

Susan has made taxable gifts totaling $900,000 by 2008. She does not have to pay any gift tax, because her total gifts are under the $1 million gift tax exemption. In 2009, Susan gives away another $300,000 subject to gift tax. Her total lifetime gifts are now $1.2 million, $200,000 over the gift tax exemption. In 2009, she must pay tax on this $200,000.

Other gifts are exempt regardless of amount, including:

- gifts between spouses who are U.S. citizens
- gifts to directly pay someone else's medical bills or school tuition, and
- gifts to tax-exempt charitable organizations.

Special Rules for Noncitizen Spouses

The unlimited marital deduction for property one spouse leaves (or gives while living) to another applies only if the recipient spouse is a citizen of the United States. It doesn't matter that a noncitizen spouse was married to a U.S. citizen or is a legal resident. While both are alive, a spouse can, however, give the other, noncitizen, spouse up to $133,000 per year free of gift tax.

The personal estate tax exemption, however, remains available no matter who inherits the property. A citizen can leave a noncitizen spouse property tax-free under this exemption.

EXAMPLE:

Lily Lim, a U.S. citizen, leaves her entire estate worth $2,200,000 to her husband, Choy Lim, a non-U.S. citizen. Lily dies in 2011, when the personal exemption is $1 million, so $1.2 million of her property is subject to estate tax. By contrast, if Choy were a U.S. citizen, all of Lily's estate would pass free of tax because of the marital deduction.

SEE AN EXPERT

Special trusts for noncitizen spouses. Property left by one spouse to a noncitizen spouse in what's called a "Qualified Domestic Trust" is allowed the marital deduction. To create one of these trusts, you'll need to see a lawyer. Indeed, if you're married to a noncitizen and have an estate worth more than the exempt amount, see a lawyer for estate tax planning.

Reducing Estate Tax

If your property is likely to be subject to estate tax, even if you use one of Nolo's AB trusts, there are a number of options you can consider. For the very rich, tax avoidance schemes can become extraordinarily twisted. Here we'll briefly look at some more common options.

Gifts

If you don't need all your income and property to live on, making tax-exempt gifts from your trust, or indeed from any of your assets, while you're alive can be a good way to reduce eventual federal estate taxes.

Every person can currently give $13,000 to any one person per year, so a couple can give $26,000 per year.

EXAMPLE:

Allen and Julia give each of their two daughters $26,000 every year for four years. They have transferred a total of $208,000 without becoming liable for gift tax.

CAUTION

Gifts made within three years of death. The gift tax exemption is not allowed for a few types of gifts made in the last three years of someone's life. The gift itself is valid, but for estate tax purposes, the value of the gift is included in the giver's estate. Most importantly, a gift of a life insurance policy is not entitled to the gift tax exemption if made within three years before death.

How to choose property to give away. It's usually wise to give away property that you think will go up in value substantially before your death. That way, you may avoid gift tax now—if the gift is worth less than the gift tax exemption—and you may avoid estate tax later, because the increased value of the property won't be included in your estate when you die. Also, if the recipient (other than a child age 14 or under) is in a lower tax bracket, you may want to give away income-generating property, so that the income will be taxed at the recipient's lower tax rates. Any income over $850 per year received by a child 14 years or under from any gift (whether from parents or anyone else) is taxed at the parents' rate.

You may not, however, want to give away property that has already appreciated greatly in value. Usually, it's wiser to hold onto it until death to take advantage of the stepped-up tax basis rules discussed above.

Gifts of life insurance. Life insurance policies you own on your own life and give away at least three years before your death are excellent gifts, from an estate planning view. Your gift tax liability is determined by the current value of the policy, which is far less than the amount the policy will pay off at death. For many policies, the present value will be less than the $13,000 annual gift tax threshold, which means that no gift tax will be assessed.

To give away a life insurance policy, you must comply with some fairly technical IRS rules, which should be available from your insurance company. The process of actually transferring ownership is simple. Insurance companies have forms you can use to make the transfer. You must make an irrevocable gift of the policy. If you keep the right to revoke the gift and get the policy back, the proceeds will be taxed as part of your estate.

If you buy a policy that requires future premium payments, you'll want to make more gifts to the new owner of the policy to cover the payments. As an alternative, you can pay for some kinds of policies all at once; these are called single-premium policies.

EXAMPLE:

Sarah buys three single-premium life insurance policies (that is, she pays the entire premium in advance) for $50,000 each and transfers ownership of the policies to her three children. She must file a gift tax return because the value of the gifts exceeds the $13,000 per person per year tax exemption. Each gift has a taxable value of $37,000. The taxable value of all three gifts is $111,000. The gift tax assessed is not due until her death. When Sarah dies, each policy pays $700,000. The total proceeds, $2.1 million, are not included as part of her estate.

Tax-Saving Trusts and Devices

As you know, this book presents Nolo's AB trusts as devices to achieve estate tax savings. Other types of tax-saving trusts and devices can be used by couples, or in some cases individuals, with larger estates. Here are some important ones:

- **Property left to spouse.** A married person with an estate worth more than the amount that can be shielded from tax by an AB trust may leave the overage outright to his or her spouse. No tax is due when the first spouse dies, because all property left to a surviving spouse is exempt.
- **QTIP trusts** (for married couples only). A QTIP trust postpones payment of estate taxes that otherwise are due when the first spouse dies. A QTIP trust can be desirable for a spouse with property over the estate tax threshold who wants:

- to leave all of his or her property to the other spouse with no payment of taxes until that surviving spouse dies, and
- wants to name final beneficiaries of the trust property (that is, doesn't want to leave the property outright to the other spouse).

One drawback of a QTIP trust is that the federal estate taxes eventually paid on the property of the first spouse to die are assessed against what the property is worth when the surviving spouse dies, not what the property was worth when the first spouse died. Usually, that means higher taxes.

EXAMPLE:

Mary Edna, a widow with three grown children, marries Roberto. Her estate has a net value of $4 million. Roberto has little property beyond his monthly Social Security check. Mary Edna wants Roberto to be able to continue to live in both her houses if she predeceases him. After his death, she wants all her property to go to her children.

If Mary Edna creates an AB trust, with Roberto having a life estate, all of her property will be subject to estate tax when she dies. Some tax probably will have to be paid, because her estate is over the exempt amount for all years except 2010. This could necessitate the sale of one of her houses. So she creates a QTIP trust. No estate taxes will be assessed against her property until Roberto dies. However, if the worth of the property has risen to $6 million when Roberto dies, estate taxes will be based on this value.

- **Generation-skipping trusts** (for individuals or couples). One of the legal devices traditionally used by the very wealthy to minimize estate taxes has been to leave the bulk of their property in trust for their grandchildren, with the income (but not the principal) from the trusts available to their children. This strategy avoids death taxes several times. Without a trust, taxes would typically be paid when the first grandparent died, then again when the second grandparent died, and then when each of their children died.

Current law imposes a tax on all "generation-skipping transfers" in excess of the amount of the personal estate tax exemption. A generation-skipping trust worth more than the exempt amount is subject to tax on the overage. This tax is assessed against the trust property when the middle (income) generation dies.

EXAMPLE:

Paul establishes a generation-skipping trust for his daughter and her children. He dies in 2009, leaving the maximum tax-free amount in a generation-skipping trust. When his daughter dies, the trust property is worth $2 million more than Paul left to the trust. Tax must then be paid on $2 million of the trust property.

Generation-skipping trusts are very complicated. These trusts are designed to have effect for at least two generations after the grantor's life, normally over 50 years, and many contingencies should be considered. Also, there are IRS requirements regarding the age of the trustee and when estate taxes will be assessed.

- **Disclaimers** (for individuals or couples). A disclaimer means that someone who has been left a gift declines to accept it. The gift is then given to an alternate beneficiary originally named by the gift-giver. A beneficiary who disclaims a gift generally does so to make the overall estate tax picture better. Of course, this means he or she doesn't need the gift he or she disclaimed to live on. Any beneficiary has the legal right to disclaim a gift, but often that right is expressly stated in estate planning documents.
- **Life insurance trusts.** An irrevocable life insurance trust is a legal entity you create for the purpose of owning life insurance you previously owned. It becomes operational during your lifetime. An irrevocable trust, like a corporation or any other trust, is a legal entity, distinct from any human being.

Transferring ownership of your life insurance policy to a new owner—the trust—can reduce federal estate taxes by removing the proceeds of the policy from your taxable estate. Why create a life insurance trust, rather than simply transfer a life insurance policy to someone else? One reason is that there may be no one you want to give your policy to. In other words, you want to get the proceeds out of your taxable estate, but you don't want the risks of having an insurance policy on your life owned by someone else. For example, the trust could specify that the policy must be kept in effect while you live, eliminating the risk that a new owner of the policy could decide to cash it in.

EXAMPLE:

Brenda is the divorced mother of two children in their 20s, who will inherit her property. Neither is sensible with money. Brenda has an estate of $1.5 million, plus life insurance that will pay $750,000 at her death. She wants to remove the proceeds of the policy from her estate. If she doesn't, her estate may be subject to estate tax. However, there's no one Brenda trusts enough to give her policy to outright. With the controls she can impose through a trust, however, she decides it's safe to allow her sister, the person she's closest to, to be the trustee of a life insurance trust for the policy. She creates an irrevocable trust and transfers ownership of the life insurance policy to that trust.

Strict federal requirements govern life insurance trusts. To gain the estate tax savings:

- The life insurance trust must be irrevocable. If you keep the right to revoke the trust, you will be considered the owner of the policy, and the proceeds will be considered part of your estate upon death.
- You cannot be the trustee. You must name either an "independent" adult (that is, someone not under your legal control) or an institution to serve as trustee.
- You must establish the trust at least three years before your death. If the trust has not existed for at least three years when you die, the trust is disregarded for estate tax purposes, and the proceeds are included in your taxable estate.
- **Charitable remainder trusts.** With a charitable remainder trust, you make an irrevocable gift of property to a tax-exempt charity while you're alive. You are entitled to receive certain income from the property as well as continue to use and control it while you're alive, with significant income tax breaks. When you die, the property, of course, must go to the charity—and therefore, no estate tax can be due.

SEE AN EXPERT

Don't try this on your own. If you want to create any of these kinds of trusts or devices, see an experienced estate planning lawyer.

RESOURCE

More about saving on taxes. *Plan Your Estate*, by Denis Clifford (Nolo), discusses these and many other advanced estate planning strategies.

Family Limited Partnerships

In the right circumstances, establishing a family limited partnership (FLP) can produce significant tax savings for inheritors. The first requirement here is that you must have a legitimate business, one that the IRS accepts as genuine. You cannot create a tax-valid family limited partnership simply to manage your regular investments, such as your securities or savings accounts.

You, as the original owner of the FLP, transfer, usually by gift, minority interests in the business to your inheritors, normally your children. The value of these minority interests can be "discounted," under IRS rules, from what the value would be if the interests had remained held by the majority owner. The theory is that minority interests, which have no legal control over the business, would be worth proportionally less to a legitimate buyer than a majority interest. The amount of the discount is subjective, and is frequently contested between the IRS and FLP owners.

EXAMPLE:

Olivia owns a successful pet food company. She intends to leave the business equally to her three children, who can maintain it or sell it, as they choose. The business is worth $2 million.

Olivia creates an FLP and transfers the business into it. There are 100 shares of the FLP. So it would seem that each share is worth $20,000. But if Olivia gives one share to each child, that share is worth less than $20,000, for gift and estate tax purposes, because, as a minority interest, it has less value to a buyer. So the gift shares may each be worth $17,000, or $15,000, depending only on the discount allowed. Olivia can transfer up to 49% ownership of the FLP to her children, and all those interests will receive minority discounts.

FLPs that save on estate taxes are tricky creatures. The FLP must be operated as a family-owned business, which means that profits must be distributed (roughly) according to legal ownership. If you create a limited partnership but continue to treat the business assets as if they were solely yours, the IRS will include the full value of the business in your estate at your death. In other words, an FLP cannot be run solely as an estate-tax-avoiding shell.

SEE AN EXPERT

You need a lawyer before giving away minority interests. If you want to explore giving interests in a family limited partnership to family members (or anyone else), you must see a lawyer. This is a difficult and rapidly changing area of the law. The IRS is not fond of discounted gifts of an FLP and tries to scrutinize them. You must be sure you do it right, and that requires working with a lawyer knowledgeable in this subject.

State Taxes

The states below impose a type of tax called an "inheritance tax." It's imposed on the recipients of property left by the deceased. (At least, that's the theory; in reality, the tax is paid out of property the deceased left.) Tax rates vary, depending on the state and the relationship of the beneficiary to the deceased. A surviving spouse, for example, commonly pays no tax or is taxed at the lowest rate. Non-family members are taxed at the highest rate. Inheritance taxes can take a significant bite from some estates.

These states impose tax on:
- all property of residents of the state, no matter where the property is located, and
- all real estate located in the state, no matter where the deceased resided.

States With Inheritance Taxes		
Indiana	Nebraska	Oklahoma
Iowa	New Jersey	Pennsylvania
Kentucky	Ohio	Tennessee
Maryland		

RESOURCE

State tax rules. State inheritance tax rules are summarized in *Plan Your Estate,* by Denis Clifford (Nolo). More detailed information is also available from state tax officials.

Because of recent changes in federal and state tax laws, a new type of state estate tax, which can be called a "pick-up replacement tax," has been adopted in a number of states. Many other states are likely to adopt a similar tax. Here's what the pick-up replacement tax is about.

Before 2002, most states collected only what was called a "pick-up" tax from estates large enough to have to pay federal estate taxes. A pick-up tax didn't increase the overall tax paid by the estate. Rather, the state was entitled, under federal law, to collect a certain percentage of the federal tax due.

But under current federal law, states can no longer claim a share of tax paid to the federal government. To make up for this loss of revenue, states are adopting the pick-up tax, now independent of federal law. The details of these new laws vary between different states. The common denominator is that some estates may have to pay state estate tax even if they are not large enough to pay federal estate tax.

This could be true even if you use an AB trust. If you leave an amount of property that exceeds your state's threshold for state estate tax, your estate will owe state tax, even though no federal tax is assessed.

EXAMPLE:

Roy and Ann are Rhode Island residents. Rhode Island has a "pick-up replacement tax." Roy and Ann make an AB trust. At Roy's death in 2009, his share of the couple's property is $2 million. That amount goes into Trust A, the deceased spouse's trust. Roy's estate is well under the 2009 federal estate tax threshold of $3.5 million, so it owes no federal tax. However, Roy's estate will owe Rhode Island estate tax, because Rhode Island imposes its own pick-up replacement tax on estates of $675,000 or more.

SEE AN EXPERT

These laws are changing fast. If you are concerned about new state pick-up replacement taxes, see a lawyer who can bring you up to date.

If you divide your time between a state that doesn't impose inheritance tax (or has a very low one) and one with high estate taxes, you may want to establish your permanent residence in the lower tax state.

To establish your legal residence in a particular state, you should register all vehicles there, keep bank and other financial accounts there, and vote there.

SEE AN EXPERT

Getting your legal residence established. Establishing residence in a no-tax state can be tricky if you also live in a high-tax one, because the high-tax state has a financial incentive to conclude that you really reside there. If you have a large estate and a complicated two-or-more-state living situation, consult a knowledgeable tax lawyer or accountant.

Planning for Incapacity

A living trust can be a big help if you become unable to manage your own financial affairs, because your successor trustee (your spouse, if you make a shared trust or an AB trust) can take over management of trust property. That person, however, has no power over any of your other financial assets or your health care decisions. For that reason, you should prepare a few other documents and coordinate them with your living trust.

Durable Power of Attorney for Finances

The best way to plan for the management of property not covered by your living trust is to use a document called a "durable power of attorney for finances." Every state recognizes this document. It gives a trusted person you choose, called your "attorney-in-fact," the

legal authority to manage your finances (except for property owned by your living trust) on your behalf. The document can be worded so that it becomes effective only if you become incapacitated, as certified in writing by a physician.

RESOURCE

Making a durable power of attorney for finances. You can use *Quicken WillMaker Plus,* software from Nolo, to prepare a durable power of attorney for finances that is valid in your state.

Medical Care Documents

If you become unconscious or mentally incapacitated and death seems close, your loved ones may have to decide what sorts of medical intervention, if any, should occur. These decisions are profound, often deeply wrenching and personal.

You can provide binding direction for what you want done regarding life-prolonging medical care. The right to die with dignity and without the agony and expense of artificial life-prolonging procedures has been confirmed by the U.S. Supreme Court, the federal government, and every state legislature. Every state authorizes individuals to create simple documents setting out their wishes concerning end-of-life medical treatment.

There are two basic documents that allow you to do this, both grouped under the broad label "health care directives." You need to prepare both. First, you need a "declaration," a written statement you make directly to medical personnel that spells out the medical care you do or do not wish to receive if you become incapacitated. Your declaration functions as a contract with the treating doctor, who must either honor your wishes for medical care or transfer you to another doctor or facility that will honor them.

Second, you'll want what's often called a "durable power of attorney for health care." In this document, you appoint someone you trust to be your "attorney-in-fact" (sometimes called your "agent" or "health care proxy") to see that your doctors and other health care providers give you the kind of medical care you wish to receive. You can also give your attorney-in-fact greater authority to make decisions about your medical care, including:

- making decisions about any issues you don't cover in your declaration
- hiring and firing medical personnel
- visiting you in the hospital or other facility, even when other visiting is restricted
- having access to medical records and other personal information, and
- getting court authorization, if it is required, to obtain or withhold medical treatment if, for any reason, a hospital or doctor does not honor your health care directives.

Several states combine the declaration and durable power of attorney for health care into a single document, usually called an "advance health care directive."

A Health Care Directive by Any Other Name …

Depending on the state, your health care documents may be called by one of several different names: Advance Health Care Directive, Medical Directive, Directive to Physicians, Declaration Regarding Health Care, Designation of Health Care Surrogate, or Patient Advocate Designation. A health care declaration may also be called a "living will," but it bears no relation to the conventional will or living trust used to leave property at death.

RESOURCE

Making health care directives. You can make a health care directive with *Quicken WillMaker Plus*, software from Nolo. Californians can also use *Living Wills & Powers of Attorney for California*, by Shae Irving (Nolo). Also, in most states, you can obtain forms from the state medical association. You can also get your state's form for free from a nonprofit organization called Caring Connections (800-658-8898; www.caringinfo.org).

Long-Term Trusts to Control Property

In certain circumstances, you may want to dictate how your property is to be managed and distributed over many years. You may want to leave property to people who, for one reason or another, may not be able to manage it for themselves, even when they are over age 35. Or you may want to impose strict controls over property left to your spouse for his or her life, to be sure it remains intact to go eventually to your children from a former marriage.

Reminder. For a discussion of how to leave property to a minor or young adult, and have someone manage it until the beneficiary is older, see Chapter 9.

SEE AN EXPERT

Long-term property management is not a do-it-yourself job. See an experienced lawyer if you want to create one of the property management trusts discussed in this section.

AB Trusts Used to Control Property

If you or your spouse have children from a previous marriage, you may want your current spouse to have use of some of your property during his or her life, but be sure that that property eventually goes to your children. One way to do this is to establish a special type of AB trust that limits the surviving spouse's use, and rights, to property in Trust A. Nolo's AB trust gives the surviving spouse, as trustee of Trust A, maximum freedom over Trust A property. Spouses in second or subsequent marriages often prefer more control over the surviving spouse's rights, to try to insure that their children will eventually receive the bulk of their property.

EXAMPLE:

Ilana and Harvey are both in their 50s. Ilana has a son from her first marriage. Harvey has two daughters from his. Ilana and Harvey purchase, equally, an $800,000 house. If one dies, each wants the other spouse to be able to live in the house for the remainder of his or her life. But after both have died, each wants his or her share of the house to go to the children of their first marriages. So Ilana and Harvey create an AB trust. Each spouse's Trust A allows the surviving spouse full use of the house, but not the right to sell it and buy another one. Then half the house goes to Ilana's son, and the other half to Harvey's two daughters.

Many questions need to be resolved in setting up the trust.

- How strict should the controls on the surviving spouse be?
- Can the spouse sell the house to pay for health needs? For any needs?
- Should the spouse be the sole trustee, or is it better to have a child share that job or to have a child be the sole trustee?
- What reports and accountings must be given to the children?

Suppose a wife wants to allow her husband the right to stay in her home while he lives. How specifically does the right need to be pinned down in the trust? Can the husband sell the house and buy another? Can he rent it out? Suppose he needs to go to a nursing home—can the house then be sold? What happens to the profits of the sale? Who gets any income from trust property?

SEE AN EXPERT

An AB trust intended to impose controls on Trust A property must be carefully drafted by a knowledgeable attorney. Inherently, you are dealing with possible conflicts—the basic concern, after all, is that the surviving spouse's desires and interests may be very different from, or directly conflict with, the desires and interests of the deceased spouse's children. To resolve these issues wisely, you need a trust geared to your desires and to the specific realities of your situation.

Spendthrift Trusts

If you want to leave property to an adult who just can't handle money, a "spendthrift trust," where an independent trustee can dole out the money little by little, is a good idea. A spendthrift trust keeps the property from being squandered by the beneficiary or seized by the beneficiary's creditors.

Special Needs Trusts

A person with a serious physical or mental disability may not be able to handle property, no matter what his or her age. Often, the solution is to establish a trust with a competent adult as trustee to manage the trust property.

RESOURCE

Trusts for disabled loved ones. *Special Needs Trusts,* by Stephen Elias (Nolo), explains how to create a trust for a disabled loved one you wish to leave money to. This trust is designed so that the loved one's inheritance will not interfere with his or her eligibility for SSI or Medicaid benefits.

Flexible Trusts

You may want the determination of how your property is spent after your death to be decided in the future by a successor trustee, not by you before you die. The usual way to do this is to create a "sprinkling trust," authorizing the trustee to decide how to spend trust money for several beneficiaries.

Wills

As I urged in chapters 3 and 15, you'll need to prepare a simple "backup" will, even if you leave most, or all, of your property by your living trust. Backup will forms are contained in Appendix B and on the CD-ROM.

Why Prepare a Backup Will?

It's always sensible to prepare a backup will for one, or probably more, of the following reasons:

- **To name a personal guardian for your minor children.** If you have young children, you need a will to achieve the vital goal of nominating a personal guardian for them. In most states, you can't use your living trust to nominate a personal guardian. Also, in your will you can appoint a property guardian for your children to manage any of their property not otherwise legally supervised by an adult. Younger people with minor children, who don't have much property, may decide that because nominating a personal guardian is the primary thing they're worried about, a simple will is all the estate planning they currently need.

- **To choose a beneficiary for suddenly acquired property.** Anyone may end up acquiring valuable property at or shortly before death, such as a sudden gift, inheritance, or (even) lottery prize. Under the will forms in this book, that property will go to the residuary beneficiary of your will. You may well not get around to, or have time to, transfer the property to your trust. Therefore, it cannot be subject to your trust. And if you didn't have a will, the property would, under your state's "intestate succession" laws, go to your closest relatives.

- **To leave property not transferred by a probate-avoidance device.** If you don't get around to planning probate avoidance for all your property (by placing it in your living trust, for example), a will is a valuable backup device. If you have a will, the property will go to whom you want to have it (the residuary beneficiary of your will) and not pass under the intestate succession laws.

- **To give away property someone left you that is still in probate.** If someone has left you property by will, and that property is still enmeshed in probate

when you die, you can't arrange to transfer it by a probate-avoidance device. Since you don't have title to the property, you have no legal right to transfer it. But again, under your will, that property will go to your residuary beneficiary when the probate court releases it.

- **To name your executor.** In your will, you name your executor (and alternate executor), the person with legal authority to supervise distribution of property left by your will and to represent your estate in probate court proceedings. It is a good idea to have an executor even if you have also set up a living trust and named a successor trustee to manage it when you die, because banks and other institutions are often reassured to know an executor exists. Normally, it's best to name the same person as your successor trustee and executor.

- **For married couples, to avoid confusion in case of simultaneous death.** The will for a member of a couple provides that if both members "die simultaneously or under such circumstances as to render it difficult or impossible to determine who predeceased the other," the will writer is conclusively presumed to have outlived the other spouse. This clause works for each spouse, in his or her own will. How can that be, you may ask? Well, the official reason is that each will is interpreted independently from the other. The real reason is that it achieves a desired goal of preventing one spouse's property from going to another's estate if one lives only a few minutes or hours longer than the other.

What You Can Do in a Backup Will

The backup will forms in this book enable you to:

- Make specific gifts—for example, "I leave my piano to Julia Rhodes." You can leave property that you haven't transferred to your living trust—for example, your personal bank account or car—to whomever you choose.

  You can leave a gift to be shared among several beneficiaries (or alternate beneficiaries) in any percentages you choose. Before doing this in your will, be sure to review "Shared Gifts" in Chapter 8.

- Name alternate beneficiaries for these specific gifts in case the primary beneficiary dies before you do.
- Name a residuary beneficiary and alternate residuary beneficiary to inherit any property subject to your will that is not specifically left to other named beneficiaries.
- Nominate a personal guardian and alternate for your minor children.
- Name a property guardian (who can be the same person as the personal guardian) to manage any of your minor children's property that isn't otherwise legally controlled by an adult. It's generally preferable to leave property to your minor children in child's trusts or under the Uniform Transfers to Minors Act rather than relying on a property guardian named in a will that you name only as a backup for property they may acquire from some other source. (See Chapter 9.)
- Appoint your executor.

> ! **CAUTION**
>
> **Disinheriting a child or spouse.** If you want to disinherit a child or your spouse, you must do so in your will. But before you decide to do this, carefully reread "Disinheritance" in Chapter 8. The law may restrict your choices.

> ! **CAUTION**
>
> **Children born or adopted after you sign your will.** If you have a child after preparing your will, prepare a new will, naming that child and leaving him or her whatever property you choose. Reread "Disinheritance" in Chapter 8, for a reminder of why this is necessary.

You may decide that you need a more complicated will. For instance, perhaps you want to appoint different personal guardians for different minor children. Or you want to arrange for care of your pets or specifically forgive debts owed you. Some people want to use a "self-proving affidavit" (legal in most states) for their witnesses, which can make it easier to probate a will without a written statement or a court appearance by a witness. If you do want a more complicated will, consult *Nolo's Simple Will Book* or *Quicken WillMaker Plus,* software from Nolo.

Pour-Over Wills

A "pour-over will" takes all the property you haven't transferred to your living trust and, at your death, leaves it ("pours it over") to that trust. Some lawyers urge all people who make living trusts to make pour-over wills, arguing that it's always best to send all your property through your living trust. There seems to be something about the name pour-over will that impresses people. The term sounds, well, sophisticated, like they're doing something really right. In fact, pour-over wills are not very desirable, in my opinion, for most people with a living trust.

When Not to Use a Pour-Over Will

Pour-over wills do not avoid probate. All property that is left through a will—any kind of will—must go through probate, unless the amount left is small enough to qualify for exemption from normal probate laws. Probate is most definitely not avoided simply because the beneficiary of a will is a living trust.

It's generally better to simply use a standard backup will to take care of your leftover (non-living trust) property rather than a pour-over will. In the backup will, you can name the people you want to get the will property, and skip the unnecessary extra step of pouring the property through the living trust after your death.

When used as a backup will, a pour-over will actually has a disadvantage that standard wills don't: It forces the living trust to go on for months after your death, because the property left through the pour-over will must normally go through probate before it can be transferred to the trust. Usually, the property left in a living trust can be distributed to the beneficiaries and the trust ended within a few weeks after the person's death.

EXAMPLE:

Joy transfers her valuable property to her living trust. She also makes a pour-over will, which states that any property she owns at death goes to the living trust. When Joy dies, the property left through her will goes to the trust and is distributed to the residuary beneficiary of her living trust, her son Louis. The living trust must be kept going until probate of the will is finished, when property left by the will is poured over into the living trust. Normally, keeping the living trust ongoing for several months, or however long probate takes, would not require filing a trust tax return, since there's no income to this trust. Still, it's better to wind up a living trust as quickly as feasible.

If Joy had simply named Louis as sole beneficiary of a simple backup will, the end result would have been the same, but the process would have been simpler. The living trust would have been ended a few weeks after Joy's death. And after probate was finished, Louis would have received whatever property passed through Joy's will.

When You May Want a Pour-Over Will

There are, however, two situations in which you might want to use a pour-over will.

If you create an AB trust, a pour-over will can be desirable. The spouses want the maximum amount of property to eventually wind up in Trust A, the marital life estate trust. So each spouse writes a pour-over will, leaving his or her will property to their Trust A. After a spouse dies, the other spouse should amend her or his will or prepare a new one, since there will no longer be a functional Trust A for the surviving spouse's property to go to.

Also, if you set up a child's subtrust for a young beneficiary in your living trust, you may want any property that child inherits through your will to go into the subtrust. Otherwise, you would create two trusts for the beneficiary: one in the will and one in your living trust.

EXAMPLE:

Jessica makes a living trust and leaves the bulk of her property to her 12-year-old son. She arranges, in the trust document, for any trust property her son inherits before the age of 30 to be kept in a child's trust, managed by Jessica's sister.

Jessica also makes a back-up will, in which she leaves everything to her son and again arranges for a child's trust to be set up if she should die before

her son reaches age 30. So if Jessica dies before her son reaches 30, two separate child's trusts will be set up to manage property for him.

If Jessica used a pour-over will, any property her son inherited through the will would go into the trust created by her living trust. With only one trust, only half the paperwork of maintaining the trust is necessary, as compared to maintaining two separate trusts.

How to Create a Pour-Over Will

You can use the will forms in this book to create a pour-over will. To do so, you leave property subject to the will to your successor trustee, as trustee of your trust. A married person usually lists two people as successor trustee—first the surviving spouse (who is technically a continuing trustee), and then the person next in line.

EXAMPLE:

Nils, married to Mercedes, wants the property he leaves through his will to go to his living trust. In his will, he lists the beneficiary as "Mercedes Janson, trustee of the Nils and Mercedes Janson Living Trust, or, if she does not survive me, to Ingemar Janson, successor trustee of the Nils and Mercedes Janson Living Trust."

Avoiding Conflicts Between Your Will and Your Living Trust

When you make both a living trust and a will, pay attention to how the two work together. If your will and your trust document contain conflicting provisions, at the least you will create confusion among your inheritors, and at the worst, bitter disputes—maybe even a lawsuit—among friends and family. Here are some guidelines to help you avoid problems:

- **Don't leave the same property in your living trust and will, even if it's to the same beneficiary.** If you transfer the property to your living trust and name a beneficiary in the trust document, that's all you need to do. Mentioning the property in your will raises the possibility of probate.
- **Name the same person to be executor of your will and successor trustee of your living trust.** There's

one important exception: If you make a basic shared trust or AB trust, you'll probably name your spouse as executor of your will, but not as successor trustee—the successor trustee takes over only after both spouses have died. The surviving spouse, however, may want to revise her will after the death of the first spouse, to name her successor trustee to be her executor.

Your beneficiaries, and your trustee/executor, don't need a conflict between your living trust and will. If you want to change a beneficiary, change it by amending the document where you named the original beneficiary, not by using your will to override it.

Simultaneous Death Clause

The will form in this book for a coupled person has a simultaneous death clause, which is effective if the couple dies together, or where it cannot be ascertained who died first. This clause is worded somewhat differently than the simultaneous death clause in the shared living trust or the AB trust, because each of those is a single document covering both spouses, whereas each spouse makes a separate will. But the simultaneous death clause in your will accomplishes the same task as the one in your living trust: Each spouse's property is treated as if he or she survived the other.

CAUTION

Watch out in Washington state. In the state of Washington, a "superwill" statute allows you to leave property held in your living trust, or in other probate avoidance devices such as joint tenancy or pay-on-death accounts, through your will. For example, if you write a will after having created a living trust, and in that will name a new beneficiary for property left to someone else in your living trust, your will prevails.

Filling in the Will Form

Here are the steps necessary to prepare your own will from a will form in Appendix B or on the CD-ROM:

Step 1. Select the correct form, depending on whether you are single (Form 11) or a member of a couple (Form 12).

As with the living trust forms, the will for a member of a couple is written in terms of a married couple, using the terms "husband" and "wife." If you are a member of an unmarried couple, please make the necessary word changes ("mate," "partner," each person's name, or whatever you feel works) in the will form, so that it makes sense for your situation.

Step 2. Read through the will form carefully. There are a number of blanks to fill in. The information called for is identified below each blank. While most of this is self-explanatory, here is what you must fill in:

- **Your name.** This should be the form of the name you use to sign such documents as deeds, checks, and loan applications. It needn't necessarily be the way your name appears on your birth or marriage certificate.
- **Your city, county, and state.**
- **The names of all your living children, and names of any children of a deceased child, if any.**
- **The names of the personal guardian, alternate personal guardian, property guardian, and alternate property guardian for your minor children.** You can name only one personal guardian and one property guardian for all your children.
- **Specific gifts.** You do not have to make any specific gifts. You can simply leave all property subject to this will to your residuary beneficiary. If you leave some property to more than one beneficiary, or alternate beneficiaries, follow the instructions in Chapter 10 for the wording of shared gifts. (Remember that in Florida, you cannot leave your house to anyone but your spouse or your children.) The will form provides three specific gift clauses. Repeat or delete these clauses as necessary.
- **The name of your residuary beneficiary and alternate residuary beneficiary.** You can name more than one residuary beneficiary if you want. For example, many people list all their children.
- **The names of your executor and alternate executor.**

You may need to renumber the clauses if you omit items that don't apply to you. Do not sign or date your will yet. You do this when you complete your final will, with your witnesses.

Step 3. Type or print out the final draft of your will. If you used the will forms in the back of the book, use a typewriter or a word processor to type out your final draft. Once your will is typed or printed, you may not make any changes by hand. A will with both handwriting and typing is not valid.

You do not need to initial each page. Your signature at the end (with the signatures of your witnesses) is all that is needed. A will with handwriting and typing combined is not valid.

> ⚠️ **CAUTION**
>
> **Don't use the form as your final will.** Do not type the information required onto the form and attempt to use it as your final will. Courts are not used to wills like this. You want your will to look normal and unthreatening to a judge, which means typed, and without the fill-in-the-blank lines and instructions. So you can see how a final draft and a typed will should look, there are samples below of Form 11, a will for a single person.

Type or print out the final draft of your will on good 8½" x 11" paper. Proofread it carefully and make sure it's letter-perfect. If you find mistakes, fix them and print out the page again. Don't ever make alterations on the face of your will by writing in words or crossing something out and initialing the change. It could make part or all of your will invalid.

Step 4. Date and sign the will in front of witnesses. (Instructions are below.)

Signing and Witnessing Your Will

To be valid, your will must be signed and dated in front of witnesses. You sign the will where the form provides. Then these witnesses must sign the will in your presence, and also in the presence of the other witnesses.

Although all states require only two witnesses, three is better because it provides one more person to establish that your signature is valid, if that becomes necessary during probate. Witnesses must be:

- Adults (18 or over) and of sound mind.
- People who won't inherit under the will. That means anyone who might inherit any gift through your will, including alternate residuary beneficiaries, cannot be a witness. But someone who will receive property from only your living trust can be a valid witness.

  Sixteen states now allow a witness to inherit will property. Still, I strongly recommend against doing that in your will. Having will witnesses who do not inherit eliminates one possible reason for challenging your will.
- People who should be easy to locate in the event of your death. This usually means people who aren't likely to move around a lot and (most of all) who are younger than you are.

Here's how to go about arranging for signing and witnessing your will:

- Have all witnesses assemble in one place.
- Tell them that the paper you hold is your will. They don't need to know what's in it.
- Sign the signature page in the witnesses' presence. Use the exact spelling of your name as you typed in the heading.
- Have each witness sign the last page in the place indicated while the other witnesses are watching. The clause immediately preceding the witnesses' signatures states ("attests") that the events outlined just above have occurred.

The witnesses list the city, county, and state of their residence (not where the will is signed). Listing the witnesses' addresses is not legally required, but can prove an aid in locating the witnesses later on, when the will becomes operational.

> ⚠️ **CAUTION**
>
> **Get the details right.** If a will doesn't comply with the technical requirements (say you had only one witness to your will), it cannot be validated by the probate court. It's not hard to do a will correctly. Double check to be sure you've done so!

~~Form 11: Basic Will for One Person~~

Will

of

Benjamin Werrin
<u>your name</u>

I, <u>Benjamin Werrin</u>, a resident of
<u>your name</u>

<u>Fairmont</u>, <u>Dutchess</u> County, <u>New York</u>,
<u>city</u> <u>county</u> <u>state</u>

declare that this is my will.

1. I revoke all wills and codicils that I have previously made.

2. I am not married.

3. (A) I am the <u>father</u> of the <u>child</u> whose <u>name</u> <u>is</u>
<u>mother/father</u> <u>child/children</u> <u>name/names</u> <u>is/are</u>

<u>Eric Werrin</u>

There are _____ living children of my deceased child _____,
<u>name</u>

whose name(s) is/are:

(B) If I fail to leave, by this will or otherwise, any property to any of the children listed above, my

failure to do so is intentional.

(C) If at my death any of my children are minors, and a personal guardian is needed, I nominate

_____ to be appointed personal guardian
                    name of personal guardian

of my minor children. If _____ cannot serve as
                                        name of personal guardian

personal guardian, I nominate _____
                                        name of alternate personal guardian

to be appointed personal guardian.

(D) If at my death any of my children are minors, and a property guardian is needed, I appoint

_____ as property guardian for my minor children.
                    name of property guardian

If _____ cannot serve as property guardian, I appoint
                    name of property guardian

_____ as property guardian.
            name of alternate property guardian

~~(E) I direct that no bond be required of any guardian.~~

4. (A) I make the following specific gifts:

I leave _____ all my cameras _____
                                        ~~property described~~

to _____ Sid Tropinsky _____ , or if
                                        ~~beneficiary's name~~

_____ Sid Tropinsky _____ fails to survive
                                        ~~beneficiary's name~~

me, to _____ Nancy Werrin _____ .
                                        ~~alternate beneficiary's name~~

I leave _____
                                        property described

to _____ , or if
                                        beneficiary's name

_____ fails to survive
                                        beneficiary's name

me, to _____ .
                                        alternate beneficiary's name

I leave _____
                                        property described

to _____ , or if
                                        beneficiary's name

_____ fails to survive
                                        beneficiary's name

me, to _____ .
                                        alternate beneficiary's name

(B) I leave all my other property subject to this will to ___Eric Werrin_____
residuary beneficiary's name

_____, or if ___he___ fails to survive me,
he/she

to ___Gil Nason_____ .
alternate residuary beneficiary's name

5. (A) I nominate ___Gil Nason_____
executor's name

to serve as executor of my will. If ___he____ is unable to serve or continue serving as executor, I nominate
he/she

___Nancy Werrin_____ to serve as executor.
alternate executor's name

(B) No bond shall be required of any executor.

I subscribe my name to this will this _____ day of _____, 20____, at

___Fairmont_____, ___Dutchess County_____, ___New York_____
city   county   state

_____
your signature

Witnesses

On the date last written above, ___Benjamin Werrin_____
your name

declared to us, the undersigned, that this was ___his___ will, and requested us to act as witnesses to it. ___He___
his/her   He/She

signed this will in our presence, all of us being present at the same time. We now, at ___his___ request and in
his/her

___his___ presence, and in the presence of each other, have signed this will as witnesses.
his/her

We declare under penalty of perjury that the foregoing is true and correct.

_____   _____
witness signature   witness printed name

_____, _____, _____
city   county   state

_____   _____
witness signature   witness printed name

_____, _____, _____
city   county   state

_____   _____
witness signature   witness printed name

_____, _____, _____
city   county   state

Final, Typed Will, Ready to Be Signed and Witnessed

Will

of

Benjamin Werrin

I, Benjamin Werrin, a resident of Fairmont, Dutchess County, New York, declare that this is my will.

1. I revoke all wills and codicils that I have previously made.

2. I am not married.

3. I am the father of the child whose name is Eric Werrin.

4. (A) I make the following specific gifts:

   I leave all my cameras to Sid Tropinsky, or if Sid Tropinsky fails to survive me, to Nancy Werrin.

   (B) I leave all my other property subject to this will to Eric Werrin, or if he fails to survive me, to Gil Nason.

5. (A) I nominate Gil Nason to serve as executor of my will. If he is unable to serve or continue serving as executor, I nominate Nancy Werrin to serve as executor.

   (B) No bond shall be required of any executor.

I subscribe my name to this will this _____ day of _____, 20_____, at Fairmont, Dutchess County, New York.

_____

Witnesses

On the date last written above, Benjamin Werrin declared to us, the undersigned, that this was his will, and requested us to act as witnesses to it. He then signed this will in our presence, all of us being present at the same time. We now at his request and in his presence, and in the presence of each other, have signed such will as witnesses.

We declare under penalty of perjury that the foregoing is true and correct.

_____   _____
witness signature   witness printed name

_____, _____, _____
city   county   state

_____   _____
witness signature   witness printed name

_____, _____, _____
city   county   state

_____   _____
witness signature   witness printed name

_____, _____, _____
city   county   state

If You Need Expert Help

Many readers, probably the majority, will find the information in this book sufficient to prepare their own living trust and backup will. But if you run into a snag of some kind, you may sensibly decide you need a lawyer's help. Throughout this book, I've indicated "red flags" that alert you to the need for professional advice. And, of course, people with an estate over the estate tax threshold need an expert's help to review all their estate tax options and prepare the living trust best geared to their needs.

Hiring a Lawyer to Review Your Living Trust

Hiring a lawyer solely to review a living trust document you've prepared sounds like a good idea. It shouldn't cost much, and seems to offer a comforting security. Sadly, though, it may be difficult or even impossible to find a lawyer who will accept the job.

While this is unfortunate, I'm not willing to excoriate lawyers who won't review a do-it-yourself living trust. From their point of view, they are being asked to accept what can turn into a significant responsibility for what they regard as inadequate compensation, given their usual fees. Any prudent lawyer sees every client as a potential occasion for a malpractice claim, or at least, serious later hassles—a phone call four years down the line that begins, "We talked to you about our living trust, and now …." Many experienced lawyers want to avoid this kind of risk. Also, many lawyers feel that if they're only reviewing someone else's work, they simply don't get deeply enough into a situation to be sure of their opinions. All you can do here is to keep trying to find a sympathetic lawyer—or be prepared to pay more, enough so the lawyer can feel he or she has been paid adequately to review your living trust.

Working With an Expert

If you have decided you want legal help, the first consideration is what type of expert you should seek out. Questions about estate taxes may be better (and less expensively) answered by an experienced accountant than by a lawyer. Or if you're wondering what type of life insurance to buy, you may be better off talking to a financial planner. But for many sophisticated living trust issues, you'll need to see a lawyer.

What Type of Lawyer Do You Need?

The type of lawyer that is right for you depends on what your problem is. Before you talk to a lawyer, decide what kind of help you really need. Do you want someone to advise you on a complete estate plan or just to go over part of your trust? If you don't clearly tell the lawyer what you want, you may find yourself agreeing to turn over all your estate planning work.

If you've prepared a trust from this book, any good estate practice lawyer should be able to help you. Do make sure that he or she is experienced with AB trusts, if you prepare that type of trust. If you want a more sophisticated document—like a QTIP trust or generation-skipping trust—it's important that you see an estate trust specialist, who'll probably cost more than a general practice estate lawyer.

If you hire an "expert," make sure that person really has the knowledge or expertise he or she claims. Many lawyers have recently discovered the profit-making potential of trusts. Lawyers who know almost nothing about living trusts (it's easy to go through law school without ever hearing of one) have found that they can charge substantial fees—$1,500 or more is common— for a simple document. Some use computer programs to churn out trusts and may or may not take into account your specific needs.

It's also important that you feel a personal rapport with your lawyer. You want one who treats you as an equal. (Interestingly, the Latin root of the word "client" translates as "to hear, to obey.") When talking with a lawyer on the phone or at a first conference, ask specific questions that concern you. Let the lawyer know that you've read this book and that you have a good understanding of estate planning. Then, see how the lawyer responds. If he or she answers you clearly and concisely—explaining, but not talking down to you—fine. If he or she acts wise, but says little except to ask that the problem be placed in his or her hands (with the appropriate fee, of course), watch out. You are either talking with someone who doesn't know the answer and won't admit it (common), or someone who finds it impossible to let go of the "me expert, you peasant" way of looking at the world (even more common).

How to Choose a Lawyer

Finding a competent estate planning lawyer who charges a reasonable fee and respects your efforts to prepare your own living trust may not be easy. Here are some suggestions on how to go about the task.

Ask Friends and Businesspeople

Personal recommendations are generally the best way to find a lawyer you'll like. If you have a close friend who's had a good experience with an estate planning lawyer, there's a good chance you'll work well with that lawyer too.

If friends can't help you, ask any businesspeople you know for referrals. Anyone who owns a small business probably has a relationship with a lawyer. Ask around to find someone you know who is a satisfied client, and get the name of his or her lawyer. Even a lawyer who does not handle estate planning will likely know someone who does. And because of the continuing relationship with your business friend, the lawyer has an incentive to recommend someone who is competent.

Also ask people in any social or other organization in which you are involved. They may well know of a good lawyer whose attitudes are similar to yours. Senior citizens' centers and other groups that advise and assist older people may have a list of local lawyers who specialize in wills and estate planning, and are well regarded.

Look Into a Group Legal Plan

Some unions, employers, and consumer groups offer group legal plans to their members or employees, who can obtain comprehensive legal assistance free or at low rates. If you are a member of such a plan, check with it first. Your problem may be covered free of charge. If it is, and you are satisfied that the lawyer you are referred to is knowledgeable in estate planning, this route is probably a good choice.

Some plans give you only a slight reduction in a lawyer's fee. In that case, you may be referred to a lawyer whose main virtue is the willingness to reduce fees in exchange for a high volume of referrals.

Try the Martindale-Hubbell Law Directory

This directory, available in most public libraries and at www.martindale.com, lists lawyers by the towns or cities they practice in, and also identifies estate planning specialists. For each lawyer or law firm listed, you'll get some information about qualifications and experience. Martindale-Hubbell tends to list established and establishment lawyers, however, so the fees they charge will not be low.

Call an Attorney Referral Service

A lawyer referral service will give you the name of an attorney who practices in your area. Usually, you can get a referral to an attorney who claims to specialize in estate planning and will give you an initial consultation for a low fee.

Most county bar associations have referral services. In some states, independent referral services, run by or for groups of lawyers, also operate.

Unfortunately, few referral services screen the attorneys they list, which means those who participate may not be the most experienced or competent. Often, the lawyers who sign up with referral services are just starting out and need clients. It may be possible to find a skilled estate planning specialist through a referral service, but be sure to take the time to check out the credentials and experience of the person to whom you're referred.

 RESOURCE

Let Nolo take the guesswork out of finding a lawyer. Nolo's Lawyer Directory provides detailed profiles of attorney advertisers, including information about the lawyer's education, experience, practice areas, and fee schedule. Go to www .lawyers.nolo.com or Nolo's main website at www.nolo.com.

Living Trust Seminars

As discussed in Chapter 3, newspapers, radio, and TV often play ads for free seminars on living trusts. Usually, these events are nothing more than elaborate pitches for paying a business or a lawyer $1,000 to $1,500 to write a living trust. Is it worth it? Probably not. For most estates, the trust forms and instructions in this book are all you need.

Often these seminars are occasions for you to be cajoled by lawyers, financial planners, and insurance agents to pay large sums of money to get your affairs in order before you die.

People are sold on the idea that much of their estate is likely to be gobbled up by estate taxes unless they set up trusts now to avoid some of the tax and buy life insurance to pay the rest. The reality is that most people don't have estates large enough to generate estate tax liability. And the seminar sponsors know it.

The sponsors try to sell:

- a lot of life insurance, to pay for supposed estate taxes, and
- their form AB trust to reduce estate taxes. (See chapters 4 and 5.)

Be sure you need these alleged benefits before paying what will be a substantial amount to acquire them. Is your estate likely to be liable for estate taxes? What type of AB trust do you need? If your situation is more complex than what can be handled by using this book, you'll probably be better off paying the money to hire a good lawyer to draft a trust geared to your needs than paying too much for the standard form offered in these seminars.

Lawyer Fees

As you already know, lawyers are expensive. They charge fees usually ranging from $150 to $500 or more per hour. While fancy office trappings, dull suits, and solemn faces are no guarantee (or even a good indication) that a particular lawyer will provide top-notch service in a style you will feel comfortable with, this conventional style almost always ensures that you will be charged at the upper end of the fee range. High fees and quality service don't necessarily go hand in hand. Indeed, the attorneys I think most highly of tend to charge moderate fees (for lawyers, that is), and seem to get along very nicely without stuffy law office trappings.

Depending on the area of the country where you live, generally, fees in the range of $200 to $300 per hour are reasonable in urban areas, given the average lawyer's overhead. In rural counties and small cities, $150 to $250 is more like it.

Be sure you've settled your fee arrangement—preferably in writing—at the start of your relationship. (In California, a written fee agreement is required by law if the bill is expected to be over $1,000.) In addition to the hourly fee, get a clear, written commitment from the lawyer stating how many hours your problem should take to handle.

Doing Your Own Legal Research

As an alternative to hiring a lawyer, you can explore doing your own legal research. This can work well for relatively simpler living trust questions, such as any specific state law about trust registration or a trustee's duty to manage trust property prudently.

Legal Research in Law Libraries

If you decide you want to do your own research in the library, how do you go about it? First, you need an introduction to how law libraries work. Since you can't hire your own law librarian, the best book explaining how nonlawyers can do their own legal work is *Legal Research: How to Find & Understand the Law,* by Stephen Elias and Susan Levinkind (Nolo). It shows you, step by step, how to find answers in the law library. It is a great legal research book written specifically for nonprofessionals.

Next, locate a law library or a public library with a good law collection. In most counties, there's a law library in the main county courthouse, although quality varies widely. Most county law libraries are supported by tax dollars or by the fees paid to file court papers. The librarians are generally most helpful and courteous to nonlawyers who are venturing to do their own legal research. If the county library is not adequate, your best bet is a law-school library. Those in state colleges and universities supported by tax dollars are almost always open to the public.

Many states have estate planning books prepared for practicing lawyers. These books contain specific clauses and forms for wills or trusts, and many other hands-on materials. The best way to locate this type of book for your state is to ask the law librarian or search the library's computerized catalogue by looking for the terms "estate planning," "wills," and "trusts."

Unfortunately, I cannot recommend doing your own research for high-end living trust issues, especially regarding estate taxes. Drafting a QTIP or generation-skipping trust that complies with all federal regulations and achieves the goals you want is truly a complicated matter that requires considerable expertise. Remember, you'll consider these types of trusts only if you have substantial assets. The risk that your trust won't be legally correct and therefore won't qualify for the tax breaks you want outweighs any possible savings gained by doing your own legal work.

Living Trust Research Books

In most states, you can find books on trusts written for the lawyers of your state.

In California, the Continuing Education of the Bar (CEB) publishes several useful estate planning books, including *Drafting California Revocable Inter Vivos Trusts* and *Estate Planning for the General Practitioner.*

Comparable books in New York, including *Income Taxation of Estates and Trusts*, by Michaelson & Blattmahr, are published by the Practising Law Institute (PLI).

If you want to wade into the murk of estate tax issues, a standard resource is the CCH (Commerce Clearing House) *Estate and Gift Tax Reporter,* available in law libraries.

Legal Information Online

It's possible to find many answers online. If you want information about a recent court decision, a new statute, a current legal issue, or more general information on some aspect of living trusts, you'll probably be able to find it somewhere on the internet. Lots of public libraries now offer online access, if you're not connected at home or at work.

Legal Research: How to Find & Understand the Law, by Stephen Elias and Susan Levinkind (Nolo), provides extensive information on how to do legal research online.

RESOURCE

Nolo's website offers information on living trusts and estate planning. You can find us at www.nolo.com.

Glossary

AB trust. An estate tax-saving trust where one spouse leaves property in what's called "Trust A," allowing the surviving spouse, during his or her lifetime, to use the income from that trust and authorizing limited rights to invade the trust principal. After the death of the surviving spouse, the trust property goes to the final beneficiaries. With an AB disclaimer trust, the surviving spouse decides how much, if any, of the deceased spouse's property to place in Trust A.

Abstract of trust. A condensed version of a living trust, which leaves out the key parts of what property is in the trust and who are the beneficiaries. An abstract of trust is used to show, to financial organizations or other institutions, that a valid living trust has been established, without revealing specifics the grantor wants to keep private and confidential.

Acknowledgment. A statement in front of a person who is qualified to administer oaths (a notary public) that a document bearing a person's signature was actually signed by that person.

Administration of an estate. The court-supervised distribution of the probate estate of a deceased person. The person who manages the distribution is called the "executor" if there is a will. If there is no will, this person is called the "administrator." In some states, the person is called "personal representative" in either instance.

Adult. A person aged 18 or older.

Affidavit. A written statement signed under oath in front of a notary public.

Augmented estate. The property left by a will plus certain property transferred outside of the will by gifts, joint tenancies, and living trusts. The augmented estate is calculated if a surviving spouse wants to claim his or her statutory share of the deceased spouse's property. In the states that use this concept, a surviving spouse is generally considered to be adequately provided for if he or she receives at least one-third of the augmented estate.

Basis. This is a tax term that has to do with the valuation of property for determining profit or loss on sale. To simplify to the basics, if you buy a house for $200,000, your tax basis is $200,000. If you later sell it for $350,000, your taxable profit is $150,000. *See also* stepped-up basis.

Beneficiary. A person or organization who is legally entitled to receive property under a will or trust. A primary beneficiary is a person who directly and certainly will benefit from the will or trust. An alternate beneficiary is a person who inherits property if a primary beneficiary dies before the person who made the will or trust does. *See* residuary beneficiary and final beneficiary.

Bond. A document guaranteeing that a certain amount of money will be paid to those injured if a person occupying a position of trust does not carry out his or her legal and ethical responsibilities.

Thus, if an executor, trustee, or guardian who is bonded (covered by a bond) wrongfully deprives a beneficiary of his or her property (say, by blowing it during a trip in Las Vegas), the bonding company will replace it, up to the limits of the bond.

Bypass trust. *See* AB trust.

Child's trust. A trust that is established by the terms of a trust form in this book. It comes into being only if, at the grantor's death, a young beneficiary hasn't yet reached the age the grantor specified in the trust document to receive his or her gift outright.

If the trust is set up, all trust property the young beneficiary is entitled to automatically goes into it. It will stay in trust until the beneficiary reaches the age specified by the grantor, or, if none is, up to 35. Then the beneficiary will receive the property outright.

Common law marriage. In a minority of states, couples may be considered married if they live together for a certain period of time and intend to be husband and wife.

Community property. Eight states follow a system of marital property ownership called "community property," and Wisconsin has a very similar "marital property" law. Very generally, all property acquired after marriage and before permanent separation is considered to belong equally to both spouses, except for gifts to and inheritances by one spouse and, in some community property states, income from property owned by one spouse prior to marriage. Spouses can, however, enter into an agreement to the contrary.

A surviving spouse automatically owns one-half of all community property. The other spouse has no legal power to affect this.

Conservator. Someone appointed by a court to manage the affairs of a mentally incompetent person. In some states, this person is called a guardian.

Creditor. A person or institution to whom money is owed. A creditor may be the person who actually lent the money, or a lawyer or bill collector who is trying to collect the money for the original creditor.

Curtesy. *See* dower and curtesy.

Custodian. A person named to care for property left to a minor under the Uniform Transfers to Minors Act. The custodian manages the property until the minor reaches the age at which state law says he or she must receive it. (In some states, the giver can specify, within limits, at what age the custodianship will end.)

The custodian has essentially the same powers as a child's trust trustee and may use the property for the minor's health, education, and support. The custodian's authority and duties are clearly set out by state law (the Uniform Transfers to Minors Act). No court supervises the custodian.

Debtor. A person who owes money.

Deceased spouse. With a shared living or AB trust created by both spouses, the first spouse to die.

Decedent. A person who has died.

Deed. The legal document by which one person (or persons) transfers title (recorded ownership) to real estate.

Disclaimer trust. A trust where a beneficiary has the specific right to disclaim all or any portion of a gift left to him or her, so the gift goes to whomever is next entitled to receive it.

Domicile. The state, or country, where one has his or her primary home.

Donee. Someone who receives a gift.

Donor. Someone who gives a gift.

Dower and curtesy. The right of a widow or widower to receive or enjoy the use of a set portion of the deceased spouse's property (usually one-third to one-half) if the surviving spouse is not left at least that share. Dower refers to the title that a surviving wife gets, while curtesy refers to what a man receives. Until recently, these amounts differed in a number of states. However, states generally provide the same benefits regardless of sex.

Durable power of attorney. A power of attorney that remains effective even if the person who created it (called the "principal") becomes incapacitated. The person authorized to act (called the "attorney-in-fact" or "agent") can make health care decisions or handle financial affairs of the principal, depending on the authority granted by the document.

Estate. Generally, all the property you own when you die. There are different kinds of estates: the taxable estate (property subject to estate taxation), the probate estate (property that must go through probate), and the net estate (the net value of the property).

Estate planning. Figuring out how to prosper when you're alive, die with the smallest taxable estate and probate estate possible, and pass property to loved ones with a minimum of fuss and expense.

Estate taxes. Taxes imposed on an estate. The federal government exempts a set amount of property, depending on the year of death. Also exempt is all property left to a surviving spouse who is a U.S. citizen. Taxes are imposed only on property actually owned at the time of death. So techniques designed to reduce taxes usually concentrate on the legal transfer of ownership of property while you are living, to minimize the amount of property owned at death. A minority of states impose a similar tax, called an inheritance tax.

Executor. The person named in a will to manage the deceased person's estate, deal with the probate court, collect assets, and distribute them as the will specifies. In some states, this person is called the "personal representative." If someone dies without a will, the probate court will appoint such a person, who is called the "administrator" of the estate.

Exemption trust. *See* AB trust.

Final beneficiary. The person(s) or institution(s) who receive the property in a marital life estate trust after the life beneficiary of that trust dies.

Financial guardian. *See* property guardian.

Funding a trust. Transferring ownership of property to a trust, in the name of the trustee.

Generation-skipping trust. An estate tax-saving trust, where the principal is left in trust for one's grandchildren, with one's children receiving only the trust income.

Gift. Any property given to another person or organization, either during the giver's lifetime, or by will or living trust after his or her death.

Gift tax. Tax on gifts made during a person's lifetime. Many gifts are exempt from tax: gifts to tax-exempt charities or the giver's spouse (if the recipient spouse is a U.S. citizen) and, currently, gifts of $13,000 or less to any one recipient in a calendar year.

Grantor. The person or persons who create a trust. Also called the "trustor," "settlor," or "creator."

Heirs. Persons who are entitled by state intestate law to inherit a deceased person's property if that person didn't make arrangements for what should happen to the property at his or her death.

Inherit. To receive property from one who dies.

Inheritors. Persons or organizations who inherit property.

Instrument. Legalese for document; sometimes used to refer to the document that creates a living trust.

Inter vivos trust. Same as living trust. ("Inter vivos" is Latin for "between the living.")

Intestate. Someone who dies without a will or other valid estate transfer device dies intestate.

Intestate succession. The method by which property is distributed when a person fails to distribute it in a will or other estate transfer device. In such cases, the law of each state provides that the property be distributed in certain shares to the closest surviving relatives. In most states, these are a surviving spouse, children, parents, siblings, nieces and nephews, and next of kin, in that order. The intestate succession laws are also used in the event an heir is found to be pretermitted (not mentioned or otherwise provided for in the will).

Irrevocable trust. Means what it says. Once you create it, that's it; it's unchangeable. A trust that cannot be revoked by the person who created it once it's created. Unlike a revocable, probate-avoidance trust, it can't be amended or changed in any way.

Joint tenancy. A way to own jointly owned real or personal property. When two or more people own property as joint tenants, and one of the owners dies, the other owners automatically become owners of the deceased owner's share. Thus, if a parent and child own a house as joint tenants, and the parent dies, the child automatically becomes full owner. Because of this "right of survivorship," a joint tenancy interest in property does not go through probate, or, put another way, is not part of the probate estate. Instead, it goes directly to the surviving joint tenant(s).

Liquid assets. Cash or assets that can readily be turned into cash.

Living trust. A trust that is set up while a person is alive and remains under the control of that person until death. Also referred to as "inter vivos trust." Living trusts are an excellent way to minimize the value of property passing through probate. This is because they enable people (called "grantors") to specify that money or other property will pass directly to their beneficiaries after their death, free of probate, and yet allow the grantors to continue to control the property during their lifetime and even end the trust or change the beneficiaries if they wish.

Living trust with marital life estate. *See* AB trust.

Living will. A document, directed to physicians, in which you state that you do not want to have your life artificially prolonged by technological means.

Marital deduction. A deduction allowed by the federal estate tax law for all property passed to a surviving spouse who is a U.S. citizen. This deduction (which really acts like an exemption) allows anyone, even a billionaire, to pass his or her entire estate to a surviving spouse without any tax at all. Tax problems, however, are usually made worse by relying exclusively on the marital deduction.

Marriage. A specific status conferred on a couple by the state. In most states, it is necessary to file papers with a county clerk and have a marriage ceremony conducted by an authorized individual to be married.

In some states, however, couples may be considered married without a ceremony in certain circumstances. *See* common law marriage.

Minor. Person under 18 years of age. All minors must be under the care of an adult (parent or guardian) unless they are "emancipated"—in the military, married, or living independently with court permission. Property left to a minor must be handled by an adult until the minor becomes an adult under the laws of the state.

Mortgage. A document that makes a piece of real estate the security (collateral) for the payment of a debt. Most house buyers sign a mortgage when they buy; the bank lends money to buy the house, and the house serves as security for the debt. If the owners don't pay back the loan on time, the bank can seize the house and have it sold to pay off the loan.

Pay-on-death account. An account, often a bank account, where you name a beneficiary to receive the account assets outside of probate when you die. Sometimes referred to as a "Totten trust."

Personal guardian. An adult appointed or selected to care for a minor child in the event no biological or adoptive parent (legal parent) of the child is able to do so. If one legal parent is alive when the other dies, the child will automatically go to the surviving parent, unless the best interests of the child require something else.

Personal property. All property other than land and buildings attached to land. Cars, bank accounts, wages, securities, a small business, furniture, insurance policies, jewelry, pets, and season baseball tickets are all personal property.

Personal representative. *See* executor.

Pour-over will. A will that "pours over" property into a trust. Property left through the will must go through probate before it goes into the trust.

Power of attorney. A legal document in which you authorize someone else to act for you. *See* durable power of attorney.

Pretermitted heir. A child (or the child of a deceased child) who is either not named or (in some states) not provided for in a will. Most states presume that persons want their children to inherit. Accordingly, children, or the children of a child who has died,

who are not mentioned or provided for in the will are entitled to a share of the estate.

Principal. Property owned by a trust, as distinguished from the income generated by that property.

Probate. The court proceeding in which (1) the authenticity of your will (if any) is established, (2) your executor or administrator is appointed, (3) your debts and taxes are paid, (4) your heirs are identified, and (5) your property in your probate estate is distributed according to your will (if there is a will).

Probate estate. All a decedent's property that passes through probate. Generally, this means all property owned at death less any property that has been placed in joint tenancy, a living trust, a bank account trust, or in life insurance.

Probate fees. Fees paid from a decedent's property to an attorney or court during probate. Typically, fees take about 5% or more of the decedent's estate.

Property guardian. The person named in a will to care for property of a minor child not supervised by some other legal method, such as a minor's trust. Also called "the guardian of the minor's estate" or "financial guardian."

QTIP trust. A type of trust that allows a surviving spouse to postpone, until his or her death, paying estate taxes that were assessed on the death of the other spouse.

Quasi-community property. A rule that applies to married couples who have moved to California, Idaho, Washington, or Wisconsin. Laws in those states require all property acquired by people during their marriage in other states to be treated as community property at their death.

Real estate. Same as real property.

Real property. All land and items attached to the land, such as buildings, houses, stationary mobile homes, fences, and trees are real property or "real estate." All property that is not real property is personal property.

Recording. The process of filing a copy of a deed with the county land records office. Recording creates a public record of all changes in ownership of property in the state.

Residuary beneficiary. The residuary beneficiary of a trust for one person, or a basic shared trust created from this book, is that beneficiary who receives any trust property not otherwise given away by the trust document. The residuary beneficiary of a will is the beneficiary who receives any property the will writer owned that was not left to beneficiaries by the will or other method.

Residuary estate. Property that goes to the residuary beneficiary of a will or trust after all specific gifts of property have been made.

Right of survivorship. The right of a surviving joint tenant (or tenant by the entirety) to take ownership of a deceased co-owner's share of the property.

Separate property. In states that have community property, all property that is not community property. *See* community property.

Special Needs Trust. A trust designed to provide for a person with a disability without interfering with that person's eligibility to receive government benefits.

Sprinkling trust. A trust that authorizes the trustee to decide how to distribute trust income or principal among different beneficiaries.

Stepped-up basis. Under current federal law, the tax basis of inherited property is "stepped up" to the market value of the property at the date of the deceased's death.

Successor trustee. The person (or institution) who takes over as trustee of a trust when the original trustee(s) have died or become incapacitated.

Surviving spouse. With a shared or AB living trust created by both spouses, the living spouse after the other spouse dies.

Surviving spouse's trust. Where a couple has created an AB trust, the revocable living trust of the surviving spouse, after the other spouse has died.

Taking against the will. State law gives a surviving spouse the right to demand a certain share (in most states, one-third to one-half) of the deceased spouse's property. The surviving spouse can take that share instead of accepting whatever he or she inherited through the deceased spouse's will. If the surviving spouse decides to take the statutory share, it's called "taking against the will." *See* dower and curtesy.

Tax basis. *See* basis.

Taxable estate. The portion of an estate that is subject to federal or state taxes.

Tenancy by the entirety. A form of property ownership available in many states. It is similar to joint tenancy, but is allowed only for property owned by a married couple (or, in Hawaii, New Jersey, Oregon, and Vermont, same-sex couples who have registered with the state).

Tenancy in common. A way for co-owners to hold title to property that allows them maximum freedom to dispose of their interests by sale, gift, or will. At a co-owner's death, his or her share goes to beneficiaries named in a will or trust or to the legal heirs, not to the other co-owners. Compare joint tenancy.

Testamentary trust. A trust created by a will.

Testate. Someone who dies leaving a valid will or other valid property transfer devices dies testate.

Testator. A person who makes a will.

Title. A document that proves ownership of property.

Totten trust. *See* pay-on-death account.

Trust. A legal arrangement under which one person or institution (called a "trustee") controls property given by another person (called a "grantor," "settlor," or "trustor") for the benefit of a third person (called a "beneficiary").

Trust corpus or **res.** Latin for the property transferred to a trust.

Trustee. The people or institutions who manage trust property under the terms of the trust document. With a revocable living trust created from the forms in this book, the creators of the trust (grantors) are the original trustees.

Trustee powers. The provisions in a trust document defining what the trustee may and may not do.

Uniform Transfers to Minors Act (UTMA). A statute, adopted by most states, that provides a method for transferring property to minors and arranging for an adult to manage it until the child is older. *See* custodian.

Will. A legal document in which a person directs what is to be done with his or her property covered by the will after the will writer's death.

How to Use the CD-ROM

The CD-ROM included with this book can be used with Windows computers. It installs files that use software programs that need to be on your computer already. It is not a standalone software program.

In accordance with U.S. copyright laws, the CD-ROM and its files are for your personal use only.

Please read this appendix and the Readme.htm file included on the CD-ROM for instructions on using the Forms CD. For a list of forms and their file names, see the end of this appendix.

Note to Macintosh users: This CD-ROM and its files should also work on Macintosh computers. Please note, however, that Nolo cannot provide technical support for non-Windows users.

Note to eBook users: You can access the CD files mentioned here from the bookmarked section of the eBook, located on the left-hand side.

How to View the README File

To view the Readme.htm file, insert the Forms CD-ROM into your computer's CD-ROM drive and follow these instructions:

Windows 2000, XP, and Vista

1. On your PC's desktop, double click the My Computer icon;
2. double click the icon for the CD-ROM drive into which the Forms CD-ROM was inserted;
3. double click the file Readme.htm.

Macintosh

4. On your Mac desktop, double click the icon for the CD-ROM that you inserted;
5. double click the file Readme.htm.

Installing the Form Files Onto Your Computer

To work with the files on the CD-ROM, you first need to install them onto your hard disk. Here's how:

Windows 2000, XP, and Vista

Follow the CD-ROM's instructions that appear on the screen.

If nothing happens when you insert the Forms CD-ROM, then

6. double click the My Computer icon;
7. double click the icon for the CD-ROM drive into which the Forms CD-ROM was inserted;
8. double click the file Setup.exe.

Macintosh

If the Living Trust Forms CD window is not open, double click the Living Trust Forms icon. Then

1. select the Living Trust Forms folder icon;
2. drag and drop the folder icon onto your computer.

Where Are the Files Installed?

Windows
By default, all the files are installed to the \Living Trust Forms folder in the \Program Files folder of your computer. A folder called Living Trust Forms is added to the Programs folder of the Start menu.

Macintosh
All the files are located in the Living Trust Forms folder.

Using the Word Processing Files to Create Documents

The CD-ROM includes word processing files that you can open, complete, print, and save with your word processing program. All word processing forms come in rich text format and have the extension ".rtf." For example, the form for Form 1: Basic Living Trust for One Person, discussed in Chapter 10, is on the file Form01.rtf. RTF files can be read by most recent word processing programs, including MS *Word*, Windows *WordPad*, and recent versions of *WordPerfect*.

The following are general instructions. Because each word processor uses different commands to open, format, save, and print documents, refer to your word processor's help file for specific instructions.

Do not call Nolo's technical support if you have questions on how to use your word processor or your computer.

Opening a File

You can open word processing files any of the three following ways:

1. Windows users can open a file by selecting its "shortcut."
   1. Click the Windows Start button;
   2. open the Programs folder;
   3. open the Living Trust Forms folder;
   4. click the shortcut to the form you want to work with.
2. Both Windows and Macintosh users can open a file by double clicking it.
   1. Use My Computer or Windows Explorer (Windows 2000, XP, or Vista) or the Finder (Macintosh) to go to the Living Trust Forms folder and
   2. double click the file you want to open.
3. Windows and Macintosh users can open a file from within their word processor.
   1. Open your word processor;
   2. go to the File menu and choose the Open command. This opens a dialog box where
   3. you will select the location and name of the file. (You will navigate to the version of the Living Trust Forms folder that you've installed on your computer.)

Editing Your Document

Here are tips for working on your document.

Refer to the book's instructions and sample agreements for help.

Underlines indicate where to enter information, frequently including bracketed instructions. Delete the underlines and instructions before finishing your document.

Signature lines should appear on a page with at least some text from the document itself.

Editing Forms That Have Optional or Alternative Text

Some forms have optional or alternative text:

- With optional text, you choose whether to include or exclude the given text.
- With alternative text, you select one alternative to include and exclude the other alternatives.

When editing these forms, we suggest you do the following:

Optional text

Delete optional text you do not want to include and keep text that you do. In either case, delete the italicized instructions. If you choose to delete an optional numbered clause, renumber the subsequent clauses after deleting it.

Alternative text

First delete all the alternatives that you do not want to include. Then delete the italicized instructions.

Printing Out the Document

Use your word processor's or text editor's Print command to print out your document.

Saving Your Document

Use the Save As command to save and rename your document. You will be unable to use the Save command because the files are "read-only." If you save the file without renaming it, the underlines that indicate where you need to enter your information will be lost, and you will be unable to create a new document with this file without recopying the original file from the CD-ROM.

Files on the CD-ROM

Form Title	File Name
Form 1: Basic Living Trust for One Person	Form01.rtf
Form 2: Basic Shared Living Trust	Form02.rtf
Form 3: AB Living Trust	Form03.rtf
Form 4: AB Disclaimer Living Trust	Form04.rtf
Form 5: Witness Statement for a Florida Living Trust	Form05.rtf
Form 6: Assignment of Property to a Trust for One Person	Form06.rtf
Form 7: Assignment of Shared Property to a Trust for a Couple	Form07.rtf
Form 8: Amendment to Living Trust for One Person	Form08.rtf
Form 9: Amendment to Basic Shared Living Trust or AB Trust	Form09.rtf
Form 10: Revocation of Living Trust	Form10.rtf
Form 11: Basic Will for One Person	Form11.rtf
Form 12: Basic Will for a Member of a Couple	Form12.rtf
Form 13: Affidavit of Successor Trustee	Form13.rtf
Property Worksheet	Property.rtf
Beneficiary Worksheet 1: Individual Living Trust	Beneficiary1.rtf
Beneficiary Worksheet 2: Basic Shared Living Trust	Beneficiary2.rtf
Beneficiary Worksheet 3: AB Trust	Beneficiary3.rtf

Tear-Out Forms

Reminder
The circled numbers on the trust forms (**1** , **4** , **7** , etc.) refer to the specific steps described in Chapter 10. These steps explain what information you need to write on the blank lines. Thus the circled **2** refers you to Step 2, "Decide How Many Property Schedules Your Trust Needs." Each step also explains how you can make appropriate revisions for that trust section. If you have any trouble completing a trust form or are puzzled by these numbers, please reread the "Step-by-Step Instructions" in Chapter 10.

Form 1: Basic Living Trust for One Person

The __1__ _____ Living Trust
                  your name (or name of trust, if different)

Declaration of Trust

I.   Trust Name

This trust shall be known as The __1__ _____ Living Trust.
                                        your name (or name of trust, if different)

II.   Trust Property

(A) Property Placed in Trust

__1__ _____ , called the grantor or trustee, declares
           your name (or name of trust, if different)

that _____ has set aside and holds in The __1__ _____
           he/she   your name (or name of trust, if different)

Living Trust all _____ interest in that property described in the attached Schedule A. __2__
                      his/her

The trust property shall be used for the benefit of the trust beneficiaries and shall be administered

and distributed by the trustee in accordance with this Declaration of Trust.

(B) Additional or After-Acquired Property

The grantor may add property to the trust at any time.

III.   Reserved Powers of Grantor

(A) Amendment or Revocation

The grantor reserves the power to amend or revoke this trust at any time during _____
                                                                                        his/her

lifetime, without notifying any beneficiary.

(B) Rights to Trust Property

Until the death of the grantor, all rights to all income, profits, and control of the trust property shall be retained by

the grantor.

(C) Homestead Rights

If the grantor's principal residence is held in this trust, grantor has the right to possess and occupy it for life, rent-free and without charge, except for taxes, insurance, maintenance, and related costs and expenses. This right is intended to give grantor a beneficial interest in the property and to ensure that grantor does not lose eligibility for a state homestead tax exemption for which grantor otherwise qualifies.

(D) Incapacity of Grantor

If the grantor becomes physically or mentally incapacitated and is no longer able to manage this trust, the person or persons named as successor trustee shall serve as trustee. The determination of the grantor's capacity to manage this trust shall be made by those of the persons listed below who are reasonably available when the successor trustee (or any of them, if two or more are named to serve together) requests their opinion. If a majority of these persons state, in writing, that in their opinion the grantor is no longer reasonably capable of serving as trustee, the successor trustee shall serve as trustee.

5A _____

(names(s) of person(s) to determine incapacity)

The successor trustee shall pay trust income at least annually to, or for the benefit of, the grantor and may also spend any amount of trust principal necessary in the trustee's discretion for the needs of the grantor, until the grantor is no longer incapacitated or until the grantor's death.

(E) Grantor's Death

After the death of the grantor, this trust becomes irrevocable. It may not be altered or amended in any respect, and may not be terminated except through distributions permitted by this Declaration of Trust.

IV. Trustees

(A) Original Trustee

The trustee of The **1** _____ Living Trust and all

your name (or name of trust, if different)

children's trusts created under this Declaration of Trust shall be **1** _____ .

your name (or name of trust, if different)

(B) Successor Trustee

Upon the death of the trustee, or _____ incapacity, the successor trustee shall be
                                              his/her

6 _____. If _____
                  name(s) of successor trustee(s)   *he/she/all of them*

_____ unable to serve or continue serving as successor trustee, the successor trustee shall be
        is/are

6 _____.
              name(s) of alternate successor trustee(s)

[If you named more than one successor trustee, include ONE of the following two paragraphs here:]

Any of the successor trustees has full and independent authority to act for and represent the trust.

[or]

All of the successor trustees must consent, in writing, to any transaction involving the trust or trust property.

(C) Trustee's Responsibility

The trustee in office shall serve as trustee of all trusts created under this Declaration of Trust, including any child's

trust.

(D) Resignation of Trustee

Any trustee in office may resign at any time by signing a notice of resignation. The resignation must be delivered

to the person or institution who is either named in this Declaration of Trust or appointed by the trustee under Section

IV, Paragraph (E), to next serve as trustee.

(E) Power to Appoint Successor Trustee

If all the successor trustees named in this Declaration of Trust cease to, or are unable to, serve as trustee, any

trustee may appoint an additional successor trustee or trustees to serve in the order nominated. The appointment

must be made in writing, signed by the trustee, and notarized.

(F) Terminology

In this Declaration of Trust, the term "trustee" includes any successor trustee or successor trustees.

(G) Bond Waived

No bond shall be required of any trustee.

(H) Compensation

No trustee shall receive any compensation for serving as trustee, except that a trustee shall be entitled to reasonable

compensation, as determined by the trustee, for serving as a trustee of a child's trust created by this Declaration of Trust,

or for serving as trustee because the grantor has become incapacitated.

(I) Liability of Trustee

With respect to the exercise or nonexercise of discretionary powers granted by this Declaration of Trust, the trustee

shall not be liable for actions taken in good faith.

V.   Beneficiaries

Upon the death of the grantor, the property listed on Schedule A shall be distributed to the beneficiaries named in this

section.

(A) Primary and Alternate Beneficiaries

1. (7) _____ shall be given
   beneficiary

_____ .
   property identified

If _____ does not survive the grantor,
   beneficiary

that property shall be given to _____
   alternate beneficiary

2. (7) _____ shall be given
   beneficiary

_____ .
   property identified

If _____ does not survive the grantor,
   beneficiary

that property shall be given to _____
   alternate beneficiary

3. (7) _____ shall be given
   beneficiary

_____ .
   property identified

If _____ does not survive the grantor,
   beneficiary

that property shall be given to _____
   alternate beneficiary

4. (7) _____ shall be given
   beneficiary

_____.
                                            property identified

If _____ does not survive the grantor,
                        beneficiary

that property shall be given to _____
                                                              alternate beneficiary

   5. **7** _____ shall be given
                                            beneficiary

_____.
                                            property identified

If _____ does not survive the grantor,
                        beneficiary

that property shall be given to _____
                                                              alternate beneficiary

(B) Residuary Beneficiary

The residuary beneficiary of the trust shall be **8A** _____,
                                                                    residuary beneficiary

who shall be given all trust property not specifically and validly disposed of by Section V, Paragraph (A).

If _____ does not survive the grantor,
                    residuary beneficiary

that property shall be given to **8A** _____.
                                                        alternate residuary beneficiary

VI. Distribution of Trust Property Upon Death of Grantor

Upon the death of the grantor, the trustee shall distribute the trust property outright to the beneficiaries named in

Section V, Paragraphs (A) and (B), subject to any provision in this Declaration of Trust that creates child's trusts or creates

custodianships under the Uniform Transfers to Minors Act.

VII. Trustee's Powers and Duties

(A) Powers Under State Law

To carry out the provisions of The **1** _____
                                                            your name (or name of trust, if different)

Living Trust, and any children's trusts created under this Declaration of Trust, the trustee shall have all

authority and powers allowed or conferred on a trustee under _____ law,
                                                                                your state

subject to the trustee's fiduciary duty to the grantor and the beneficiaries.

(B) Specified Powers

The trustee's powers include, but are not limited to:

1. The power to sell trust property, and to borrow money and to encumber that property, specifically including trust real estate, by mortgage, deed of trust, or other method.

2. The power to manage trust real estate as if the trustee were the absolute owner of it, including the power to lease (even if the lease term may extend beyond the period of any trust) or grant options to lease the property, to make repairs or alterations, and to insure against loss.

3. The power to sell or grant options for the sale or exchange of any trust property, including stocks, bonds, debentures, and any other form of security or security account, at public or private sale for cash or on credit.

4. The power to invest trust property in property of any kind, including but not limited to bonds, debentures, notes, mortgages, stocks, stock options, stock futures, and buying on margin.

5. The power to receive additional property from any source and add to any trust created by this Declaration of Trust.

6. The power to employ and pay reasonable fees to accountants, lawyers, or investment experts for information or advice relating to the trust.

7. The power to deposit and hold trust funds in both interest-bearing and non-interest-bearing accounts.

8. The power to deposit funds in bank or other accounts uninsured by FDIC coverage.

9. The power to enter into electronic fund transfer or safe deposit arrangements with financial institutions.

10. The power to continue any business of the grantor.

11. The power to institute or defend legal actions concerning the trust or grantor's affairs.

12. The power to execute any document necessary to administer any child's trust created in this Declaration of Trust.

13. The power to diversify investments, including authority to decide that some or all of the trust property need not produce income.

(C) Payment by Trustee of the Grantor's Debts and Taxes

The grantor's debts and death taxes shall be paid by the trustee. The trustee shall pay these from the following trust property: **9** _____

_____

_____ .

If the property specified above is insufficient to pay all the grantor's debts and death taxes, the trustee shall determine how such debts and death taxes shall be paid from trust property.

VIII. General Administrative Provisions

(A) Controlling Law

The validity of The ① _____
                                    your name (or name of trust, if different)

Living Trust shall be governed by the laws of _____
                                                                  your state

(B) Severability

If any provision of this Declaration of Trust is ruled unenforceable, the remaining provisions shall nevertheless remain in effect.

(C) Amendments

The term "Declaration of Trust" includes any provisions added by amendments.

(D) Accountings

No accountings or reports shall be required of the trustee.

IX. Child(ren)'s Trust(s)

All trust property left to any of the minor or young adult beneficiaries listed below in Section IX, Paragraph (A), shall be retained in trust for each such beneficiary in a separate trust of this

① _____ Living Trust.
             your name (or name of trust, if different)

Each trust may be identified and referred to by adding the name of that trust's beneficiary to the name of this trust. The following terms apply to each child's trust:

(A) Trust Beneficiaries and Age Limits

A child's trust shall end when the beneficiary of that trust, listed below, becomes 35, except as otherwise specified in this section:

_____   _____

_____   _____

_____   _____

_____   _____

_____   _____

_____   _____

(B) Powers and Duties of a Child's Trust Trustee

1. Until a child's trust ends, the trustee may distribute to or use for the benefit of the beneficiary as much of the net income or principal of the child's trust as the trustee deems necessary for the beneficiary's health, support, maintenance, or education. Education includes, but is not limited to, college, graduate, professional, and vocational studies, and reasonably related living expenses.

2. In deciding whether to make a distribution to the beneficiary, the trustee may take into account the beneficiary's other income, resources, and sources of support.

3. Any child's trust income that is not distributed to a beneficiary by the trustee shall be accumulated and added to the principal of the trust for that beneficiary.

4. The trustee of a child's trust is not required to make any accounting or report to the trust beneficiary.

(C) Assignment of Interest of Beneficiary Prohibited

The interests of the beneficiary of a child's trust shall not be transferable by voluntary or involuntary assignment or by operation of law before actual receipt by the beneficiary. These interests shall be free from the claims of creditors and from attachments, execution, bankruptcy, or other legal process to the fullest extent permitted by law.

(D) Compensation of Trustee

Any trustee of a child's trust created under this Declaration of Trust shall be entitled to reasonable compensation out of the trust assets for ordinary and extraordinary services, and for all services in connection with the termination of any trust.

(E) Termination of a Child's Trust

A child's trust shall end when any of the following events occur:

1. The beneficiary reaches the age specified in Section IX, Paragraph (A). If the trust ends for this reason, the remaining

principal and accumulated income of the trust shall be given outright to the beneficiary.

2. The beneficiary dies. If the trust ends for this reason, the trust property shall pass to the beneficiary's heirs.

3. The trustee distributes all trust property under the provisions of this Declaration of Trust.

X. Custodianships Under the Uniform Transfers to Minors Act

1. All property **10B** _____ becomes entitled to
beneficiary

under this trust document shall be given to _____ as
custodian's name

custodian for _____ under the _____
beneficiary   state

Uniform Transfers to Minors Act, until _____ reaches age _____.
beneficiary

2. All property **10B** _____ becomes entitled to
beneficiary

under this trust document shall be given to _____ as
custodian's name

custodian for _____ under the _____
beneficiary   state

Uniform Transfers to Minors Act, until _____ reaches age _____.
beneficiary

3. All property **10B** _____ becomes entitled to
beneficiary

under this trust document shall be given to _____ as
custodian's name

custodian for _____ under the _____
beneficiary   state

Uniform Transfers to Minors Act, until _____ reaches age _____.
beneficiary

Certification by Grantor

I certify that I have read this Declaration of Trust and that it correctly states the terms and conditions under which the

trust property is to be held, managed, and disposed of by the trustee, and I approve the Declaration of Trust.

Dated: _____

_____
Grantor and Trustee

Notary's Acknowledgment

State of _____

County of _____

On _____, _____, before me, _____, a notary public, personally appeared_____, who proved to me on the basis of satisfactory evidence to be the person(s) whose name(s) is/are subscribed to the within instrument and acknowledged to me that he/she/they executed the same in his/her/their authorized capacity(ies), and that by his/her/their signature(s) on the instrument the person(s), or the entity upon behalf of which the person(s) acted, executed the instrument.

I certify under PENALTY OF PERJURY under the laws of the State of California that the foregoing paragraph is true and correct.

WITNESS my hand and official seal.

_____
Signature of Notary Public

_____
Printed Name

Notary Public for the State of _____

Residing at _____

[NOTARY SEAL]   My commission expires _____

All the grantor's interest in the following property:

Form 2: Basic Shared Living Trust

The ⟨1⟩ _____ Living Trust

your names (or name of trust, if different)

Declaration of Trust

I. Trust Name

This trust shall be known as The ⟨1⟩ _____ Living Trust.

your names (or name of trust, if different)

II. Trust Property

(A) Property Placed in Trust

⟨1⟩ _____ , called the grantors

your names

or trustees, declare that they have set aside and hold in The ⟨1⟩ _____

your names (or name of trust, if different)

_____ Living Trust all their interest in the property

described in the attached Schedules A, B, and C. ⟨2⟩

The trust property shall be used for the benefit of the trust beneficiaries, and shall be administered and distributed by

the trustees in accordance with this Declaration of Trust.

(B) Rights Retained by Grantors

As long as both grantors are alive, both grantors retain all rights to all income, profits, and control of the trust property

listed on Schedule A of The ⟨1⟩ _____

your names (or name of trust, if different)

_____ Living Trust.

(1) As long as _____ is alive, she shall retain all

wife's name

rights to all income, profits, and control of her separate property listed on Schedule B of The _____

⟨1⟩ _____ Living Trust.

your names (or name of trust, if different)

(2) As long as _____ is alive, he shall retain all

husband's name

rights to all income, profits, and control of his separate property listed on Schedule C of The _____

⟨1⟩ _____ Living Trust.

your names (or name of trust, if different)

(C) Additional or After-Acquired Property

Either grantor, or both, may add property to the trust at any time.

(D) Character of Property Placed in Trust

While both grantors are alive, property transferred to this trust shall retain its original character. If the trust is revoked, the trustee shall distribute the trust property to the grantors based on the same ownership rights they had before the property was transferred to the trust, as specified below.

1. Shared Property

All trust property listed on Schedule A was shared property:

4 _____

identify the character of shared property listed in Schedule A

_____

_____

_____ .

2. Separate Property

The trust property listed on Schedule B shall retain its character as the separate property of _____

_____ . The trust property listed on Schedule C

wife's name

shall retain its character as the separate property of _____ .

husband's name

[Make appropriate deletions if wife and/or husband has no separate property.]

(E) Revocation

As long as both grantors live, either grantor may revoke The **1** _____

your names (or name of trust, if different)

_____ Living Trust at any time by writing given to the

grantor. No beneficiary need be given any notice of revocation. After the death of a spouse, the surviving spouse can

amend his or her continuing revocable living trust, Trust 2, as defined in Section V, Paragraph (B).

(F) Amendment

As long as both grantors live, The **1** _____

your names (or name of trust, if different)

Living Trust may be altered, amended, or modified only by a writing signed by both grantors.

(G) Homestead Rights

If the grantors' principal residence is held in this trust, grantors have the right to possess and occupy it for life, rent-free and without charge, except for taxes, insurance, maintenance, and related costs and expenses. This right is intended to give grantors a beneficial interest in the property and to ensure that the grantors, or either of them, do not lose eligibility for a state homestead tax exemption for which either grantor otherwise qualifies.

III. Trustees

(A) Original Trustees

The trustees of The **1** _____

your names (or name of trust, if different)

Living Trust and any other trust or child's trusts created under this Declaration of Trust shall be _____

1 _____.

your names

Either trustee may act for, and represent, the trust in any transaction.

(B) Trustee on Death or Incapacity of Original Trustee

Upon the death or incapacity of _____or

wife's name

_____, the other spouse shall

husband's name

serve as sole trustee of this trust and any child's trust created under this Declaration of Trust.

(C) Trustee's Responsibility

The trustee in office shall serve as trustee of all trusts created under this Declaration of Trust, including any child's trust.

(D) Terminology

In this Declaration of Trust, the term "trustee" includes any successor trustee or trustees. The singular "trustee" also includes the plural.

(E) Successor Trustee

Upon the death or incapacity of the surviving spouse, or the incapacity of both spouses, the successor trustee shall be **6** _____. If _____

name(s) of successor trustee(s)   he/she/all of them

_____ unable to serve or to continue serving as successor trustee, the next successor trustee shall be

is/are

⑥ _____ .

name(s) of alternate successor trustee(s)

[If you named more than one successor trustee, include ONE of the following two paragraphs here:]

Any of the successor trustees has full and independent authority to act for and represent the trust.

[or]

All of the successor trustees must consent, in writing, to any transaction involving the trust or trust

property.

(F) Resignation of Trustee

Any trustee in office may resign at any time by signing a notice of resignation. The resignation must be delivered to

the person or institution who is either named in this Declaration of Trust, or appointed by the trustee under Section III,

Paragraph (G), to next serve as trustee.

(G) Power to Appoint Successor Trustee

If all the successor trustees named in this Declaration of Trust cease to, or are unable to, serve as trustee, any

trustee may appoint an additional successor trustee or trustees to serve in the order nominated. The appointment must

be made in writing, signed by the trustee, and notarized.

(H) Bond Waived

No bond shall be required of any trustee.

(I) Compensation

No trustee shall receive any compensation for serving as trustee, except that a trustee shall be entitled to

reasonable compensation, as determined by the trustee, for serving as a trustee of a child's trust created by this

Declaration of Trust, or for serving as trustee because the grantors or a grantor becomes incapacitated.

(J) Liability of Trustee

With respect to the exercise or nonexercise of discretionary powers granted by this Declaration of Trust, the trustee

shall not be liable for actions taken in good faith.

IV. Beneficiaries

(A) Husband's Primary and Alternate Beneficiaries

Upon the death of _____ ,
                                                  husband's name

trust property owned by _____ ,
                                                  husband's name

as his share of the trust property listed on Schedule A and any separate property listed on Schedule C,

shall be distributed as specified to the beneficiaries named in this section.

1. Husband's Specific Beneficiaries

a. **7** _____ shall be given
                                       beneficiary

_____ .
                        property identified

If _____ does not survive _____ ,
              beneficiary   husband's name

that property shall be given to _____ .
                                                     alternate beneficiary

b. **7** _____ shall be given
                                       beneficiary

_____ .
                        property identified

If _____ does not survive _____ ,
              beneficiary   husband's name

that property shall be given to _____ .
                                                     alternate beneficiary

c. **7** _____ shall be given
                                       beneficiary

_____ .
                        property identified

If _____ does not survive _____ ,
              beneficiary   husband's name

that property shall be given to _____ .
                                                     alternate beneficiary

d. **7** _____ shall be given
                                       beneficiary

_____ .
                        property identified

If _____ does not survive _____ ,
              beneficiary   husband's name

that property shall be given to _____ .
                                                     alternate beneficiary

e. **7** _____ shall be given
beneficiary

_____ .
property identified

If _____ does not survive _____ ,
beneficiary   husband's name

that property shall be given to _____ .
alternate beneficiary

2. Husband's Residuary Beneficiary

The residuary beneficiary of any trust property owned by _____
husband's name

_____ as his share of the trust property listed on Schedule A or any separate property

listed on Schedule C, and not specifically and validly disposed of by Section IV, Paragraph (A)1, shall be

8A _____ . If _____
residuary beneficiary   residuary beneficiary

_____ does not survive _____
husband's name

that property shall be given to **8A** _____ .
alternate residuary beneficiary

(B) Wife's Primary and Alternate Beneficiaries

Upon the death of _____ ,
wife's name

trust property owned by _____ ,
wife's name

as her share of the trust property listed on Schedule A and any separate property listed on Schedule B,

shall be distributed as specified to the beneficiaries named in this section.

1. Wife's Specific Beneficiaries

a. **7** _____ shall be given
beneficiary

_____ .
property identified

If _____ does not survive _____ ,
beneficiary   wife's name

that property shall be given to _____ .
alternate beneficiary

b. **7** _____ shall be given
beneficiary

_____ .
property identified

If _____ does not survive _____ ,
               beneficiary   wife's name

that property shall be given to _____ .
                                            alternate beneficiary

c. **7** _____ shall be given
                                  beneficiary

_____ .
                                  property identified

If _____ does not survive _____ ,
               beneficiary   wife's name

that property shall be given to _____ .
                                            alternate beneficiary

d. **7** _____ shall be given
                                  beneficiary

_____ .
                                  property identified

If _____ does not survive _____ ,
               beneficiary   wife's name

that property shall be given to _____ .
                                            alternate beneficiary

e. **7** _____ shall be given
                                  beneficiary

_____ .
                                  property identified

If _____ does not survive _____ ,
               beneficiary   wife's name

that property shall be given to _____ .
                                            alternate beneficiary

2. Wife's Residuary Beneficiary

The residuary beneficiary of any trust property owned by _____
                                                                         wife's name

_____ as her share of the trust property listed on Schedule A or any separate property

listed on Schedule B, and not specifically and validly disposed of by Section IV, Paragraph (B)1, shall be

8A _____ . If _____
                          residuary beneficiary   residuary beneficiary

_____ does not survive _____
                                                              wife's name

that property shall be given to **8A** _____ .
                                            alternate residuary beneficiary

V. Administration of Trust Property

(A) Terminology

The first grantor to die shall be called the "deceased spouse." The living grantor shall be called the "surviving spouse."

(B) Division and Distribution of Trust Property on Death of Spouse

1. Upon the death of the deceased spouse, the trustee shall divide the property of The **1** _____

_____ Living Trust listed on Schedules A, B, and C

your names (or name of trust, if different)

into two separate trusts, Trust 1 and Trust 2. The trustee shall serve as trustee of Trust 1 and Trust 2.

2. Trust 1 shall contain all the property of The **1** _____

your names (or name of trust, if different)

Living Trust owned by the deceased spouse at the time it was transferred to the trustee, plus shared

ownership property with a total value equal to one-half of the total value at the time of the deceased spouse's death of

shared ownership property, plus accumulated income, appreciation in value, and the like, attributable to the ownership

interest of the deceased spouse, and his or her share of all property acquired in the trust's name or the trustees' names.

Trust 1 becomes irrevocable at the death of the deceased spouse. The trustee shall distribute the property in Trust 1 to

the beneficiaries named by the deceased spouse in Section IV of this Declaration of Trust, subject to any provision of this

Declaration of Trust that creates children's trusts or creates custodianships under the Uniform Transfers to Minors Act.

3. Trust 2 shall contain all the property of The **1** _____

your names (or name of trust, if different)

_____ Living Trust owned by the surviving spouse at the time it was transferred to the

trust, plus accumulated income, appreciation in value, and the like attributable to the ownership interest of the

surviving spouse and any trust property left by the deceased spouse to the surviving spouse.

4. The trustee shall have exclusive authority to determine the paperwork and record keeping necessary to establish

Trust 1 and Trust 2.

(C) Property Left to the Surviving Spouse

Any trust property left by the deceased spouse to the surviving spouse shall remain in the surviving spouse's

revocable trust, Trust 2, without necessity of a formal transfer to that trust.

(D) Administration of Trust 2

1. Rights Retained by Surviving Spouse

Until the death of the surviving spouse, all rights to all income, profits, and control of property in Trust 2 shall be

retained by or distributed to the surviving spouse.

2. Revocation

The surviving spouse may amend or revoke Trust 2 at any time during his or her lifetime, without notifying any beneficiary.

3. Distribution of Property in Trust 2

Upon the death of the surviving spouse, Trust 2 becomes irrevocable, and the property in Trust 2 shall be distributed to the beneficiaries listed in Section IV, subject to any provision of this Declaration of Trust that creates child's trusts or creates custodianships under the Uniform Transfers to Minors Act.

VI. Incapacity

 (A) Incapacity of Both Grantors

If both grantors become physically or mentally incapacitated and are no longer able to manage this trust, the person or persons named as successor trustee shall serve as trustee. The determination of the grantors' capacity to manage this trust shall be made by those of the persons listed below who are reasonably available when the successor trustee (or any of them, if two or more are named to serve together) requests their opinion. If a majority of these persons state, in writing, that in their opinion the grantors are no longer reasonably capable of serving as trustee, the successor trustee shall serve as trustee.

_____
name(s) of person(s) to determine incapacity

The successor trustee shall pay trust income at least annually to, or for the benefit of, the grantors and may also spend any amount of trust principal necessary, in the successor trustee's discretion, for the needs of the grantors, until the grantors, or either of them, are no longer incapacitated, or until their deaths.

 (B) Incapacity of Surviving Spouse

If, after the death of the deceased spouse, the surviving spouse becomes physically or mentally incapacitated and is no longer able to manage Trust 2, the person or persons named as successor trustee shall serve as trustee. The determination of the grantor's capacity to manage the trust shall be made by those of the persons listed below who are reasonably available when the successor trustee (or any of them, if two or more are named to serve together) requests their opinion. If a majority of these persons state, in writing, that in their opinion the grantor is no longer reasonably capable of serving as trustee, the successor trustee shall serve as trustee.

The successor trustee shall pay trust income at least annually to, or for the benefit of, the surviving spouse and may also spend any amount of the trust principal necessary in the successor trustee's discretion, for the needs of the surviving spouse, until the surviving spouse is again able to manage his or her own affairs, or until his or her death.

VII. Simultaneous Death

If both grantors should die simultaneously, or under such circumstances as to render it difficult or impossible to determine who predeceased the other, for purposes of this living trust, it shall be conclusively presumed that both died at the same moment, and neither shall be presumed to have survived the other. The trustee shall distribute the trust property to the named beneficiaries.

VIII. Trustee's Powers and Duties

(A) Powers Under State Law

To carry out the provisions of this Declaration of Trust, and to manage the trust property of The

1

_____ Living Trust, Trust 1, Trust 2, and

your name(s) (or name of trust, if different)

any child's trust created under this Declaration of Trust, the trustee shall have all authority and power allowed or

conferred under _____ law, subject to the rights retained by

your state

each grantor in Section II (B) and to the trustee's fiduciary duty to the grantors and the beneficiaries.

(B) Specified Powers

The trustee's powers include, but are not limited to:

1. The power to sell trust property, and to borrow money and to encumber property, specifically including trust real estate, by mortgage, deed of trust, or other method.

2. The power to manage trust real estate as if the trustee were the absolute owner of it, including the power to lease (even if the lease term may extend beyond the period of any trust) or grant options to lease the property, to make repairs or alterations, and to insure against loss.

3. The power to sell or grant options for the sale or exchange of any trust property, including stocks, bonds, debentures, and any other form of security or security account, at public or private sale for cash or on credit.

4. The power to invest trust property in property of any kind, including but not limited to bonds, debentures, notes, mortgages, stocks, stock options, stock futures, and buying on margin.

5. The power to receive additional property from any source and add to any trust created by this Declaration of Trust.

6. The power to employ and pay reasonable fees to accountants, lawyers, or investment experts for information or advice relating to the trust.

7. The power to deposit and hold trust funds in both interest-bearing and non-interest-bearing accounts.

8. The power to deposit funds in bank or other accounts uninsured by FDIC coverage.

9. The power to enter into electronic fund transfer or safe deposit arrangements with financial institutions.

10. The power to continue any business of either grantor.

11. The power to institute or defend legal actions concerning the trust or grantors' affairs.

12. The power to execute any document necessary to administer any trust created in this Declaration of Trust.

13. The power to diversify investments, including authority to decide that some or all of the trust property need not produce income.

(C) Payment by the Trustee of the Grantors' Debts and Taxes

1. Wife's Debts and Taxes

_____'s debts and
wife's name

death taxes shall be paid by the trustee. The trustee shall pay these from the following trust property:

9 _____.

2. Husband's Debts and Taxes

_____'s debts and
husband's name

death taxes shall be paid by the trustee. The trustee shall pay these from the following trust property:

9 _____.

3. If Specified Property Insufficient

If the property specified above is insufficient to pay all a grantor's debts and death taxes, the trustee shall determine how such debts and death taxes shall be paid from that grantor's trust property.

IX. General Administrative Provisions

(A) Controlling Law

The validity of The **1** _____ Living Trust and

your names (or name of trust, if different)

construction of its provisions shall be governed by the laws of _____.

your state

(B) Severability

If any provision of this Declaration of Trust is ruled unenforceable, the remaining provisions shall nevertheless remain in effect.

(C) Amendments

The term "Declaration of Trust" includes any provisions added by valid amendment.

(D) Accountings

No accountings or reports shall be required of the trustee.

X. Child(ren)'s Trust(s)

All trust property left to any of the minor or young adult beneficiaries listed below in Section X, Paragraph (A), shall be retained in trust for each such beneficiary in a separate trust of this **1** _____

_____ Living Trust. Each trust may

your names (or name of trust, if different)

be identified and referred to by adding the name of that trust's beneficiary to the name of this trust. The

following terms apply to each child's trust:

(A) Trust Beneficiaries and Age Limits

A trust shall end when the beneficiary of that trust, listed below, becomes 35, except as otherwise specified in this

section:

Trust for	Shall end at age
_____	_____
_____	_____
_____	_____
_____	_____
_____	_____

(B) Powers and Duties of a Child's Trust Trustee

1. Until a child's trust ends, the trustee may distribute to or use for the benefit of the beneficiary as much of the net income or principal of the child's trust as the trustee deems necessary for the beneficiary's health, support, maintenance, or education. Education includes, but is not limited to, college, graduate, professional, and vocational studies, and reasonably related living expenses.

2. In deciding whether to make a distribution to the beneficiary, the trustee may take into account the beneficiary's other income, resources, and sources of support.

3. Any child's trust income that is not distributed to a beneficiary by the trustee shall be accumulated and added to the principal of the trust for that beneficiary.

4. The trustee of a child's trust is not required to make any accounting or report to the trust beneficiary.

(C) Assignment of Interest of Beneficiary Prohibited

The interests of the beneficiary of a child's trust shall not be transferable by voluntary or involuntary assignment or by operation of law before actual receipt by the beneficiary. These interests shall be free from the claims of creditors and from attachments, execution, bankruptcy, or other legal process to the fullest extent permitted by law.

(D) Compensation of Trustee

Any trustee of a child's trust created under this Declaration of Trust shall be entitled to reasonable compensation without court approval out of the trust assets for ordinary and extraordinary services, and for all services in connection with the termination of any trust.

(E) Termination of a Child's Trust

A child's trust shall end when any of the following events occurs:

1. The beneficiary reaches the age specified in Section X, Paragraph (A). If the trust ends for this reason, the remaining principal and accumulated income of the trust shall be given outright to the beneficiary.

2. The beneficiary dies. If the trust ends for this reason, the trust property shall pass to the beneficiary's heirs.

3. The trustee distributes all trust property under the provisions of this Declaration of Trust.

XI. Custodianships Under the Uniform Transfers to Minors Act

1. All property ^{10B} _____ becomes entitled to
beneficiary

under this trust document shall be given to _____ as
custodian's name

custodian for _____ under the _____
beneficiary   state

Uniform Transfers to Minors Act, until _____ reaches age _____ .
beneficiary

2. All property ^{10B} _____ becomes entitled to
beneficiary

under this trust document shall be given to _____ as
custodian's name

custodian for _____ under the _____
beneficiary   state

Uniform Transfers to Minors Act, until _____ reaches age _____ .
beneficiary

3. All property ^{10B} _____ becomes entitled to
beneficiary

under this trust document shall be given to _____ as
custodian's name

custodian for _____ under the _____
beneficiary   state

Uniform Transfers to Minors Act, until _____ reaches age _____ .
beneficiary

Certification by Grantors

We certify that we have read this Declaration of Trust and that it correctly states the terms and conditions under which the trust property is to be held, managed, and disposed of by the trustees and we approve the Declaration of Trust.

Dated: _____

_____
Grantor and Trustee

_____
Grantor and Trustee

Notary's Acknowledgment

State of _____

County of _____

On _____, _____, before me, _____, a notary public, personally appeared_____, who proved to me on the basis of satisfactory evidence to be the person(s) whose name(s) is/are subscribed to the within instrument and acknowledged to me that he/she/they executed the same in his/her/their authorized capacity(ies), and that by his/her/their signature(s) on the instrument the person(s), or the entity upon behalf of which the person(s) acted, executed the instrument.

I certify under PENALTY OF PERJURY under the laws of the State of _____ that the foregoing paragraph is true and correct.

WITNESS my hand and official seal.

_____
Signature of Notary Public

_____
Printed Name

Notary Public for the State of _____

Residing at _____

[NOTARY SEAL]   My commission expires _____

Schedule B
Wife's separate property placed in trust

All Wife's interest in the following property:

Schedule C
Husband's separate property placed in trust

All Husband's interest in the following property:

Form 3: AB Living Trust

The ① _____ AB Living Trust
your names (or name of trust, if different)

Declaration of Trust

I. Trust Name

This trust shall be known as The ① _____ Living Trust.
your names (or name of trust, if different)

II. Trust Property

(A) Property Placed in Trust

① _____ , called the grantors
your names

or trustees, declare that they have set aside and hold in The ① _____
your names (or name of trust, if different)

_____ Living Trust all their interest in the property described in the attached Schedules A, B, and C. ②

The trust property shall be used for the benefit of the trust beneficiaries, and shall be administered and distributed

by the trustees in accordance with this Declaration of Trust.

(B) Rights Retained by Grantors

As long as both grantors are alive, both grantors retain all rights to all income, profits, and control of the trust

property listed on Schedule A of The ① _____
your names (or name of trust, if different)

① _____ Living Trust.

(1) As long as _____ is alive, she shall retain all
wife's name

rights to all income, profits, and control of her separate property listed on Schedule B of The _____

① _____ Living Trust.
your names (or name of trust, if different)

(2) As long as _____ is alive, he shall retain all
husband's name

rights to all income, profits, and control of his separate property listed on Schedule C of The _____

① _____ Living Trust.
your names (or name of trust, if different)

(C) Additional or After-Acquired Property

Either grantor, or both, may add property to the trust at any time.

(D) Character of Property Placed in Trust

While both grantors are alive, property transferred to this trust shall retain its original character. If the trust is revoked, the trustee shall distribute the trust property to the grantors based on the same ownership rights they had before the property was transferred to the trust, as specified below.

Specifically:

1. Shared Property

All trust property listed on Schedule A was shared property:

4 _____

identify the character of shared property listed in Schedule A

_____

_____

_____ .

2. Separate Property

The trust property listed on Schedule B shall retain its character as the separate property of

_____ . The trust property listed on Schedule C

wife's name

shall retain its character as the separate property of _____ .

husband's name

[Make appropriate deletions if wife and/or husband has no separate property.]

(E) Revocation

For as long as both grantors live, either grantor may revoke The **1** _____

your names (or name of trust, if different)

Living Trust at any time by writing given to the other grantor. No beneficiary need be given any notice

of revocation.

(F) Amendment

Except as provided in Section VII, Paragraph (B), for as long as both grantors live, The _____ may be altered, amended, or modified only by a writing signed by both grantors.

   After the death of a spouse, the surviving spouse can amend his or her revocable living trust, Trust B, The Surviving Spouse's Trust, as defined in Section V, Paragraphs (A)3 and (B)3, and in Section VI.

(G) Homestead Rights

   If the grantors' principal residence is held in this trust, grantors have the right to possess and occupy it for life, rent-free and without charge, except for taxes, insurance, maintenance, and related costs and expenses. This right is intended to give grantors a beneficial interest in the property and to ensure that the grantors, or either of them, do not lose eligibility for a state homestead tax exemption for which either grantor otherwise qualifies.

III. Trustees

(A) Original Trustees

   The trustees of The **1** _____

your names (or name of trust, if different)

Living Trust and any AB trust or other trusts, including child's trusts, created under this Declaration of

Trust shall be **1** _____.

your names (or name of trust, if different)

Either trustee may act for, and represent, the trust in any transaction.

(B) Trustee on Death or Incapacity of Original Trustee

   Upon the death or incapacity of _____or

wife's name

_____, the other spouse shall serve

husband's name

as sole trustee of this trust and all trusts and any child's trust created under this Declaration of Trust.

(C) Trustee's Responsibility

   The trustee in office shall serve as trustee of this trust and all trusts and any child's trust created under this Declaration of Trust.

(D) Terminology

   In this Declaration of Trust, the term "trustee" includes any successor trustee or trustees. The singular "trustee" also includes the plural.

(E) Successor Trustee

5A Upon the death or incapacity of the surviving spouse, or the incapacity of both spouses, the successor trustee

shall be **6** _____. If _____

name(s) of successor trustee(s)   he/she/all of them

_____ unable to serve or to continue serving as successor trustee, the next successor trustee shall be

is/are

6 _____ .

name(s) of alternate successor trustee(s)

[If you named more than one successor trustee, include ONE of the following two paragraphs here:]

Any of the successor trustees has full and independent authority to act for and represent the trust.

[or]

All of the successor trustees must consent, in writing, to any transaction involving the trust or trust

property.

(F) Resignation of Trustee

Any trustee in office may resign at any time by signing a notice of resignation. The resignation must be delivered to

the person or institution who is either named in this Declaration of Trust, or appointed by the trustee under Section III,

Paragraph (G), to next serve as the trustee.

(G) Power to Appoint Successor Trustee

If all the successor trustees named in this Declaration of Trust cease to, or are unable to, serve as trustee, any trustee

may appoint an additional successor trustee or trustees to serve in the order nominated. The appointment must be

made in writing, signed by the trustee, and notarized.

(H) Bond Waived

No bond shall be required of any trustee.

(I) Compensation

No trustee shall receive any compensation for serving as trustee, except that a trustee shall be entitled to

reasonable compensation, as determined by the trustee, for serving as a trustee of Trust A, or a child's trust created by

this Declaration of Trust, or for serving as trustee because the grantors or a grantor has become incapacitated.

(J) Liability of Trustee

With respect to the exercise or nonexercise of discretionary powers granted by this Declaration of Trust, the trustee shall not be liable for actions taken in good faith.

IV. Specific Beneficiaries

(A) Wife's Specific and Alternate Beneficiaries

Upon the death of _____ , the following gifts

wife's name

shall be made from trust property owned by _____ .

wife's name

1. **7** _____ shall be given

beneficiary

_____ .

property identified

If _____ does not survive _____ ,

beneficiary · wife's name

that property shall be given to _____ .

alternate beneficiary

2. **7** _____ shall be given

beneficiary

_____ .

property identified

If _____ does not survive _____ ,

beneficiary · wife's name

that property shall be given to _____ .

alternate beneficiary

3. **7** _____ shall be given

beneficiary

_____ .

property identified

If _____ does not survive _____ ,

beneficiary · wife's name

that property shall be given to _____ .

alternate beneficiary

(B) Husband's Specific and Alternate Beneficiaries

Upon the death of _____ , the following gifts

husband's name

shall be made from trust property owned by _____ .

husband's name

1. **7** _____ shall be given

beneficiary

_____ .

property identified

If _____ does not survive _____ ,
       beneficiary   husband's name

that property shall be given to _____ .
                                                alternate beneficiary

2. **(7)** _____ shall be given
                                        beneficiary

_____ .
                                         property identified

If _____ does not survive _____ ,
       beneficiary   husband's name

that property shall be given to _____ .
                                                alternate beneficiary

3. **(7)** _____ shall be given
                                        beneficiary

_____ .
                                         property identified

If _____ does not survive _____ ,
       beneficiary   husband's name

that property shall be given to _____ .
                                                alternate beneficiary

(C) Remaining Trust Property

Except as provided by Section IV, Paragraph (A) or (B), all other trust property of the deceased spouse shall be

transferred to, and administered as part of, Trust A, defined in Section V.

V. Creation of Trust A on Death of Deceased Spouse

(A) Terminology

1. The first grantor to die shall be called the "deceased spouse." The living grantor shall then be called the "surviving

spouse."

2. The "trust property of the deceased spouse" shall consist of all property of The

(1) _____ Living Trust
                             your names (or name of trust, if different)

individually owned by the deceased spouse at the time it was transferred to the trustee, plus shared ownership

property with a total value equal to one-half of the total value at the time of the deceased spouse's death of the shared

ownership trust property, plus accumulated income, appreciation in value, and the like, attributable to the ownership

interest of the deceased spouse, and his or her share of all property acquired in the trust's name or the trustees' names.

3. The "trust property of the surviving spouse" shall consist of all property of The _____

1 _____ Living Trust

your names (or name of trust, if different)

individually owned by the surviving spouse at the time it was transferred to the trustee, plus shared ownership

property with a total value equal to one-half of the total value at the time of the deceased spouse's death of the shared

ownership trust property, plus accumulated income, appreciation in value, and the like, attributable to the ownership

interest of the surviving spouse, and his or her share of all property acquired in the trust's name or the trustees' names.

(B) Division of Trust Property on Death of Deceased Spouse

1. Upon the death of the deceased spouse, the trustee shall divide the property of The _____

1 _____ Living Trust

your names (or name of trust, if different)

listed on Schedules A, B, and C into two separate trusts, Trust A and Trust B.

2. All trust assets of the deceased spouse, as defined in Section V, Paragraph (A)2, shall be placed in a trust known

as Trust A, after making any specific gifts provided for in Section IV, Paragraph (A) or (B), subject to any provision in this

Declaration of Trust that creates child's trusts or creates custodianship under the Uniform Transfers to Minors Act.

3. The trustee shall place all trust assets of the surviving spouse, as defined in Section V, Paragraph (A)3, in a trust

known as Trust B (The Surviving Spouse's Trust).

4. Physical segregation of the assets of The **1** _____

your names (or name of trust, if different)

_____ Living Trust is not required to divide that trust's property into

Trust A and Trust B. The trustee shall exclusively determine what records, documents, and actions are required to

establish and maintain Trust A and Trust B.

(C) Administration of Trust A

All property held in Trust A shall be administered as follows:

1. Upon the death of the deceased spouse, Trust A shall be irrevocable.

2. The life beneficiary of Trust A shall be the surviving spouse.

3. If _____ is the deceased spouse,
wife's name

the final beneficiaries of Trust A shall be:

8B
_____
name(s) of final beneficiary(ies)

_____

_____

_____

If _____ is the deceased spouse,
wife's name

the alternate final beneficiaries of Trust A shall be:

8B
_____
name(s) of alternate final beneficiary(ies)

_____

_____

_____

4. If _____ is the deceased spouse,
husband's name

the final beneficiaries of Trust A shall be:

8B
_____
name(s) of final beneficiary(ies)

_____

_____

_____

If _____ is the deceased spouse,
husband's name

the alternate final beneficiaries of Trust A shall be:

8B
_____
name(s) of alternate final beneficiary(ies)

_____

_____

_____

5. The trustee shall pay to or spend for the benefit of the surviving spouse the net income of Trust A at least quarterly. The trustee shall also pay to or spend for the benefit of the surviving spouse any sums from the principal of Trust A necessary for the surviving spouse's health, education, support, and maintenance, in accord with his or her accustomed manner of living.

6. [11] No accounting of Trust A shall be required of the trustee, except that the final beneficiaries shall be provided with copies of the annual federal income tax return.

7. The trustee shall be entitled to reasonable compensation from assets of Trust A for services rendered managing Trust A, without court approval.

8. Upon the death of the life beneficiary, the trustee shall distribute the property of Trust A to the final or alternate final beneficiary or beneficiaries, as named in Section V, Paragraph C(3) or C(4).

VI. Trust B: The Surviving Spouse's Trust

(A) Creation of Trust B, The Surviving Spouse's Trust

Upon the death of the deceased spouse, all trust property owned by the surviving spouse, as defined in Section V, Paragraph (A)3, shall be held in Trust B, The Surviving Spouse's Trust.

(B) Administration of Trust B

Until the death of the surviving spouse, the surviving spouse retains all rights to all income, profits, and control of the property in Trust B. The surviving spouse may amend or revoke Trust B at any time during his or her lifetime, without notifying any beneficiary.

(C) Distribution of Property in Trust B

1. Upon the death of the surviving spouse, Trust B becomes irrevocable.

2. The trustee shall first distribute any specific gifts of the surviving spouse to the beneficiaries named in Section IV, Paragraph (A) or (B). The trustee shall then distribute all remaining property of Trust B to his or her final, or alternate final, beneficiaries, as named in Section V, Paragraph (C)3 or (C)4.

3. All distributions under Section VI, Paragraph (C), are subject to any provision in this Declaration of Trust that creates child's trusts or creates custodianships under the Uniform Transfers to Minors Act.

VII. Incapacity

5A

(A) Incapacity of Grantors

If both grantors become physically or mentally incapacitated and are no longer able to manage this trust, the person or persons named as successor trustee shall serve as trustee. The determination of the grantors' capacity to manage this trust shall be made by those of the persons listed below who are reasonably available when the successor trustee (or any of them, if two or more are named to serve together) requests their opinion. If a majority of these persons state, in writing, that in their opinion the grantors are no longer reasonably capable of serving as trustee, the successor trustee shall serve as trustee.

_____

name(s) of person(s) to determine incapacity

The successor trustee shall pay trust income at least annually to, or for the benefit of, the grantors and may also spend any amount of trust principal necessary, in the successor trustee's discretion, for the needs of the grantors, until the grantors, or either of them, are no longer incapacitated, or until their deaths.

5B

(B) Amending AB Trust If Estate Tax Law Changes

Notwithstanding any other provision of this trust, if Congress changes the estate tax law, this trust may be amended as follows:

1. If both grantors are alive but one is incapacitated, the competent spouse may amend this AB trust in order to take best advantage of the new tax law.

2. If both grantors are alive but incapacitated, the successor trustee may amend this AB trust in order to take best advantage of the new tax law.

5A

(C) Incapacity of Surviving Spouse

If, after the death of the deceased spouse, the surviving spouse becomes physically or mentally incapacitated and is no longer able to manage Trust B, the person or persons named as successor trustee shall serve as trustee.

1. The determination of the grantor's capacity to manage the trust shall be made by those of the persons listed below who are reasonably available when the successor trustee (or any of them, if two or more are named to serve together) requests their opinion. If a majority of these persons state, in writing, that in their opinion the grantor is no longer reasonably capable of serving as trustee, the successor trustee shall serve as trustee.

2. The successor trustee shall pay trust income at least annually to, or for the benefit of, the surviving spouse, and spend any amount of that trust's principal necessary, in the successor trustee's discretion, for the needs of the surviving spouse, until the surviving spouse is no longer incapacitated, or until his or her death. Any income not spent for the benefit of the surviving spouse shall be accumulated and added to the property of Trust B.

3. The successor trustee shall manage Trust A, under the terms of this Declaration of Trust, until the surviving spouse is again able to serve as trustee of that trust, or until the death of the surviving spouse.

4. The successor trustee shall manage any operational child's trust created by this Declaration of Trust.

VIII. Simultaneous Death

If both grantors should die simultaneously, or under such circumstances as to render it difficult or impossible to determine who predeceased the other, for the purposes of this living trust it shall be conclusively presumed that both died at the same moment, and neither shall be presumed to have survived the other. The trustee shall make any specific gifts left by either spouse, and then distribute all remaining property to each spouse's final beneficiaries.

IX. Trustee's Powers and Duties

(A) Powers Under State Law

To carry out the provisions of this Declaration of Trust, and to manage the trust property of The _____

1 _____ Living Trust,

your names (or name of trust, if different)

Trust A, Trust B, and any child's trust created under this Declaration of Trust, the trustee shall have all authority and power allowed or conferred under _____ law, subject to the

your state

rights retained by each grantor in Section II (B) and to the trustee's fiduciary duty to the grantors and the beneficiaries.

(B) Specified Powers

The trustee's powers include, but are not limited to:

1. The power to sell trust property, and to borrow money and to encumber property, specifically including trust real estate, by mortgage, deed of trust, or other method.

2. The power to manage trust real estate as if the trustee were the absolute owner of it, including the power to lease (even if the lease term may extend beyond the period of any trust) or grant options to lease the property, to make

repairs or alterations, and to insure against loss.

3. The power to sell or grant options for the sale or exchange of any trust property, including stocks, bonds, debentures, and any other form of security or security account, at public or private sale for cash or on credit.

4. The power to invest trust property in property of any kind, including but not limited to bonds, debentures, notes, mortgages, stocks, stock options, stock futures, and buying on margin.

5. The power to receive additional property from any source and add to any trust created by this Declaration of Trust.

6. The power to employ and pay reasonable fees to accountants, lawyers, or investment experts for information or advice relating to the trust.

7. The power to deposit and hold trust funds in both interest-bearing and non-interest-bearing accounts.

8. The power to deposit funds in bank or other accounts uninsured by FDIC coverage.

9. The power to enter into electronic fund transfer or safe deposit arrangements with financial institutions.

10. The power to continue any business of either grantor.

11. The power to institute or defend legal actions concerning the trust or grantors' affairs.

12. The power to execute any document necessary to administer any trust created in this Declaration of Trust.

13. The power to diversify investments, including authority to decide that some or all of the trust property need not produce income.

(C) Payment by the Trustee of the Grantors' Debts and Taxes

1. Wife's Debts and Taxes

_____'s debts and
wife's name

death taxes shall be paid by the trustee. The trustee shall pay these from the following trust property:

9 _____.

2. Husband's Debts and Taxes

_____'s debts and
husband's name

death taxes shall be paid by the trustee. The trustee shall pay these from the following trust property:

9 _____.

3. If Specified Property Insufficient

If the property specified above is insufficient to pay all a grantor's debts and death taxes, the trustee shall determine how such debts and death taxes shall be paid from that grantor's trust property, except as limited by any law or IRS regulation controlling the property in Trust A.

X. General Administrative Provisions

(A) Controlling Law

The validity of The  _____ Living Trust and
your names (or name of trust, if different)

construction of its provisions shall be governed by the laws of _____.
your state

(B) Severability

If any provision of this Declaration of Trust is ruled unenforceable, the remaining provisions shall nevertheless remain in effect.

(C) Amendments

The term "Declaration of Trust" includes any provisions added by valid amendment.

XI. Child(ren)'s Trust(s)

All trust property left to any of the minor or young adult beneficiaries listed below in Section XI, Paragraph (A), shall be retained in trust for each such beneficiary in a separate trust of this  _____

_____ Living Trust.
your names (or name of trust, if different)

Each trust may be identified and referred to by adding the name of that trust's beneficiary to the name of this trust. The following terms apply to each child's trust:

(A) Trust Beneficiaries and Age Limits

A trust shall end when the beneficiary of that trust, listed below, becomes 35, except as otherwise specified in this section:

Trust for

Shall end at age

_____   _____

_____   _____

_____   _____

_____   _____

_____   _____

(B) Powers and Duties of a Child's Trust Trustee

1. Until a child's trust ends, the trustee may distribute to or use for the benefit of the beneficiary as much of the net income or principal of the child's trust as the trustee deems necessary for the beneficiary's health, support, maintenance, or education. Education includes, but is not limited to, college, graduate, professional, and vocational studies, and reasonably related living expenses.

2. In deciding whether to make a distribution to the beneficiary, the trustee may take into account the beneficiary's other income, resources, and sources of support.

3. Any child's trust income that is not distributed to a beneficiary by the trustee shall be accumulated and added to the principal of the trust for that beneficiary.

4. The trustee of a child's trust is not required to make any accounting or report to the trust beneficiary.

(C) Assignment of Interest of Beneficiary Prohibited

The interests of the beneficiary of a child's trust shall not be transferable by voluntary or involuntary assignment or by operation of law before actual receipt by the beneficiary. These interests shall be free from the claims of creditors and from attachments, execution, bankruptcy, or other legal process to the fullest extent permitted by law.

(D) Compensation of Trustee

Any trustee of a child's trust created under this Declaration of Trust shall be entitled to reasonable compensation without court approval out of the trust assets for ordinary and extraordinary services, and for all services in connection with the termination of any trust.

(E) Termination of a Child's Trusts

A child's trust shall end when any of the following events occurs:

1. The beneficiary reaches the age specified in Section XI, Paragraph (A). If the trust ends for this reason, the remaining principal and accumulated income of the trust shall be given outright to the beneficiary.

2. The beneficiary dies. If the trust ends for this reason, the trust property shall pass to the beneficiary's heirs.

3. The trustee distributes all trust property under the provisions of this Declaration of Trust.

XII. Custodianships Under the Uniform Transfers to Minors Act

1. All property **10B** _____ becomes entitled to
beneficiary

under this trust document shall be given to _____ as
custodian's name

custodian for _____ under the _____
beneficiary   state

Uniform Transfers to Minors Act, until _____ reaches age _____.
beneficiary

2. All property **10B** _____ becomes entitled to
beneficiary

under this trust document shall be given to _____ as
custodian's name

custodian for _____ under the _____
beneficiary   state

Uniform Transfers to Minors Act, until _____ reaches age _____.
beneficiary

3. All property **10B** _____ becomes entitled to
beneficiary

under this trust document shall be given to _____ as
custodian's name

custodian for _____ under the _____
beneficiary   state

Uniform Transfers to Minors Act, until _____ reaches age _____.
beneficiary

Certification by Grantors

We certify that we have read this Declaration of Trust and that it correctly states the terms and conditions under which the trust property is to be held, managed, and disposed of by the trustees, and we approve the Declaration of Trust.

Dated: _____

_____
Grantor and Trustee

_____
Grantor and Trustee

Notary's Acknowledgment

State of _____

County of _____

On _____, _____, before me, _____, a notary public, personally appeared_____, who proved to me on the basis of satisfactory evidence to be the person(s) whose name(s) is/are subscribed to the within instrument and acknowledged to me that he/she/they executed the same in his/her/their authorized capacity(ies), and that by his/her/their signature(s) on the instrument the person(s), or the entity upon behalf of which the person(s) acted, executed the instrument.

I certify under PENALTY OF PERJURY under the laws of the State of California that the foregoing paragraph is true and correct.

WITNESS my hand and official seal.

_____
Signature of Notary Public

_____
Printed Name

Notary Public for the State of _____

Residing at _____

[NOTARY SEAL]   My commission expires _____

Schedule A 3
Shared property placed in trust

All Wife's interest in the following property:

All Husband's interest in the following property:

Form 4: AB Disclaimer Living Trust

The **1** _____ AB Living Trust
your names (or name of trust, if different)

Declaration of Trust

I. Trust Name

This trust shall be known as The **1** _____ Living Trust.
your names (or name of trust, if different)

II. Trust Property

(A) Property Placed in Trust

1 _____, called the grantors
your names

or trustees, declare that they have set aside and hold in The **1** _____
your names (or name of trust, if different)

_____ Living Trust all their interest in the property described in the attached Schedules A, B, and C. **2**

The trust property shall be used for the benefit of the trust beneficiaries, and shall be administered and distributed

by the trustees in accordance with this Declaration of Trust.

(B) Rights Retained by Grantors

As long as both grantors are alive, both grantors retain all rights to all income, profits, and control of the trust

property listed on Schedule A of The **1** _____
your names (or name of trust, if different)

1 _____ Living Trust.

(1) As long as _____ is alive, she shall retain all
wife's name

rights to all income, profits, and control of her separate property listed on Schedule B of The _____

_____ Living Trust.
your names (or name of trust, if different)

(2) As long as _____ is alive, he shall retain all
husband's name

rights to all income, profits, and control of his separate property listed on Schedule C of The _____

1 _____ Living Trust.
your names (or name of trust, if different)

(C) Additional or After-Acquired Property

Either grantor, or both, may add property to the trust at any time.

(D) Character of Property Placed in Trust

While both grantors are alive, property transferred to this trust shall retain its original character. If the trust is

revoked, the trustee shall distribute the trust property to the grantors based on the same ownership rights they had

before the property was transferred to the trust, as specified below.

Specifically:

1. Shared Property

All trust property listed on Schedule A was shared property:

④ _____

identify the character of shared property listed in Schedule A

_____

_____

_____.

2. Separate Property

The trust property listed on Schedule B shall retain its character as the separate property of _____

_____. The trust property listed on Schedule C

wife's name

shall retain its character as the separate property of _____.

husband's name

[Make appropriate deletions if wife and/or husband has no separate property.]

(E) Revocation

For as long as both grantors live, either grantor may revoke The ① _____

your names (or name of trust, if different)

Living Trust at any time by writing given to the other grantor. No beneficiary need be given any notice of revocation.

(F) Amendment

Except as provided in Section VII, Paragraph (B), for as long as both grantors live, The

① _____ Living Trust

your names (or name of trust, if different)

may be altered, amended, or modified only by a writing signed by both grantors.

After the death of a spouse, the surviving spouse can amend his or her revocable living trust, Trust B, The Surviving Spouse's Trust, as defined in Section V, Paragraph (B)1, and in Section VI.

(G) Homestead Rights

If the grantors' principal residence is held in this trust, grantors have the right to possess and occupy it for life, rent-free and without charge, except for taxes, insurance, maintenance, and related costs and expenses. This right is intended to give grantors a beneficial interest in the property and to ensure that the grantors, or either of them, do not lose eligibility for a state homestead tax exemption for which either grantor otherwise qualifies.

III. Trustees

(A) Original Trustees

The trustees of The ❶ _____
                                                    your names (or name of trust, if different)

Living Trust and any AB trust or other trusts, including child's trusts, created under this Declaration of

Trust shall be ❶ _____ .
                                                    your names (or name of trust, if different)

Either trustee may act for, and represent, the trust in any transaction.

(B) Trustee on Death or Incapacity of Original Trustee

Upon the death or incapacity of _____ or
                                                                                  wife's name

_____ , the other spouse shall serve
                                    husband's name

as sole trustee of this trust and all trusts and any child's trust created under this Declaration of Trust.

(C) Trustee's Responsibility

The trustee in office shall serve as trustee of this trust and all trusts and any child's trust created under this Declaration of Trust.

(D) Terminology

In this Declaration of Trust, the term "trustee" includes any successor trustee or trustees. The singular "trustee" also includes the plural.

(E) Successor Trustee

5A Upon the death or incapacity of the surviving spouse, or the incapacity of both spouses, the successor

trustee shall be **6** _____ . If _____

name(s) of successor trustee(s)   he/she/all of them

_____

unable to serve or to continue serving as successor trustee, the next successor trustee shall be
   is/are

6 _____

.

name(s) of alternate successor trustee(s)

[If you named more than one successor trustee, include ONE of the following two paragraphs here:]

Any of the successor trustees has full and independent authority to act for and represent the trust.

[or]

All of the successor trustees must consent, in writing, to any transaction involving the trust or trust

property.

(F) Resignation of Trustee

Any trustee in office may resign at any time by signing a notice of resignation. The resignation must be delivered

to the person or institution who is either named in this Declaration of Trust, or appointed by the trustee under

Section III, Paragraph (G), to next serve as the trustee.

(G) Power to Appoint Successor Trustee

If all the successor trustees named in this Declaration of Trust cease to, or are unable to, serve as trustee, any

trustee may appoint an additional successor trustee or trustees to serve in the order nominated. The appointment

must be made in writing, signed by the trustee, and notarized.

(H) Bond Waived

No bond shall be required of any trustee.

(I) Compensation

No trustee shall receive any compensation for serving as trustee, except that a trustee shall be entitled to

reasonable compensation, as determined by the trustee, for serving as a trustee of Trust A, or a child's trust created by

this Declaration of Trust, or for serving as trustee because the grantors or a grantor has become incapacitated.

(J) Liability of Trustee

With respect to the exercise or nonexercise of discretionary powers granted by this Declaration of Trust, the

trustee shall not be liable for actions taken in good faith.

IV. Specific Beneficiaries

(A) Wife's Specific and Alternate Beneficiaries

Upon the death of _____ , the following gifts

wife's name

shall be made from trust property owned by _____ .

wife's name

1. ⑦ _____ shall be given

beneficiary

_____ .

property identified

If _____ does not survive _____ ,

beneficiary   wife's name

that property shall be given to _____ .

alternate beneficiary

2. ⑦ _____ shall be given

beneficiary

_____ .

property identified

If _____ does not survive _____ ,

beneficiary   wife's name

that property shall be given to _____ .

alternate beneficiary

3. ⑦ _____ shall be given

beneficiary

_____ .

property identified

If _____ does not survive _____ ,

beneficiary   wife's name

that property shall be given to _____ .

alternate beneficiary

(B) Husband's Specific and Alternate Beneficiaries

Upon the death of _____ , the following gifts

husband's name

shall be made from trust property owned by _____ .

husband's name

1. **7** _____ shall be given

_____ .
beneficiary

property identified

If _____ does not survive _____ ,
beneficiary husband's name

that property shall be given to _____ .

alternate beneficiary

2. **7** _____ shall be given

_____ .
beneficiary

property identified

If _____ does not survive _____ ,
beneficiary husband's name

that property shall be given to _____ .

alternate beneficiary

3. **7** _____ shall be given

_____ .
beneficiary

property identified

If _____ does not survive _____ ,
beneficiary husband's name

that property shall be given to _____ .

alternate beneficiary

(C) Remaining Trust Property

All other trust property of the deceased spouse shall be transferred and administered as provided by Section V.

V. Division of Trust Property Upon Death of Deceased Spouse

(A) Terminology

1. The first grantor to die shall be called the "deceased spouse." The living grantor shall then be called the "surviving spouse."

2. The "trust property of the deceased spouse" shall consist of all property of The _____

1 _____ Living Trust

your names (or name of trust, if different)

individually owned by the deceased spouse at the time it was transferred to the trustee, plus shared ownership

property with a total value equal to one-half of the total value at the time of the deceased spouse's death of the shared

ownership trust property, plus accumulated income, appreciation in value, and the like, attributable to the ownership

interest of the deceased spouse, and his or her share of all property acquired in the trust's name or the trustees' names.

3. The "trust property of the surviving spouse" shall consist of all property of The _____

1 _____ Living Trust

your names (or name of trust, if different)

individually owned by the surviving spouse at the time it was transferred to the trustee, plus shared ownership

property with a total value equal to one-half of the total value at the time of the deceased spouse's death of the shared

ownership trust property, plus accumulated income, appreciation in value, and the like, attributable to the ownership

interest of the surviving spouse, and his or her share of all property acquired in the trust's name or the trustees' names,

plus any property acquired pursuant to the terms of this trust.

(B) Division of Trust Assets

After the death of the deceased spouse, the trustee shall divide the trust assets into three shares, called the

Survivor's Share, the Marital Deduction Share, and the Bypass Trust Share.

1. Survivor's Share. This share consists of the trust assets of the surviving spouse, as defined in Section V,

Paragraph (A)3. These assets shall be held in and administered as part of Trust B, the Surviving Spouse's Trust.

2. Marital Deduction Share. This share consists of the assets that pass to the surviving spouse under this

declaration of trust that are not disclaimed by the surviving spouse within nine months of the deceased spouse's death.

These assets shall be held in and administered as part of Trust B.

3. The Bypass Trust Share. This share consists of assets that pass to the surviving spouse under this Declaration

of Trust that are disclaimed by the surviving spouse. The assets shall be held and administered in Trust A, the Deceased

Spouse's Trust.

(C) Disclaimer of Trust Assets

The surviving spouse has the authority to disclaim any trust assets left to him or her by the deceased spouse.

The surviving spouse is not required to disclaim any of these trust assets. If the surviving spouse chooses to disclaim

property, he or she shall do so within nine months after the deceased spouse's death. Any disclaimed property shall be

called the "Bypass Trust Share," and shall be held and administered in Trust A. If the surviving spouse does not disclaim

any assets left to him or her by the deceased spouse's trust, the trustee shall not establish Trust A.

(D) Property of Trust A

1. If the trustee does establish Trust A, that trust shall contain all assets disclaimed by the surviving spouse.

2. The deceased spouse's trust property placed in Trust A shall exclude any specific gifts provided for in Section IV, Paragraph (A) or (B).

3. Physical segregation of the assets of The  _____

your names (or name of trust, if different)

Living Trust is not required to divide that trust's property into Trust A and Trust B. The trustee shall exclusively determine what records, documents, and actions are required to establish and maintain Trust A and Trust B.

(E) Administration of Trust A

All property held in Trust A shall be administered as follows:

1. Upon the death of the deceased spouse, Trust A shall be irrevocable.

2. The life beneficiary of Trust A shall be the surviving spouse.

3. If _____ is the deceased spouse,

wife's name

the final beneficiaries of Trust A shall be:

8B _____

name(s) of final beneficiary(ies)

_____

_____

If _____ is the deceased spouse,

wife's name

the alternate final beneficiaries of Trust A shall be:

8B _____

name(s) of alternate final beneficiary(ies)

_____

_____

4. If _____ is the deceased spouse,

husband's name

the final beneficiaries of Trust A shall be:

_____

name(s) of final beneficiary(ies)

_____

_____

_____

If _____ is the deceased spouse,

husband's name

the alternate final beneficiaries of Trust A shall be:

_____

name(s) of alternate final beneficiary(ies)

_____

_____

_____

5. The trustee shall pay to or spend for the benefit of the surviving spouse the net income of Trust A at least quarterly. The trustee shall also pay to or spend for the benefit of the surviving spouse any sums from the principal of Trust A necessary for the surviving spouse's health, education, support, and maintenance, in accord with his or her accustomed manner of living.

6. **11** No accounting of Trust A shall be required of the trustee, except that the final beneficiaries shall be provided with copies of the annual federal income tax return.

7. The trustee shall be entitled to reasonable compensation from assets of Trust A for services rendered managing Trust A, without court approval.

8. Upon the death of the life beneficiary, the trustee shall distribute the property of Trust A to the final or alternate final beneficiary or beneficiaries, as named in Section V, Paragraph E(3) or E(4).

VI. Trust B, The Surviving Spouse's Trust

(A) Creation of Trust B, The Surviving Spouse's Trust

Upon the death of the deceased spouse, all trust property owned by the surviving spouse, as defined in Section V, Paragraph (A)3, shall be held in Trust B. Trust B shall include any trust property of the deceased spouse left to the surviving spouse and not disclaimed by her or him.

(B) Administration of Trust B

Until the death of the surviving spouse, the surviving spouse retains all rights to all income, profits, and control of the property in Trust B. The surviving spouse may amend or revoke Trust B at any time during his or her lifetime, without notifying any beneficiary.

(C) Distribution of Property in Trust B

1. Upon the death of the surviving spouse, Trust B becomes irrevocable.

2. The trustee shall first distribute any specific gifts of the surviving spouse to the beneficiaries named in Section IV, Paragraph (A) or (B). The trustee shall then distribute all remaining property of Trust B to his or her final, or alternate final, beneficiaries, as named in Section V, Paragraph (E)3 or (E)4.

3. All distributions under Section VI, Paragraph (C), are subject to any provision in this Declaration of Trust that creates child's trusts or creates custodianships under the Uniform Transfers to Minors Act.

VII. Incapacity

(A) Incapacity of Grantors

If both grantors become physically or mentally incapacitated and are no longer able to manage this trust, the person or persons named as successor trustee shall serve as trustee. The determination of the grantors' capacity to manage this trust shall be made by those of the persons listed below who are reasonably available when the successor trustee (or any of them, if two or more are named to serve together) requests their opinion. If a majority of these persons state, in writing, that in their opinion the grantors are no longer reasonably capable of serving as trustee, the successor trustee shall serve as trustee.

_____

name(s) of person(s) to determine incapacity

The successor trustee shall pay trust income at least annually to, or for the benefit of, the grantors and may also spend any amount of trust principal necessary, in the successor trustee's discretion, for the needs of the grantors, until the grantors, or either of them, are no longer incapacitated, or until their deaths.

(B) Amending AB Trust If Estate Tax Law Changes

Notwithstanding any other provision of this trust, if Congress changes the estate tax law, this trust may be amended as follows:

1. If both grantors are alive but one is incapacitated, the competent spouse may amend this AB trust in order to take best advantage of the new tax law.

2. If both grantors are alive but incapacitated, the successor trustee may amend this AB trust in order to take best advantage of the new tax law.

5A (C) Incapacity of Surviving Spouse

If, after the death of the deceased spouse, the surviving spouse becomes physically or mentally incapacitated and is no longer able to manage Trust B, the person or persons named as successor trustee shall serve as trustee.

1. The determination of the grantor's capacity to manage the trust shall be made by those of the persons listed below who are reasonably available when the successor trustee (or any of them, if two or more are named to serve together) requests their opinion. If a majority of these persons state, in writing, that in their opinion the grantor is no longer reasonably capable of serving as trustee, the successor trustee shall serve as trustee.

_____

name(s) of person(s) to determine incapacity

2. The successor trustee shall pay trust income at least annually to, or for the benefit of, the surviving spouse, and spend any amount of that trust's principal necessary, in the successor trustee's discretion, for the needs of the surviving spouse, until the surviving spouse is no longer incapacitated, or until his or her death.

Any income not spent for the benefit of the surviving spouse shall be accumulated and added to the property of Trust B.

3. The successor trustee shall manage Trust A, under the terms of this Declaration of Trust, until the surviving spouse is again able to serve as trustee of that trust, or until the death of the surviving spouse.

4. The successor trustee shall manage any operational child's trust created by this Declaration of Trust.

VIII. Simultaneous Death

If both grantors should die simultaneously, or under such circumstances as to render it difficult or impossible to determine who predeceased the other, for the purposes of this living trust it shall be conclusively presumed that both died at the same moment, and neither shall be presumed to have survived the other. The trustee shall make any specific gifts left by either spouse, and then distribute all remaining property to each spouse's final beneficiaries.

IX. Trustee's Powers and Duties

(A) Powers Under State Law

To carry out the provisions of this Declaration of Trust, and to manage the trust property of The _____

1 _____ Living Trust,

your names (or name of trust, if different)

Trust A, Trust B, and any child's trust created under this Declaration of Trust, the trustee shall have all authority

and power allowed or conferred under _____ law, subject to the

your state

rights retained by each grantor in Section II (B) and to the trustee's fiduciary duty to the grantors and the beneficiaries.

(B) Specified Powers

The trustee's powers include, but are not limited to:

1. The power to sell trust property, and to borrow money and to encumber property, specifically including trust real estate, by mortgage, deed of trust, or other method.

2. The power to manage trust real estate as if the trustee were the absolute owner of it, including the power to lease (even if the lease term may extend beyond the period of any trust) or grant options to lease the property, to make repairs or alterations, and to insure against loss.

3. The power to sell or grant options for the sale or exchange of any trust property, including stocks, bonds, debentures, and any other form of security or security account, at public or private sale for cash or on credit.

4. The power to invest trust property in property of any kind, including but not limited to bonds, debentures, notes, mortgages, stocks, stock options, stock futures, and buying on margin.

5. The power to receive additional property from any source and add to any trust created by this Declaration of Trust.

6. The power to employ and pay reasonable fees to accountants, lawyers, or investment experts for information or advice relating to the trust.

7. The power to deposit and hold trust funds in both interest-bearing and non-interest-bearing accounts.

8. The power to deposit funds in bank or other accounts uninsured by FDIC coverage.

9. The power to enter into electronic fund transfer or safe deposit arrangements with financial institutions.

10. The power to continue any business of either grantor.

11. The power to institute or defend legal actions concerning the trust or grantors' affairs.

12. The power to execute any document necessary to administer any trust created in this Declaration of Trust.

13. The power to diversify investments, including authority to decide that some or all of the trust property need not produce income.

(C) Payment by the Trustee of the Grantors' Debts and Taxes

1. Wife's Debts and Taxes

_____'s debts and
wife's name

death taxes shall be paid by the trustee. The trustee shall pay these from the following trust property:

⑨ _____.

2. Husband's Debts and Taxes

_____'s debts and
husband's name

death taxes shall be paid by the trustee. The trustee shall pay these from the following trust property:

⑨ _____.

3. If Specified Property Insufficient

If the property specified above is insufficient to pay all a grantor's debts and death taxes, the trustee shall

determine how such debts and death taxes shall be paid from that grantor's trust property, except as limited by any law

or IRS regulation controlling the property in Trust A.

X. General Administrative Provisions

(A) Controlling Law

The validity of The ① _____ Living Trust and
your names (or name of trust, if different)

construction of its provisions shall be governed by the laws of _____.
your state

(B) Severability

If any provision of this Declaration of Trust is ruled unenforceable, the remaining provisions shall nevertheless

remain in effect.

(C) Amendments

The term "Declaration of Trust" includes any provisions added by valid amendment.

XI. Child(ren)'s Trust(s)

All trust property left to any of the minor or young adult beneficiaries listed below in Section XI, Paragraph (A),

shall be retained in trust for each such beneficiary in a separate trust of this ① _____

_____ Living Trust.

your names (or name of trust, if different)

Each trust may be identified and referred to by adding the name of that trust's beneficiary to the name of this trust.

The following terms apply to each child's trust:

(A) Trust Beneficiaries and Age Limits

A trust shall end when the beneficiary of that trust, listed below, becomes 35, except as otherwise specified in this

section:

10A Trust for   Shall end at age

Trust for	Shall end at age
_____	_____
_____	_____
_____	_____
_____	_____
_____	_____

(B) Powers and Duties of a Child 's Trust Trustee

1. Until a child's trust ends, the trustee may distribute to or use for the benefit of the beneficiary as much of

the net income or principal of the child's trust as the trustee deems necessary for the beneficiary's health, support,

maintenance, or education. Education includes, but is not limited to, college, graduate, professional, and vocational

studies, and reasonably related living expenses.

2. In deciding whether to make a distribution to the beneficiary, the trustee may take into account the beneficiary's

other income, resources, and sources of support.

3. Any child's trust income that is not distributed to a beneficiary by the trustee shall be accumulated and added to

the principal of the trust for that beneficiary.

4. The trustee of a child's trust is not required to make any accounting or report to the trust beneficiary.

(C) Assignment of Interest of Beneficiary Prohibited

The interests of the beneficiary of a child's trust shall not be transferable by voluntary or involuntary assignment or by operation of law before actual receipt by the beneficiary. These interests shall be free from the claims of creditors and from attachments, execution, bankruptcy, or other legal process to the fullest extent permitted by law.

(D) Compensation of Trustee

Any trustee of a child's trust created under this Declaration of Trust shall be entitled to reasonable compensation without court approval out of the trust assets for ordinary and extraordinary services, and for all services in connection with the termination of any trust.

(E) Termination of a Child's Trust

A child's trust shall end when any of the following events occurs:

1. The beneficiary reaches the age specified in Section XI, Paragraph (A). If the trust ends for this reason, the remaining principal and accumulated income of the trust shall be given outright to the beneficiary.

2. The beneficiary dies. If the trust ends for this reason, the trust property shall pass to the beneficiary's heirs.

3. The trustee distributes all trust property under the provisions of this Declaration of Trust.

XII. Custodianships Under the Uniform Transfers to Minors Act

1. All property [10B] _____ becomes entitled to
beneficiary

under this trust document shall be given to _____ as
custodian's name

custodian for _____ under the _____
beneficiary   state

Uniform Transfers to Minors Act, until _____ reaches age _____.
beneficiary

2. All property [10B] _____ becomes entitled to
beneficiary

under this trust document shall be given to _____ as
custodian's name

custodian for _____ under the _____
beneficiary   state

Uniform Transfers to Minors Act, until _____ reaches age _____.
beneficiary

3. All property ^{10B} _____ becomes entitled to
                                              beneficiary

under this trust document shall be given to _____ as
                                                              custodian's name

custodian for _____ under the _____
                        beneficiary   state

Uniform Transfers to Minors Act, until _____ reaches age _____.
                                                    beneficiary

Certification by Grantors

We certify that we have read this Declaration of Trust and that it correctly states the terms and conditions under

which the trust property is to be held, managed, and disposed of by the trustees, and we approve the Declaration of Trust.

Dated: _____

_____
                Grantor and Trustee

_____
                Grantor and Trustee

Notary's Acknowledgment

State of _____

County of _____

On _____, _____, before me, _____, a notary public, personally appeared _____, who proved to me on the basis of satisfactory evidence to be the person(s) whose name(s) is/are subscribed to the within instrument and acknowledged to me that he/she/they executed the same in his/her/their authorized capacity(ies), and that by his/her/their signature(s) on the instrument the person(s), or the entity upon behalf of which the person(s) acted, executed the instrument.

I certify under PENALTY OF PERJURY under the laws of the State of _____ that the foregoing paragraph is true and correct.

WITNESS my hand and official seal.

_____
Signature of Notary Public

_____
Printed Name

Notary Public for the State of _____

Residing at _____

[NOTARY SEAL]   My commission expires _____

Schedule B
Wife's separate property placed in trust

All Wife's interest in the following property:

Schedule C
Husband's separate property placed in trust

All Husband's interest in the following property:

Form 5: Witness Statement for a Florida Living Trust

Statement of Witness

On this _____ day of _____, 20____ , _____

your name(s)

_____ declared to me, the undersigned, that

this Declaration of Trust was _____ living trust and requested me to act as witness to it.

his/her/their

_____ then signed this living trust in my presence. I now

your name(s)

at _____ request, in _____ presence, subscribe my name as witness and declare I understand this

his/her/their   his/her/their

to be _____ living trust.

his/her/their

      I declare under penalty of perjury that the foregoing is true and correct, this _____ day of

_____, 20_____ .

_____

witness's signature

_____

witness's typed name

_____, _____, _____

   city   county   state

Form 6: Assignment of Property to a Trust for One Person

Assignment of Property

I, _____ , as grantor,
your name

hereby assign and transfer all my rights, title, and interest in the following property _____

_____

_____

to _____ , as trustee of the
your name

_____ Living Trust,
your name (or name of trust, if different)

dated _____ , 20_____ .

Executed at _____ , _____ , on
city   state

_____ , 20_____ .
date

_____
Grantor and Trustee

Form 7: Assignment of Shared Property to a Trust for a Couple

Assignment of Property

We, _____ ,

your names

as grantors, hereby assign and transfer all our rights, title, and interest in the following property

_____

_____

_____ to

_____ , as trustees of

your names

The _____

your names (or name of trust, if different)

Living Trust, dated _____ , 20 _____ .

    Executed at _____ , _____ , on

city   state

_____ , 20 _____ .

date

_____

Grantor and Trustee

_____

Grantor and Trustee

Form 8: Amendment to Living Trust for One Person

Amendment to Living Trust

This Amendment to The **1** _____
　　　　　　　　　　　　　　　　　　　　　　your name (or name of trust, if different)

Living Trust dated _____, 20_____, is made this _____ day of
　　　　　　　　　　　date Declaration of Trust signed

_____, 20_____, by _____,
　　　　　　　　　　　　　　　　　　　　　　　　　　　　your name

the grantor and trustee of the trust. Under the power of amendment reserved to the grantor by Section III,

Paragraph (A), of the trust, the grantor amends the trust as follows:

1. The following is added to the Declaration of Trust:

　　_____

　　_____

2. The following is deleted from the Declaration of Trust:

　　_____

　　_____

[Repeat as needed]

In all other respects, the Declaration of Trust as executed on _____,

20_____, by the grantor is affirmed.

Executed at _____, _____, on
　　　　　　　　　　　　city　　　　　　　　　　　　　　　　　　　　state

_____, 20_____.
　　　　　date

_____
　　　　Grantor and Trustee

Notary's Acknowledgment

State of _____

County of _____

On _____, _____, before me, _____, a notary public, personally appeared_____, who proved to me on the basis of satisfactory evidence to be the person(s) whose name(s) is/are subscribed to the within instrument and acknowledged to me that he/she/they executed the same in his/her/their authorized capacity(ies), and that by his/her/their signature(s) on the instrument the person(s), or the entity upon behalf of which the person(s) acted, executed the instrument.

I certify under PENALTY OF PERJURY under the laws of the State of California that the foregoing paragraph is true and correct.

WITNESS my hand and official seal.

_____
Signature of Notary Public

_____
Printed Name

Notary Public for the State of _____

Residing at _____

[NOTARY SEAL]   My commission expires _____

Form 9: Amendment to Basic Shared Living Trust or AB Trust

Amendment to Living Trust

This Amendment to The ①_____

_____
your names (or name of trust, if different)

Living Trust dated _____, 20_____, is made this _____ day of_____ ,

date Declaration of Trust signed

20_____, by _____ ,

your names

_____ the grantors and trustees of the trust. Under the power of amendment reserved to

the grantors by Section II, Paragraph (F), of the Declaration of Trust, the grantors amend the trust as follows:

1. The following is added to the Declaration of Trust:

_____

_____

2. The following is deleted from the Declaration of Trust:

_____

_____

[Repeat as needed]

In all other respects, the Declaration of Trust as executed on _____, 20_____

date

by the grantors is affirmed.

Executed at _____, _____, on

city   state

_____, 20_____.

date

_____
Grantor and Trustee

_____
Grantor and Trustee

Notary's Acknowledgment

State of _____

County of _____

On _____, _____, before me, _____, a notary public,
personally appeared_____, who proved to me on the basis
of satisfactory evidence to be the person(s) whose name(s) is/are subscribed to the within instrument and acknowledged to
me that he/she/they executed the same in his/her/their authorized capacity(ies), and that by his/her/their signature(s) on the
instrument the person(s), or the entity upon behalf of which the person(s) acted, executed the instrument.

I certify under PENALTY OF PERJURY under the laws of the State of California that the foregoing paragraph is true and correct.

WITNESS my hand and official seal.

_____
Signature of Notary Public

_____
Printed Name

Notary Public for the State of _____

Residing at _____

[NOTARY SEAL]   My commission expires _____

Form 10: Revocation of Living Trust

Revocation of Living Trust

On _____, 20_____, _____

your name(s)

_____ created a revocable living trust, called

"The _____

your name(s) (or name of trust, if different)

Living Trust," with _____

your name(s)

_____ as the grantor(s) and trustee(s).

Under the terms of the trust, the grantor(s) reserved to _____ the full power to revoke the

himself/herself/themselves

trust.

     According to the terms of the Declaration of Trust, and the laws of the State of _____

your state

_____ the grantor(s) hereby revoke the Declaration of Trust and state

that the trust is completely revoked. All property of The _____

your name(s) (or name of trust, if different)

_____ Living Trust shall be returned to the grantor(s)

and legally owned by _____ as defined in the Declaration of Trust.

him/her/them

Dated: _____

_____

Grantor and Trustee

_____

Grantor and Trustee

Notary's Acknowledgment

State of _____

County of _____

On _____, _____, before me, _____, a notary public,
personally appeared_____, who proved to me on the basis
of satisfactory evidence to be the person(s) whose name(s) is/are subscribed to the within instrument and acknowledged to
me that he/she/they executed the same in his/her/their authorized capacity(ies), and that by his/her/their signature(s) on the
instrument the person(s), or the entity upon behalf of which the person(s) acted, executed the instrument.

I certify under PENALTY OF PERJURY under the laws of the State of California that the foregoing paragraph is true and correct.

WITNESS my hand and official seal.

_____
Signature of Notary Public

_____
Printed Name

Notary Public for the State of _____

Residing at _____

[NOTARY SEAL]   My commission expires _____

Form 11: Basic Will for One Person

Will

of

_____
your name

I, _____, a resident of

_____, _____ County, _____,
city   county   state

declare that this is my will.

1. I revoke all wills and codicils that I have previously made.

2. I am not married.

3. (A) I am the _____ of the _____ whose _____ _____
         mother/father   child/children   name/names   is/are

    _____

    _____

    _____

    _____

    _____ .

    There are _____ living children of my deceased child _____ ,
                                                                                          name

whose name(s) is/are:

    _____

    _____

    _____

    _____ .

    (B) If I fail to leave, by this will or otherwise, any property to any of the children listed above, my failure to do so is

intentional.

(C) If at my death any of my children are minors, and a personal guardian is needed, I nominate _____

_____ to be appointed personal guardian
name of personal guardian

of my minor children. If _____ cannot serve as
name of personal guardian

personal guardian, I nominate _____
name of alternate personal guardian

to be appointed personal guardian.

(D) If at my death any of my children are minors, and a property guardian is needed, I appoint

_____ as property guardian for my minor children.
name of property guardian

If _____ cannot serve as property guardian, I appoint
name of property guardian

_____ as property guardian.
name of alternate property guardian

(E) I direct that no bond be required of any guardian.

4. (A) I make the following specific gifts:

I leave _____
property described

to _____ , or if
beneficiary's name

_____ fails to survive
beneficiary's name

me, to _____ .
alternate beneficiary's name

I leave _____
property described

to _____ , or if
beneficiary's name

_____ fails to survive
beneficiary's name

me, to _____ .
alternate beneficiary's name

I leave _____
property described

to _____ , or if
beneficiary's name

_____ fails to survive
beneficiary's name

me, to _____ .
alternate beneficiary's name

(B) I leave all my other property subject to this will to _____
residuary beneficiary's name

_____, or if _____ fails to survive me,
he/she

to _____ .

alternate residuary beneficiary's name

5. (A) I nominate _____

executor's name

to serve as executor of my will. If _____ is unable to serve or continue serving as executor, I nominate

he/she

_____ to serve as executor.

alternate executor's name

(B) No bond shall be required of any executor.

I subscribe my name to this will this _____ day of _____, 20_____, at

_____, _____, _____

city   county   state

_____

your signature

Witnesses

On the date last written above, _____

your name

declared to us, the undersigned, that this was _____ will, and requested us to act as witnesses to it. _____

his/her   He/She

signed this will in our presence, all of us being present at the same time. We now, at _____ request and in

his/her

_____ presence, and in the presence of each other, have signed this will as witnesses.

his/her

We declare under penalty of perjury that the foregoing is true and correct.

_____ _____

witness signature   witness printed name

_____, _____, _____

city   county   state

_____ _____

witness signature   witness printed name

_____, _____, _____

city   county   state

_____ _____

witness signature   witness printed name

_____, _____, _____

city   county   state

Form 12: Basic Will for a Member of a Couple

Will

of

_____
your name

I, _____, a resident of
your name

_____, _____ County, _____,
city   county   state

declare that this is my will.

1. I revoke all wills and codicils that I have previously made.

2. I am married to _____.
                                              name

3. (A) I am the _____ of the _____ whose _____ _____
                       mother/father   child/children   name/names   is/are

_____

_____

_____

_____

    There are _____ living children of my deceased child _____,
                                                                    name

whose name(s) is/are:

_____

_____

_____

_____

    (B) If I fail to leave, by this will or otherwise, any property to any of the children listed above, my failure to do so is

intentional.

    (C) If at my death any of my children are minors, and a personal guardian is needed, I nominate

_____ to be appointed personal guardian
name of personal guardian

of my minor children. If _____ cannot serve as
                                       name of personal guardian

personal guardian, I nominate _____

name of alternate personal guardian

to be appointed personal guardian.

       (D) If at my death any of my children are minors, and a property guardian is needed, I appoint

_____ as property guardian for my minor children.

name of property guardian

If _____ cannot serve as property guardian, I appoint

name of property guardian

_____ as property guardian.

name of alternate property guardian

       (E) I direct that no bond be required of any guardian.

      4. (A) I make the following specific gifts:

I leave _____

property described

to _____ , or if

beneficiary's name

_____ fails to survive

beneficiary's name

me, to _____ .

alternate beneficiary's name

I I leave _____

property described

to _____ , or if

beneficiary's name

_____ fails to survive

beneficiary's name

me, to _____ .

alternate beneficiary's name

I leave _____

property described

to _____ , or if

beneficiary's name

_____ fails to survive

beneficiary's name

me, to _____ .

alternate beneficiary's name

      (B) I leave all my other property subject to this will to _____

residuary beneficiary's name

_____ , or if _____ fails to survive me,

he/she

to _____ .

alternate residuary beneficiary's name

5. (A) I nominate _____
                            executor's name

to serve as executor of my will. If _____ is unable to serve or continue serving as executor, I nominate
                                          he/she

_____ to serve as executor.
                    alternate executor's name

(B) No bond shall be required of any executor.

6. If my spouse and I should die simultaneously, or under such circumstances as to render it difficult or impossible to

determine who predeceased the other, I shall be conclusively presumed to have survived my spouse for purposes of this will.

I subscribe my name to this will this _____ day of _____, 20_____, at

_____, _____, _____
            city   county   state

_____
            your signature

Witnesses

On the date last written above, _____
                                                      your name

declared to us, the undersigned, that this was _____ will, and requested us to act as witnesses to it. _____
                                                        his/her   He/She

then signed this will in our presence, all of us being present at the same time. We now, at _____ request and in
                                                                                                                    his/her

_____ presence, and in the presence of each other, have signed this will as witnesses.
      his/her

We declare under penalty of perjury that the foregoing is true and correct.

_____   _____
witness signature   witness printed name

_____, _____, _____
            city   county   state

_____   _____
witness signature   witness printed name

_____, _____, _____
            city   county   state

_____   _____
witness signature   witness printed name

_____, _____, _____
            city   county   state

Form 13: Affidavit of Successor Trustee

Affidavit of Assumption of Duties by Successor Trustee

State of _____, County of _____.
　　　　　　　　　state　　　　　　　　　　　　　　　　　　county of successor trustee

_____, of legal age, first being duly sworn, declares:
　　　　　　　　successor trustee's name

On _____, 20_____, _____
　　　　　　　date　　　　　　　　　　　　　　　　　　name(s) of grantor(s)

_____ created The

_____ Living Trust.
　　　　　　name(s) of grantor(s) (or name of trust, if different)

On _____, 20_____, _____
　　　　　　　date　　　　　　　　　　　　　　　　　　grantor's name

died, as established in the attached certified copy of the Certificate of Death.

[For a shared or AB trust, add:]

On _____, 20_____, _____
　　　　　　　date　　　　　　　　　　　　　　　　　　second grantor's name

died, as established in the attached certified copy of the Certificate of Death.

The Declaration of Trust creating The _____
　　　　　　　　　　　　　　　　　　　　　　　name(s) of grantor(s) (or name of trust, if different)

_____ Living Trust provides that upon the death of the grantors, I,

_____ become the trustee of the trust.
　　　　　　successor trustee's name

I hereby accept the office of trustee of the trust, and am now acting as trustee of the trust.

Dated: _____

_____

Successor Trustee

Notary's Acknowledgment

State of _____

County of _____

On _____, _____, before me, _____, a notary public, personally appeared_____, who proved to me on the basis of satisfactory evidence to be the person(s) whose name(s) is/are subscribed to the within instrument and acknowledged to me that he/she/they executed the same in his/her/their authorized capacity(ies), and that by his/her/their signature(s) on the instrument the person(s), or the entity upon behalf of which the person(s) acted, executed the instrument.

I certify under PENALTY OF PERJURY under the laws of the State of California that the foregoing paragraph is true and correct.

WITNESS my hand and official seal.

_____

Signature of Notary Public

_____

Printed Name

Notary Public for the State of _____

Residing at _____

[NOTARY SEAL]   My commission expires _____

Property Worksheet

I. Assets

Description of Your Property	Net Value of Your Ownership	Who Owns It	Transfer to Trust?

A. Liquid Assets

1. cash (dividends, etc.)

_____ _____ _____ _____
_____ _____ _____ _____
_____ _____ _____ _____
_____ _____ _____ _____

2. savings accounts

_____ _____ _____ _____
_____ _____ _____ _____
_____ _____ _____ _____
_____ _____ _____ _____

3. checking accounts

_____ _____ _____ _____
_____ _____ _____ _____
_____ _____ _____ _____
_____ _____ _____ _____

4. money market accounts

_____ _____ _____ _____
_____ _____ _____ _____
_____ _____ _____ _____
_____ _____ _____ _____

5. certificates of deposit

_____ _____ _____ _____
_____ _____ _____ _____
_____ _____ _____ _____
_____ _____ _____ _____

6. treasury bills or notes

_____ _____ _____ _____
_____ _____ _____ _____
_____ _____ _____ _____

7. promissory notes (owed to you)

_____ _____ _____ _____
_____ _____ _____ _____
_____ _____ _____ _____
_____ _____ _____ _____

Description of Your Property	Net Value of Your Ownership	Who Owns It	Transfer to Trust?

B. Other Personal Property
(all your property except liquid assets, business interests, and real estate)

1. listed (private corporation) stocks and bonds

_____

2. unlisted stocks and bonds

_____

3. government bonds and securities

_____

4. automobiles and other vehicles, including planes, boats, and recreational vehicles

_____

5. precious metals

_____

6. household goods

_____

7. clothing

_____

Description of Your Property	Net Value of Your Ownership	Who Owns It	Transfer to Trust?
8. jewelry and furs			
9. artworks, collectibles, and antiques			
10. tools and equipment			
11. valuable livestock/animals			
12. life insurance proceeds			
13. money owed you (personal loans, etc.)			
14. retirement accounts, including IRAs, 401(k)s, and profit-sharing plans			
15. life insurance (proceeds payable on death)			no

Description of Your Property	Net Value of Your Ownership	Who Owns It	Transfer to Trust?
16. other valuable personal property			

C. Miscellaneous Receivables

(mortgages, deeds of trust, or promissory notes held by you; any rents due from income property owned by you; and any payments due for professional or personal services, or property sold by you that are not fully paid by the purchaser)

D. Real Estate

1. address

2. address

3. address

4. address

5. address

E. Total Net Value of Your Assets $ _____

II. Liabilities

To Whom Debt Is Owed   **Amount**

A. Personal Property Debts

1. personal loans (banks, major credit cards, etc.)

_____   _____
_____   _____
_____   _____
_____   _____
_____   _____
_____   _____
_____   _____
_____   _____

2. other personal debts

_____   _____
_____   _____
_____   _____
_____   _____
_____   _____
_____   _____
_____   _____
_____   _____
_____   _____

B. Taxes (include only taxes past and currently due; do not include taxes due in the future or estimated estate taxes)

_____   _____
_____   _____
_____   _____
_____   _____
_____   _____
_____   _____

C. Any Other Liabilities (legal judgments, accrued child support, etc.)

_____   _____
_____   _____
_____   _____

D. Total Liabilities (excluding those liabilities already deducted in Section I) $ _____

III. Net Worth (Total Net Value of Your Assets, from Section I.E, above, minus Total Liabilities, from Section II.D, above) $ _____

Beneficiary Worksheet 1: Individual Living Trust

1. Specific Gifts

Item of Property

Primary Beneficiary

Alternate Beneficiary

Item of Property

Primary Beneficiary

Alternate Beneficiary

Item of Property

Primary Beneficiary

Alternate Beneficiary

Item of Property

Primary Beneficiary

Alternate Beneficiary

Item of Property

Primary Beneficiary

Alternate Beneficiary

Item of Property

Primary Beneficiary

Alternate Beneficiary

Item of Property

Primary Beneficiary

Alternate Beneficiary

Item of Property

Primary Beneficiary

Alternate Beneficiary

Item of Property

Primary Beneficiary

Alternate Beneficiary

Item of Property

Primary Beneficiary

Alternate Beneficiary

2. Residuary Beneficiary or Beneficiaries

Residuary Beneficiary(ies)

Alternative Residuary Benficiary(ies)

Beneficiary Worksheet 2: Basic Shared Living Trust

Wife's Beneficiaries

1. Specific Gifts

Item of Property
_____

Primary Beneficiary
_____

Alternate Beneficiary
_____

Item of Property
_____

Primary Beneficiary
_____

Alternate Beneficiary
_____

Item of Property
_____

Primary Beneficiary
_____

Alternate Beneficiary
_____

Item of Property
_____

Primary Beneficiary
_____

Alternate Beneficiary
_____

Item of Property
_____

Primary Beneficiary
_____

Alternate Beneficiary
_____

Item of Property
_____

Primary Beneficiary
_____

Alternate Beneficiary
_____

Item of Property
_____

Primary Beneficiary
_____

Alternate Beneficiary
_____

Item of Property
_____

Primary Beneficiary
_____

Alternate Beneficiary
_____

Item of Property
_____

Primary Beneficiary
_____

Alternate Beneficiary
_____

2. Residuary Beneficiary or Beneficiaries

Residuary Beneficiary(ies)
_____

_____

Alternative Residuary Benficiary(ies)
_____

Husband's Beneficiaries

1. Specific Gifts

Item of Property
_____

Primary Beneficiary
_____

Alternate Beneficiary
_____

Item of Property
_____

Primary Beneficiary
_____

Alternate Beneficiary
_____

Item of Property
_____

Primary Beneficiary
_____

Alternate Beneficiary
_____

Item of Property
_____

Primary Beneficiary
_____

Alternate Beneficiary
_____

Item of Property
_____

Primary Beneficiary
_____

Alternate Beneficiary
_____

Item of Property
_____

Primary Beneficiary
_____

Alternate Beneficiary
_____

Item of Property
_____

Primary Beneficiary
_____

Alternate Beneficiary
_____

Item of Property
_____

Primary Beneficiary
_____

Alternate Beneficiary
_____

Item of Property
_____

Primary Beneficiary
_____

Alternate Beneficiary
_____

2. Residuary Beneficiary or Beneficiaries

Residuary Beneficiary(ies)
_____

_____

_____

Alternative Residuary Benficiary(ies)
_____

Beneficiary Worksheet 3: AB Trust

1. Wife's Specific Beneficiaries

Item of Property

Primary Beneficiary

Alternate Beneficiary

Item of Property

Primary Beneficiary

Alternate Beneficiary

Item of Property

Primary Beneficiary

Alternate Beneficiary

2. Wife's Final Beneficiaries

3. Wife's Alternate Final Beneficiaries

4. Husband's Specific Beneficiaries

Item of Property

Primary Beneficiary

Alternate Beneficiary

Item of Property

Primary Beneficiary

Alternate Beneficiary

Item of Property

Primary Beneficiary

Alternate Beneficiary

5. Husband's Final Beneficiaries

6. Husband's Alternate Final Beneficiaries

Index

N

Get the Latest in the Law

(1) Nolo's Legal Updater
We'll send you an email whenever a new edition of your book is published!
Sign up at **www.nolo.com/legalupdater**.

(2) Updates at Nolo.com
Check **www.nolo.com/update** to find recent changes in the law that
affect the current edition of your book.

(3) Nolo Customer Service
To make sure that this edition of the book is the most recent one, call us at
800-728-3555 and ask one of our friendly customer service representatives
(7:00 am to 6:00 pm PST, weekdays only). Or find out at **www.nolo.com**.

(4) Complete the Registration & Comment Card ...
... and we'll do the work for you! Just indicate your preferences below:

Registration & Comment Card

NAME _____ DATE _____

ADDRESS _____

CITY _____ STATE _____ ZIP _____

PHONE _____ EMAIL _____

COMMENTS _____

WAS THIS BOOK EASY TO USE?   (VERY EASY)   5   4   3   2   1   (VERY DIFFICULT)

☐ Yes, you can quote me in future Nolo promotional materials. *Please include phone number above.*

☐ Yes, send me **Nolo's Legal Updater** via email when a new edition of this book is available.

Yes, I want to sign up for the following email newsletters:

    ☐ **NoloBriefs** (monthly)
    ☐ **Nolo's Special Offer** (monthly)
    ☐ **Nolo's BizBriefs** (monthly)
    ☐ **Every Landlord's Quarterly** (four times a year)

☐ Yes, you can give my contact info to carefully selected
partners whose products may be of interest to me.

LITR9

Send to: **Nolo** 950 Parker Street, Berkeley, CA 94710-9867, Fax: (800) 645-0895,
        or include all of the above information in an email to regcard@nolo.com
        with the subject line "LITR9."

more from

NOLO and USA TODAY

Cutting-Edge Content, Unparalleled Expertise

The Busy Family's Guide to Money
by Sandra Block, Kathy Chu & John Waggoner

The Busy Family's Guide to Money will help you make the most of your income, handle major one-time expenses, figure children into the budget—and much more. **$19.99**

The Work From Home Handbook
Flex Your Time, Improve Your Life
by Diana Fitzpatrick & Stephen Fishman

If you're one of those people who need to (or simply want to) work from home, let this book help you come up with a plan that both you and your boss can embrace! **$19.99**

Retire Happy
What You Can Do NOW to Guarantee a Great Retirement
by Richard Stim & Ralph Warner

You don't need a million dollars to retire well, but you do need friends, hobbies and an active lifestyle. This book shows how to make retirement the best time of your life. **$19.99**

The Essential Guide for First-Time Homeowners
Maximize Your Investment & Enjoy Your New Home
by Ilona Bray & Alayna Schroeder

This reassuring resource is filled with crucial financial advice, real solutions and easy-to-implement ideas that can save you thousands of dollars. **$19.99**

Easy Ways to Lower Your Taxes
Simple Strategies Every Taxpayer Should Know
by Sandra Block & Stephen Fishman

Provides useful insights and tactics to help lower your taxes. Learn how to boost tax-free income, get a lower tax rate, defer paying taxes, make the most of deductions—and more! **$19.99**

Prices subject to change.

800-728-3555 or www.nolo.com

NOLO More Help from **Nolo.com**

ONLINE LEGAL DOCUMENTS *NOW*

Preparing legal documents used to be time consuming and expensive. Not anymore. Created by Nolo's experienced legal staff, these documents can now be prepared in a matter of minutes at: **www.nolo.com**

BUSINESS FORMATION

Form your business right now with our easy-to-use online service. Simply follow our detailed, step-by-step instructions and leave the rest to us.

Online LLC Formation	from $149
Online Corporation Formation	from $149

ESTATE PLANNING

Plan your estate, and save on legal fees at the same time with Nolo's comprehensive online forms. Don't delay—get your affairs in order now!

Online Will	from $69.95
Online Living Trust	from $169.99

INTELLECTUAL PROPERTY

Got a terrific idea? The fastest and safest way to establish proof of creation is a Provisional Patent Application. File a PPA now!

Online PPA	from $169.99

100s more business and consumer legal forms available at www.nolo.com—from $4.99 to $16.99

Related Books

Plan Your Estate
Protect Your Loved Ones, Property & Finances
$44.99

Nolo's Simple Will Book
$36.99

The Executor's Guide
Settling a Loved One's Estate or Trust
$39.99

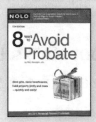

8 Ways to Avoid Probate
$21.99

All titles are also available in downloadable format at nolo.com.

Find an Estate Planning Attorney

- *Qualified lawyers*
- *In-depth profiles*
- *Respectful service*

If you have questions about planning your estate, you don't need just any lawyer. You want a qualified attorney to answer your questions about living trusts, wills, powers of attorney, probate, executors, life insurance and taxes, who can provide up-to-the-minute legal advice and strategic help to protect your loved ones.

Nolo's Lawyer Directory is designed to help you search for the right attorney. Lawyers in our program are in good standing with the State Bar Association and have created extensive profiles that feature their professional histories, credentials, legal philosophies, fees and more.

Check out **Nolo's Lawyer Directory** to find an estate planning lawyer who is right for you.

www.lawyers.nolo.com

The attorneys shown above are fictitious. Any resemblance to an actual attorney is purely coincidental.